D0390845

Government at Risk

Government at Risk

CONTINGENT LIABILITIES AND FISCAL RISK

Hana Polackova Brixi
Allen Schick
editors

A COPUBLICATION OF
THE WORLD BANK AND
OXFORD UNIVERSITY PRESS

© 2002 The International Bank for Reconstruction and Development /
The World Bank
1818 H Street, NW
Washington, DC 20433

All rights reserved.

1 2 3 4 04 03 02 01

A copublication of the World Bank and Oxford University Press.

Oxford University Press
198 Madison Avenue
New York, NY 10016

The findings, interpretations, and conclusions expressed here are those of the author(s) and do not necessarily reflect the views of the Board of Executive Directors of the World Bank or the governments they represent.

The World Bank cannot guarantee the accuracy of the data included in this work. The boundaries, colors, denominations, and other information shown on any map in this work do not imply on the part of the World Bank any judgment of the legal status of any territory or the endorsement or acceptance of such boundaries.

Rights and Permissions

The material in this work is copyrighted. No part of this work may be reproduced or transmitted in any form or by any means, electronic or mechanical, including photocopying, recording, or inclusion in any information storage and retrieval system, without the prior written permission of the World Bank. The World Bank encourages dissemination of its work and will normally grant permission promptly.

For permission to photocopy or reprint, please send a request with complete information to the Copyright Clearance Center, Inc., 222 Rosewood Drive, Danvers, MA 01923, USA, telephone 978-750-8400, fax 978-750-4470, www.copyright.com.

All other queries on rights and licenses, including subsidiary rights, should be addressed to the Office of the Publisher, World Bank, 1818 H Street NW, Washington, DC 20433, fax 202-522-2422, e-mail pubrights@worldbank.org.

Library of Congress Cataloging-in-Publication Data *has been applied for.*

Contents

Foreword

IN PUBLIC FINANCE, it no longer suffices for analysts and institutions to focus solely on budget revenues and expenditures. Recent history demonstrates that fiscal performance and, in turn, economic development can be seriously disrupted by the sudden, unexpected costs of hidden contingent liabilities and other unanticipated fiscal risks.

During the second half of the 1990s, unreported contingent liabilities and related fiscal risks contributed to economic crises and disrupted growth in a number of developing countries, motivating stepped-up efforts at the World Bank to devise new concepts and tools for analyzing and managing public finance. With the aim of improving the analysis of fiscal risks and supporting policy advice in this area, the Economic Policy Unit of the Bank's Poverty Reduction and Economic Management Network established the Quality of Fiscal Adjustment Thematic Group. This book was produced as part of the effort by this Thematic Group to promote new thinking about public finance.

We now know that conventional frameworks for fiscal analysis that concentrate on direct, explicit liabilities fail to address contingent fiscal risks. For example, fiscal sustainability analysis that focuses, as is typically the case, on the officially reported budget deficits fails to detect possible future increases in government debt and payments that may emerge from both explicit and implicit government guarantees on enterprise credit, state insurance schemes, exchange rate guarantees, and commitments to assist failed banks. Similarly, the government budget process and documentation generally fail to scrutinize the substantial claims on public resources that are associated with contingent liabilities, realized and potential.

This book is a notable step forward in filling gaps in our understanding of fiscal risks and in developing suitable frameworks for managing them. Through country cases and advances in conceptual design, the book provides a menu of practical ideas for policymakers and scholars for bringing fiscal risk within the ambit of public finance. It demonstrates that government fiscal analysis needs to cover the entire portfolio of direct and contingent liabilities, as well as assets and the revenue base. This in turn requires the government to identify, classify, and assess its fiscal risks so that it can provide reliable estimates of future payments that may ensue from past and pending liabilities. Only by identifying and measuring its exposure can a government bring its risks under effective control. This task has been facilitated by the availability of new methodologies, such as value-at-risk analysis and options pricing. But despite these advances, governments still face technical challenges in dealing with risk. However, the greater challenges are political and informational. Governments must care enough about fiscal and economic performance beyond the short term to impose limits on future risk-taking and to invest resources in identifying and controlling fiscal risks.

The essential challenge for governments is to launch a full and forthright effort to avoid excessive risk-taking and to prudently manage the risks that they do take. Doing so typically requires governments to commit themselves to greater transparency and broader fiscal discipline than they have had in the past.

The benefits for governments that make the effort are enormous, not only with respect to their future fiscal stability, but also with respect to their capacity to achieve broader policy objectives. The ideas and cases presented in this book should prompt governments to undertake this effort.

At the World Bank, the analysis and control of fiscal risks has now become an integral part of its assistance to member countries. Working closely with policymakers, the Bank tailors its analytic support and policy advice to country-specific circumstances, taking into account the technical challenges (few countries have a reasonably complete inventory of government contingent liabilities and other fiscal risks), the institutional set-up (fiscal and quasi-fiscal institutions and relationships), and the political sensitivity of the issues (a full accounting of fiscal risks often shows a government to be in a less favorable financial condition than is reported in official statements).

There is no single approach to dealing with contingent liabilities and fiscal risk. As the studies in this book indicate, governments that have sought to control their risk exposure have taken several different approaches. This book points the way ahead by setting out general principles of sound fiscal management and by providing specific examples of innovative country practices.

Nicholas H. Stern
Senior Vice President
   Development Economics
   and Chief Economist
The World Bank

Gobind T. Nankani
Vice President and Head of Network
   Poverty Reduction and Economic
   Management Network
The World Bank

Acknowledgments

WE WOULD LIKE TO EXPRESS our sincere gratitude to all the distinguished authors for their valuable contributions to this book. We also thank our many colleagues and friends who provided helpful advice and suggestions. We acknowledge in particular the support and feedback on the papers that we received from the Quality of Fiscal Adjustment Thematic Group (QFA TG) of the Economic Policy division of World Bank's Poverty Reduction and Economic Management (PREM) Network. Assistance from other World Bank staff, staff of other international institutions, government officials, academics, and researchers, who provided valuable feedback on earlier drafts of the chapters, is also gratefully acknowledged. Finally, we would like to thank the anonymous reviewers of this book whose challenging comments and suggestions have greatly improved this text.

We acknowledge with thanks the financial support we received for this book and related research and dissemination from the Economic Policy division of World Bank's PREM Network through the QFA TG. Support received from the Public Expenditure Thematic Group of the Public Sector Division is also gratefully acknowledged.

The views expressed in this book are those of the authors and should not be attributed to any particular institution, including institutions with which individual authors may be associated, including the World Bank, International Monetary Fund, the Federal Reserve System, and others.

Government at Risk: Contingent Liabilities and Fiscal Risks

Hana Polackova Brixi
World Bank

Allen Schick
University of Maryland

ONE DOES NOT HAVE TO SEARCH far to see evidence of governments at risk. In some countries, a long spell of seemingly sound fiscal management was followed by a fast-moving crash that forced the government to spend unbudgeted resources to pay obligations that few knew existed. When economic conditions stabilized, the government was left with elevated levels of debt and other obligations. Similarly, in other countries government debt soared much faster than the official deficit would have suggested, because the government was compelled to make good on obligations that had been assumed to be outside the budgetary framework. Today, in still other countries, the public finances are facing a difficult future as the off-budget obligations accumulated in the past come due in the decades immediately ahead. In all these scenarios, governments at risk have faced or are facing major fiscal challenges as a result of their contingent liabilities, which tend to remain outside the framework of conventional public finance analysis and institutions.

When risks come due in developed countries, they impose costs on government budgets and sometimes temporarily reduce economic output. When governments in less-affluent countries take imprudent risks, the effects of such risks may spread quickly across the economy, cause capital to flow out to safer havens, possibly compel the government to change economic course, and so retard or even reverse the country's development. Moreover, if the mechanisms for information disclosure are weak and market institutions not well developed, the risks assumed by government generate a bias in the behavior of economic agents and moral hazard in the markets, and thus work against development even before they are realized.

In many countries, the reality or prospect of unbudgeted fiscal risks coming due has been a wakeup call to extend fiscal management beyond the budget to all actions and transactions that put the government in financial jeopardy. Doing so is difficult, however, because it requires government to enter uncharted fiscal territory, where analytical frameworks are sometimes difficult to apply, accounting standards are underdeveloped or poorly enforced, and the data are inadequate or hidden from public scrutiny. And, because contingent liabilities often grow from fiscal opportunism, when policymakers seek to hide the real fiscal cost of their decisions and to reduce the reported budget deficit, bringing them under control may become first of all a question of political will.

This book aims to provide motivation and practical guidance to governments seeking to improve their management of fiscal risks. Among other things, it addresses some of the difficult analytical and institutional challenges that face reformers tooling up to manage government fiscal risks, and it describes the inadequacies of conventional practices as well as recent advances in dealing with fiscal risk. It also presents several untested ideas for developing new instruments for regulating and valuing fiscal risks. In so doing, the authors recognize that some novel schemes are not yet sufficiently developed to warrant immediate application by governments. But pushing forward the frontier of public finance today, the book aims to enhance the practice of fiscal analysis and management in the future.

This volume has grown out of World Bank initiatives to assist countries that are working to understand and manage the fiscal risks facing their governments. These initiatives, led by the World Bank Quality of Fiscal Adjustment Thematic Group during 1998–2001, covered over 40 interested countries and involved partnerships with many government agencies, leading universities, research institutions, international agencies, and associations of practitioners around the world.

The Magnitude of the Problem

We define fiscal risk as a source of financial stress that could face a government in the future. The book focuses particularly on the fiscal risks that are realized when uncertain events occur—such fiscal risks are often associated with government contingent liabilities. Recent history has brought with it many examples of contingent liabilities that challenge government finances. The explicit and implicit government insurance schemes in the domestic banking sector that emerged from the 1997 financial crisis in East Asia added some 50 percent of gross domestic product (GDP) to the stock of government debt in Indonesia, 30 percent in Thailand, and over 20 percent in Japan and Korea. In the 1980s, similar schemes generated a fiscal cost of over 40 percent of GDP in Chile and around 25 percent of GDP in Côte d'Ivoire, Uruguay, and República Bolivariana de Venezuela.[1] In the 1990s, Brazil and Argentina saw their government debt escalate when the central government had to bail out commitments made by subnational governments. Government debt in Malaysia, Mexico, and Pakistan soared from unexpected defaults on government guarantees that had been issued to promote private participation in infrastructure. Several chapters of this book illustrate that contingent liabilities may become the most critical factor in a country's fiscal performance.

Empirical analysis of past increases in the stock of government debt confirms that realized government contingent liabilities account for a large share of those increases. Kharas and Mishra (2001) illustrate across nearly 50 countries that large increases in the stock of government debt cannot be explained by the governments' reported budget deficits (see Figure 1). Calling the annual increase in government debt that is in excess of budget deficit a "hidden deficit," Kharas and Mishra show that hidden deficits have stemmed mainly from the cost of realized contingent liabilities and realized risks in the government debt portfolio (particularly the currency risk of government foreign debt instruments). In some developing and transition countries, contingent liabilities have contributed on average to hidden deficits of more than 2 percent of GDP annually over a period of more than 10 years. The analysis by Kharas and Mishra also indicates that contingent liabilities tend to be associated with speculative attacks and currency crises.

In the recent past, several factors have worked to increase governments' exposure to fiscal risk and their tendency to incur hidden deficits. The rapidly increasing volumes and volatility of international private capital flows have accelerated the growth of domestic financial systems but also have made these systems, and thus implicitly the countries' fiscal authorities, more vulnerable. This condition was clearly illustrated during the three years following the 1997 outflow of foreign capital from East Asia. Privatization and reduction of the explicit financial role of the state allowed many governments to cut their budgeted expenditures, but required either explicit or implicit promises that the government would come to the rescue should the private sector fail to deliver expected outcomes. Such guarantees and promises, in turn, have increased the uncertainty of future public financing

Figure 1. Average Annual "Hidden" Deficits
(percent of GDP over different 5- to 20-year periods from 1970s to 1990s)

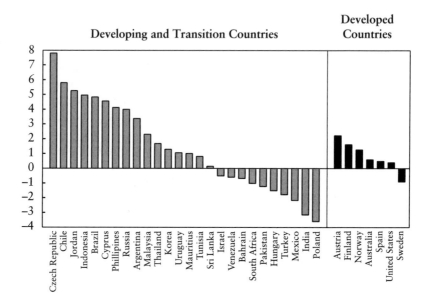

Note: Graphs represent average annual increases in government debt unexplained by reported deficits.
Source: Kharas and Mishra (2001).

requirements. Furthermore, these guarantees have boosted moral hazard in the markets. Loans and investments with a full guarantee suffer from insufficient analysis and supervision by creditors. Moreover, the beneficiaries of poorly designed state insurance schemes tend to expose themselves to excessive risks. For example, in the United States the generous benefits of the federal flood insurance program have resulted in the excessive construction of homes in flood-prone areas (U.S. GAO 1998). This market behavior makes it more likely that later the government will be asked to provide financial support.

The Political Economy of Contingent Liabilities and Fiscal Risk

Often fiscal risks, particularly those in the form of contingent liabilities, arise from politics and fiscal opportunism rather than economic policy. Policymakers tend to build up government contingent liabilities to avoid difficult adjustment and painful structural reforms. In this process, credit guarantees replace budgetary subsidies; take-or-pay contracts come in lieu of liberalizing prices and restructuring the energy, water, and other vital sectors; "letters of comfort" allow insolvent enterprises and banks to avoid bankruptcies; and so on.

In some instances, government support in the form of contingent liabilities may be justified. In Europe and the United States, few would argue against the immediate provision of a government guarantee to cover the legal liability of airlines after the September 2001 terrorist attacks in the United States. Government support was deemed justified for the political risk negatively affecting the airlines. Government guarantees, as the form of support, also were appropriate because the airlines would, in their own interest, try to avoid further terrorism onboard.[2]

In many cases, however, governments have assumed contingent liabilities either in pursuing low-priority objectives—that is, on programs that would not have withstood public scrutiny—or in using off-budget support when other forms would have been more appropriate. Some governments have provided letters of comfort to cover the commercial risk of foreign investors that have taken a position in domestic financial institutions or enterprises. But with the ensuing moral hazard, bailouts have often followed, frequently financed directly from special government funds rather than through the budget, and have tended not to be a good use of public money.

A common example of off-budget forms of support that are not appropriate is the provision of credit guarantees to enterprises that continually incur losses. While the government may have a good reason to support some of such enterprises (for example, the national railways, if their losses are the result of government fare pricing policy), budgetary subsidies or direct government loans would sometimes be more effective and almost always less expensive.

Whether for railways or airlines, often the best response to calls for government support is to encourage restructuring, privatize enterprises and financial institutions (and recapitalize them in the process if needed), break down monopolies, and liberalize prices. But the ease of issuing government guarantees and other promises of future possible government support allows the government to postpone these sometimes difficult and, in the short term, costly actions.

In most countries, government is able to offer a promise of future contingent support without seriously considering the future cost to the taxpayer. Governments doing their accounting and budgeting on a cash basis have particularly wide scope to behave opportunistically.[3] In contrast to commercial accounting practices, which in most developed countries require firms to recognize the future cost of pensions and other risks on their balance sheets, few governments disclose the prospective costs of their off-budget commitments. At the time of signing a letter of comfort or a guarantee contract, the government is able to claim no cost to the budget. In some countries, a variety of government entities are able to take on such commitments—sometimes without even informing the ministry of finance or any other authority. Other countries have centralized the guarantee-issuing authority at the ministry of finance or similar entity, but still do not require such an entity to report the government's off-budget commitments until they fall due. And even after they fall due, government may just issue more debt or find alternative ways to cover them, without ever recording the event in any reports. As a result, guarantees and similar forms of off-budget support that create contingent liabilities turn out to be a relatively easy way for government to avoid scrutiny of the risks inherent in channeling its support.

As these examples of the inappropriate use of off-budget forms of government support indicate, fiscal opportunism that gives rise to government contingent liabilities tends to grow out of a narrow scope of conventional fiscal analysis and fiscal management. Scrutiny that focuses solely on the government's cash-basis budget and deficit invites policymakers to generate contingent liabilities and other fiscal risks outside the budgetary framework (see Box 1). Many countries have learned firsthand that a narrow focus on cash-basis budget, deficit, and debt compels governments to delay investments and structural reforms, run down public assets, raise temporary revenues (sometimes by assuming long-term liabilities in exchange for cash), and distort spending priorities and the timing as well as the form of government support (see, for example, Forte 1998, Polackova 1998, and Easterly 1999). As reforms (such as pension reform, the downsizing of public employment, and enterprise and bank restructuring) that may require higher deficits in the short term are put on hold, fiscal opportunism puts economic growth at risk. Whether contingent liabilities are assumed in the effort to maintain the status quo and avoid reforms, or just to provide government support outside the budget and thus conceal its cost and financing, their existence generates uncertainties about future public financing requirements and so threatens future fiscal stability and the country's development. In this context, Selowsky (1998) has emphasized that reported deficit reduction does not necessarily imply "quality" of fiscal adjustment, which has the dimension of sustainability as well as efficiency.

Overall, development tends to be correlated with a shift in risk from individuals and individual economic agents and sectors to the state. As governments promote development and economic conditions improve, policymakers are pressured to take on commitments they may have avoided earlier. Social security programs, various state insurance schemes (targeting various beneficiaries, including enterprises, developers, farmers, and depositors), umbrella guarantees covering agen-

Box 1. Fiscal Risks as a By-product of Deficit Targeting

When loose rules for fiscal management are accompanied by pressure for fiscal adjustment, vote-seeking politicians and budget-seeking bureaucrats have additional cause for opportunism. Paradoxically, the incentive to mask the true cost of risks often rises when government comes under pressure to tighten its budget constraints. When pressure for adjustment is slack, the government may have little incentive to hide the costs of its financial commitments. But when stringent fiscal targets are imposed, wily spenders have incentive to substitute illusory adjustments for actual ones. And when proper accounting rules and strong enforcement mechanisms do not accompany the targets, the spenders have ample opportunity to evade the controls.

Various studies have shown that weak enforcement produces budgetary opportunism. In 1985 the United States enacted the Gramm-Rudman-Hollings law, which promised to progressively reduce the size of the deficit and to produce a balanced budget by 1991. But, as Schick (1995) points out, instead of genuine austerity, the law spawned budgetary legerdemain that increased the government's exposure to fiscal risk. The volume of loan guarantees escalated, the government was slow in responding to a costly crisis in the banking sector, and it adopted policies (such as asset sales) that weakened its long-term fiscal posture. In effect, as Rubin (1997) shows, faced with the Gramm-Rudman constraint on fiscal deficits, the U.S. Congress has reduced direct lending by $50 billion and increased loan guarantees by $178 billion, replacing budgetary outlays by explicit contingent liabilities.

In the process of fulfilling all the criteria for EU membership, the Maastricht criteria on government deficit and debt were applied by some countries in ways that escalated fiscal risk. The ploys, well described by Forte (1999), included defining government narrowly, so that the finances of various state-owned or controlled institutions were not included in the calculation; hiding a portion of the governments debt in various nongovernmental accounts; substituting guarantees for loans and grants; recording subsidies as purchases of assets; devising off-budget expenditures in lieu of direct financing; and deferring expenditures on infrastructure and maintenance. Some European Union governments received one-time payments from enterprises in exchange for assuming future pension liabilities; others reduced their reported public debt by reclassifying certain state enterprises as private entities. in Italy, the railways have raised funds through the financial markets to cover their deficits for many years with government agreement and an explicit guarantee from the treasury. Yet, those operations had no impact on the measured fiscal deficit or on the measured stock of government liabilities (Glatzel, 1998).

(Box continues on the following page.)

Box 1 *(continued)*

Creative accounting and budgeting practices have been used also in developing countries to portray their fiscal condition in a much more favorable light than is warranted. When pressured by adjustment programs administered by the World Bank or IMF, some developing countries have privatized assets, disinvested in infrastructure and other public goods, and replaced subsidies by directed credit and credit guarantees. Widespread recourse to illusory adjustments has led Easterly (1999) to conclude that when outside institutions demand a reduction in the deficit or debt, the affected government often responds by creating a fiscal illusion: achieving more favorable deficit and debt figures while divesting assets, accumulating contingent liabilities, and in other ways eroding the government's net worth.

cies in particular lines of business (for example, agricultural credit and guarantee funds, housing funds, and export credit funds), and specific guarantees that cover anything from borrowing by state-owned enterprises to commercial risks facing private investors, all tend to grow significantly as countries progress in their development.

Transition and emerging market economies face particularly large fiscal risks. Their dependence on foreign private financing, weak regulatory and legal enforcement systems, opaque ownership and distorted incentive structures, inadequate information disclosure, and the weak disciplinary effects of the international financial markets tend to increase the incidence of failures in the financial and corporate sectors. Such failures in turn often generate political pressure on governments to intervene through bailouts. A history of bailouts, particularly if coupled with a lengthy tradition as a paternalistic state, only contributes to the spread of moral hazard in the markets.

In addition, transition and the emergence of new markets involve enormous risks: by entrepreneurs in starting new businesses or acquiring old ones; by investors in providing venture capital; by importers and exporters in building new trade opportunities; by farmers in facing volatile prices and competition; by state-owned enterprises in taking on excessive risk pursuing profit or being barred from charging market prices; by workers in seeking employment free of government intervention. Understandably, some economic agents seek to transfer the risk to government explicitly by obtaining guarantees or other forms of assurance that government support will be forthcoming. Without extensive guarantees, there is some likelihood that private enterprise will be stillborn or stunted, the inflow of capital will be inadequate, investors will be unwilling to acquire state enterprises, and depositors will be reluctant to place their money in domestic banking institutions.

Markets that have a short history and offer limited information restrict the understanding that investors as well as politicians have of the risks they are taking. Imperfect knowledge induces both investors and politicians to underestimate the future potential cost of their decisions. Underestimation tends to be greatest when costs are contingent on future occurrences, such as repayment of loans or the performance of enterprises, and when the government bears implicit obligations that depend on future decisions, such as on whether to make good on uninsured bank deposits. This factor explains in part why in many transition and emerging market economies creditors have tolerated excessive risk exposure by domestic financial institutions and enterprises before fleeing. During the early years of change in an economic system, it is tempting for politicians to take the position that risks are justified because they enable the economy to grow more robustly. Later, politicians often feel that they have no choice but to assist troubled enterprises and financial institutions. As economies integrate with the international markets, more reliable data become available and more scrutiny is demanded. This tendency enhances the ability of both governments and investors to estimate risks with standard methodologies. Investors are then more likely to become more cautious in buying government debt instruments and thus to subject governments to greater discipline.

Scope for Fiscal Opportunism

Across countries, the main sources of fiscal risk and their underlying political economy tend to be similar. We now review the most common examples and highlight the *scope* for fiscal opportunism that exists in the various cases. We do not claim, however, that fiscal opportunism *actually* arises in all countries and in all such cases.

The largest scope for fiscal opportunism is traditionally offered by the financial sector. Governments are accustomed to using financial institutions, private or state-owned, to finance various projects and support programs. Development banks, policy banks, and credit and guarantee funds are authorized by the government to borrow in the markets to finance its programs. They raise resources to build roads, power plants, or schools; provide credit to farmers, enterprises, or health insurance funds—sometimes for new investment projects, other times to cover operating losses; and offer guarantees to exporters or developers. Because many such programs, although sometimes justifiable on policy grounds, are not profitable financially, financial institutions accumulate liabilities without securing the revenues to pay them

off. For the government, financial institutions appear to be a convenient channel for promoting various agendas without directly burdening the budget. But later, when the financial institution is unable to
roll over its debt, it ultimately needs government resources. If these
resources are provided directly from the proceeds of government borrowing, the budget deficit remains unaffected. In some countries, government exercises substantial influence over the banking sector, and
financial institutions do not pursue the interest of their creditors and
depositors (without relying on government bailout). As noted earlier,
the result is widespread losses and possibly a banking crisis. In resolving a banking crisis, many governments again use the financial sector
to create a fiscal illusion. Often asset and management companies are
created for the sole purpose of raising revenues to recapitalize banks
outside the budgetary framework of the government (Klingebiel 2000).

In some countries, state-owned enterprises are the vehicle used to
implement programs of a fiscal nature. By giving state-owned enterprises the responsibility for providing unemployment benefits, pensions, schooling, housing, and such, the government may again ensure
service delivery without directly burdening its budget. Later on, should
enterprises be short of resources to cover the cost of all these services,
the government would provide support—possibly through a financial
institution. When privatizing an enterprise, the government may have
to take over its obligations, which sometimes can be done in the form
of a guarantee issued by an autonomous privatization fund or credit
and guarantee fund (for example, by an environment fund to cover the
future environmental liabilities of the enterprise). On the other hand,
the government may be able to obtain a cash payment for assuming
some of the enterprise obligations, as was recently done in France for
enterprise pension obligations (Forte 1998). The government also may
require enterprises to charge artificially low prices for "necessities," in
effect avoiding the need to pay family transfers from the budget. To
cover the ensuing losses, the government may then issue a guarantee
on a credit to be taken by the enterprise from a commercial bank.
Ultimately, when the government has to provide financing it may do
so via a guarantee fallen due—again outside the budgetary framework.

Subnational governments are able to devise similar routes for op-
portunistic fiscal behavior. Many create their own financial institutions to raise revenues for off-budget programs, issue guarantees, or
borrow directly in the financial markets. Because their obligations
appear to be backed implicitly by the central government, they find it
possible to raise funds even if the financial sustainability of their activities raises doubts. Fiscal risks taken by subnational governments
are complicated by the fact that subnational policymakers may themselves rely on an implicit promise of the central government's help.
Depending on the political clout of each individual subnational gov-

ernment, it may be untenable for a central government to let a subnational government go bankrupt. Because most countries do not have clear regulations or a monitoring system for subnational government risk-taking, as financial markets develop, subnational governments tend to accumulate excessive obligations that eventually may compel the central government to provide a bailout.[4]

In recent years, government promotion of private participation in infrastructure, although often justified on policy grounds, has become a major source of fiscal risks. The justifiable objective of promoting private initiative may be diluted by the lack of political will to establish an adequate pricing mechanism, unbundle monopolies, and introduce a risk-sharing mechanism with the private developers and creditors. Explicitly through build-operate guarantee contracts, or implicitly through a perceived responsibility for the provision of core services, the government may be called on to step in with financing in case of failure.[5]

Public pension and health schemes are another common, albeit predictable, source of fiscal risk for governments. Arguably, society is better off when such risks are pooled and when the pool is expanded to cover all citizens or residents. But whatever its advantages, pooling transfers the risk to future rather than current government budgets. In an aging society, a promise of high pension and health benefits affects future government finances enormously. Most governments, however, still do not consider this intergenerational impact.

Reforms

Reforming any of these areas or, more broadly, how government deals with fiscal risk is likely to be costly politically, because constituencies from pensioners to bank owners have reasons to oppose such reforms. The average taxpayer would benefit—but he or she usually lacks lobbying power. Furthermore, such reforms imply that policymakers might have considerably less scope for fiscal maneuvering in the future. Chapters of this book address the various aspects of fiscal opportunism as they arise in different circumstances and make recommendations for improvements in the light of their political feasibility.

This book has been prepared in recognition of the probability that national governments will continue to shoulder various fiscal risks. The contributors to this volume recognize that risk-taking by the government is justified in some instances. But they take the position that if risks are here to stay, they should be properly regulated and managed, with appropriate information and oversight and full accounting for the costs that may be imposed on government.

It is assumed here that a necessary first step toward fiscally prudent policies is for policymakers to identify, classify, and understand the fiscal risks facing the government. Comprehension of the fiscal risks and their consequences may encourage governments to avoid the risks that are bound to surface within a politically meaningful time horizon. For risks that extend beyond that time frame, achievement of fiscally sound behavior may depend on market discipline. In particular, policymakers are more likely to gravitate toward fiscally sound decisions if the media, the public, investors, credit-rating agencies, and multilateral institutions understand the government's fiscal performance in its entirety and if there are sanctions when politicians expose the state to excessive risks and then conceal those risks.

The contributors to this volume seek to identify institutional mechanisms that can be applied domestically and internationally to optimize the amount of risk-taking by government. Domestically, an agency that is insulated from direct political pressures—for example, a supreme audit institution or an autonomous government debt management office—can assess and report on the direct and contingent fiscal risks of each government agency and of government as a whole. Although voters do not necessarily care about government fiscal risk, public explanation of the fiscal risks by an independent audit office may encourage the international forces of restraint. To be effective, international restraint should be used to ensure that the government applies the international rules for fiscal analysis not only to the budget and debt, but also to contingent liabilities. Specifically, international pressure may compel the government to meet certain quality standards: to define, measure, and monitor its full fiscal performance, using sound indicators and methods as defined by international authorities such as the International Monetary Fund, World Bank, European Commission, or sovereign credit rating agencies and investors.

Organization of This Book

This book explores the problem of fiscal risk along two dimensions. One dimension is that of the entire government portfolio of fiscal risks; the other is that of selected specific sources of government fiscal risk. Accordingly, the book is divided into two parts, each offering a conceptual treatment of the issues along with country examples.

Part I begins with an overview of different approaches to dealing with government fiscal risks (Chapter 1 by Hana Polackova Brixi and Ashoka Mody). The overview offers a classification of fiscal risks (the Fiscal Risk Matrix) and, with extensive references to the existing literature and country practice, summarizes various analytical and institutional approaches toward government management of fiscal risk. In particular, it outlines an approach to managing government fiscal risk in the context of the portfolio of government assets, sources of future revenues, and direct and contingent liabilities; sets

policy formulation in the context of fiscal risk management; and offers some guidance on structuring guarantees and government programs to minimize their risk.

Next, the book explores the institutional factors affecting the op-
portunistic behavior of policymakers and suggests corrective measures
with examples of good practice across countries. In this context, Chapters 2 and 3 by Murray Petrie and Allen Schick, respectively, illustrate
the inadequacies of conventional cash-basis reporting, accounting, and
budgeting, and call for more comprehensive and sounder approaches.
These chapters particularly highlight the usefulness of requiring government to publish a statement of contingent liabilities and fiscal risk.
They also outline the benefits of accrual-basis accounting and budgeting for government fiscal risk management.[6] These chapters provide
many examples of country practice from developed, transition, and
developing countries.

Subsequent chapters explore the practice of risk management in the
private sector and its applicability to government. Chapter 4 by Suresh
Sundaresan provides an overview of the analytical tools and practices
used by financial institutions and corporations to manage their risk
exposures, and then applies the methodology to valuing government
guarantees. Similarly, Chapter 5 by Krishna Ramaswamy applies a
factor model to government risk analysis—particularly for risk-taking
by public sector entities, including state-owned enterprises.

Then, linking the discussion of government and private sector practice, the chapters that follow focus on approaches to expanding fiscal
analysis to incorporate fiscal risks and to bringing market incentives
into the government's thinking about fiscal sustainability. Chapter 6
by Daniel Cohen integrates contingent liabilities with the traditional
fiscal sustainability analysis and offers an institutional arrangement to
introduce market discipline into government risk-taking. Chapter 7 by
Richard Hemming and Murray Petrie further expands the fiscal
sustainability framework and introduces a framework for assessing
the exposure of a government's future fiscal performance to risks.

The country examples in Part I offer additional conceptual approaches and illustrate some of the discussion in the earlier chapters.
Reflecting on the ability of policymakers to generate fiscal illusion,
Chapter 8 by William Easterly and David Yuravlivker applies a comprehensive approach to fiscal analysis in the form of evaluating the net
worth of the governments of Colombia and República Bolivariana de
Venezuela. Chapter 9 by Hana Polackova Brixi, Allen Schick, and Leila
Zlaoui recognizes the special challenges in fiscal risk management facing transition countries and evaluates various aspects of the quality of
fiscal adjustment and fiscal management related to government contingent liabilities in the Czech Republic, Bulgaria, and Hungary. In Chapter 10, Kathie Krumm and Christine Wong incorporate contingent

liabilities into the fiscal sustainability analysis for China. Looking at the portfolio of contingent liabilities and risks from the perspective of government debt, Chapter 11 by Hana Polackova Brixi and Sudarshan Gooptu presents scenarios for government debt management in Indonesia and Thailand. In a similar spirit, Chapter 12 by Juan Carlos Echeverry and others discusses reforms in dealing with contingent liabilities as implemented under the leadership of the Colombia Treasury.

Part II presents analytical and institutional approaches that governments might consider when facing risks in specific government programs or sectors. Chapter 13 by George Pennacchi focuses on the risk of guarantees that are often taken on by governments implementing pension reforms and utilizes an option-pricing methodology to value a government's risk exposure. In Chapter 14, Stijn Claessens and Daniela Klingebiel analyze the ways in which to measure and reduce the government's risk exposure in the banking sector. Chapter 15 by Ron Feldman discusses risks arising from government insurance programs. Recognizing the implicit responsibility of the fiscal authorities (and thus of the government budget) for the central bank's positive net worth, Chapter 16 by Mario I. Blejer and Liliana Schumacher utilizes a value-at-risk approach to assessing the central bank's own risk exposure.

Looking at country experience and practice, Chapter 17 by Ashoka Mody analyzes the lessons of the 1997 East Asian financial crisis for private participation in infrastructure and associated government contingent liabilities. For fiscal risks taken on by subnational governments, Chapter 18 by Jun Ma offers a framework that would allow the central government to monitor and discipline the subnational governments' risk exposure and thereby reduce the associated exposure by the central government. Chapter 19 by Sweder van Wijnbergen and Nina Budina applies option-pricing methodology to evaluating government foreign debt restructuring agreements for Bulgaria. Finally, the fiscal risk of floods, particularly in the case of Argentina, is explored in Chapter 20 by Alcira Kreimer.

Reflecting on available country experience and on the new concepts presented in the book, the concluding chapter by Allen Schick draws together a list of policy recommendations for governments seeking to bring their fiscal risks under control.

The descriptions and discussions in this book of the concepts and practices of dealing with contingent liabilities and other fiscal risk suggest that a broad range of approaches for governments to use in analyzing and managing such risks are available. In this respect, the book illustrates that contemporary practices have yet to be standardized. Under these circumstances, the book seeks to motivate policymakers and policy analysts to pay attention to the fiscal risks governments face, and it provides a rich menu of practices that may be applied in countries that are serious about confronting such risks.

Notes

1. For an overview and analysis of the cost of banking crises, see Honohan and Klingebiel (2000).

2. In addition, countries argued that they could not afford to let several big airlines go under simultaneously, because the effect on jobs and confidence could be too great. A temporary, targeted government subsidy to overcome the temporary financial shock may be appropriate to smooth job reductions and allow the strongest to survive. It should be acknowledged, however, that the credit guarantees for which the airlines lobbied may have the additional effects of delaying the restructuring in the airline industry that, given the increasing losses of many airlines even before the attacks, was considered overdue. For analysis of the pros and cons of various scopes and forms of government support to the airline industry after the terrorist attacks, see, for example, the *Economist* ("More Pain Ahead," September 22, 2001, and "Uncharted Airspace," September 28, 2001).

3. In cash-basis accounting, expenses and liabilities are accounted not when the obligation is incurred, but only when the government makes the actual cash transfer. Thus a government collecting a fee for assuming a liability (for example, when it issues a guarantee or accepts the pension liability of an enterprise under privatization) reports the transaction as a net revenue gain.

4. Dillinger (1999) discusses the economics and political economy of central government bailouts of subnational governments in South America.

5. Irwin and others (1998) provide examples and analysis of public risk in private infrastructure.

6. An accrual-basis accounting system without accrual budgeting will not ensure that governments adequately consider contingent fiscal risks in policy. Although this system encourages governments to prepare a statement of contingent liabilities and financial risks, it generally does not require that the liabilities be included in the balance sheet and that the associated risks be evaluated and quantified. International accrual accounting standards require that liabilities be accounted only when the obligation is due with certainty. For a discussion of the rules of probability and risk assessment, see International Accounting Standards Committee (1997).

References

Dillinger, William. 1999. "Fiscal Management in Federal Democracies: Argentina and Brazil." Policy Research Working Paper 2121. World Bank, Washington, D.C.

Easterly, William. 1999. "When Is Fiscal Adjustment an Illusion?" *Economic Policy* (April).

Forte, Francesco. 1998. "Accounting and Financial Practices in Light of Context of the Maastricht Treaty." In *European Union Accession: The Challenges for Public Liability Management in Central Europe*. Washington, D.C.: World Bank.

Honohan, Patrick, and Daniela Klingebiel. 2000. "Controlling Fiscal Cost of Banking Crises." Policy Research Working Paper 2441. World Bank, Washington, D.C.

International Accounting Standards Committee. 1997. *International Accounting Standards 1997*. London.

Irwin, Timothy, Michael Klein, Guillermo Perry, and Mateen Thobani, eds. 1998. *Dealing with Public Risk in Private Infrastructure*. World Bank Latin American and Caribbean Studies. Washington, D.C.: World Bank.

Kharas, Homi, and Deepak Mishra. 2001. "Fiscal Policy, Hidden Deficits, and Currency Crises." In S. Devarajan, F. H. Rogers, and L. Squire, eds. *World Bank Economists' Forum*. Washington, D.C.: World Bank.

Klingebiel, Daniela. 2000. "The Use of Asset Management Companies in the Resolution of Banking Crises: Cross-country Experience." Policy Research Working Paper 2284. World Bank, Washington, D.C.

Polackova, Hana. 1998. "Contingent Government Liabilities: A Hidden Risk for Fiscal Stability." Policy Research Working Paper 1989. World Bank, Washington, D.C.

Rubin, Irene. 1997. *The Politics of Public Budgeting: Getting and Spending, Borrowing and Balancing*. Chatham, N.J.: Chatham House.

Schick, Allen. 1995. *The Federal Budget: Politics, Policy, and Process*. Washington, D.C.: Brookings Institution.

Selowsky, Marcelo. 1998. "Fiscal Deficits and the Quality of Fiscal Adjustment." In *The Challenges for Public Liability Management in Central Europe*. Washington, D.C.: World Bank.

U.S. GAO (General Accounting Office). 1998. *Budgeting for Federal Insurance Programs*. Washington, D.C.: Government Printing Office.

PART I

Learning to Deal with Fiscal Risks in Government Portfolio

*Possible Analytical
and Institutional Frameworks*

CHAPTER I

Dealing with Government Fiscal Risk: An Overview

Hana Polackova Brixi
World Bank

Ashoka Mody*
International Monetary Fund

MANY GOVERNMENTS HAVE FACED serious macroeconomic instability as a result of obligations that were not recorded in any fiscal documents. Governments may have taken advantage of guarantees and financial companies to implement their policies outside the budgetary system, or they may have just been blind to risk spreading in the markets. Whether the result of fiscal opportunism to conceal the true fiscal cost of government programs, or of an effort to find more efficient ways to achieve policy objectives (by, for example, offering guarantees instead of direct loans and cash subsidies), or of lenience toward moral hazard in the behavior of market agents, such obligations often turn out to be very costly. At some point in time, many guarantees fall due, state insurance programs require subsidies, and banks involved in policy lending or exposed to excessive risk with the hope of government bailout eventually file for such a bailout. And, as illustrated in Mexico in 1994, in East Asia in 1997, and, to some extent, around the world after the September 2001 terrorist attack on the United States, these hidden obligations tend to surface and require public resources all at once in times of crises and economic slowdown.[1]

---

*The author was with the World Bank when he wrote this article; he is currently with the IMF.

But the conventional approaches to public finance analysis fail to reveal hidden government obligations and the associated fiscal risks. Similarly, public finance institutions, including systems for government budget management, debt management, accounting, financial control, and public scrutiny, often remain blind to government contingent liabilities. Thus a string of years in which government has reported a balanced budget and low public debt suggests neither that the government has been fiscally prudent nor that it will enjoy fiscal stability in the near future.[2]

This chapter begins by discussing a simple typology of sources of fiscal risk—the Fiscal Risk Matrix. It then introduces the Fiscal Hedge Matrix and expands on the standard government asset and liability management framework. Using this framework, it outlines principles for dealing with fiscal risks in their policy and institutional contexts. The chapter then explores the possibilities for governments to reduce their risk exposure by enabling market agents to better manage their own risks, developing risk-sharing mechanisms, hedging, and building reserves. Finally, the chapter offers a set of questions to assist policymakers in learning about fiscal risks in their own country. Overall, this chapter introduces a number of topics that will be further elaborated in the rest of the chapters in this volume.

The Fiscal Risk Matrix

The Fiscal Risk Matrix presented in Table 1.1 divides sources of fiscal risk—that is, sources of future possible financing pressure on the fiscal authorities of a country—into four groups according to the following characteristics: direct versus contingent, and explicit versus implicit.[3] *Direct liabilities* are predictable obligations that will arise in any event. *Contingent liabilities* are obligations triggered by a discrete but uncertain event. For government policies, the probability of a contingency occurring and the magnitude of the required public outlay are exogenous (for example, the occurrence of a natural disaster) or endogenous (for example, the implications of market institutions and of the design of government programs on moral hazard in markets). Contingent liabilities also rise with weaknesses in the macroeconomic framework, financial sector, and regulatory and supervisory systems, and with weak information disclosure in the markets. They also emerge from so-called quasi-fiscal activities—that is, activities of a fiscal nature that the government pursues outside its budgetary framework.[4] *Explicit liabilities* are specific government obligations defined by law or contract. The government is legally mandated to settle such an obligation when it becomes due. *Implicit liabilities* represent a moral obligation or expected burden for the government not in the legal sense, but based on public expectations and political pressures.

Table 1.1 Government Fiscal Risk Matrix

Sources of obligations	Direct liabilities (obligation in any event)	Contingent liabilities (obligation if a particular event occurs)
Explicit Government liability as recognized by a law or contract	• Sovereign debt (loans contracted and securities issued by central government) • Expenditure composition (nondiscretionary spending) • Expenditures legally binding in the long term (civil service salaries and pensions)	• State guarantees for non-sovereign borrowing by and other obligations of sub-national governments and public and private sector entities (development banks) • Umbrella state guarantees for various types of loans (mortgage loans, student loans, agriculture loans, small business loans) • Trade and exchange rate guarantees issued by the state • State guarantees on private investments • State insurance schemes (deposit insurance, income from private pension funds, crop insurance, flood insurance, war-risk insurance)
Implicit A moral obligation of government that reflects public and interest group pressures	• Future public pensions (as opposed to civil service pensions)[a] • Social security schemes[a] • Future health care financing[a] • Future recurrent costs of public investment projects	• Default of a subnational government or public/private entity on nonguaranteed debt/obligations • Banking failure (support beyond government insurance, if any) • Cleanup of liabilities of entities being privatized • Failure of a nonguaranteed pension fund, employment fund, or social security fund (protection of small investors) • Possibly negative net worth and/or default of central bank on its obligations (foreign exchange contracts, currency defense, balance of payments) • Other calls for bailouts (for example, following a reversal in private capital flows) • Environmental recovery, disaster relief, military financing

a. In this framework, these services fall in the category of government direct implicit liabilities if their provision is not mandated by law. If mandated by law, then these services fall in the category of government direct explicit liabilities.

Source: Polackova (1998).

Government *direct explicit liabilities* are legal or contractual obligations of the government that will arise in any event. These obligations constitute the main subject of conventional fiscal analysis. They are: the repayment of sovereign debt, expenditures based on budget law in the current fiscal year, and expenditures in the long term for legally mandated items such as civil service salaries and pensions and, in some countries, even the overall social security system. Among these items, recent literature has focused on risks embedded in the size and structure of the government debt portfolio (see Nars 1997, World Bank and IMF 2000, and Dooley 2000 for an overview).

Government *direct implicit liabilities* will also arise in any event, but the government will not be legally obliged to act on them. Such obligations often arise as a presumed consequence of public expenditure policies in the longer term. Given their implicit nature, these obligations are not captured in government balance sheets. Typically, they are high for demographically driven expenditures. For example, future pensions payable in a public pay-as-you-go scheme, unless guaranteed by law, constitute a direct implicit liability. Its size reflects the expected generosity of and eligibility for pensions and future demographic and economic developments. Among direct implicit liabilities, recent literature has particularly explored public pension liabilities (World Bank 1994; IMF 1996; OECD 2000; Bodie and Davis 2000).

Contingent explicit liabilities are government legal obligations to make a payment only if a particular event occurs. Because the fiscal cost of contingent explicit liabilities is invisible until they are triggered, they represent a hidden subsidy, blur fiscal analysis, and drain government finances only later. For that reason, *state guarantees* and financing through *state-guaranteed institutions* look politically more attractive than budgetary support even if they are more expensive later. In the markets, contingent government obligations may immediately create moral hazard, particularly if the government guarantee covers the whole rather than a part of the underlying assets and all rather than selected political or commercial risks. *State insurance schemes* often cover uninsurable risks of infrequent losses that are enormous in total magnitude. Thus, rather than financing themselves from fees, they redistribute wealth and rely on government net financing. To date, research has focused on issues of measurement and management of loan guarantees (Mody and Patro 1996; Lewis and Mody 1997), investment guarantees in infrastructure (Chase Manhattan Bank 1996; Irwin and others 1998), state development finance institutions (Yaron 1992), pension guarantees (see Chapter 13 by Pennacchi in this volume), deposit insurance (Leaven 2000; World Bank 2001a), crop insurance (Hueth and Furtan 1994), and other state insurance schemes (U.S. GAO 1998, and Chapter 15 by Feldman in this volume).

Contingent implicit liabilities depend on the occurrence of a particular future event and on government willingness to act on them. Such obligations are typically not officially recognized until *after* a failure occurs. The triggering event, the cost at risk, and the required size of government outlay are uncertain. In most countries, the *financial system* represents the most serious contingent implicit government liability. Experiences have indicated that markets expect the government to help financially far beyond its legal obligation if stability of the financial system is at risk (for examples, see Chapter 14 by Claessens and Klingebiel in this volume and World Bank 2001a). Fiscal authorities also are often compelled to cover losses and obligations of the *central bank, subnational governments, state-owned and large private enterprises, budgetary and extrabudgetary agencies,* and any other *agencies of political significance.*[5]

The effect of fiscal risks arising from government direct and contingent liabilities can best be analyzed in the context of an extended government balance sheet that includes future revenues as well as contingent liabilities, and assets as well as direct liabilities. This approach builds on the assets and liabilities management literature (Cassard and Folkerts-Landau 1997; OECD 1999; World Bank and IMF 2000) and can be referred to as an *extended assets and liabilities management framework.* In this approach, a Fiscal Hedge Matrix (Table 1.2) complements the Fiscal Risk Matrix to illustrate the different sources of potential revenues that can serve to cover government obligations. Sources of government financial safety also can be divided into direct and contingent, explicit and implicit. Direct explicit sources reflect the government's legal power to raise income from its existing, tangible assets. Direct implicit sources also are based on the existing assets, but these are not under the government's direct control and thus may offset fiscal risks to a limited degree only. Contingent explicit sources relate to the government's legal power to raise finances in the future from sources other than its own assets. Finally, contingent implicit sources are not available to the government until a particular situation occurs and, even then, require the government to make a special case for their utilization. The two matrixes (Tables 1.1 and 1.2), once filled with country-specific items, would help a government to identify the exact scope for its fiscal analysis and management.

The value of government assets and future revenues and the cost of government obligations are associated with different types of risk. Clearly, the government's residual, unhedged exposure to fiscal risk is the result of the correlation among, rather than a simple summation of, the effects of the different types of risks on the individual items in its extended balance sheet. The types of risk include: *refinancing risk* (constraints on the government's ability to issue debt—exacerbated particularly by short

Table 1.2 Government Fiscal Hedge Matrix

Sources of financial safety	Direct sources of safety (based on the stock of existing assets)	Contingent sources of safety (dependent on future events, such as value generated in the future)

Explicit Based on government legal powers (ownership and the right to raise revenues)	• Assets recovery (work-out and sales of non-performing loans and sales of equity)
	 • Privatization of state-owned enterprises and other public resources
	 • Recovery of government loan assets (resulting from earlier direct government lending)
		• Government revenues from resource extraction and sales
		 • Government customs revenues
		 • Tax revenues
		   - minus tax expenditures (exclusions, exemptions, and deductions, which reduce taxable income)
		   - minus revenue commitment (to subnational governments)
		   - minus revenues sold forward (commodity forward sales) and pledged as collateral (partly at risk)
		 • Hedging instruments and (re-)insurance policies purchased by the government from financial institutions

Implicit Based on government indirect control	• Stabilization and contingency funds[a] • Positive net worth of central bank	• Profits of state-owned enterprises • Contingent credit lines and financing commitments from official creditors • Current account surpluses across currencies

a. Stabilization and contingency funds may be designated for a general or very specific purpose and can be under direct or indirect government control. Thus their classification may be different in each case.
Source: The authors.

maturities of and maturity bunching in government obligations), *liquidity risk* (risk of having to sell assets at loss—intensified by maturity mismatch between assets and liabilities and by rigidities in the government's capacity to raise revenues and cut expenditures), *currency risk* (exchange rate risk and cross-currency risk, exposure to short-term exchange rate volatility—arising from the currency structure of government debt and exchange rate guarantees, which is partly offset by the currency structure of government assets and revenues), *interest rate risk* (particularly associated with floating interest rates), *commodity price risk* (swings in the price of oil, rice, and similar commodities), *derivative risk* (risk of large losses from the use of derivative instruments), *medium- and long-term sustainability risk* (risk arising from adverse trends that underlie government finances), *political risk* (risk of policy reversals and political instability), and *operational risk* (poor valuation and risk assessment, system errors, poor organizational structures, corruption, and fraud). The literature has mainly explored the impact of most of these types of risk on government direct liabilities (World Bank and IMF 2000) and of selected types of risk on government revenues and expenditures (see, for example, Larson, Varangis, and Yabuki 1998 on the impact of commodity price). To analyze the overall government risk exposure and its sensitivity to different risk types, taking into account possible correlations among risks across the entire extended government balance sheet, public finance will need to build on tools developed in finance, such as portfolio optimization and factor analysis (see Chapter 4 by Sundaresan and Chapter 5 by Ramaswamy in this volume).

Dealing with Risk in Fiscal Analysis and Fiscal Management

Because it is impossible for governments in a market environment to avoid fiscal risk, they need to control and manage their risk exposure. Dealing with fiscal risk is important not only from the perspective of future fiscal stability. With respect to allocative efficiency, for example, only with a view toward its likely full fiscal cost in the future can a proposed government guarantee be properly scrutinized against other competing programs. As for operational efficiency, only with a full understanding of the various types of risk involved can such a guarantee be structured in a way to provide the desired support without unnecessarily generating moral hazard and exposing the government to risk.

But do governments have the incentives and capacity to reflect fiscal risks in their policy choices and to carry out a good fiscal risk management strategy? It depends on how well they understand the issues and on the kind of scrutiny and pressures policymakers face in dealing with fiscal risks and their consequences. There are good examples to build on. Australia and South Africa use a medium-term expenditure framework to enhance predictability of fiscal performance and, particularly in the case of South Africa, to make their governments accountable for their risk analysis as well as macroeconomic and demographic assumptions.[6] Canada, the Netherlands, and the United States have incorporated analysis of selected contingent liabilities and tax expenditures into their budgetary frameworks, requiring budget allocations and reserve funds to reflect the present value of future potential outlays and foregone revenues (Congressional Research Service 1998). Sweden and Colombia have authorized their government debt management agencies to track and manage the risk of contingent liabilities, and they require the beneficiaries of government guarantees to pay the full present value of their expected fiscal cost up-front into a reserve fund, which also is managed by the debt management agency (see Calderon Zuleta 1999 and Chapter 12 by Echeverry and others in this volume). In India, the Federal Reserve Bank and Ministry of Finance have carefully assessed the government's exposure to fiscal risk across the entire Fiscal Risk Matrix and, as a consequence, established a Guarantee Redemption Fund to cushion the future fiscal cost of central government's guarantees. They also implemented rules on subnational government guarantees and on subnational guarantee funds to provide for the future expected cost of subnational guarantees (Commonwealth Secretariat 2001).

The analysis and management of government exposure to fiscal risks have three dimensions: the macroeconomic context, specific fiscal risks, and the institutional framework. The *macroeconomic context* of the government's exposure to fiscal risks relates to its capacity to absorb financial pressures that it may realize in the future. How much room for maneuver does the government have to absorb fiscal risks? Limits on the government's absorption capacity for fiscal risks are determined by possible macroeconomic constraints, such as the existence of a currency board and fixed exchange rate arrangements, and by the trends, rigidity, and sensitivities of the general government's expenditures and revenues, the size and liquidity of its assets, the structure of its obligations, and its future possible borrowing constraints. For example, does the government have access to reliable sources of financing, such as deep domestic bond markets, or is it critically dependent on the confidence of foreign investors?

In this context, fiscal performance relates to developments in the government's entire extended balance sheet (across the two matrixes presented above). Thus fiscal sustainability analysis would be replaced by an analysis of government net worth and of the future financial pressures and financing options. In this volume, Chapter 8 by William Easterly and David Yuravlivker applies the net worth approach to Colombia and República Bolivariana de Venezuela. Focusing on obligations, in Chapter 10 Kathie Krumm and Christine Wong integrate contingent liabilities with fiscal sustainability analysis for China. In Chapter 9 Hana Polackova Brixi, Allen Schick, and Leila Zlaoui try to overcome the shortcomings of conventional deficit measurement and calculate the "true fiscal deficit" and "hidden debt" of the government of the Czech Republic, reflecting the cost of contingent liabilities. For Bulgaria, they discuss the impact of the currency board arrangement on the government's vulnerability to fiscal risks. Chapter 7 by Richard Hemming and Murray Petrie outlines a framework for analyzing fiscal vulnerability, which is broadly defined as the ability of government to achieve its fiscal policy objectives.

Dealing with *specific fiscal risks* requires addressing the following three areas of questions: First, what are the *sources of fiscal risk*? Particularly, which budgetary and off-budget government programs may generate unexpected financial pressure on the government in the future? Second, what *types of risk* is the government exposed to? For example, are the cost of the government's debt service, the value of its revenues, or the likelihood that government contingent liabilities will become reality affected by movements in the exchange rate, domestic or foreign interest rate, and commodity prices, or by the risks of its own fiscal mismanagement and operational failure (institutional risks)? Third, how *sensitive* is the overall fiscal position to the various sources and types of risk? What are the possible stress scenarios linking the realization of different fiscal risks, and what are the possible consequences for the government fiscal position?

The goal of government fiscal risk analysis (and management) is to ensure that government has the cash available to meet its obligations and deliver on its policies, under any more or less likely conditions. Therefore, less likely stress scenarios require as much attention as the most likely baseline scenario.[7] Results of stress testing, reestimated periodically for changes in the underlying assumptions (to mark the expected fiscal outcomes to market), will be critical for government risk management in deciding, for example, on an appropriate level of reserves and hedging strategy. In Chapter 11 in this volume, Brixi and Gooptu, taking into account the correlation in the sensitivity of the different items in the Fiscal Risk and Fiscal Hedge Matrixes to the different types of risk, build a stress scenario for the government of Indonesia.

For major contingent liabilities, how does one assess their size, probability of realization, and possible future fiscal effects? The literature on valuing credit and project guarantees and state insurance programs has built on contingent claims analysis (see Mody and Patro 1996, Lewis and Mody 1997, Arthur Andersen 2000, and Marrison 2001 for an overview). Contingent claim analysis uses two basic concepts: the expected costs (that is, the most likely or average cost) and the unexpected costs (that is, the maximum likely cost with a particular small probability, also referred to as value at risk or cost at risk) of the contingent liabilities.

To reveal both the average and the maximum likely fiscal cost of government contingent liabilities, one would generate a large number of random scenarios (for example, using Monte Carlo simulations, as described in Arthur Andersen 2000 and Marrison 2001). In the distribution of outcomes of the different scenarios, scenarios that occurred most often would indicate the average fiscal cost and scenarios (also referred to as stress scenarios) that occurred at a predetermined probability (usually 5 percent or 10 percent) would indicate the cost at risk. (In this volume, valuation of contingent liabilities using value-at-risk and option-pricing approaches are discussed particularly in Chapter 4 by Sundaresan, Chapter 13 by Pennacchi, and Chapter 19 by van Wijnbergen and Budina. For an overview of different approaches as they have already been applied, see U.S. GAO 1993, 1998.)

As such, the average cost of contingent liabilities is a measure of government subsidy implied by the issuance of a government guarantee or other program of contingent government support. Thus from a policy point of view, the average cost estimate can be used to judge whether the government would be willing to support the project through an equivalent up-front cash subsidy (in which case, as further discussion will point out, the government also should be willing to budget for the expected cost of contingent liabilities at the time of assuming them). The stress scenario implies a fiscal cost that the government has to consider in its risk management approach and has to be prepared to pay in the future.

The *institutional framework* for dealing with fiscal risks mainly relates to the rules and practice of information disclosure, monitoring, fiscal planning, and budgeting. The institutional framework affects the government's incentives and ability to constrain, control, and manage its fiscal risks. The framework must be such that it promotes a risk-awareness culture in government and minimizes the scope for fiscal opportunism. Whether or not policymakers extend the focus of public finance institutions to cover fiscal risks depends on several factors, including the definition and measurement of internationally recognized fiscal indicators (that is, the pressure of institutions such as EUROSTAT, the International Monetary Fund, the World Bank, the Organisation for Economic Co-operation and Development, and the United Nations), public pressure (by the media, independent audit institutions, watchdog agencies, and legislators), investors' demands and preferences (for example, to what extent sovereign credit rating agencies pay attention to fiscal risks, and investors punish the government for concealing relevant data and exposing the country to excessive fiscal risk), and whether or not fiscal risks attract the attention of reform-minded policymakers.

Fiscal risks are likely to attract more attention if the government is required to *disclose* them. Disclosure can be in the form of a simple statement of contingent liabilities and tax expenditures, or full-fledged financial statements based on an accrual accounting system. The governments of Australia, Canada, the Netherlands, New Zealand, and the United States offer good practices to follow. The fiscal statements of these countries list the various sources of fiscal risk; discuss their nature and sensitivities, implications for future fiscal position, and allocative efficiency (compared with budgetary spending); and, where applicable, provide their face value or estimated future fiscal cost or both (see Chapter 2 by Petrie for examples and references). Governments also should enforce requirements that market agents disclose information about their risk exposures. Particularly agencies that may appear to be implicitly guaranteed by the government should be subject to strict disclosure requirements. In this context, for example, subnational governments should report on their guarantees and on the activities of their own financial enterprises; state-owned enterprises should report on their environmental commitments; and financial institutions should report on their off–balance sheet items. Such broad disclosure would allow market agents as well as the government to conduct proper monitoring and analysis and to react to possible moral hazard.

Although the *organizational setup for fiscal risk management* will be specific to every country, some general principles apply (see Box 1.1). These include: centralize the risk-taking authority (possibly the

---

Box 1.1 Division of Responsibilities for Fiscal Risk Management

Large banks, including J. P. Morgan and Deutsche Bank, have divided the functions of designing and authorizing new transactions, analysis, and record-keeping among three different offices. The front office serves as the central point for the design of financial instruments, and it has the exclusive authority to enter into new derivative and debt transactions. Its objective is to ensure the required levels of available cash and optimize the overall return-risk ratio. The middle office provides analysis of future obligations and payoffs and their sensitivities for the entire portfolio. Finally, the back office is responsible for record-keeping and maintaining comprehensive databases.

Maintaining these functions independent of each other improves transparency and the control of portfolio risks and prevents the front office from exceeding its predetermined risk exposure limits. The governments of Ireland and Sweden, for example, have successfully applied such a division of responsibilities to their debt management.

Many governments have centralized the authority to issue debt, guarantees, tax exemptions, and other off-budget programs. Now they should expand the scope of risk management and adjust organizational structures and responsibilities accordingly. See Nars (1997).

ministry of finance to oversee any risk-taking in the public sector); separate risk-monitoring (for example, internally by the debt management office and externally by the supreme audit institution) from risk-taking; and connect risk-taking with budgeting and debt management practice. Obviously, accountability structures are crucial to ensure the best efforts and reduce the scope for fraud and corruption. Policymakers and civil servants need to be accountable for the adequacy of their risk analysis and the assumptions underlying decisions that involve fiscal risks and for managing the overall government risk exposure. Therefore, the role of the independent audit (and the supreme audit institution), as it is in the case of the U.S. General Accounting Office, would extend beyond its conventional limits to cover all aspects of government risk analysis and risk management (see Chapter 2 by Petrie).

Budgeting and accounting rules influence the allocation of resources, affect the timing and recognition of transactions, and may provide opportunities and incentives to shift costs and risks from one period to another and from one part of a government to another. Cash flow budgeting, for example, makes guarantees and other contingent forms of government support look more attractive than direct loans or cash subsidies. It treats direct loans and subsidies as outlays, but does not recognize contingent liabilities until default occurs, at which point the government has little choice but to make good on past commitments.[8] Direct loans and subsidies thus appear expensive and the contingent form of support cheap. To make matters worse, in cash flow budgeting income earned from origination fees on guarantees is booked as current revenue, making it appear that the government is profiting by taking these risks.

In contrast, an accrual-based budgeting and accounting system requires that the net present fiscal cost associated with individual government programs, including programs that generate a contingent liability, be included in budget documents and thus be made visible from the moment government decides to launch them. Moreover, for contingent liabilities it encourages the government to set aside resources up-front at the time of their launching (see Box 1.2 for a private sector analog and Chapter 3 by Schick for a detailed discussion).[9] To strengthen accountability, the budget would be set in the context of a publicly announced medium-term fiscal framework, which would later make any departures from the original risk analysis apparent.

The experience of a number of countries (most of which is discussed in this book), including Canada, Colombia, Hungary, the Netherlands, South Africa, Sweden, and the United States, has indicated that a comprehensive shift of the accounting and budgeting systems to accrual basis is not necessary in order for government to take control

---

Box 1.2 Budgeting for Risk in the Private Sector

Programs of contingent support are often akin to put options, which create the obligation, but not the right, to buy an asset at certain pre-defined strike levels. Charging the full option price when writing (selling) an option, as is typical in the private sector, amounts to immediately fully provisioning the expected cost of contingent support. The price of an option reflects the present value of the future possible loss, which may be incurred by the underwriting institution. As illustrated by the Black-Scholes formula, the price increases with the time to expiry (for example, maturity of the guaranteed loan) and with the volatility of the underlying asset (for example, share price of the enterprise whose debt is under the guarantee). Financial institutions charge the full option price immediately at the time of selling the option. The amount is then used either to build reserves or to buy a hedge. See Hull (1997).

---

of its fiscal risks.[10] Tables 1.3 and 1.4 summarize measures to enhance policymakers' understanding of fiscal risks and their incentives as well as capacity for dealing with them. These measures can be built upon any decent public finance management system.

Reducing Government Risk Exposure

A number of commodity-exporting nations have tried to manage their risk exposure by building reserves in booms and creating stabilization funds, but the results have been mixed (Davis and others 2001 provide an overview). With more success, several governments have used derivatives and "exotic" debt instruments (such as debt instruments linking the amount of debt repayment to commodity prices) to hedge risks in the government assets and liabilities portfolio.[11] Other governments also have successfully purchased reinsurance for risks (such as weather risks) from a large international reinsurer.[12] In recent years, increasing market integration has made it possible to pool risk across countries and thus has enabled financial markets to provide insurance against risks, such as crop risks and disaster risks, that had been considered uninsurable before. Financial markets have typically welcomed government risk management initiatives (in the early 1990s, for example, the government of New Zealand witnessed a rapid improvement in the terms of its sovereign borrowing once it announced and implemented

Table 1.3 Systemic Measures to Reduce Government
Exposure to Fiscal Risk

Fiscal policy	*Fiscal management*
First— • Identify and reconsider government programs and promises that imply significant risks, no longer serve a significant social or economic purpose, or can be replaced by market instruments such as private insurance, derivatives. • Identify, classify, and analyze all major sources of fiscal risk and financial safety (build an extended government balance sheet). • Announce that only those contingent liabilities included in a public statement of fiscal risk will be honored. • As a context to policy decision-making, introduce the concept of fiscal vulnerability.	*First—* • Assign responsibility for identifying, recording, and reporting government obligations, assessing the future likely fiscal cost, and monitoring government exposure to fiscal risk. • Analyze the sensitivity of the government's fiscal position to the different types of risks and create a list of early warning indicators that signal possible future fiscal pressures (for example, exchange rate movements, rate of credit growth in the banking system, and demand growth vis-à-vis the existing capacity in infrastructure). • Establish nominal, nonbudgetary control mechanisms for fiscal risks such as information disclosure on government obligations and tax expenditures, exposure limits (for example, maximum amount of guarantees outstanding), and earmarking of future funds to cover the likely costs of contingent liabilities.
Later— • For policy decisions, analyze full fiscal performance and its vulnerability to risks and expand the medium-term fiscal framework to cover the effects of fiscal risks. • Identify the government's risk absorption capacity and (according to its risk preference and its capacity to absorb and manage risk) determine the government's optimal risk exposure and reserve and hedging policy. • Develop a government risk management strategy that would guide policymakers and staff in day-to-day decisions involving government risk exposure. • Consider private sector coverage to replace existing and proposed government programs.	*Later—* • Recognize and disclose information about government full fiscal performance, including exposure to fiscal risk. • Scrutinize fiscal risks in the budget process before they are taken. • Consider government risk exposure in structuring programs. • Build capacity for analyzing and managing risk (including mitigation of the risk at source, transferring the risk to parties better able to bear the risk, and monitoring and managing any residual risk that cannot be mitigated or transferred) and for auditing government dealing with fiscal risk. • Build a mechanism to enforce the disclosure, monitoring, and regulation of risks in both the public and private sectors.

Source: Polackova (1998) and the authors.

Table 1.4 Measures to Control the Fiscal Risks of Individual Government Programs

Fiscal policy	Fiscal management
Before accepting— • Assess how the program fits with policy objectives. • Consider the program's risks and likely future fiscal cost and compare alternative forms of government support, including actions to enable private sector coverage. • Outline and announce the limits of government responsibility with respect to the program in order to minimize moral hazard.	*Before accepting—* • As part of fiscal planning and budgeting, evaluate the risks and estimate the likely future fiscal cost. • Design the program well, providing for risk mitigation and risk transfer, to minimize government risk exposure and moral hazard in the markets. • Decide on the management of residual risk (for example, set a hedge and an additional reserve requirement).
When accepted— • Stick to the preset limits of the scope of the program and of the associated government responsibility. • Reconsider the program's relevance in the context of the evolving needs, changing structure of the economy and role of the government, and advances in technology and financial markets.	*When accepted—* • Report the risk (for example, issue a statement of fiscal risks). • Budget for the net present value of the expected fiscal cost of the program. • Continuously monitor the performance under the program, including the program's risk factors, reserve adequacy, and behavioral effects. • Update the risk analysis and risk management strategy. • Audit the validity of the risk analysis and the quality of risk management. • Draw consequences if a bias in the original risk analysis and government decision is revealed. • Prepare contingency plans for dealing with the program (whether explicit or implicit) if fiscal risks are realized.
Upon execution— • Execute strictly within the preset limits of government responsibility. • If implicit, assess the fit with policy priorities and possible moral hazard effects before executing.	*Upon execution—* • Evaluate performance under the program, compare and report the actual fiscal cost versus the original cost estimates, and punish for failures (including a bias in risk analysis and deficiency in risk management).

Source: Polackova (1998) and the authors.

its risk management strategy). Since the 1997 crisis in Asia, investment banks and sovereign credit rating agencies have increasingly discussed government risk exposure in their country risk analyses (see,
for example, Standard and Poor's 1997).

For governments and for enterprises, the objective of risk management is to align the demand for funds with revenues (Froot, Scharfstein,
and Stein 1994). Private companies and financial institutions have
benefited from using enterprise-wide risk management strategies and
financial markets to manage and hedge risk. In addition to learning
from their experience, which is discussed in Chapter 4 by Sundaresan,
governments often also have the option of supporting broader reforms
that reduce risks or make them insurable in the markets.

For governments, the management of risk entails three complementary tasks: involving the private sector (mitigating the risk at source
and developing financial risk markets), transferring the risk to parties
better able to bear the risk (creating risk-sharing arrangements), and
managing any residual risk that cannot be mitigated or transferred
(monitoring, building reserves, and hedging).

Ultimately, *risk mitigation* with private sector involvement is the
most desirable long-run strategy, because it not only reduces the
government's exposure to fiscal risk but also reduces the vulnerability
of the economy to shocks. Instead of assuming risk, governments would
enable markets to deal with it. For example, a power sector that is
organized to permit competitive generation and distribution will foster efficient use of resources while at the same time lowering the risk
arising from excessive installation of capacity (for other examples, see
Table 1.5).

Similarly, by supporting the development of the *markets for risk
instruments,* the government can effectively withdraw from its direct
role in dealing with many risks. In this regard, policymakers need to
ask: Are the risks for which government coverage is sought truly uninsurable in the private sector? How can these risks be made insurable?
For example, regulatory changes can encourage large international
insurers to access the local market and pool risks uninsurable in a
small economy and can make derivatives accessible to local market
agents. Private risk markets reduce the need for the traditional government programs such as disaster risk insurance, crop insurance, and
minimum price policies. Similarly, new financial instruments may help
domestic financial institutions to better manage risk, thereby reducing
their demand for government guarantees. However, risk mitigation
strategies and markets for risk instruments may require fundamental
sectoral reforms and thus cannot be developed overnight. (For a discussion linking fiscal risk with sectoral reform, see, for example, Irwin
and others 1998). Therefore, more effective risk-sharing may be the
practical short-term strategy.

Table 1.5 Risk, Possible Fiscal Cost, and Private Sector
Solution

Type of risk	Coverage	Possible fiscal cost	Private sector solution
Credit guarantees	Debt service and losses due to default	Principal plus interest plus possible penalties by the creditor for default	Credit enhancement Risk-sharing with creditors
Guarantee on minimum return of pension funds	Minimum absolute amount (monetary value)	Guaranteed amount times the number of pensioners	Sound regulatory framework for pension funds and the overall financial markets
	Minimum relative amount (share of average wage)	Average wage share times the number of pensioners	
Project guarantees	Design and development Construction risk Operating risk (cost overrun, delays) Demand/revenue risk Financial risk (exchange rate, interest rate) Force majeure Environmental risk Political and policy risk	Very large if not capped	Correcting for any market failures that reduce access of investors to adequate risk protection mechanisms in the markets Risk-sharing with investors and creditors
Disaster Insurance	Losses due to disasters	Very large if not capped	Environment allowing direct access to international insurers and reinsurers, catastrophe bonds and derivatives
Deposit Insurance	Bank deposits	Face value of all deposits if not capped	Regulations allowing bank access to risk protection and risk markets Disclosure of information on bank performance and management, international competition, low limits on the deposit amounts guaranteed

(Table continues on the following page.)

Table 1.5 (continued)

Type of risk	Coverage	Possible fiscal cost	Private sector solution
Price support	Minimum price of a product/ commodity	Guaranteed min- imum price minus actual price, multiplied by quantity	Encourage direct access to interna- tional derivatives markets
Implicit guarantee on various obligations	Explicitly: none Implicitly: obliga- tions of subnation- al governments, state-owned finan- cial institutions, enterprises and funds, large mar- ket agents, etc.	Almost unlimited	Sound regulatory frame- work for accounting, information dis- closure, and audit Credible announce- ments and actions by the government to minimize expecta- tions of a bailout

Source: The authors.

Risk transfer and a good *risk-sharing mechanism* require clear policy objectives and understanding of all the underlying risks in a program. In the private sector in the last 20 years, the possibilities for transfer-ring risk have been growing rapidly. Derivative products have allowed firms to subdivide, isolate, and swap various risks, but they also have created new risk exposures that are not easy to quantify (Garber 1998). So far, for governments the primary method of transferring risk has been through risk-sharing provisions in their guarantees and insurance contracts. Recent practice and literature have suggested that carving out commercial risk from government coverage significantly reduces the negative behavioral effects of such government programs in the markets as well as limits government risk exposure (U.S. GAO 1998; World Bank 1999c, 2000). For example, in the banking sector, should the government provide deposit insurance, then a relatively low cap on government protection would increase the incentives of bankers to improve due diligence and project selection, lowering risk and the wasteful use of resources. Similarly, price support programs require their own risk-sharing arrangement with, for example, farmers (see Box 1.3).

For implicit contingent liabilities, risk-sharing tends to be applied ex post. As Honohan (1999) argues, however, fiscal cost is lower (and government crisis management more efficient) if government has an ex ante, confidential contingency plan (for example, deciding ex ante which stakeholders—domestic depositors in local currency, domestic depositors in foreign currency, foreign depositors, creditors, and share-holders—to assist and how much before a crisis occurs). Similarly, the

Box 1.3 Government Price Support Programs for Farmers

International markets are not always able to offer adequate instruments, such as futures, options, or insurance policies, to protect farmers against the volatility of their particular product. In reality, it may be difficult for a farmer to sell (short hedge) futures on his or her product in order to make the final selling price certain and thus protect against losses from a possible future reduction in its price. Thus the government may still be the only source of protection. (Even when markets do not offer instruments of adequate protection to individual farmers, they may offer hedging or reinsurance instruments on a larger scale and customized basis to government—for example, customized derivatives contracts over-the-counter or a reinsurance policy). In many countries, government protection comes in the form of a price support program, which guarantees farmers a minimum price for their output. Such programs generate for the government an obligation to pay farmers the difference between the market price and the guaranteed minimum price should the price of their product drop below the minimum price.

If price support turns out to be the preferred choice of government support, how should the program be designed to minimize both moral hazard on the side of the farmers and the future fiscal cost on the side of the government? To deter overproduction, the amount of product guaranteed must be limited—by imposing a nominal ceiling and quotas and by charging the farmers a fee per unit of guaranteed product. (For a particular minimum price, the Black Scholes options-pricing formula allows one to determine the fee. As Cox and Rubinstein 1985 explain, the only required variables for the calculation will be the given minimum price, the actual price, the volatility of actual prices over past years, and the time to expiration—that is, the number of days ahead for the minimum price to apply. Alternatively, the government may sell the limited amount of per-unit price guarantees in an auction). If the objective is to provide subsistence to temporarily impoverished farmers and encourage them to sustain a limited amount of land or number of bushels or livestock (rather than flood the market with excess production), the program may be efficiently designed as a put spread, setting not only the minimum price but also the maximum amount of support paid to farmers per unit of product. For example, if the minimum price is set at 100 and the maximum amount of government support at 20, government pays 15 if the actual price is 85, but no more than 20 even if the actual price drops well below 80.

Changing tastes that may cut demand for a particular commodity (such as lamb and beef in the early 21st century) and cause it to drop in price erode the rationale of the commodity's strategic importance. Thus the risk of a continual drop in demand should not belong to the government. Also, risks that the quality of (and thus the price that can be charged for) a domestic product drops compared with the quality and price of that sold by international competitors, or that new technology and fertilizers drive prices down permanently, should not belong to the government. These are reasonably well under the farmers' control. Thus a price support program would become effective only if the reasons for a low price are temporary and clearly and entirely out of the farmers' control.

central government can impose limits, either confidentially or publicly, for its responsibilities in the event a subnational government goes bankrupt (for example, to ensure the water supply but not the mayor's salary).

As for *dealing with any residual risk that cannot be mitigated or transferred*, this also is best done within the expanded assets and liabilities framework (for literature on the portfolio approach to risk management, see Cassard and Folkerts-Landau 1997; World Bank 2000; World Bank and IMF 2000). Across the two matrixes presented in Tables 1.1 and 1.2, analysis and stress testing of the impact of various types of risks help to account for the correlation in the value of government spending pressures and proceeds under different scenarios, and to identify the government's residual, unhedged risk exposure (the types of risk that have the strongest overall fiscal effect).

The government then has two basic approaches to dealing with its risk exposure and to protecting itself against rare events: building up reserves and using financial hedges. Once a government determines the level of loss it is capable of and willing to absorb, it can establish *reserves* against unexpected losses. Several concerns, though, are associated with provisioning. First, setting reserves on the basis of portfolio risk analysis (as opposed to the additive loss exposure of each government program) is advantageous but it has yet to be fully tested by governments (Lewis and Mody 1997). Second, reserves have an opportunity cost—and one that is particularly high in bad times and in poor countries. The challenge is to acknowledge the opportunity cost of not having reserves—when government is stuck, unprepared for a sudden increase in its obligations or a drop in its revenues. For governments that find themselves unable to obtain favorable credit in such situations, fiscal crises become a reality with all their negative consequences. Furthermore, how should reserves be invested, and who will be responsible for investment decisions? How does government ensure reserve adequacy? And how does government prevent the misuse of reserves? Arguably, politicians will always find ways to tap reserves even for purposes other than those originally intended. The experience in many countries, particularly with stabilization funds, indicates that neither laws nor rules prevent misuse.

Analysts have been searching for possible approaches to improving reserve adequacy and reducing possible misuse. In Chapter 6 of this volume, Daniel Cohen proposes that countries with developed capital markets create a transparent reserve fund and sell its shares to private owners. Market mechanisms would serve to discover the share price of the reserve fund, primarily reflecting on the adequacy of its capitalization and of its use. For countries with underdeveloped capital markets, a reputable foreign institution may be entrusted with the task of

---

Box 1.4 Margin Calls to Collateralize Risk

Learning from the practice of margin calls applied by investment banks, government may be able to reduce moral hazard in the markets and its own risk exposure by requiring beneficiaries of its programs to make collateral payments when their performance deteriorates. The collateral "penalty" would be calculated as the increase in the mark-to-market fiscal cost. This practice would encourage the beneficiaries of government programs to limit their own risk exposure and generate resources for the government contingency reserve fund when the government's risk exposure increases. But it would demand tight monitoring of performance in the real and financial sectors.

Investment banks periodically monitor their credit risk exposure on clients' portfolios against predetermined, uncollateralized limits and require clients to make collateral "penalty" payments for the excess mark-to-market value of a potential loss over the limit. The limit is defined ex ante, as part of the contractual agreement between the bank and the client, often in terms of both the most likely loss and value at risk facing the bank with respect to a specific sector, region, or market segment. For a specific portfolio, when assumptions underlying its risk analysis deteriorate, the bank requires the client (a "margin" call) to immediately make a collateral payment equal to the excess of the mark-to-market potential loss over the limit.

---

managing the reserves under predetermined parameters of risk and returns. A contract would specify permissible claims on reserves and make other claims subject to a penalty and ex ante public disclosure. Both approaches could be complemented with margin calls to collaterize risk (see Box 1.4).

Hedging does not fully substitute for reserves, because all contingencies cannot be foreseen and market hedges are not available for contingencies that can be visualized.[13] However, where hedging is possible, it may be superior to building reserves for governments with good capacities and control mechanisms. The fiscal costs of different government programs may be negatively correlated,[14] but creating additional government programs with the sole objective of risk-pooling would be a questionable practice for government. Therefore, hedging and purchase of reinsurance may be needed to complement pooling.

Take, for example, a government that largely depends on tax revenues from copper sales. When the price of copper goes down, the government is short on revenues. If its access to borrowing is limited, it has to cut public expenditures abruptly. Instead of building a revenue stabilization fund, the government can look for possibilities to stabilize its fiscal performance by structuring its obligations to reflect copper prices. For example, the government may attempt to link its liabilities to the source of volatility—that is, to issue bonds that offer a yield inversely linked to copper price. Structuring liabilities according to the sources of volatility in the government portfolio of contingent liabilities and revenues reduces the overall volatility in the future fiscal outlook and thus offers an alternative to stabilization reserve funds. When revenues are low, debt service will become less expensive and vice versa. Private insurance companies have similar experience in issuing catastrophe bonds, which offer lower yields when a hurricane occurs than when it does not.[15] The government also may purchase customized derivatives that will deliver a positive payoff, inversely related to the copper price, when the price of copper drops below a specific threshold.

Similarly, governments have found ways to hedge their risks through derivatives applied to their obligations portfolio. Many governments—most notably, Belgium, Colombia, Hungary, Ireland, New Zealand, and Sweden—have experimented with asset and liability management approaches in order to match currency, interest rate, and maturity risks in the portfolios of their liabilities and assets. They have utilized interest rate swaps, currency swaps, currency forwards, and other derivatives to achieve the desired risk profile in their debt portfolio.

Possibilities to hedge risks of contingent liabilities have been explored mainly with respect to minimum price support policies and crop insurance. To hedge their risk exposure, several governments (for example, of Colombia and Mexico) have been purchasing futures and customized forward contracts. (For an example of the use of options to hedge price support policy, see Box 1.5). Ideally, the price of the hedge would be passed on to the program beneficiaries (for example, as a fee to be charged the farmers discussed in Box 1.3). Some financial instruments, such as catastrophe bonds, which link their yield inversely to the occurrence of a particular catastrophe, would help to hedge risks of associated contingent liabilities and revenue decline. For more examples, using a combination of the above approaches, see Table 1.6.

The borderline between hedging and speculation is, however, sometimes difficult to draw. Recent experiences of companies and hedge funds have reconfirmed that derivatives that provide less than a perfect hedge may generate risks on their own. Also, the use of derivatives is dangerous if there is not a clear strategy on which specific risks to hedge and to what extent to hedge them. For government as well as for private companies, the ad hoc availability of new hedging instruments, and the attractions of financial engineering, should never drive risk management decisions. Potentially risky hedging techniques in-

---

Box 1.5 Securitizing Government Risk

How does a government hedge the risk of price support policies? Suppose the government offers a minimum price guarantee on a commodity. Assuming the floor price is set at $10 per unit, the government pays the difference between the floor and actual price if the actual price falls below $10 per unit (see graph).

This payoff exactly illustrates that providing a price support policy is equal to shorting a put option (selling the right to sell a commodity at a specified minimum price). To hedge against possible losses, the replicating strategy suggests buying puts from international financial intermediaries. The cost to the government is the difference between the total fees collected by the government from the commodity producers (if possible in an auction) and the price paid by the government for the put. The strategy allows the government to convert its fiscal cost from the form of an unknown contingent liability to a fixed, up-front payment.

---

clude a dynamic hedging strategy, which requires readjusting the hedging mechanism as its underlying assumptions change (Hull 1997).

Therefore, before a treasurer or debt managers launch sophisticated risk management techniques, top policymakers need to decide to what extent the government should be exposed to risk—that is, to what extent should the government require that its expected fiscal pressures be matched with its actual resources? Addressing this question, in turn, will depend on the extent to which government can rely on ad hoc borrowing and tax increases and on the extent to which the government can afford to restructure or default on its budget programs (are arrears permissible?) and on its contingent and direct liabilities. And what is the government's risk management capability?

Table 1.6 Reducing Government Risk Exposure

Source of risk	Reduce risk in design	Reduce exposure for risks taken
Guarantees	Cover only selected risks such as political/policy risks.	Adjust risk exposures in direct liability and assets portfolio (for example, reduce exposure to the pertinent currency if exchange rate risk is covered by the guarantee). Establish a reserve fund for all guarantees. Limit total benefits paid to the amount available in the reserve fund. Ensure reserve adequacy by transforming the reserve fund into a public company with shares freely traded.[a]
Disaster insurance	Cap maximum benefit. Insure middle rather than first portion of loss.	Issue catastrophe bonds (possibly for a basket of likely disasters). Purchase reinsurance for risks in excess of a threshold that is deemed fiscally bearable.
Deposit insurance	Require information disclosure, sound regulation, supervision, and enforcement before introducing deposit insurance. Cap maximum benefit. Insure middle rather than first portion of loss.	Establish separate reserve fund. Limit total benefits paid to the amount available in the reserve fund. Ensure reserve adequacy by transforming the reserve fund into a public company with shares freely traded.[a]
Price support	Auction policies. Cover only selected risks such as political/policy risks.	Purchase payoff-replicating derivatives. Purchase reinsurance.
Implicit guarantees to banks and enterprises	Make announcements and act to minimize moral hazard.	Seek contingent credit line from IMF.
Privatization and asset sale	Find a strategic investor (future revenue). Maximize privatization revenue.	Use proceeds to reduce government liabilities or future obligations.

(Table continues on the following page.)

Table 1.6 (continued)

Source of risk	Reduce risk in design	Reduce exposure for risks taken
Purchase of bad assets	Pay only estimated market price (a part of recapitalization objectives). Allow for market mechanisms to deal with bad assets (strengthening the position of creditor, bankruptcy processes, and so forth). Make announcements and act to minimize expectations of future possible repeated purchases.	Sell bad assets quickly.
Commodity tax	Demand base payment independent of commodity price.	Issue commodity-linked bonds. Purchase commodity-linked derivatives. Purchase insurance.
Repayment of direct lending	Require collateral.	Purchase default insurance.

a. The interests of the fund shareholders would contribute to ensuring reserve adequacy—that is, to charging guarantee beneficiaries, such as banks, adequate premiums. This arrangement loosely imitates the arrangement suggested in Chapter 6 by Daniel Cohen in this volume.

Source: The authors.

The Fiscal Risk Questionnaire: An Example

For many governments, the objective to understand and manage their exposure to fiscal risk is likely to require major efforts throughout an extended period of time. The fiscal risk questionnaire that follows provides a set of questions that analysts and policymakers may find useful in dealing with government fiscal risk.

🙷 🙷 🙷

Fiscal Risk Questionnaire

A. Macroeconomic Context

1. What are the macroeconomic constraints on the government's future fiscal performance?
   Identify constraints such as a currency board or other inflexible exchange rate arrangement, high public debt levels, low sovereign credit rating, or shallow domestic debt markets that risk the government's future ability to issue debt.

2. What trends are affecting the government's general fiscal position?
   Analyze medium-term and long-term trends to provide a consolidated picture inclusive of all levels of government, off-budget funds, public assets, and liabilities.

3. How sensitive are these fiscal trends to the underlying macroeconomic, demographic, and policy assumptions?
   Build stress scenarios for the medium-term and long-term fiscal outlooks with respect to the underlying assumptions.

B. Sources of Fiscal Risk

1. What are the major sources of fiscal risk? What are the largest and riskiest contingent government liabilities in the country? Are they explicit or implicit? Fill in the Fiscal Risk Matrix (Table 1.1) with specific items.

2. What are the main types of risks determining the size and urgency of the items in the Fiscal Risk Matrix?
   Consider currency risk, interest rate risk, commodity price risk, refinancing risk, operational risk, political risk, policy risk, and similar risks.

3. Overall, are the items identified in the Fiscal Risk Matrix likely to raise significantly the future financing requirement of the government? If so, under which circumstances mainly?
   Consider the overall size of contingent liabilities (face values) and a stress scenario if these obligations are realized. Compare the overall face value of contingent liabilities with the reported government debt and with the government's future borrowing capacity.

C. Analysis of Selected Risks

1. How clearly defined are the public sector and the spheres of government responsibility? Is there a precise legal delineation of the

public sector (for example, in the form of a full list of public sector agencies) and of government responsibilities? If not legally defined, is it clearly understood which services are guaranteed by the government?

2. State-guaranteed institutions and directed credit
   Identify institutions that fulfill orders of the government to extend financing to enterprises, banks, agencies of any kind, or households. Review their balance sheets and statements of contingent liabilities.
   What type of government support do these institutions receive (for example, privatization revenues, cheap financing via the central bank, state guarantee for borrowings)?

3. Guarantees
   Review government guarantees, their issuer (the ministry of finance or other government agency), beneficiaries, creditors, face values, the type of risks and their shares covered, currency of denomination, and risk estimates if any.

4. State-owned enterprises and banks
   Review the largest state-owned enterprises and their balance sheets and risk statements and the largest state-owned banks and their balance sheets and risk statements.

D. Sources of Government Financial Safety

1. What are the major sources of government financial safety? What are the largest tradable government assets and other sources of future revenues? Fill in the Fiscal Hedge Matrix (Table 1.2) with specific items.

2. How sensitive are these financial sources to the respective types of risks? What are the likely scenarios for the future government revenue stream?

3. Taking into account the correlation in the sensitivity of government finances to the different types of risks, compare the scenarios of the likely future government revenue stream with the likely financing pressures to emerge from the items identified in the Fiscal Risk Matrix. What is the worst-case scenario?

E. Recording and Reporting: Transparency

1. For each item in the matrixes, which agencies are responsible for final approval, recording, monitoring, and data consolidation?

2. Which agencies and authorities are informed ex ante about contingent liabilities and, overall, about the fiscal risks associated with programs under government consideration?
   • The issuing agency only?
   • The related sector ministry?
   • The finance ministry?
   • The cabinet?
   • The parliament?
   • Others?

3. Which agencies can instantaneously retrieve up-to-date information about the items listed in the matrixes? Which documents report such information? What is the time lag in reporting?

4. Which sources of fiscal risks are *not* reported to the:
   • Ministry of finance
   • Cabinet
   • Central bank
   • Parliament
   • Foreign investors
   • Public?

F. Institutional Arrangements: Accountability

1. Do any legal requirements apply to the government with respect to estimating, accounting, and reporting the *future* fiscal costs associated with its direct and contingent liabilities?
   No
   Yes, in the budget process
   • when the government is called on to pay
   • when cash is transferred
   • other.

2. Which of the obligations identified in the Fiscal Risk Matrix are *not* regulated by any law and depend fully on ad hoc government decisions?

3. What is the legal and regulatory framework for:
   • *State guarantees:* the requirements for their design (the type of risks that can be covered, the extent of the required risk-sharing), issuance (is only the ministry of finance authorized?), government control mechanism (required reports from the creditor and beneficiary, audit and valuation requirements), and the realization mechanism if they fall due.

- *Subnational governments, public sector agencies and enterprises, and state-guaranteed institutions:* the financial management and reporting requirements and government control mechanism.
- *Demands on the government to extend ad hoc previously unforeseen financial support:* the legal requirements and practice for deliberation in government decisionmaking.

4. Is the government legally required to explain increases in public liabilities (particularly increases above the levels explained by budget deficit figures)?
   No
   Yes,
   - to the parliament
   - to the public
   - other.

5. What is the authority and capacity of the supreme audit institution with respect to the government's risk exposure and risk management?
   Is the supreme audit institution authorized to review and capable of reviewing the quality and assumptions of the government's fiscal risk analysis, fiscal risk management strategy, and fiscal risk management practice?

G. Policy: Practice

1. When the government considers new promises of contingent government support, how much attention does it pay to risk analysis, to the issues of moral hazard in the markets, and similar things? In particular, do the ministry of finance, cabinet, central bank, or parliament quantify the future fiscal cost of alternative options in a single medium-term fiscal framework? Describe the risks of alternative options (direct versus contingent support program, possibilities for risk-sharing in guarantee contracts, and others).

2. In which areas and under what circumstances do the public or interest groups expect the government to provide financial support beyond the budget?

3. Identify examples of times at which the government withstood political pressure and did not provide financial support beyond the budgeted figures (for example, when the government refused to solicit financial support for a failed enterprise or bank).

4. Are public enterprises and banks, state-guaranteed institutions, and creditors and beneficiaries under state guarantees "rewarded" and "punished" for the quality of their management of risk? *Provide examples.*

H. Fiscal Risk Management: Capacities

1. Describe the capacities of the ministry of finance, other government agencies, public sector institutions and enterprises, and state-guaranteed institutions to analyze, monitor, and control the risks of government programs and contingent liabilities.
   What methodologies have been used to analyze the size and risks of specific contingent liabilities? What have been the challenges and results in applying these methodologies? What has been the process of monitoring and controlling risk?

2. Describe the process of designing a state guarantee, a state insurance program, or any other program that involves fiscal risk.
   Particularly focus on the risk analysis and treatment of moral hazard in the design process. For example, to what extent are risks shared between the government and the program beneficiaries?

3. What measures have been implemented by the parliament, cabinet, ministry of finance, sector ministries, and other public agencies to prevent and reduce fiscal risks arising from the public and private sectors?
   For example, are there any limits on enterprise debt, subnational government obligations, or central bank obligations? Are any actions taken if they appear too high? Does the government have an explicit risk management strategy with respect to its overall fiscal risk exposure?

4. Does the government build contingency reserves, purchase reinsurance, or hedge to mitigate its fiscal risk exposure?
   Who determines the required size of the contingency reserves and how? What is the hedging practice?

Conclusion

Dealing with contingent liabilities and other fiscal risks has recently surfaced as an increasingly important issue in public finance analysis and public finance management. Learning from country experience and from new research (both discussed in the chapters of this book), this chapter has outlined a framework to guide analysts and policymakers in their attempts to understand and improve the management of fiscal risk. Further research and long-term efforts by governments will be needed, however, for public finance analysis and public finance institutions to truly come to terms with government fiscal risk, and for policymakers and civil servants to acquire the incentives and capacity to optimize government exposure to risks.

Notes

1. The literature discussing the ultimate fiscal and economic costs of hidden government obligations is large. Kharas and Mishra (2001) illustrate the fiscal cost of contingent liabilities across over 30 countries. Works by Brock (1992), Kryzanowski and Roberts (1993), Caprio and Klingebiel (1997), and World Bank (2001a) discuss government bailouts in the banking sector. Freeman and Mendelowitz (1982) illustrate a bailout in the private corporate sector. U.S. GAO (1998) draws lessons from the past fiscal cost of credit guarantees and government insurance programs. Townsend (1977), Salant (1983), and Bardsley (1994) analyze adverse behavioral effects and the ex post fiscal cost of price-fixing schemes. Dillinger (1999) and Fornasari, Webb, and Zou (2000) analyze bailouts of subnational governments by the central government.

2. The conventional approach to the analysis of fiscal sustainability is limited in two ways: first, it looks only at the liability side of the public sector balance sheet, and, second, it considers only direct liabilities, ignoring contingent liabilities, both explicit and implicit. Under the conventional approach, the actual deficit is compared with the estimated sustainable deficit level that will keep the debt-to-GDP (gross domestic product) ratio constant for feasible rates of growth, real interest, and inflation. This approach assumes that keeping a constant ratio of public debt to GDP will ensure public sector solvency and avoid debt crises in the future. Another, less-stringent requirement is to test for the no-Ponzi-scheme condition for public debt, followed up by the neoclassical solvency approach. This methodology checks for public solvency by comparing the annual rate of growth of the government debt-to-GDP ratio with the real interest rate. If the debt ratio systematically grows faster than the real interest rate, the public sector is considered insolvent. Conventional fiscal analysis also tends to neglect the sensitivity of the fiscal position to risks, such as macroeconomic volatility, called contingent liabilities, and unclear expenditure commitments, and the ability of the government to cope with shocks.

For a critique of standard approaches to fiscal sustainability analysis and deficit measurement, see Eisner and Pieper (1984), Buiter (1985), Bean and Buiter (1987), Fischer and Easterly (1990), Blejer and Cheasty (1991), Easterly, Rodriguez, and Schmidt-Hebbel (1994), Selowsky (1998), Easterly (1999), and Kharas and Mishra (2001). These studies reflect the fact that, depending on the definition and measurement methodology, deficit measures may mean very different things. They explore the impact of the coverage of a government budget, the definition of government, and the accounting and budgeting frameworks, as well as the impact of inflation, seasonality, structural changes in the economy, and the business cycle on the results of fiscal analysis. Doubts have been expressed about the feasibility of incorporating hidden government obligations in fiscal analysis. For example, Eisner (1984) notes that the valuation of contingent liabilities of government in the calculation of deficits is subject to the criticism that the government can legislate actions that may seriously change their future value.

For a critique of how public finance management frameworks treat contingent liabilities and fiscal risk, see, for example, World Bank (1997), Schick (1998, 2001), and Schiavo-Campo and Tommasi (1999).

3. This section draws on Polackova (1998).

4. In Chapter 7 of this book, Richard Hemming and Murray Petrie try to differentiate quasi-fiscal activities from contingent liabilities, using a narrower definition for contingent liabilities.

5. Dillinger (1999) provides examples of the subnational government risk of Argentina and Brazil. Hutchinson (2000) and World Bank (2001b) illustrate the fiscal risks of state-owned enterprises. In the United States, an interesting body of literature has been developed around the so-called government-sponsored enterprises (GSEs), which provide guarantees in housing and agriculture markets. The best-known GSEs are Fannie Mae and Freddie Mac. Creditors have perceived GSEs as beneficiaries of an implicit guarantee of the U.S. government and thus have been willing to offer cheap financing. For an overview, see Stanton and Moe (2001) and Van Order (2000).

6. The Medium-Term Expenditure Framework (MTEF), as first applied in Australia, tackles fiscal opportunism with respect to government expenditures and revenues by requiring policymakers to analyze and disclose the assumptions and medium-term (three to five years) implications of their budget proposals and to be accountable for any departures from their targeted levels in year-by-year decisionmaking. In South Africa, MTEF extends further to cover consequences of off-budget items such as government guarantees. For a discussion, see World Bank (1997), Schiavo-Campo and Tommasi (1999), Kruger (1999), and Schick (2001).

7. Stress scenarios illustrate the sensitivity of expected fiscal outcomes to normal and abnormal changes in the underlying assumptions. For a specific program, stress testing will show how normal and extreme changes in the underlying factors (such as commodity price) over the next 3, 6, and 12 months will affect its fiscal cost. More broadly, applied to the government's fiscal position stress testing helps detect key fiscal vulnerabilities of government. A convenient way to generate less likely scenarios and stress scenarios is the value-at-risk (cost-at-risk) approach. For an introduction to the value-at-risk literature, see, for example, Best (1998) and Butler (1999); for an application to contingent liabilities, see Blejer and Schumacher (1998).

A baseline scenario would reflect the expected, most likely outcomes and utilize actuarial, econometric, or contingent claim analysis methods (see Lewis and Mody 1997 and Mody and Patro 1996 for a summary and Hull 1997 for a textbook introduction).

8. Many governments pay the cost of defaulted contingent liabilities directly from borrowing proceeds. In such cases, contingent liabilities never affect the budget and budget deficit. After they fall due, they are only reflected in an increase in government debt.

9. The use of present value budgeting may or may not affect cash-based estimates of the government's fiscal deficit. It depends on whether the effect on the deficit is recorded when money is transferred from the budget to a contingency fund (then no effect is recorded when a guarantee is called and paid for from the contingency fund) or only when actual cash payments are disbursed from the program account. For more discussion on accounting and budgeting for risk, see also Lewis and Mody (1997), Brixi, Ghanem, and Islam (1999), Brixi, Papp, and Schick (1999), and World Bank (1999b).

10. A full accrual-based accounting system, though desirable, is neither necessary nor sufficient to ensure that governments adequately report and consider contingent fiscal risks in policy. Although an accrual accounting system encourages governments to prepare a statement of contingent liabilities and financial risks, it generally does not require that contingent liabilities be included in the balance sheet and that the associated risks be evaluated and quantified. International accounting standards, for example, require only *probable* contingent liabilities (contingencies with a relatively high probability of realization) to be included in the balance sheet, leaving the others in a separate statement of contingent liabilities without requiring analysis of the underlying risks. In the case of budgeting, budgeting for the present value of the future fiscal cost of contingent liabilities may be combined with cash budgeting for budgetary spending (cash-based) programs. Countries successfully combining reporting on contingent liabilities with cash accounting include the Czech Republic, Hungary, and South Africa, and those budgeting for contingent liabilities within a cash-based budgeting system include Canada, the Netherlands, and the United States.

11. Derivatives can be designed in many different ways to fit the risk management objectives. Basic derivatives include futures and forwards, swaps, and options. A *future contract* is an arrangement between two parties to buy or sell an asset at a predetermined future time and price. These contracts are normally traded on an exchange. A similar arrangement, a *forward contract*, can be made with a financial intermediary over-the-counter, without involving an exchange. A *swap* is an arrangement in which two parties exchange the stream of payment of two different assets. For background on futures, forwards, and swaps, see Hull (1997). An *option contract* gives the holder the right but not the obligation to buy (call option) or to sell (put option) an asset at a predetermined future time and price. This predetermined price is known

as the *strike price* and the predetermined date is known as the *expiration* or *maturity date*. At the time of purchase, the buyer of an option contract pays an *option price* to the option writer. *Option-pricing analysis*, most often employing the Black-Scholes formula, serves to set the option price. For background on options, see Cox and Rubinstein (1985). On the actual and possible use of derivatives as hedging instruments by governments, see, for example, Claessens (1993), Nars (1997), World Bank (1999a, 2000), and Patterson (2001).

12. Mody (2000), for example, describes the experience with rainfall insurance purchased by the government of Nicaragua from a private reinsurer.

13. *Hedging* refers to the strategy of protecting oneself against losses arising from changes in market conditions. It involves relatively safe *perfectly offsetting transactions* (that would "perfectly" offset gaines/losses arising from changes in market conditions) and relatively risky *dynamic hedging strategies* (that require continual rebalancing as market conditions evolve). For an introduction, see Hull (1997).

14. Pooling less than perfectly correlated risks (for example, hurricane, drought, and fire) would allow the government to reduce the volatility in the total long-term cost of its insurance programs.

15. Catastrophe bonds are obligations whose interest and principal payments are linked to a catastrophic event. For example, they could call for a reduction in the interest or principal, or for extension of maturity if losses related to the underlying event exceed the trigger level. This arrangement is called reinsurance protection (see Insurance Services Office 1999).

References

The word *processed* describes informally reproduced works that may not be commonly available through libraries.

Arthur Andersen. 2000. *General and Specific Methodologies for Valuing Contingent Liabilities*. Washington, D.C.

Bardsley, Peter. 1994. "The Collapse of the Australian Wool Reserve Price Schemes." *Economic Journal* 104 (426): 1087–1105.

Bean, Charles, and William Buiter. 1987. "The Plain Man's Guide to Fiscal and Financial Policy." Employment Institute, London, October.

Best, Philip. 1998. *Implementing Value at Risk*. Chichester; New York: John Wiley.

Blejer, Mario, and Adrienne Cheasty. 1991. "The Measurement of Fiscal Deficits: Analytical and Methodological Issues." *Journal of Economic Literature* 29: 1644–78.

Blejer, Mario, and Liliana Schumacher. 1998. "Central Bank Vulnerability and the Credibility of Commitments: A Value-at-Risk Approach to Currency Crises." IMF Working Paper WP/98/65. International Monetary Fund, Washington, D.C.

Bodie, Zvi, and Philip Davis. 2000. *The Foundations of Pension Finance.* 2 vols. Cheltenham; Northampton: Elgar Reference Collection.

Brixi, Hana Polackova, Hafez Ghanem, and Roumeen Islam. 1999. "Fiscal Adjustment and Contingent Government Liabilities." Policy Research Working Paper 2177. World Bank, Washington, D.C.

Brixi, Hana Polackova, Anita Papp, and Allen Schick. 1999. "Fiscal Risks and the Quality of Fiscal Adjustment in Hungary." Policy Research Working Paper 2176. World Bank, Washington, D.C.

Brock, Philip. 1992. "External Shocks and Financial Collapse: Foreign Loan Guarantees and Intertemporal Substitution of Investment in Texas and Chile." *American Economic Review* 82 (2): 168–73.

Buiter, Willem. 1985. "A Guide to Public Sector Debt and Deficits." *Economic Policy* (November): 14–79.

Butler, Cormac. 1999. *Mastering Value at Risk: A Step-By-Step Guide to Understanding and Applying Var.* London; New York: Financial Times/ Prentice Hall.

Calderon Zuleta, Alberto. 1999. "Valuing and Managing Risk Associated with Government Contingent Liabilities." In *Proceedings of the Second Sovereign Debt Management Forum.* Washington, D.C., November 1–3. World Bank.

Caprio Jr., Gerard, and Daniela Klingebiel. 1997. "Bank Insolvency: Bad Luck, Bad Policy, or Bad Banking?" In Michael Bruno and Boris Pleskovic, eds., *Annual World Bank Conference on Development Economics 1996.* Washington, D.C.: World Bank.

Cassard, Marcel, and David Folkerts-Landau. 1997. "Risk Management of Sovereign Assets and Liabilities." IMF Working Paper WP/97/166. International Monetary Fund, Washington, D.C.

Chase Manhattan Bank. 1996. *Risk Management Handbook, Private Sector Participation in Urban Infrastructure.* Washington, D.C.: U.S. Agency for International Development.

Claessens, Stijn. 1993. "Risk Management in Developing Countries." Technical Paper 235. World Bank, Washington, D.C.

Commonwealth Secretariat. 2001. *External Sector Contingent Liabilities— A Study on India.* London, January.

Congressional Research Service. 1998. *Tax Expenditures. Compendium of Background Material on Individual Provisions.* Committee on the Budget, U.S. Senate, Washington, D.C.

Cox, John, and Mark Rubinstein. 1985. *Options Markets.* Upper Saddle River, N.J.: Prentice Hall.

Davis, Jeffrey, Rolando Ossowski, James Daniel, and Steven Barnett. 2001. "Stabilization and Savings Funds for Nonrenewable Resources. Experience and Fiscal Policy Implications." Occasional Paper 205. International Monetary Fund, Washington, D.C.

Dillinger, William. 1999. "Fiscal Management in Federal Democracies: Argentina and Brazil." Policy Research Working Paper 2121. World Bank, Washington, D.C.

Dooley, Michael. 2000. "Debt Management and Crisis in Developing Countries." *Journal of Development Economics* 63 (October): 45–58.

Easterly, William. 1999. "When Is Fiscal Adjustment an Illusion?" *Economic Policy* (April).

Easterly, William, Carlos Alfredo Rodriguez, and Klaus Schmidt-Hebbel. 1994. *Public Sector Deficits and Macroeconomic Performance.* Washington, D.C.: World Bank.

Eisner, Robert. 1984. "Which Budget Deficit? Some Issues of Measurement and Their Implications." *American Economic Review* 74 (2):138–43.

Eisner, Robert, and Paul Pieper. 1984. "A New View of the Federal Debt and Budget Deficits." *American Economic Review* 74 (2): 11–29.

Fischer, Stanley, and William Easterly. 1990. "The Economics of the Government Budget Constraint." *World Bank Research Observer* 5 (2).

Fornasari, Francesca, Steven Webb, and Heng-fu Zou. 2000. "The Macroeconomic Impact of Decentralized Spending and Deficits: International Evidence." *Annals of Economics and Finance* 1 (November): 403–33.

Freeman, Brian, and Allan Mendelowitz. 1982. "Program in Search of a Policy: The Chrysler Loan Guarantee." *Journal of Policy Analysis and Management* 1 (summer): 443–53.

Froot, K. A., D. S. Scharfstein, and J. C. Stein. 1994. "A Framework for Risk Management." *Harvard Business Review* (November–December).

Garber, Peter. 1998. "Derivatives in International Capital Flows." Working Paper 6623. National Bureau of Economic Research, Cambridge, Mass., June.

Honohan, Patrick. 1999. "Fiscal Contingency Planning for Banking Crises." Policy Research Working Paper 2228. World Bank, Washington, D.C.

Hueth, Darrell L., and William H. Furtan. 1994. *Economics of Agricultural Crop Insurance: Theory and Evidence.* Norwell, Mass.: Kluwer Academic Publishers.

Hull, John. 1997. *Options, Futures, and Other Derivatives.* Upper Saddle River, N.J.: Prentice Hall.

Hutchinson, Gladstone. 2000. "The Challenge of Fiscal Sustainability: Public Enterprise Financial Relationship with Government in Jamaica." Lafayette College. Processed.

IMF (International Monetary Fund). 1996. "Aging Populations and the Fiscal Consequences of Public Pension Schemes." Washington, D.C.

Insurance Services Office. 1999. "Insuring Catastrophic Risk." Processed.

Irwin, Timothy, Michael Klein, Guillermo Perry, and Mateen Thobani. 1998. *Public Risk in Private Infrastructure.* Washington, D.C.: World Bank.

Kharas, Homi, and Deepak Mishra. 2001. "Fiscal Policy, Hidden Deficits, and Currency Crises." In S. Devarajan, F. H. Rogers, and L. Squire, eds. *World Bank Economists' Forum.* Washington, D.C.: World Bank.

Kruger, Coen. 1999. "Valuing and Managing Risk Associated with Government Contingent Liabilities." Presentation at the Second Sovereign Debt Management Forum, Washington, D.C., November 1–3. World Bank.

Kryzanowski, L., and G. S. Roberts. 1993. "Canadian Banking Solvency." *Journal of Money, Credit and Banking* 25 (3): 361–76.

Larson, Donald F., Panos Varangis, and Nanae Yabuki. 1998. "Commodity Risk Management and Development." Policy Research Working Paper 1963. World Bank, Washington, D.C.

Leaven, Luc. 2000. "Banking Risks around the World: The Implicit Safety Net Subsidy Approach." World Bank. Processed.

Lewis, Christopher, and Ashoka Mody. 1997. "The Management of Contingent Liabilities: A Risk Management Framework for National Governments." In Timothy Irwin, Michael Klein, Guillermo Perry, and Mateen Thobani, eds., *Dealing with Public Risk in Private Infrastructure*. World Bank Latin American and Caribbean Studies. Washington, D.C.: World Bank.

Marrison, Christopher. 2001. "Risk Measurement for Project Finance Guarantees." Capital Markets Company. Processed.

Mody, Ashoka. 2000. "Nicaragua: Rainfall Risk Management Project." World Bank. Processed.

Mody, Ashoka, and Dilip Patro. 1996. "Valuing and Accounting for Loan Guarantees." *World Bank Research Observer* 11 (February): 119–42.

Nars, Kari. 1997. *Excellence in Debt Management*. London: Euromoney.

OECD (Organisation for Economic Co-operation and Development). 1999. *How Should Governments Invest Financial Assets and Manage Debt*. PUMA/SBO/RD (99). Paris: OECD.

———. 2000. *Reforms for an Aging Society*. Paris: OECD.

Patterson, Linda. 2001. "The State of Texas Hedging Program: A Long Position and a Long Perspective." Presentation delivered at World Bank, June 25. Patterson and Associates. Processed.

Polackova, Hana. 1998. "Contingent Government Liabilities: A Hidden Risk for Fiscal Stability." Policy Research Working Paper 1989. World Bank, Washington, D.C.

Salant, S. W. 1983. "The Vulnerability of Price Stabilization Schemes to Speculative Attack." *Journal of Political Economy* 91: 1–38.

Schiavo-Campo, Salvatore, and Daniel Tommasi. 1999. *Managing Government Expenditure*. Manila: Asian Development Bank.

Schick, Allen. 1998. *A Contemporary Approach to Public Expenditure Management*. Washington, D.C.: World Bank.

———. 2001. "Does Budgeting Have a Future?" Presentation at OECD Senior Budget Officials' Meeting, Paris, May. Organisation for Economic Co-operation and Development.

Selowsky, Marcelo. 1998. "Fiscal Deficits and the Quality of Fiscal Adjustment." In *The Challenges for Public Liability Management in Central Europe*. Washington, D.C.: World Bank.

Standard and Poor's. 1997. "Criteria: Financial System Stress and Sovereign Credit Risk." *Sovereign Ratings Service* (December).

Stanton, Thomas, and Ronald Moe. 2001. "Government Corporations and Government Sponsored Enterprises." In Lester M. Salamon, ed., *The Tools of Government: A Public Management Handbook for the Era of Third-Party Government.* New York: Oxford University Press.

Townsend, R. M. 1977. "The Eventual Failure of Price Fixing Schemes." *Journal of Economic Theory* 14: 190–99.

U.S. GAO (General Accounting Office). 1993. *Bank Insurance Fund: Review of Loss Estimation Methodologies.* Washington, D.C.

———. 1998. *Budgeting for Federal Insurance Programs.* Washington, D.C.

Van Order, Robert. 2000. "The Structure and Evolution of American Secondary Mortgage Markets, with Some Implications for Developing Markets." Freddie Mac, Washington, D.C. Processed.

World Bank. 1994. *Averting the Old Age Crisis.* Washington, D.C.

———. 1997. *Public Expenditure Management Handbook.* Washington, D.C.

———. 1999a. "Dealing with Commodity Price Volatility in Developing Countries: A Proposal for a Market-based Approach?" Discussion Paper for the Roundtable on Commodity Risk Management in Developing Countries, Washington, D.C., September 24.

———. 1999b. *Malaysia: Public Expenditure Review.* Washington, D.C.

———. 1999c. *Toolkits for Private Participation in Water and Sanitation.* Washington, D.C.

———. 2000. *Proceedings of the Second Sovereign Debt Management Forum.* Washington, D.C., November 1–3.

———. 2001a. *Finance for Growth: Policy Choices in a Volatile World.* Policy Research Report, May.

———. 2001b. "Parastatal Performance and Strategy in Bangladesh." Processed.

World Bank and IMF (International Monetary Fund). 2000. "Guidelines for Public Debt Management" *<www.worldbank.org/fps/>.*

Yaron, Jacob. 1992. "Assessing Development Finance Institutions—A Public Interest Analysis." World Bank Discussion Paper 174. World Bank, Washington, D.C.

CHAPTER 2

Accounting and Financial Accountability to Capture Risk

Murray Petrie
The Economics and Strategy Group

THE TRADITIONAL CASH-BASED accounting and reporting systems used by many governments provide inadequate information within the executive for the management of fiscal risks.[1] They also do not produce enough information for the legislature and the public to hold governments accountable for the management of fiscal risks. The traditional focus on cash has been consistently associated with fiscal management practices that are short term and reactive. Poor information has interacted with poor incentives to discourage decisionmakers from taking a longer-term view of fiscal risks and their management.

In recognition of these shortcomings, a range of initiatives has been introduced in different countries and by international agencies that, while not motivated solely by a desire for better risk management, has important implications for the management of fiscal risk. The initiatives taken include: greater overall transparency in fiscal management, supplementary reporting of noncash information in budget documents and the final accounts, changes to the basis of accounting, and moves by governments to tighten control over fiscal risks.

This chapter discusses these initiatives. It does so within a framework that focuses on risk to the aggregate fiscal position—that is, on sources of variability in the overall level of government spending, revenues, the fiscal balance, and value of assets and liabilities. While these sources of variability manifest themselves through variability in individual spending, revenue, and financing programs, it is the impact on the aggregate fiscal position that is the chief object of concern.

Risk is defined here as any situation in which there is a range of possible outcomes around the expected fiscal position. Inherent uncertainty about which of a number of different possible states of nature will apply in the future creates a range of possible fiscal outcomes. This approach captures forecasting risk, in addition to uncertain obligations such as guarantees and other contingent liabilities.[2] The focus in this chapter is on the annual budget and the short- to medium-term fiscal position.

In general, the objective of financial risk management for any entity is to improve the entity's financial position and performance, while protecting the entity from unacceptable variance in returns—and in particular from the risk of unacceptable losses. It is clear that the specification of what is an unacceptable level of fiscal risk will vary from country to country. It will depend on the initial fiscal position, the degree of fiscal flexibility, the nature and extent of fiscal risks, the quality of the information available, the capacity for risk management, and on the perceived "return" to risk-taking. Assessing what a government's appetite for risk should be is an extremely complex issue, which at present is at the boundary of public finance theory, let alone practice (for a discussion of these issues, see OECD 1999 and Polackova 1998). For most governments, determining optimal risk exposure will not be of practical relevance until major progress has been made in identifying, analyzing, quantifying, reporting, and managing existing fiscal risks. This is the subject of the rest of this chapter.

The chapter is structured as follows. The next section describes the weaknesses in traditional cash-based budget management systems with respect to the management of fiscal risks. That section is followed by one that outlines a framework for fiscal risk management, comprising both macro-level and micro-level elements, and provides country examples. The chapter ends with some concluding remarks.

Weaknesses in the Treatment of Risk under Traditional Cash-based Accounting Systems

Governments have historically reported their financial performance using cash-basis accounting.[3] The reasons for this include simplicity, compliance with legal requirements, and the government's borrowing requirement and the macroeconomic impact of the budget.

Cash-basis accounting has, however, a number of well-recognized weaknesses. Some relate specifically to inadequacies in the treatment of fiscal risks. For example:

• The cash basis results in the incomplete or inaccurate measurement of current transactions. In many instances, there is a discrepancy between when a commitment is entered into, when resources are used and the economic effects are felt, and when a cash payment is made. For example, contingent liabilities are not reflected in pure cash-basis financial statements until and if they have to be paid.[4] The real effects of government lending and insurance programs and of civil service pension schemes are distorted by cash-basis reporting.[5]

• There is a lack of information on stocks of assets and liabilities and the relationship between flow and stock variables. Although most governments provide at least some information on public debt, depreciation is not reported, and risks relating to an impending need for capital replacement may remain hidden.

In addition, there has generally been no reporting of the sensitivity of the fiscal position to changes in key forecasting assumptions.

More seriously, the deferred recognition of expenditures can hide an accumulation of problems until they reach massive proportions. The classic example of this is regulatory forbearance in banking supervision. Regulators and politicians may be tempted to defer dealing with insolvent banks in the hope the banks will recover, or, if not, that the cost will fall on a future administration.[6] With the expectation of future government support, the managers of distressed banks may take on even higher levels of risk in the knowledge they are in effect gambling with public money. The cost of financial sector reconstruction in the last two decades has been massive in many countries and constitutes a major source of fiscal risk.

In general, therefore, pure cash-basis accounting and reporting result in inadequate information for use by the executive in managing fiscal risks and for use by the legislature and the public in holding the government accountable for such management. Moreover, it often leaves financial markets guessing about the true state of public finances and the likely (as opposed to the budgeted) fiscal deficit. In recognition of these shortcomings, some countries have introduced in recent years a range of initiatives in fiscal risk management. These include overall transparency in the public accounts[7]; supplementary reporting of information on fiscal risks in budget documents, in the final accounts, or in both; a change to the basis of accounting; and a centralized approach to implementing fiscal risk management within the government. These initiatives are discussed in detail in the next section.

Recent Initiatives to Build Accountability in Fiscal Risk Management

The approach to fiscal risk management outlined below contains what might be thought of as both macro- and micro-level elements. The macro-level element covers broad transparency to the public in the conduct of fiscal policy. The more micro-level elements comprise specific reporting of information on fiscal risks, the choice of an appropriate basis of accounting, and a centralized approach to the implementation of fiscal risk management.

Greater Overall Fiscal Transparency

Conducting fiscal policy in a transparent and open manner is a high-level approach that has the potential to reduce significantly fiscal risk and improve risk management. Making information available publicly requires institutional capacity and systems within government so that the information is available within government in the first instance.[8] Such "internal transparency" is capable on its own of producing major gains in the management of fiscal risk through improving the information base within the executive for fiscal decisionmaking and strengthening accountability within government for risk management.

In the absence of public transparency, however, there is limited external accountability and less assurance that there will be a sustainable improvement in the management of fiscal risk. And in the absence of external accountability, there may be less incentive for the government to implement sound internal risk management systems in the first place.

Construed broadly, fiscal transparency requires much more than just the timely publication of the budget and final accounts. It also covers clarity of roles and responsibilities; commitment to the timely publication of complete information on the past, present, and projected fiscal position; open budget preparation, execution, and reporting; and independent assurances of the integrity of fiscal information.[9]

Transparency in all these dimensions is a critically important element of a medium-term fiscal risk management strategy. While there are elements of transparency that relate specifically to the reporting of fiscal risks (see below), there are also broader elements that can significantly reduce fiscal risk. For example, the main source of fiscal risk in many countries is debt servicing. Transparency in the conduct of debt management is an important element in effectively managing risks and ensuring the accountability of those responsible. Transparency in this respect involves clarity of roles and responsibilities and clear objectives for debt management; open processes for conducting debt management operations; and regular and timely reporting of a range of details of government debt.[10]

A further problem in many countries has been the lack of clarity of roles within the public sector. Directives to state-owned enterprises (SOEs) to conduct a proliferation of quasi-fiscal activities have often resulted in these institutions accumulating losses and needing to be bailed out.[11] In formal terms, such potential spending can be seen as a type of implicit contingent liability (as illustrated by the Fiscal Risk

Matrix in Chapter 1). A transparent, arms-length governance framework for SOEs, with separate identification (and funding from the government budget) of noncommercial obligations, can reduce what is in many countries a major source of fiscal risk. A lack of clarity in the respective roles of the central government and lower-level governments and ad hoc mechanisms for determining intergovernmental transfers are also sources of fiscal risk in many countries.

A more general point is that greater transparency in the conduct of fiscal policy reduces the risk of errors. In a situation in which functions such as macroeconomic forecasting, fiscal forecasting, and macrofiscal analysis are conducted entirely within the government, there may be no independent check on the quality and accuracy of fiscal information and analysis.

Supplementary Reporting of Information on Risks

In view of the deficiencies in cash-basis reporting, a number of countries have in recent years initiated supplementary reporting of information on fiscal risks. Some international standard-setting agencies also have been revising or developing standards for fiscal reporting that bear on the management of fiscal risks.

For example, the Code of Good Practices on Fiscal Transparency issued by the International Monetary Fund (IMF) contains a requirement that countries publish a fiscal risk statement with the annual budget. The Fund's "Manual on Fiscal Transparency" indicates that the statement should contain information on specific fiscal risks—such as contingent liabilities—and on general forecasting risks.

The International Federation of Accountants (IFAC) is undertaking a medium-term project to develop a core set of standards for financial reporting by governments. The standards are for the cash and accrual bases of accounting. As part of this project, IFAC published the study *Governmental Financial Reporting: Accounting Issues and Practices.* Rather than prescribing particular accounting treatments, it describes the types of additional disclosures that some governments using cash-basis reporting make on contingent liabilities. It also notes that reporting of information on contingencies is required under accrual accounting (see IFAC 2000: 47–49, 171).

The IMF is also revising its *Government Finance Statistics Manual.*[12] Some major changes are proposed, including use of an accrual basis of recording and compilation of information on contingent liabilities in a supplement to the balance sheet.

There are different ways in which to categorize fiscal risks as a useful way of organizing supplementary reporting. One of the possibilities would be according to whether they are *forecasting risks* (these are related to the types of risk discussed in Chapter 1) or *specific fiscal risks* (discussed as sources of risk in the Fiscal Risk Matrix of Chapter 1). Forecasting risks are the inherent risks involved in forecasting the fiscal aggregates. Budget forecasts are normally highly sensitive to the assumptions made about a small number of key parameters. Governments also are typically exposed to specific fiscal risks. These include contingent liabilities such as guarantees, indemnities, uncalled capital, and legal action against the government.

Forecasting Risks. Forecasting risks should be disclosed in the central government's annual budget documents. The realism and reliability of the budget are generally highly dependent on the quality of the underlying macroeconomic forecasts on which the budget forecasts are based. Typically, there also will be a small number of key forecasting assumptions related to particular revenue sources or expenditure programs (for example, the price of oil or the exchange rate). Variability in the annual cost of debt servicing due to factors such as exchange rate, interest rate, and maturity structure risk can be a major source of exposure as well.

The budget documents should therefore provide information on the key assumptions on which the budget forecasts are based, and they should illustrate the sensitivity of the budget to variations in these key assumptions. Periodic assessments also should be published of the reliability of budget macroeconomic and fiscal forecasts compared with outturn, with an analysis of deviations by major category. For example, information should be provided on the effects on forecast revenues, expenditures, and the overall balance of, say, a 1 percent decrease in growth of the gross domestic product (GDP) from that assumed in the budget. Half of the member countries of the Organisation for Economic Co-operation and Development (OECD) publish a fiscal sensitivity analysis.[13] U.S. budget documents, for example, contain detailed information about and discussion of the economic assumptions underlying the budget, including comparisons with the assumptions developed by the Congressional Budget Office and with the assumptions contained in the administration's budget for the previous year (see United States 1999: chap. 1, Economic Assumptions).

In addition to sensitivity analysis, it is desirable to publish some alternative medium-term scenarios in which different economic growth and aggregate fiscal developments are combined. These can illustrate the robustness of the budget in the face of broad alternative developments. An example of scenario analysis reporting by the New Zealand government is shown in Table 2.1.

In this context, a government might go the further step and discuss its fiscal strategy in the event that the economic and fiscal outlook turns out to be less favorable than that contained in the budget forecasts. Discussion of broad fiscal contingency plans could help to re-

Table 2.1 Fiscal Scenario Reporting: Summary of Alternative Scenarios, New Zealand

	1997/98 actual	1998/99 forecast	1999/00 projection	2000/01 projection	2001/02 projection
Production GDP (%)					
Central forecast	2.0	(0.3)	2.9	3.5	3.0
Export-led recovery	2.0	(0.3)	3.8	4.4	2.7
Weak recovery	2.0	(0.4)	2.0	1.8	3.7
Nominal expenditure GDP (%)					
Central forecast	3.3	0.4	3.8	5.2	4.6
Export-led recovery	3.3	0.4	4.9	6.5	5.1
Weak recovery	3.3	0.3	2.7	2.6	5.2
Operating balance (billion $)					
Central forecast	2.5	2.2	(0.0)	0.8	1.5
Export-led recovery	2.5	2.2	0.3	1.7	2.8
Weak recovery	2.5	2.1	(0.6)	(0.7)	(0.3)

Source: Based on Table 3.1 in Government of New Zealand (1999: 59).

duce market uncertainty about the possible path of fiscal policy. Providing markets with a broad indication of what sort of fiscal adjustments will be made in response to possible adverse developments—for example, spending cuts or deferrals, tax increases, a bigger deficit, or some combination of these elements—may reduce the risk of abrupt market reactions to adverse market developments. Such an indication also may make it more likely that a government will be ready to take quick action when and if an adverse event does occur.

Specific Fiscal Risks. For contingent liabilities, supplementary reporting should take the form of a statement of the outstanding stock of contingent liabilities of the central government. In addition to its publication with the final accounts, a statement of contingent liabilities should be included with the annual budget documents in order to provide a complete picture of the fiscal position at the time the budget is presented. To qualify as a contingent liability, the amount of expenditure at risk should be material,[14] and the likelihood that the item will result in future expenditure should be more than remote. Under accrual accounting, to qualify as a contingent liability a possible future expenditure must also be less than likely.[15]

For each such contingent liability, or pooled program of contingent liabilities, information should be presented on its nature and potential fiscal significance. For example, for a loan guarantee (or a portfolio of similar loans) reporting should cover the amount of the loan, to whom the loan has been advanced, and the duration of the loan. Whether there have been any changes in the details of the item since the previous reporting date also should be noted. Where possible, an estimate should be provided of the expected cost of each contingent liability—desirably in the form of a range rather than just a point estimate. Some contingent liabilities are nonquantifiable, however, while an estimate of expected cost for others would not be sufficiently reliable. An example of contingent liability reporting, taken from the first trial balance sheet of the Japanese government, is shown in Box 2.1.

Other specific, short-term fiscal risks that should be reported with the budget include the following:

• Where there is an unusual degree of uncertainty about the likely cost of a material expenditure item in the budget, this should be disclosed. For example, perhaps the government has made provision for meeting the costs of reconstruction following a major disaster. At the time of finalizing the budget the cost allowed in the budget may be very uncertain.

• Where items have not been included in the budget at all because of the extent of uncertainty about their timing, magnitude, or eventuality, these items should be disclosed. For example, the government may have announced its intention to increase food subsidies or public pensions, but the details of the decision may not have been finalized sufficiently for inclusion in the budget. The government of New Zealand reports these sorts of specific fiscal risks in its *Budget Economic and Fiscal Update* report accompanying the annual budget (Government of New Zealand 1999).

A Change to the Basis of Accounting

The basis of accounting refers to the set of accounting principles for recording transactions that determine when the effects of transactions or events are recognized for financial reporting purposes. The accrual basis of accounting entails recognition of transactions or events at the time the transaction or event occurs rather than at the time a cash payment is made. Accrual accounting also entails the production of a full balance sheet. These two differences between cash and accrual accounting have important implications for the management of fiscal risk. In addition, the disclosure of supplementary information on contingent liabilities and commitments is required under IFAC's Generally Accepted Accounting Practice (as reflected in international accounting standards).[16]

A balance sheet encapsulates a longer-term perspective on the government's financial position. In principle, it represents the estimated present value of future cash flows—provided they meet the accounting

Box 2.1 Reporting of Contingent Liabilities in Japan

The following table is an extract from the Japanese government balance sheet (preliminary trial), as of March 31, 1999 (Japan, Study Group on Explanatory Methods of Fiscal Position 2000).

I. Contingent liabilities.

   (1) **Liabilities for loan guarantees and loss compensation contracts (million yen)**

Items	Amount in foreign currency	Amount in yen
Compensation for Nuclear Energy Business		798,000
Guarantee for principal and interest payment for bonds of Japan Finance Corporation for Small Business		400,350
Total		48,928,627

   (2) **Claims for damages in pending cases (million yen)**

Cases	Amount claimed
Claim for injunction in Amagasaki Air Pollution Case (Kobe District Court, (wa) No. 2217, 1988; (wa) No. 1766, 1995)	12,168
Appeal case for restitution of unjust enrichment (Endless Money Chain Case) (Fukuoka High Court, (administrative; ko) No. 11, 1996)	10,396
Total	88,510

   Note 1: All the amounts claimed are mentioned in this table, whether or not the Government is expected to win the case.
   Note 2: In cases where the claimed amount is more than 1 billion yen, case names are mentioned.

   (3) **Other major contingent liabilities**

Title	Outline
Project for providing aid money to assist victims' recovery from disasters.	When natural disasters occur and prefectural authorities provide aid money to the head of each household affected by disasters, the Government shall be liable to share part of the aid money under the provisions of Cabinet orders.

definition and recognition criteria and can be reliably measured. A balance sheet therefore provides significant additional information about the future implications of current policies. For example, under accrual accounting information is provided on the full cost of current civil service pension policies, the accumulating burden on future budgets, and the variability in the value of the liability from year to year. Such information can help focus debate on the appropriate design of pension schemes. The choice between defined-contribution and defined-benefit pension schemes, for example, involves significant differences in the amount of fiscal risk borne by the government.[17]

However, accrual accounting on its own does not provide all the information that a fiscal economist would wish. This can be a source of confusion because of the sometimes different use of the word *accrual* by economists and accountants. To some economists, accrued expenditures mean any real consumption or outflow of resources. To an accountant, an accrued expenditure must meet the definition of a liability and the recognition criteria of a liability—chiefly, that it can be reliably measured. The effect of the definition and recognition criteria in accrual accounting is that there is a significant difference between the information that would be contained in a "comprehensive balance sheet"[18] and that contained in a balance sheet produced in accordance with current internationally recognized accounting practices. For example, the expected cost of possible obligations such as one-off guarantees is not generally recognized as a liability and integrated into the budget by governments that have adopted accrual budgeting. A guarantee does not meet the recognition criteria for an expense, unless it is judged more likely than not that the expense will in fact occur and the expected cost of the guarantee can be estimated with sufficient reliability. In general, this means that one-off guarantees will not normally be recognized as expenses in the budget.

The desirable approach to accounting (and budgeting) for specific fiscal risks requires balancing two important principles in public finance. First, decisionmaking is best informed, and incentives are best aligned, if governments recognize the cost of commitments at the time they are made. Second, budget appropriations should be based on reliable information compiled on the basis of widely accepted accounting policies and supported by credible institutional arrangements.[19]

The best approach seems likely to depend on the particular circumstances in individual countries, including the significance and nature of specific fiscal risks, the existing accounting system, and the country's financial management capacity. Introducing an annual contingency fund and expanding the reporting of information on fiscal risks—both fiscal sensitivity and specific fiscal risks—can be readily done in the context of a cash-basis accounting and budgeting system. Malaysia and Japan are examples of countries using a modified cash basis of accounting, but which report supplementary information on guarantees.[20] Much of the information on fiscal risks is in any case provided through such supplementary reporting even in those countries that have adopted full accrual accounting. The adoption of accrual accounting is a large undertaking, and it should be guided by broader considerations than the management of fiscal risk alone.

A Centralized Approach to Implementing Fiscal Risk Management

The nature of the fiscal risk management function lends itself to a centralized policy setting and oversight. The links to the budget process, and the need (at least in principle) to take a portfolio approach to the analysis of risk, suggest that a completely decentralized approach would not be effective. Depending on the overall public sector management framework, however, some combination of central oversight and decentralized accountabilities will be appropriate.

A further important source of fiscal risk in most countries, as noted, is the sensitivity of the fiscal position to changes in the economic environment. An early step in a risk management strategy should be reporting the fiscal sensitivity analysis. This requires close coordination between those responsible for fiscal and macroeconomic forecasting, particularly in generating realistic alternative macroeconomic scenarios to test the sensitivity of the fiscal baseline.

In generating alternative fiscal scenarios, allowance should be made in one scenario for a combination of adverse events to stress test the medium-term fiscal baseline. Such a scenario might include a fall in economic growth, a drop in government revenues, an increase in routine government spending, a shortening of the maturity structure of public debt, the calling of some guarantees, and expenditure demands from implicit contingent liabilities. The likely correlations between these adverse developments mean that while such a scenario may not be likely, it will nevertheless be very much within the range of possibilities (as is all too often demonstrated by actual country experiences).

At the same time, information should be aggregated across the central government on the specific fiscal risks to which individual government agencies are currently exposed. The information should include, to the extent possible, an estimate of the likely range of expected cost to the government for each risk or pooled program of risks. This task might best be achieved as a component of the fiscal reporting individual agencies must provide to the ministry of finance.[21] This requires a clear, common framework defining fiscal risks—for example, in the government's accounting policies (for contingent liabilities) and in the budget instructions sent to departments. It requires communication of a clear expectation that agency heads will be accountable for complying and of a means to verify compliance. It also requires careful central monitoring. For example, the maturity profile of the different risks and guarantees must be analyzed to avoid any undesirable bunching of exposures. Identification of priorities is required to facilitate choices between competing proposals for government guarantees. And, once sound governance arrangements are in place, ongoing central monitoring is required of the performance of individual agencies in mitigating the fiscal risks to which they are exposed. Compliance by individual agencies will, in turn, mean they must have the necessary accounting and information systems to capture and report the relevant information, and an effective internal control environment.

Kazakhstan provides a good example of a centralized approach to the ongoing management of existing guarantees (see Box 2.2). Every entity whose foreign borrowing is guaranteed by government is required to provide quarterly financial statements to a special monitoring unit in the Ministry of Finance. They also must lodge the funds required for loan repayment installments into a restricted account one month before each installment is due and maintain the equivalent of one installment in the account at all times. This provides scope for the government to take action in the event of a failure to lodge a payment, before a call is made on the budget to honor the guarantee.

Another measure that would strengthen the accountability of policymakers and civil servants for prudent management of risks would be to incorporate risk-taking and risk management within the scope of the external audit. This would mean that the supreme audit institution would audit the information provided by each government agency on the fiscal risks to which it is exposed. In New Zealand, each government department must maintain a Register of Contingent Liabilities in which the details of all contingent liabilities are recorded. Each minister responsible for a department is required to sign a certification twice each year that the department's schedule of contingent liabilities is complete and accurate to the best of his or her knowledge. These documents are subject to external audit. The New Zealand controller and auditor general also has reported to Parliament on the performance of individual entities in managing specific fiscal risks (see New Zealand Controller and Auditor General 1999). Similarly, the U.S. General Accounting Office reports to the U.S. Congress on contingent liabilities and other risks facing the federal government and on the analysis and management of the risks by the responsible departments.[22]

There may still be a problem with guarantees "in the bottom drawer" that never see the light of day until they are presented as a fait accompli to the ministry of finance. This is likely to be a problem in countries with a history of hidden guarantees and off-budget activities. One way to try to break out of this low-level equilibrium might be to take the approach sometimes adopted for expenditure arrears—that is, the

---

Box 2.2 Management of Fiscal Risks in Kazakhstan

Kazakhstan provides a good example of a concerted approach to strengthening the management of fiscal risks (Kazakhstan 2000). The impetus for reform came after a proliferation of guarantees culminated in a large call on the budget during a difficult period of fiscal consolidation. This situation focused attention on the need to bring guarantees under effective centralized control. Kazakhstan also faces substantial variability of budget revenues, in part because of its reliance on oil revenues.

Reforms introduced to improve the management of fiscal risks include the following:

• All guarantees now require the prior approval of the minister of finance.

• Every entity whose foreign borrowing is guaranteed by government is required to provide an annual business plan and quarterly financial statements to a special monitoring unit in the Ministry of Finance. They also must lodge the funds required for loan repayment installments in a restricted account one month before each installment is due and maintain the equivalent of one installment in the account at all times. The Ministry of Finance reports quarterly to the government on the financial condition of guarantee recipients. This reporting provides scope for the government to ensure timely action is taken to prevent a call on its budget for covering such debts in the event of a failure by the guarantee recipient to lodge a payment.

• The government has introduced an annual ceiling on the stock of new guarantees that can be issued. This ceiling has resulted in careful scrutiny of all new guarantee proposals. A number of foreign-financed new capital projects have not gone ahead because, on closer examination, it was decided that it was not appropriate for the government to issue a guarantee.

• An allowance is made within net lending in the central government budget for the estimated cost of guarantees in the next year. This allowance comprises a mixture of one-off guarantees that are very difficult to estimate and some large guarantee programs for which some historical loss information is available. If the funds are not required, the spending authority lapses at the end of the year.

• A revenue-dependent contingency fund has been established within the budget. It contains a list of worked-up capital projects that can only proceed as and when interim budget revenue targets are met during the year.

---

government announces that any government guarantees that have not been declared to the minister of finance by a particular date will not be honored. If combined with a commitment by the government to publish a statement containing all guarantees, this approach might be sufficiently credible to flush out the legitimate government guarantees. The recipients of legitimate guarantees would have both a strong incentive to ensure that the guarantee's existence was declared and the means to monitor whether it was declared. The success of such an approach would, however, be critically dependent on the presence of sufficient political will to enforce the strategy.

The next step would be the imposition of a control framework for the management of existing fiscal risks. This step might be taken on a decentralized basis, in which each agency would be responsible and accountable for managing its own fiscal risks in a prudent manner. Central agencies would monitor performance, but might require that a prior clear and comprehensive risk management strategy be in place in each agency. Alternatively, or in addition, the ministry of finance might impose specific risk management policies and practices for generic or significant risks (for example, a foreign exchange risk management policy to which each agency with significant foreign exchange exposure must adhere). Specific responsibilities should be assigned within government for monitoring fiscal risks across the SOE and financial sectors.

Central controls also should be imposed on taking on new specific fiscal risks. Because of the potential for budget discipline to be circumvented, and for a loss of fiscal control through the issuing of guarantees, centralized processes should be put in place to enable the government to control the issuing of new guarantees and indemnities. Depending on the country concerned, this control might mean a requirement for prior approval of the minister of finance, the cabinet, or parliament.[23] In Japan, the Parliament approves an annual ceiling on the face value of new guarantees issued in each fiscal year (Japan, Ministry of Finance 2001).

Approval of a new guarantee also might depend in part on the circumstances of the recipient of the guarantee—such as its financial soundness or the quality of its governance. In South Africa, policy restricts the issuing of guarantees to certain situations (see Box 2.3). For example, no guarantees are provided to private institutions unless management decisions can be influenced directly by the government. Processes also might be put in place to constrain the issuing of new guarantees to the annual budget round. Such a step would at least allow some comparison of the merits of individual spending and guarantee proposals in terms of cost-effectiveness. It also could facilitate broad judgments about the consistency of the total "spending and guarantee package" with the government's budget and medium-term fiscal strategy.

Some Concluding Remarks

There is a hierarchy of approaches to improving the management of fiscal risk. A fundamental first step is developing an understanding of

---

Box 2.3 Management of Fiscal Risks in South Africa

South Africa's approach to fiscal risk management comprises both a *macro-level framework* and provisions at the *micro level* (Kruger 1999). The macro-level framework includes:

- full transparency of fiscal management to ensure accountability (failure to comply with reporting requirements is a criminal offence);
- a medium-term expenditure framework, which enhances transparency and predictability;
- intergovernmental fiscal arrangements involving constitutional restrictions on the ability of provincial governments to borrow and powers for the national government to intervene in the event a province incurs an unauthorized expenditure;
- a coordinating and supervisory role in borrowing by state-owned enterprises (SOEs); and
- a regulatory environment for the banking and financial sector so that systemic risks do not pose a threat to planned fiscal outcomes.

The framework for managing fiscal risks at the micro level includes:

- quantification of all financially related assets and liabilities;
- a clear distinction between contingent liabilities and actual liabilities;
- strict guidelines for issuing guarantees—no guarantees to assist private institutions unless management decisions can be influenced directly; guarantees may be provided where there is an obligation in terms of international treaties, or where foreign loans are considered to be in the national interest (guarantees for commercial entities are in the process of being phased out);
- guarantee fees to act as a disincentive to use guarantees and to create a level playing field where SOEs are competing with the private sector;
- a Public Finance Management Act that establishes full accountability, clear reporting responsibilities, and the use of accrual accounting principles, including the production of a consolidated balance sheet; and
- management of implicit fiscal risks through classifying SOEs on the basis of the tolerable risk appetite per institutional type—for example, through restructuring commercial enterprises for privatization; through full cost recovery in public utility pricing with cross subsidization to be transparent; and through insurance providers charging risk-related premiums.

---

the main sources of fiscal risk in a particular country. Such an understanding requires aggregation and centralization of information across the central government on the specific fiscal risks to which individual government agencies and the central government itself are currently exposed (using, for example, the Fiscal Risk Matrix presented in Chapter 1). This step in itself is a demanding exercise. From this step should follow attempts to assess at least the broad order of magnitude of the most significant risks and how they affect different elements of the government's revenues, expenditures, assets, and liabilities. This assessment enables ongoing monitoring of risks, identification of priority areas for reducing exposure to existing risks, and some control over taking on new risks.

Major gains might be made at this stage in many countries through reexamining some basic policies from the perspective of fiscal risk management. For example, the framework for intergovernmental fiscal relations, the need to retain government ownership of some SOEs and banks, the management of public debt, and the quality of prudential supervision of the financial sector are all areas where good policy design and transparency can make a major contribution to reducing fiscal risk.

Reporting detailed information on specific fiscal risks, and on the sensitivity of the fiscal position, should be an early part of a risk management strategy. Another objective is to publish information on broad alternative macrofiscal scenarios. Such reporting requires a supporting public management infrastructure. In addition to ensuring better information for the executive on which to base fiscal policy, it provides the crucial added discipline of external accountability. Efforts to improve the management of fiscal risks also might benefit from incorporating risk management into the scope of the external audit. At the same time, improvements should be initiated on key deficiencies in broader fiscal transparency arrangements.

Central controls over who is authorized to take on new risks, such as issuing guarantees, should be put in place. The possibility of avoiding the risk altogether, or of shifting it partially to other agents, should be examined at the outset. Consideration of many guarantees also might be held over for deliberation alongside other fiscal priorities in the annual budget round. Specific responsibilities should be assigned within the government for monitoring fiscal risks across the SOE and financial sectors and for monitoring the financial position of agencies with government-guaranteed debt. Charging a fee for the issuance and maintenance of a guarantee might be a useful additional means of ensuring sound scrutiny of proposals for new guarantees. Moreover, some attempt should be made to compare the merits of guarantees against competing fiscal priorities. This might involve setting a limit on the value of new guarantees entered into.

A change in the basis of accounting toward accrual accounting can result in better information and accountability for fiscal risk management. From an implementation risk perspective, however, it would in general seem prudent to move first from pure cash-basis reporting to supplementary reporting of fiscal risks, and the implementation of a general budget contingency reserve, before considering the establishment of dedicated reserve funds for contingent liabilities or introducing full accrual accounting.

There is great scope for improvements in fiscal performance in many countries through better management of fiscal risks. The deficiencies of traditional pure cash reporting have reinforced the tendency of governments to take a short-term and reactive approach to fiscal management. New and expanded sources of fiscal risk increase the imperative for better fiscal control, and new techniques offer the possibility of improved management and better outcomes.

Notes

1. The author would like to acknowledge helpful comments on earlier drafts from David Webber, Ian Ball, Jon Blondal, and Istvan Szekely.

2. Contingencies are defined by the International Accounting Standards Committee (IASC) as conditions or situations whose ultimate outcome, gain or loss, will be confirmed only on the occurrence, or nonoccurrence, of one or more uncertain events. See IFAC (1998: paras. 692–701).

3. See IFAC (1998) for a discussion of the definitions of the different bases of accounting (cash, modified cash, modified accrual, and accrual accounting).

4. With the exception of origination fees, which, if charged, show as a favorable cash impact at the time the guarantee is issued, further distorting the picture.

5. See U.S. GAO (1998a: 5) for a discussion of the distortions of insurance and lending programs under cash accounting. "Cash-based budgeting for federal insurance programs may provide neither the information nor incentives necessary to signal emerging problems, make adequate cost comparisons, control costs, or ensure the availability of resources to pay future claims."

6. See U.S. GAO (1998a: 6): "Many analysts believe that the cash-based budget treatment of deposit insurance exacerbated the savings and loan crisis by creating a disincentive to close failed institutions. Since costs were not recognized in the budget until cash payments were made, leaving insolvent institutions open avoided recording outlays in the budget and raising the annual deficit but ultimately increased the total cost to the government."

7. The move to greater overall fiscal transparency, supplementary reporting, and the choice of accounting basis are, of course, motivated by many considerations in addition to risk management objectives.

8. Effective accountability also may require a change in attitudes to embed a feeling of personal responsibility for fiscal risk management in the public service culture. Such a change should perhaps be seen in the broader context of civil service reform. This is beyond the scope of this chapter, but may be a key element in bringing about an improvement in fiscal risk management.

9. These are the four general principles of the International Monetary Fund's Code of Good Practices on Fiscal Transparency. See the IMF website <www.imf.org/external/np/fad/trans/index.htm>.

10. See the IMF's "Fiscal Transparency Manual" for a discussion of reporting public debt. The manual can be found on the IMF website <www.imf.org/external/np/fad/trans/index.htm>.

11. Quasi-fiscal activities (QFAs) are activities undertaken under the direction of government by a central bank or state-owned financial or commercial enterprise that are fiscal in character—that is, the effects of the activity could in principle be duplicated by budgetary measures in the form of a tax, subsidy, or direct expenditure. Examples are guarantees, subsidized lending, and financial sector bailouts. These activities have similar economic effects whether they are undertaken by a central government agency or a central bank or a public financial enterprise. They can be very large, and they need to be taken into account in assessing fiscal performance and fiscal risk.

12. See IMF (1996: 85–87). Also available on the Fund's website <www.imf.org/external/pubs/ft/gfs/manual/index.htm>.

13. Some OECD countries take additional steps to ensure the integrity and quality of the macroeconomic forecasts. These range from an expert independent review panel that comments publicly on the forecasts; to a review of the macroeconomic assumptions by the National Audit Office and a legal requirement to publish the entire Treasury macroeconomic model (United Kingdom); to basing the government's official forecasts on private sector consensus forecasts (Canada); to fully contestable fiscal forecasts produced by a separate entity, the Congressional Budget Office, which reports directly to the legislature (United States).

14. It would seem desirable, however, to report contingent liabilities where the likelihood of actual expenditure is very small but the amount potentially at risk is very large.

15. Where accrual or modified accrual-basis accounting is used, only those events that are judged less than likely to result in future expenditure are included in supplementary reporting as contingent liabilities. Those events judged likely to result in future expenditure are recognized immediately as a liability—that is, they are defined as liabilities rather than contingent liabilities.

16. See IFAC (2000: 171). In accounting, commitments are defined as a government's responsibility for a future liability based on an existing contractual agreement. Examples include long-term leases or multiyear contracts for the purchase of capital equipment.

17. Under a defined-benefit scheme, the government bears the risk of a mismatch between the return on any scheme assets and the defined pension obligation. Under a defined-contribution scheme, the contributor bears the risk of uncertain return on pension fund assets.

18. That is, a balance sheet containing all the prospective cash inflows and outflows compiled using realistic projections based on current policies.

An example of a comprehensive balance sheet is the Fiscal Risk Matrix and Fiscal Hedge Matrix shown in Chapter 1.

19. Valuing risk may be a demanding exercise; it requires a modeling capacity that is not readily available in government offices. And even the results of the best models need to be treated as rough estimates of future values rather than predictions. The U.S. General Accounting Office, for example, has commented critically on the ability of U.S. federal agencies to reasonably estimate subsidy costs in their credit programs: "Until weaknesses are addressed the credibility of loan program cost information they submit will continue to be questionable" (U.S. GAO 1998b). Therefore, scenario analysis may be more useful for policymakers than a single expected cost figure.

20. See IFAC (2000: 51) for a discussion of the additional reporting prepared in Malaysia in the context of a modified cash basis of accounting. A feature typical of the modified cash basis system is holding the books open for a specified period after year-end to overcome some of the timing problems of pure cash-basis accounting.

21. References to the ministry of finance are a generic reference to the ministry or department with primary responsibility for fiscal policy coordination and budget management.

22. For examples of such reports, see U.S. GAO (1998a, 1998b, 1998c) and the U.S. General Accounting Office website <*www.gao.gov*>.

23. A recent survey of OECD countries found that in three the approval of only the minister of finance was required for the granting of a guarantee, while in the great majority the approval of parliament was required (Blondal 1999).

References

Blondal, Jon. 1999. "Management of Fiscal Risk in OECD Member Countries." Presentation at World Bank Course on Managing Fiscal Risks, Washington, D.C., June 8–11.

Government of New Zealand. 1999. *Budget Economic and Fiscal Update 1999.* Wellington.

IFAC (International Federation of Accountants), Public Sector Committee. 1998. *Draft Guideline for Governmental Financial Reporting.* New York.

———. 2000. *Governmental Financial Reporting: Accounting Issues and Practices.* New York.

IMF (International Monetary Fund), Fiscal Affairs Department. 2001. "Code of Good Practices on Fiscal Transparency" and "Manual on Fiscal Transparency"<*www.imf.org/external/np/fad/trans/index.htm*>.

IMF (International Monetary Fund), Statistics Department. 1996. *Government Finance Statistics Manual: An Annotated Outline.* Washington, D.C.

Japan, Ministry of Finance, Financial Bureau. 2001. *FILP Report 2000.* February.

Japan, Study Group on Explanatory Methods of Fiscal Position. 2000. "The Japanese Government Balance Sheet (Preliminary trial)." Tokyo, October.

Kazakhstan. 2000. "Rules for Carrying Out the Monitoring of the Financial Condition of Legal Entities that Have Received Non-governmental Foreign Loans under Republic of Kazakhstan Government Guarantees." Astana.

Kruger, Coen. 1999. "Managing Fiscal Risks: The South African Approach." Presentation at World Bank Course on Managing Fiscal Risks. Washington, D.C., June 8–11.

New Zealand Controller and Auditor General. 1999. *How Are State-Owned Enterprises Managing Foreign Exchange Risk.* Chapter 8, First Report for 1999. Wellington.

OECD (Organisation for Economic Co-operation and Development). 1999. *How Should Governments Invest Financial Assets and Manage Debt?* PUMA/SBO/ RD (99). Paris.

Polackova, Hana. 1998. "Contingent Government Liabilities: A Hidden Risk for Fiscal Stability." Policy Research Working Paper 1989. World Bank, Washington D.C.

U.S. GAO (General Accounting Office). 1998a. *Budgeting for Federal Insurance Programs.* GAO/T-AIMD-98-147. Washington, D.C.

———. 1998b. *Credit Reform: Greater Effort Needed to Overcome Persistent Cost Estimation Problems.* GAO/AIMD-98-14. Washington, D.C., March.

———. 1998c. *Report on US Government's Consolidated Financial Statements for FY97.* GAO/AIMD-98-127. Washington, D.C.

United States. 1999. *Budget of the United States Government, Analytical Perspectives. Fiscal Year 1999.* Washington, D.C.: Government Printing Office.

CHAPTER 3

Budgeting for Fiscal Risk

Allen Schick
University of Maryland

As MEASURES OF FISCAL RISK, conventional budgets are deficient on two counts. First, they have a short time frame—one year in countries that have only annual budgets, three to five years in countries that budget within medium-term fiscal frameworks. These time horizons are too short to account for the downstream risks taken by governments when they establish pension systems and other entitlements, issue or guarantee loans, or promise to make good on shortfalls in financial performance. Second, conventional budgets record only cash flows; they do not account for the buildup of liabilities, contingent obligations, or the future cost of past commitments.

Because budgets measure cash flows rather than liabilities and short-term payments rather than long-term risks, politicians have an incentive and opportunity to provide benefits to those who seek assistance from government in ways that mask the true cost, leading to policies and actions that worsen future fiscal conditions. Governments create fiscal illusions, beneficiaries behave in morally hazardous ways, and the upshot is escalation in fiscal jeopardy. This pattern is widespread; it occurs in developed, transitional, and developing countries. In developed countries, the failure to properly control and account for risk may burden future budgets and take a bite out of economic growth. In transitional and newly developed countries, however, the failure may retard development and reverse recent economic gains. In developing countries, failure to deal adequately with risk may diminish already dim economic prospects.

The study of fiscal risks held by government is in its infancy. Building on work done by Hana Polackova Brixi and others, this chapter discusses means by which national budgets might be transformed into more effective instruments to control fiscal risk (Polackova 1998a).

The first section briefly outlines alternative approaches for dealing with fiscal risk, and the two sections that follow examine alternative approaches for incorporating risk into financial statements and budget decisions. The final sections consider options for controlling fiscal risks through market-type arrangements.

Approaches to Managing Fiscal Risk

Governments determined to manage the risks they take can choose from a variety of approaches. Some have been tried by a few governments, some by none. This section clarifies the various approaches, which are elaborated later in this chapter.

The first approach is for government to be open about the types of risks it faces, the volume and possible costs of these liabilities, and the probability that various commitments will come due. This approach is in line with the contemporary drive for transparency in fiscal matters, but it requires distinguishing between explicit and implicit risks.

The second approach is to incorporate decisions on risks into the ongoing budget process, thereby enabling the government to compare direct and contingent expenditures without biasing the outcome in favor of one or another type of transaction. Not all risks can be managed through the budget, however. The more direct and explicit the risk, the greater is the suitability of budgeting for estimating the cost to government and setting aside resources for this purpose.

Third, government can manage risk by limiting risks before they are taken. This approach would entail establishing criteria for determining whether the government should issue guarantees or enter into other contingent commitments, assessing the degree of risk in the light of these criteria, and refusing to take on risks that do not meet the government's standards.

Finally, government may rely on market-type mechanisms to shift all or a portion of the risk to private entities. Some of the innovations in this area have had little or no application in government. Although they are commonly used by commercial enterprises, the aim here is not to recommend particular reforms but to stimulate innovative thinking on how governments might come to grips with practices and conditions that may jeopardize their future fiscal health. Table 3.1 summarizes features of the four approaches.

The four approaches are differentiated not only in method but in objective as well. This first is based on the notion that government should be informed before it takes on new risk. The second emphasizes budget neutrality—the rules of budgetary accounting should not bias policy in favor of any particular instrument. The third approach rests on the notion that government should be risk-averse and should

Table 3.1 Comparison of Four Approaches to Managing
Fiscal Risk

Approach	Main objective	Limitation(s)
1. Reporting on financial statements	Transparency: fuller account of financial condition and risks.	Many governments do not have accurate, comprehensive financial statements. These statements cannot cover implicit risks or risks with low probability. Just publishing statements does not itself change risk-taking behavior by government.
2. Cost-based budgeting	Budget allocations reflect prospective cost to government; risk-taking competes with other claims on budget.	Costing methodology is not well developed, and cost estimates may be unreliable. Does not cover implicit risks. May be treated as a technical exercise rather than as a real allocation of resources.
3. Rules for taking fiscal risks	Applies to guarantees and other contingent liabilities; criteria applied before risk is taken.	Political pressure may override the criteria. Very few governments have rules determining when to enter contingent liabilities.
4. Market-type arrangements	Relies on market to reduce risk held by government and to more accurately estimate the cost of risks taken by it.	Governments typically take on contingent liabilities because of a decision not to rely on the market.

Source: The author.

accept new risk only when stringent criteria have been fulfilled. The
fourth approach takes the view that in the best of circumstances government is inherently a poor assessor and regulator of risk, and so it
should turn these tasks over to the market.

Transparency in Reporting on Fiscal Risk

Liabilities and expectations, which are neither known nor recorded,
cannot be effectively controlled. An essential first step, then, in making risks held by government transparent is to inventory the array of

risks and liabilities borne by it. This is not an easy task, however, and so the first effort may not yield a comprehensive or completely accurate account. Several governments, including that of South Africa, have used the Fiscal Risk Matrix presented in Chapter 1 to identify the risks they are holding and the policy remedies that might be applied. In South Africa, the official charged with this responsibility has indicated that striving to fill in each of the boxes in the matrix made government aware of significant risks that were previously unknown. Table 3.2 shows the results of this work. Note that for most of the entries the government has been unable to estimate the downstream costs it might face. Nevertheless, filling in the matrix has been a useful early step in mapping out the government's exposure and response.

In compiling an inventory, it is necessary to canvass state entities and programs in order to identify the agencies authorized to enter into commitments, the transactions or conditions that have been insured, the contingencies that would trigger government payments, and the volume of outstanding liabilities. Although a comprehensive account may be out of reach, government can identify most of its direct and contingent obligations by concentrating on those sectors and programs in which these risks typically occur: agriculture, housing finance, banking, small business, state enterprises, imports and exports, insurance schemes, and infrastructure development.

There are two schools of thought on whether government should acknowledge implicit liabilities. One urges transparency; the other counsels fuzziness. Both aim to discourage moral hazard, but they differ on how this is best accomplished. The case for openness and disclosure rests on the argument that moral hazard abates when the government clearly and credibly signals how it will respond to possible failures and events—for example, whether it will indemnify uninsured depositors or pay for essential services provided by bankrupt municipalities. It might declare that depositors will be compensated for losses only up to a certain amount or that it will finance certain municipal services but not others. These signals, it is argued, will deter affected parties from behaving in ways that add to the government's potential liabilities. Of course, signaling its intentions is effective only if the government holds a credible position and acts as promised. Wrong signals provide added incentives for misbehavior.

It would be appropriate for the government to take further action to discourage moral hazard when it makes implicit liabilities explicit. For example, if the government steps in to pay for the ongoing services of insolvent municipalities, it also should enact laws or regulations that deter local governments from spending beyond their means, as well as legislation extending bankruptcy rules and procedures to these entities. If it accepts responsibility for expected (but not legally required) future pensions, the government should restructure the pension

Table 3.2 South African Policy Approach

Type of risks	Policy approach
Explicit direct risks	
Sovereign borrowing (ZAR380 billion)	Identify risks and formulate risk-averse strategy.
Medical schemes	Adjust policy in budget.
Civil pensions	Adjust policy in budget.
Explicit contingent risks	
Loan guarantees (ZAR73 billion)	Phase out guarantees. Revise authority to borrow and issue guarantees. Cap borrowing authorities and approve and coordinate borrowing strategies.
Guarantees on private investment	Share risk (contracts). Establish joint project limits. Establish country limits. Cap limits per institution.
State insurance schemes	Cap government risk exposure. Share risks (also offshore).
Implicit direct risks	
Socioeconomic expenditure	Analyze policies. Establish medium-term expenditure framework also to reflect contingent liabilities. Better reflect cost in annual budget.
Recurrent expenditure of public investment (also state-owned enterprises)	Incorporate in fiscal planning and budgeting. Introduce "corporate governance" in projects.
Implicit contingent risks	
Default of subnationals	Monitor and introduce ex ante warning signals.
Systemic risks	Monitor.
Liabilities and risks of policy failure from privatization/commercialization	Consider fiscal risks when restructuring. Monitor.
Disaster relief/unavoidable expenditure	Build contingency reserves. Establish contingent credit lines and purchase reinsurance.
Monetary/exchange management	Rethink interest rate and exchange rate policy to contain government risk exposure. Monitor central bank reserve management, derivative use, and risk exposure.

Source: The author.

system to put it on a sound financial basis. Without corrective measures, making implicit costs explicit would almost certainly worsen the fiscal posture.

The counterargument is that the government should not divulge its intentions on implicit risk because doing so would greatly increase moral hazard. This is the position taken by the International Monetary Fund (IMF) in statements elaborating on its new Code of Good Practices on Fiscal Transparency (IMF 1999). The IMF code vigorously promotes openness on fiscal matters, but it nevertheless recommends that "implicit guarantees, such as the possibility that a government may in the future bail out a public enterprise or private sector bank" be excluded from statements on contingent liabilities (paragraph 67). The statement adds that implicit guarantees should be excluded "because of the potential *moral hazard* to which being transparent about such provisions could give rise" (emphasis in original).

When a government considers whether to make implicit liabilities explicit, it must take account of the credibility of its position. More than one government has announced that it will not pay depositor claims on failed financial institutions only to be compelled by political or economic circumstances to provide assistance.

Indeed, there can be no blanket rule for all implicit liabilities. In some cases, maintaining a fuzzy position will shift a portion of the risk to market actors if they bet wrong on what the government will do. In other cases, fuzziness will leave the government with higher costs in the end when it makes good on implicit commitments. Implicit pension liabilities should not be treated the same as implicit exchange rate guarantees. For the former, the government might do well to recognize the liabilities and to provide for them in the budget; for the latter, the government might be better off keeping importers and exporters uncertain about its intentions.

Accounting for Contingent Liabilities

Public accounting systems generally recognize direct liabilities, not contingent ones. The *Draft Guideline for Governmental Financial Reporting* issued by the International Federation of Accountants (IFAC) in 1998 takes the position in paragraph 443 that "commitments and contingencies are items which do not meet the definition and recognition criteria" for incorporation in financial statements (IFAC 1998). These criteria define a liability as "a present obligation of the enterprise arising from past events, the settlement of which is expected to result in an outflow . . . of resources." According to IFAC, a liability should be recognized in financial statements when "it is probable that an outflow of resources . . . will result from the settlement of a present obligation and the amount at which the settlement will take place can be measured reliably" (paragraph 443). Contingent liabilities do not satisfy these criteria, because they depend on future rather than past events and cannot be reliably measured. Nevertheless, the IMF Code of Good Practices on Fiscal Transparency specifies in Statement 2.1.3. that "[s]tatements should be published with the annual budget giving a description of the nature and fiscal significance of contingent liabilities, tax expenditures, and quasi-fiscal activities" (IMF 1999). (For a more detailed discussion of accounting and reporting of contingent liabilities and other fiscal risks, see Chapter 2 by Petrie in this volume.)

Measuring Risks

The IMF fiscal transparency code urges that each nation present in its annual budget a statement of fiscal risks, including those deriving from guarantees and insurance schemes, and that, where feasible, these risks be quantified. Doing so is a challenging task, for risk assessment and measurement are much more advanced in the business sector, where various statistical tools and hedging strategies are widely used. Few governments have had much experience in this area, but there is no reason why they cannot adapt relevant commercial practices to their needs. As governments gain experience in assessing risks, the quality of their estimates is likely to improve.

Reporting the estimated costs of contingent liabilities and other fiscal risks in budgets or on financial statements may spur governments to produce point estimates, which specify a definite cost but are almost always wrong and misleading. Few (if any) governments have the capacity to measure accurately the probability that future contingencies will come due and the cost they will incur if they have to make payments pursuant to these obligations. Less than a decade after it spent more than US$100 billion resolving widespread insolvency in the banking sector, the U.S. government issued in fiscal 2000 a provisional balance sheet estimating the present value of future deposit insurance liabilities at only $1 billion (United States, OMB 1999: Table 2-1). It may be that measures adopted to regulate the lending practices of financial institutions and fees paid for deposit insurance will protect the U.S. government against future losses. But surely one cannot rule out the possibility of widespread distress in the banking industry or capital markets that would cause insured losses to escalate.

Ideally, risks should be estimated in terms of a range, with the key assumptions and probabilities published alongside the estimates. In addition, given the difficulty of estimating future costs, the following suggestions may be useful for governments with limited capacity to manage risks. First, concentrate on the riskiest endeavors, the ones likely to account for most downstream liabilities. Second, make precise cost estimates only when warranted by experience and when the risks are pooled rather than concentrated. And, third, report fiscal risks, even when it is not possible to quantify costs.

Formulating Financial Statements

Although IMF recommends that a statement on contingent liabilities be included in a country's budget, there is a modest trend toward publishing them as notes to financial statements. Three contemporary developments have given new prominence to government financial statements: (a) the shift underway from cash-based public accounting to the accrual basis; (b) the growing reliance on financial statements to report on a government's financial condition; and (c) the broadened role of auditors in reviewing these financial statements and in assessing the government's performance.

New Zealand pioneered in accrual accounting and budgeting a decade ago when its Public Finance Act (1989) mandated that all government entities apply commercial accounting principles. The conversion was swift and relatively painless and has led to the publication of audited financial statements for all departments as well as a combined financial statement for the government; a supporting schedule to this statement lists both quantifiable and nonquantifiable contingent liabilities. Over the past decade, approximately a dozen national governments have followed suit, and more are likely to join the movement to the accrual basis under prodding from international organizations.

In commercial practices, contingent risks have an impact on the balance sheet when provision is made for expected losses. To the extent, therefore, that losses on contingent liabilities can be measured, it would be appropriate to make provision for them on the balance sheet. But at this stage, cost estimates for these liabilities usually lack the precision associated with recording direct liabilities. The most sensible approach, therefore, may be to list contingent liabilities in the notes, not in the financial statement.

Budgetary Neutrality

The rationale that has led some governments to introduce accrual accounting also applies to the budget. Cost-based budgeting is designed to make a government responsible for the resources it uses and strengthens the government's capacity to manage risks that are taken in current budgets but payment for which emerges in subsequent fiscal years. Polackova (1998b: 50) correctly argues that an "accrual-based accounting system without accrual budgeting is neither necessary nor sufficient to ensure adequate policy consideration for contingent liabilities and other fiscal risks." But there are several impediments to budgeting for contingencies on a cost basis. One is that the development of accounting standards for government budgets is still in its infancy. Another, already noted, is that cost estimates tend to be less reliable for contingent rather than direct liabilities. As long as cost is based on budget estimates rather than market prices, combining direct and contingent expenditures in a single cost measure may be highly misleading as to the resources actually expended or risked by government. A third issue is that the time horizon of budgeting may be too short for allocating costs arising from contingent liabilities. Even in countries that have a medium-term timeframe, budget projections typically extend out only three to five years. Fiscal risks often spill over well beyond this period.

There are four basic approaches to budgeting for contingent liabilities. One is to present background information on contingent liabilities and other financial risks in the budget, but to make budget decisions only for direct expenditures and for payments pursuant to existing commitments. Another is to devise a separate budget for contingent liabilities and risks. The third is to integrate direct and contingent liabilities on a cash basis. And the fourth option is to integrate the two types of liabilities on a cost basis. The first three options are discussed briefly, and the final one is considered in the light of novel U.S. budgetary procedures for direct and guaranteed loans.

Presenting Information in the Budget

The first option is to publish information on contingent liabilities and risks in the supporting schedules, but not in the budget estimates. The inclusion of supplementary information is a common practice in budgeting. Many national budgets provide background data on the economy, grants to subnational governments, programs and activities, and other matters. Although the supplementary information is not voted, it assists parliament, attentive groups, and the public in assessing the government's budgetary intentions. Similarly, background information could be provided on contingent liabilities, but these data would not be combined with the estimates. For most governments, providing such information would be a significant advance, even if the budget listed only the various risks and liabilities but did not provide cost estimates.

Parallel Budgeting for Contingent Liabilities

Alternatively, the government would compile a parallel budget for contingent liabilities and related risks. Although separate from the regular budget, the "contingent liabilities" budget would be voted by parliament. This parallel budget would, like a regular budget, specify all the commitments authorized for the fiscal year; it might also limit the amount of contingent liabilities outstanding and set aside cash resources for expected calls on contingent liabilities during the year.

During the 1980s, a parallel budget system was introduced by the U.S. government for direct and guaranteed loans. This parallel budget set a total limit on the amount of new loan commitments and allocated this total among particular programs and agencies. This separate system was replaced in the early 1990s by the integrated arrangement described below. This U.S. system is limited to risk associated with direct and guaranteed loans; it is not applied to other contingent liabilities.

Clearly, few governments have sufficient information to compile a comprehensive budget for all contingent liabilities. It may be appropriate, therefore, to budget only for those contingencies for which reasonably reliable data are available. For example, government may have reasonably accurate and complete information on the loans it guarantees, but know little about the debt incurred or guaranteed by state-owned enterprises. In such a situation, it would be prudent for the budget to cover only the former, even though the latter may pose greater risk. Of course, government should endeavor to progressively improve its coverage of fiscal risk by investigating areas where information is meager but the risk of loss is great.

An alternative approach would be to budget for changes in the volume of known contingent liabilities and to concentrate on those prospective losses that can be reasonably estimated rather than all such liabilities. To do this, the government might construct a baseline (similar to the baselines used for expenditure projections in medium-term frameworks) that would estimate future payouts for previously authorized or outstanding contingent liabilities. Each year the baseline would be adjusted for changes in projected payouts stemming from new government actions (such as the issuance of additional guarantees, changes in economic conditions affecting the probability that the government will have to make future payments, and reestimates of the losses expected from existing contingent liabilities). The baseline data would be presented for government decision. Each year the government would decide on new explicit contingent liabilities by adjusting the baseline. But the government would not control total contingent liabilities; instead, it would focus on year-to-year changes in estimated payouts for those risks included in the baseline.

Integrating Contingent Liabilities into the Cash-based Budget

The third option would go further and combine payments on contingent liabilities with the conventional cash-based budget. In this arrangement, the government would set aside resources in the budget to pay for losses expected during the year or over the medium term. It also would use the budget to regulate the total volume of guarantees or the amount of new guarantees to be issued during the fiscal year.

A comparison of the approach initially taken by the Netherlands and that applied by Hungary shows various ways of integrating guarantees with direct expenditures. When it initially incorporated guarantees in the budget, the Netherlands recorded total new guarantees as expenditures. Thus within a fixed budget constraint, the issuance (or authorization) of new guarantees crowded out an equivalent amount of direct expenditure. In effect, the budget made provision for the full value of guarantees, not for expected payouts. Clearly, this treatment was intended to discourage the issuance of guarantees in lieu of conventional grants and subsidies. Once this practice was developed, the Netherlands shifted to a "cost" basis that budgeted for estimated payouts.

The government of Hungary has adopted seven interlocking budget controls on guarantees (see Chapter 9 by Brixi, Schick, and Zlaoui in this volume). First, the volume of guarantees authorized in the budget is limited to a certain percentage of state revenues. Second, the volume of outstanding guarantees issued by various state entities (such as the Hungarian Development Bank) is limited by law. Third, the budget sets aside funds for payments expected to be made during the fiscal year pursuant to existing guarantees. Fourth, guarantee contracts are reviewed by the Ministry of Finance, which closely monitors the issuance of guarantees by departments and other entities. Fifth, material information on new guarantees (such as the amount, conditions, justification, lender, and borrower) are published in a government resolution. Sixth, the annual budget reports the probability of default and expected payments on each guarantee program. Finally, the issuance of guarantees is reported to the State Audit Office.

Although the system is not perfect—for example, some major guarantees are exempted from the limit on the total volume issued each year—it has greatly reduced the exposure of government to losses from contingent liabilities. In fact, disbursements for calls on defaulted guarantees have been below the amounts set aside in the budget for this purpose. The main problem for Hungary has been dealing with implicit contingent liabilities. These are not covered by the new budget control system, and payments to cover these losses have far exceeded those made for explicit liabilities.

Budgeting for the Cost of Contingent Liabilities

Budgeting for contingent liabilities on a cash basis may result in either too much or too little control of the government's risk of loss. The early approach taken by the Netherlands overstated the cost, because the government was likely to be liable for only a fraction of the losses it was guaranteeing. By contrast, the Hungarian method may understate cost, because the government will have to make good on its commitments even if the amounts provisioned in the budget are inadequate.

Moreover, when contingent liabilities are budgeted on a volume and cash basis, politicians may have an incentive to substitute them for grants and other disbursements. While cash payments are budgeted as outlays in the year they are made, payments for guarantees do not appear as outlays until later years, when default or other events occur. On a cash basis, guarantees are inexpensive relative to grants, even though they may cost more in the long run.

To deal with this problem, the U.S. government introduced new budgetary rules for direct and guaranteed loans in 1992. These rules are designed to neutralize budgetary incentives and to make politicians indifferent to whether they choose grants, direct loans, or guarantees. These three types of transactions are budgeted on a cost basis, rendering the timing of cash payments less relevant in allocating government resources. The Netherlands now uses a similar system.

The current U.S. system, which has not been altered since its introduction in 1992, shifts the budgetary basis of loans and guarantees from cash flow to subsidy cost. This cost is defined in law as "the estimated long-term cost to the Government of a direct loan or a loan guarantee, calculated on a net present value basis, excluding administrative costs." Net present value is calculated by discounting estimated future cash outflows (loan disbursements and payments on defaults) and inflows (origination fees, repayment of principal and interest on direct loans, and recoveries), using a discount rate equal to the interest rate paid by the U.S. government on borrowings of a comparable maturity. A separate appropriation is made for the projected subsidy cost of each loan program; this appropriation is included in the budget as an outlay, even though money might not be disbursed until years later. Subsidy costs are included in the computation of total budget expenditures and in the surplus or deficit.

Budgeting for direct and guaranteed loans entails complex procedures for estimating subsidy costs and new accounting procedures for recording the cash flows associated with loan transactions. The process is designed to differentiate between the subsidized portion of loans that is budgeted as a cost and the unsubsidized portion that is budgeted as a below-the-line transaction. Budget resources are provided only for the subsidy cost, which almost always is significantly less than the face value of the loan or guarantee. The subsidy cost of direct loans is the present value of the amounts not repaid (minus fees and recoveries) and the difference between the interest rate charged borrowers and the cost of money to government. The subsidy cost of guaranteed loans is the present value of the difference between cash payments for defaults and cash received from fees and recoveries.

The subsidy cost is estimated at the time a direct loan is obligated or a loan guarantee commitment is made. Actual loan performance, however, often varies from early estimates, sometimes significantly. Accordingly, the subsidy cost is annually reestimated during the lifetime of loans and guarantees, and an automatic appropriation is provided to cover overruns. Because this appropriation is automatic, government agencies are not penalized in their budgets if they underestimate subsidy cost. Since fiscal 1992 when the credit system was first implemented, underestimates have been relatively minor, but it is important to bear in mind that this entire period has been largely one of robust economic growth in the United States.

As noted, a key objective of the subsidy approach is to ensure that budget decisions are neutral—that is, they are not skewed in favor of or against any particular type of transaction. Budgeting for subsidy cost puts direct loans, guaranteed loans, and grants on an equal basis. All are budgeted in terms of cost to government rather than in terms of cash exchanged. The hypothetical example below contracts the cash basis and subsidy cost treatment of these transactions (in millions of U.S. dollars).

Transaction		*Amount budgeted*	
Type	*Amount*	*Cash basis*	*Subsidy cost*
Loan	$100	$100	$15
Guaranteed loan	100	–2	30
Grant	20	20	20

This hypothetical case compares a direct loan of $100 million, a guaranteed loan of $100 million, and a grant of $20 million. On a cash basis, the direct loan would appear in the budget as the most costly transaction, because the entire amount disbursed is recorded as an outlay. By contrast, the guaranteed loan would be budgeted as a revenue gain for the government, because it receives income from origination fees in the year the guarantee is issued. On a subsidy cost basis, however, budgeted outlays for the direct loan would be reduced from $100 million to $15 million, because projected repayments of principal and interest would be included in the measurement of subsidy costs. Budget outlays for the guaranteed loan would rise from -$2 million to $30 million, because projected defaults in later years would be included in the subsidy cost, making it the costliest type of transaction. The amount recorded for a grant would not change, but the cost basis would make it more readily comparable to direct and guaranteed loans. Note, however, that the hypothetical amount shown here for a grant is based on disbursements, while the cost reported for a loan and a guarantee is based on projections of future discounted cash flows.

Conversion to the subsidy cost basis entails maintaining separate budgetary accounts for the subsidized and unsubsidized portions of loans and guarantees. Program accounts receive appropriations for subsidy costs; financing accounts handle the cash flows associated with the nonsubsidized portion. Program accounts are included in the budget; financing accounts are recorded as "means of financing" and their cash flows are not included in budget receipts or outlays.

The subsidy cost basis is currently used in the United States only for direct and guaranteed loans, not for other contingent liabilities. However, legislation tabled in the U.S. Congress in 1999 (but not enacted) would have shifted all U.S. government insurance programs to this basis (H.R. 853, sec. 604, 106th Cong., 1st sess., 1999). The legislation provided that beginning with fiscal 2006, insurance commitments would be made only to the extent that budget resources were appropriated to cover their "risk-assumed cost." In the legislation, this cost is defined as "the net present value of the estimated cash flows to and from the Government resulting from an insurance commitment or modification thereof." Inasmuch as the volume of insurance commitments is many times greater than that of loan guarantees, enactment of this legislation might have an enormous impact on the budgetary treatment of contingent liabilities. Although no action has been taken, this type of proposal is likely to be revived in the future.

Criteria for Contingent Liabilities

The two broad approaches discussed thus far—accounting and budgeting for fiscal risks—would significantly enhance government's understanding of the contingent liabilities it faces. But they do not deal with the critical issue in risk management: whether government should commit itself to the contingent liability in the first instance. In the business sector, financial institutions rigorously partition decisions on risk from risk assessment. One decisionmaking entity is responsible for negotiating insurance contracts, loans, and other commitments; the other assesses the credit-worthiness of borrowers, the risk inherent in the activity, and other risk factors. Moreover, the institution would finalize its commitment only if the risk factors were assessed to be within acceptable parameters. In government, however, risk commitment and risk assessment are often done by the same entity. In the United States, for example, the government agency that guarantees loans also estimates the subsidy cost by assessing the probability of default.

Canadian Principles for Regulating Risk

The best time to manage risk is before the commitment is made; afterward, all government can do is to account for the risk it has undertaken in financial statements or the budget and to manage its portfolio of liabilities in ways that mitigate losses. The government of Canada introduced a set of principles in the mid-1980s to regulate the risks it takes on loans and loan guarantees. For this discussion, the most salient principles are the following:

- In the case of loans, any concessional terms, such as a below-market interest rate, are treated as budgetary expenditures. In some cases, the subsidy is so high that the entire loan is budgeted as an expenditure.
- Before a loan or guarantee is tendered, the sponsoring department must analyze the project and demonstrate that it cannot be financed without government assistance, and that cash flow will be adequate to cover repayment of the debt as well as interest and operating costs and yield a satisfactory rate of return.
- Risk must be shared with private equity sponsors who supply a substantial portion of the required funds from their own resources. Moreover, guarantees must provide that in the event of default, the government shall recover its losses from private equity sponsors.
- Bankers should share risk by bearing a minimum of 15 percent of the net loss associated with any default. This arrangement would give them an incentive to undertake a rigorous assessment of their risk exposure.
- Interest rates on loans should be set to cover the government's cost of money and estimated future losses on loan guarantees. Fees should be imposed to recover estimated future losses and to defray administrative expenses.
- Provision should be made for loans and guarantees at the time they are issued. The amount provisioned should be based on an assessment of risk, and sponsoring departments must pay for these provisions out of fees earned in issuing guarantees or their annual appropriations.
- New loans and loan guarantee programs must be approved by the minister of finance and authorized by Parliament.
- Departments and Crown corporations are required to report on their contingent liabilities. These reports are published as notes to the government's annual financial statement. Moreover, estimates of contingent liabilities and losses are audited by the auditor general who reports directly to Parliament.

Certain exceptions to these rules exist, but the overall effect has been to compel government to consider its risk exposure before guaranteeing loans.

Limiting the Government's Liability to the Amount Provisioned for Losses

The U.S. and Canadian methods for budgeting for fiscal risks rely on loss estimates made at the time loans are issued or guaranteed. Inasmuch as future defaults cannot be known perfectly ex ante, it is possible they will be underestimated. If this occurs, the amount appropriated for subsidy cost in the United States or the amount provisioned for losses in Canada will be immediate. In fact, politicians may have a strong incentive to underestimate risks, especially in the American system where an automatic appropriation is available to cover unbudgeted losses. They do not pay a budget penalty when costs are underestimated.

In Chapter 6 of this volume, Daniel Cohen has proposed a novel scheme to impel government to disclose the true risk deriving from guarantees and other contingent liabilities. He would have the government provision for projected losses by setting aside money equal to its estimated liability in a reserve fund. Once this money is reserved, the government would have no further liability. All claims against guarantees would be paid by the reserve fund, not by government. Most important, claims would be limited to the resources available in the reserve fund; if the reserve fund were depleted, no further claims would be paid.

This arrangement would provide lenders and others seeking government guarantees with a strong incentive to demand that risk be accurately assessed. An underestimate would devalue guarantees and shift risk from the government's reserve fund to private parties. Cohen also has suggested that the reserve fund be privatized, with its shares traded publicly. The share price would reflect the market's assessment of whether adequate provision has been made for the risk insured by the reserve fund.

The Cohen proposal has not been implemented by any government, though doing so would not be a difficult technical feat. It is not certain, however, that his mechanism would effectively constrain the government's liability to the amount provisioned. Ex ante valuation of risk is inherently inaccurate, and barring government from adjusting the amount provisioned as it gains additional information may be impractical. Firms often adjust the amount provisioned for bad debt and other losses in response to new information, and there is little reason to expect the government to behave otherwise. One can foresee enormous political pressure on a government to bail out underfunded reserve funds; in fact, it is likely to be blamed for the underfunding. Of course, if government has the option of replenishing the reserve fund, it would lose much of the incentive to provision adequately for losses.

Even if it were to curtail explicit risk, the Cohen arrangement would not curtail the government's exposure to implicit contingent liabilities. In these cases, there may be strong pressure on the government to compensate for losses even if it were not legally obligated to do so, and even if the reserve fund lacked sufficient resources to cover these claims.

Using the Market to Regulate Risk

An alternative to the Cohen plan would be to allow the market to assess and allocate risk rather than the government. The main advantages to bringing the market into play would be less political opportunism, diversified risk, and lower government losses. Every risk insured by government can be insured commercially at some cost, or not at all if the probability of loss were so high that no private insurer would be willing to take it. When government replaces the market, it shifts the cost to itself. Understandably, private risk takers actively search for opportunities to shift the cost to government, and they often have little difficulty recruiting politicians to go along. Any market-type remedy, therefore, must return all or a portion of the cost to private risk-takers. The easiest way to accomplish this would be for the government to refrain from tendering guarantees; another would be to adopt the rigorous screening criteria applied by Canada. But assuming the government was bent on accepting risk, it might take several measures to reduce its exposure.

Risk-sharing

One simple way for government to reduce risk is to share it with lenders, borrowers, importers/exporters, enterprises, or others seeking guarantees. If the government were to enforce a rule that it would assume no more than 50 percent of the risk, the private parties holding the other half (or more) of the risk would have to think about their own exposure before proceeding with the transaction. A bank would have to consider the credit-worthiness of borrowers; it would no longer suffice to care only about the quality of the guarantee. Some guaranteed transactions might still proceed, but others surely would be aborted if the government limits its liability.

In a variation on this approach, the government would insure the last rather than the first loss. Risk-sharing would be promoted by the use of high deductibles, which would require the insured party to pay for the loss up to a certain monetary value. Government liability would take effect only after the deductible is satisfied.

Risk-based Premiums

One of the anomalies of risk-taking is that government often charges less for its riskiest guarantees. A well-established enterprise might be charged market interest rates or an initiation fee; startup ventures might receive concessional interest rates and have the fee waived. As perverse as this seems, there is a certain political-economic logic to this behavior. Risky borrowers, the argument runs, need government assistance because they have no recourse to private markets. They cannot afford to pay up-front fees or at-market interest rates. Therefore, the government should assist them by forgoing these charges or offering concessionary terms. In effect, the guarantee serves as a subsidy. Arguably, guarantees are an inefficient form of subsidy. Assistance might be better provided through grants rather than contingent liabilities that mask the true cost of government. On this basis, government would do well to charge risk-adjusted premiums for its guarantees. Some lenders and borrowers, importers and exporters, and other risk-takers would be deterred by high premiums, thereby reducing government's exposure.

Reinsurance of Government Risk

One of the most common means used in the private sector to limit liability is the purchase of reinsurance. This practice is rarely applied in government, however. There is no technical impediment to government purchasing reinsurance when it guarantees loans, agricultural prices, or any other event or outcome. As in markets, the amount paid by government would reflect the risk it has taken. The cost of reinsurance not only would give government a powerful signal about the risk it is holding, but also might dissuade it from taking risks that would require very high reinsurance premiums. In other words, the practice of immediately reinsuring itself would deter government from underwriting transactions adjudged by the market to have the highest probability of loss.

The reinsurance model can accommodate several variations. For example, government could reinsure only a portion of risk, or it could base premiums on the cost of reinsurance. In both cases, reinsurance would be a means of promoting risk-sharing.

Conclusion

Risk management is still in its infancy in public finance. Governments have little of the experience and few of the instruments used by firms and markets to assess and control risk. Some techniques perfected in the private sector may be adapted for government use in the years ahead, and some of the cutting-edge practices introduced by Canada and the United States might be tried in other countries. But dealing with contingent liabilities is not easy in any country and is especially difficult in developing and some transitional countries where the markets and insurance sectors are relatively undeveloped and where the margin for error is narrow.

Some critics have urged that the best posture is for governments to take few risks. Clearly, risk-sharing can be more broadly applied by insuring only a portion of possible loss, levying risk-adjusting premiums, and purchasing reinsurance. But in modern times, even well-managed governments in sturdy economies are called on to accept risks that in an earlier age might have been held by the household or enterprise. Many positive things, including economic improvement, have happened because governments have taken fiscal risks. It is precisely because governments will continue to expose themselves to various contingencies that they should be more transparent about the risk they face, more willing to make provision for these risks in their budgets, and more insistent on sharing the risk with others.

References

IFAC (International Federation of Accountants), Public Sector Committee. 1998. *Draft Guideline for Governmental Financial Reporting.* New York.

IMF (International Monetary Fund), Fiscal Affairs Department. 1999. "Manual on Fiscal Transparency." Washington, D.C.

Polackova, Hana. 1998a. "Contingent Government Liabilities: A Hidden Risk for Fiscal Stability." Policy Research Working Paper 1989. World Bank, Washington, D.C.

———. 1998b. "Government Contingent Liabilities: A Hidden Risk to Fiscal Stability—A Consideration for EU Accession." In European Commission, *European Union Accession: The Challenges for Public Liability Management in Central Europe.* Washington, D.C.: World Bank.

United States, OMB (Office of Management and Budget).1999. *Analytical Perspectives, Budget of the United States Government, Fiscal Year 2000.* Washington, D.C.: Government Printing Office.

CHAPTER 4

Institutional and Analytical Framework for Measuring and Managing Government Contingent Liabilities

Suresh M. Sundaresan
Graduate School of Business, Columbia University

THE MANAGEMENT OF RISK in the process of earning an attractive return on the capital employed is a challenge that confronts many organizations in the private and public sectors. For private corporations, which are widely regarded to be profit-maximizing (or value-maximizing) entities, this task has assumed paramount importance with the increased level of competition, globalization, and securitization of the markets where risks are priced and traded. The institutional and analytical frameworks used to manage and measure the risks of corporations and set the right incentives for managers have been studied extensively. As for the public sector, economists have widely investigated the problems associated there with the measurement of deficits and contingent liabilities, but no operational guidelines have emerged on how contingent liabilities should be reported in any measure of government deficit.

The measurement of risk and its accurate reporting in the calculation of federal, state, and city deficits are important to many organizations such as the International Monetary Fund (IMF), World Bank, lenders in the private sector, and ultimately citizens of different generations. Fiscal liabilities tremendously influence the deficit and thus the actual risk and opportunities faced by a country. An example of a liability that may result in intergenerational transfers is the social security system and the aging of the population. The percentage of retired people in the population is increasing in many countries. This increase will lead to a greater burden on the working population even when other factors are held constant.

This chapter reviews the literature on measurement of fiscal deficits, government liabilities, and the analytical tools for measuring government contingent liabilities. It also discusses the merits of measuring a liability accurately in the context of the fact that governments typically have much discretion to legislate actions that can drastically affect the future value of its liabilities (which cannot be predicted ahead). Despite valid concerns about relying on a single measure of deficit, I argue that an accurate measure of liability is very important to lending institutions and legislative bodies. In this context, I argue that the valuation of contingent liabilities in reporting the fiscal risk of governments is *qualitatively different* from a standard loan guarantee (put option-pricing) problem. This is rooted in the observation that the presence of a guarantee (an example of a contingent liability of the government) alters the stochastic process of the variable on which the guarantee is provided in the first place.

An example should amplify this point. Suppose the government decides to guarantee loans of private sector companies in an infrastructure area such as power. This guarantee covers the repayment of interest and principal, which may be denominated in a foreign currency. The presence of the guarantee results in an excess supply of power, leading to a supply response. In anticipation of this supply response, the consumer demand for power-intensive goods also goes up, leading to a demand response. In equilibrium, this response will affect the price of power at which the demand is equal to supply. This situation makes the valuation of loan guarantees a challenging problem.

This chapter is organized as follows. The next section reviews the economics literature on deficits as well as the operational concerns of development institutions. It is followed by a description of the institutional features that monitor the risks taken by corporations. The next section contrasts the institutional arrangements that governments face in addressing the risk management problem. It also explores the differences between the objectives of a corporation and of a government and how such differences may affect their propensity toward risk-bearing. A description of the tools of risk management used in the private sector follows, along with my argument that many of these tools need to be recast in a fundamental way to be relevant to managing the risks faced by governments. The final section outlines a model for measuring the exposure of a government's contingent liabilities. Most of the technical arguments are presented in the Appendix.

Economic Theory on Deficits

Economic theory has much to say about the measurement of deficits, the relevance of any deficit measures, and the role of deficits in the welfare of the economy. This section briefly reviews the literature.

Accounting, Reporting, and Policy Flexibilities

The construction of an ideal balance sheet for a country has engaged the attention of economists for over 20 years. Papers by Buiter (1983) and Bean and Buiter (1987) have attempted to lay down some conceptual groundwork to address this issue. The conceptual and methodological issues in the measurement of fiscal deficits, which are materially affected by the way in which the liabilities are measured and reported, have been discussed in an extensive review paper by Blejer and Cheasty (1991). At the heart of measuring liabilities is the issue of measuring revenues and expenditures of governments, on the one hand, and financing, on the other. Blejer and Cheasty (1991) point out that "the government debt criterion" assumes that if a transaction extinguishes a liability or creates a liability, then it is considered as financing. Under "the public policy criterion," transactions that further the goals of policymakers are classified as taxing and spending. Depending on the doctrine used, then, the deficit measures may mean very different things. Another item that introduces a variation in the deficit measure is the choice between cash accounting and accrual accounting. Under strict cash deficit accounting, only those government outlays for which cash has been distributed within one year is part of the budget balance. Likewise, only those actual cash revenues received within the year go to the budget balance. In the accrual measure of deficits, the actual net resource preemption is accounted for regardless of the cash flows during the year. Depending on the concept used (which may be closer to either the cash or the accrual concept), the measure of deficit will represent different things.

The issues surrounding the measurement of deficit and their implications have been articulated in papers by Eisner (1984) and Eisner and Pieper (1984). An insight that emerges from this strand of literature is that a single measure of deficit may never be adequate for public policy debate or cross-country comparisons. Moreover, deficits can display seasonal patterns, may vary with the growth rate of the economy, and are easily changed through legislative actions and tax policies. Eisner (1984) notes that the valuation of a government's contingent liabilities in the calculation of deficits is subject to the criticism that the government can legislate actions that may seriously change the future value of its contingent liabilities. Inflation also can significantly affect the reported budget deficit in a significant manner. Finally, when the economy is growing and undergoing structural changes, any measure of deficit is likely to be not very informative. Thus the measure of deficit should control for factors such as seasonality, the stage of the economy, and inflation levels.

Ricardian View of Deficit Measurement

The standard approach to budget deficits makes the following case: if the government borrows money (and effectively reduces taxes), it may promote aggregate demand by the consumers. An implication is that the private savings will be lower than the implied tax cut. This will call for an increase in the real rate of interest to restore savings. But the higher real rate will crowd out investment, leading to a lower stock of capital. *In this sense, a budget deficit induced by borrowing is a burden, especially for future generations who will face a diminished stock of capital.*

At the heart of any discussions of government liabilities and deficits lies the Ricardian equivalence theorem, which argues for the perfect substitutability of tax and debt financing under some simplifying assumptions. In a seminal contribution, Barro (1974) argues that intergenerational altruism is a key factor in restoring the neutrality of fiscal policies. The present value of government expenditures (broadly defined to include hidden contingent liabilities) must equal the present value of tax revenues, because the government budget constraint must hold intertemporally. It then follows that the present value of taxes cannot change unless the present value of all expenditures also changes. In short, any deficit-induced tax cut must result in a future tax increase with the same present value. An important implication of the Ricardian equivalence theorem is that any current budget deficit leads to an increase in private savings, which exactly offsets the decrease in the government's savings. This has important implications for the role of deficits and their measurement. *Under the Ricardian view, an accurate measurement of a deficit may help forecast future taxation policies.* (For discussion, also see Barro 1979, 1989; Bean and Buiter 1987; Bernheim 1987; Bernheim and Bagwell 1988; Abel and Bernheim 1991.)

Corporations have the choice of issuing debt or equity, and the Modigliani-Miller theorem sets the benchmark for any debate on whether a specific combination of debt and equity is value-maximizing from the perspective of the corporation. The government can run a deficit or cut taxes, and the Ricardian equivalence theorem defines the circumstances under which fiscal policy choices matter. Because deviations from the Ricardian equivalence result may be expected, whether there is a budget deficit or a tax cut may no longer be a matter of indifference.

Effects of Government Guarantees

The volume of government contingent liabilities is of concern to private sector lenders, the IMF, the World Bank, and future generations of citizens. Loan guarantees, which are an example of a state contingent liability, may lead to moral hazard and excessive risk-taking and an oversupply of loans. The impact of government guarantees on foreign investments was examined by Wu (1950), who argued that the threat of expropriation and nonconvertibility of currency earnings were the biggest risks of concern to the guaranteeing institutions. The possibility that government actions may affect the allocations of resources and the response by private sector entities has been well recognized in the literature. Brock (1992) points out that government guarantees on foreign loans have led to investment booms that have affected the level and the path of the outputs in the economy whose risks are being measured. Brock (1992) also notes that "loan guarantees may also distort an economy's macroeconomic adjustment by permitting a postponement of the liquidation process." He presents case studies from Chile and Texas to show that some delays in the closure of insolvent financial institutions have had disastrous macroeconomic consequences. A similar argument has been advanced by Kryzanowski and Roberts (1993) to suggest that the absence of bank runs in the Canadian banking system may not be due to the bank branching system but to "the forbearance of regulators coupled with an implicit guarantee of all deposits." The fact that loan guarantees and subsidies lead to actions by entities in the private sector has been well articulated by economists. Insightful papers by Townsend (1977) and Salant (1983) note how price-fixing schemes are doomed to fail and are prone to speculative attack by agents in the economy. Bardsley (1994), who examined the collapse of Australia's Wool Reserve Price Scheme, points out that price-fixing schemes can fail even when they are not backed by a fixed, exogenously set financial limit as assumed by Townsend (1977). It is clear that lenders would like to have accurate information about what the valuations of contingent liabilities are even if the government is able to pursue tax and other fiscal policies in the future to dramatically change the future valuation of these liabilities. The point is that any current valuation of such liabilities must be viewed within the context of dynamic actions that can be taken by the government to significantly affect the valuation. With this caveat in mind, we turn to some important papers in the realm of valuing contingent liabilities.

Valuation of Loan Guarantees

The presence of contingent liabilities in the private sector and their effects have been studied in a variety of different contexts. In a pioneering paper, Merton (1977) investigated the effect of deposit insurance and its valuation. His insightful analysis showed that loan guarantees are basically put options written on the underlying assets backing the loans. Later Merton (1978) extended his analysis to value deposit insurance when there are costs of surveillance. In a related contribution, Borensztein and Pennacchi (1990) examine the valuation of interest payment guarantees on debt issued by a developing country. They exploit the market prices of debt in the secondary market to infer an unobservable state variable whose realizations depend on whether there will be contractual debt service or default. Borensztein and Pennacchi assume that the stochastic process followed by the state variable is unaffected by the presence of a guarantee.

A direct application of the insights of such papers to the measurement of the contingent liabilities of government is precluded for several reasons. First, the announcement of a guarantee produces a supply response. For example, government loan guarantees end up increasing the stock of debt because of the supply response. This is not modeled in option pricing. Second, and perhaps more important, because of this supply response, the level and the path of outputs and prices change, leading to an endogenous shift in the underlying path of the economy. This implies that the standard option-pricing paradigm, which assumes an exogenous stochastic process for the underlying assets that is invariant to the presence of the guarantees, cannot be applied in a "cookbook" style to valuing the government's contingent liability. The moral hazard problems associated with price subsidies and guarantees make the valuation much more difficult.

Summary of Insights from the Economics Literature

In summarizing the insights of the economics literature, I argue for the following priorities in research on fiscal risk measurement in general and the valuation of contingent liabilities in particular:

• The neutrality of fiscal policy under some conditions implies that a dollar of debt financing is no different from a dollar raised through taxes. Although this may not strictly hold, it forms a useful theoretical basis for examining how one should assess a federal deficit. The ability of the government to legislate future actions that may significantly alter the current valuations of contingent liabilities makes any isolated valuation measure less relevant for policy debates.

• Government actions such as subsidies and loan guarantees lead to private actions and responses that may affect the level and path of the outputs of the economy. They may induce moral hazard—for example, a government guarantee on debt issued by entities in the private sector may reduce the incentive of these entities to stay current in their debt obligations. (But this is mitigated by the fact that private sector issuers may care about their reputations if they are repeated participants in credit markets.) Another possibility is that the guaranteeing entity is able to extract significant rents from the debtors because of the dire need to get the scarce capital. These observations underscore the need to evaluate the costs of government actions in a general equilibrium or a more inclusive setting than just viewing the measurement of contingent liability as an isolated problem.

• Some government actions such as loan guarantees and price-fixing schemes may lead to a harmful response by agents in the economy, such as speculative attacks on buffer stocks and subsidy programs and inefficient liquidation of insolvent firms in the presence of guarantees. This observation leads to the possibility that the conventional measures of valuing such contingent liabilities may underestimate their true costs.

• A corollary to this observation is that the valuation of contingent liabilities cannot be conducted in isolation of their effects on the asset side, as well as the liability side, of the government's balance sheet. This is particularly challenging because the present value of benefits and other costs generated by government actions is often difficult to quantify but nonetheless very important.

Operational Guidelines for Measuring Risk

Economic theory thus offers important guidelines in the measurement and management of risks assumed by government's implicit and explicit guarantees and subsidies. The focus of this literature is to provide a conceptual and a methodological basis for understanding and reporting deficits. However, for policymakers and institutions such as the World Bank and the IMF, which extend loans and assistance to developing and underdeveloped economies, the issue of correctly measuring the risks assumed by such economies is of *practical and operational concern* because it affects their lending and assistance policies. A recent contribution by Brixi and Zlaoui (1999) and Chapter 3 by Allen Schick and Chapter 9 by Hana Polackova Brixi, Allen Schick, and Leila Zlaoui in this volume have explored risk measurement issues applied to specific countries as well as to the general issue of contingent and hidden government liabilities. The key contributions in this strand of work can be summarized as follows:

• Practical measures of liabilities can be put in the context of a Fiscal Risk Matrix (see Polackova 1998 and Chapter 1 of this volume). Four types of risks are recognized in this framework: (a) direct explicit liabilities, (b) direct implicit liabilities, (c) explicit contingent liabilities, and (d) implicit contingent liabilities. Direct explicit liabilities are government obligations such as government employee wages that are clearly identifiable and fall under the rubric of the national legal framework. Direct implicit liabilities are future obligations of government that do not necessarily constitute legal obligations but rather moral obligations. Explicit contingent liabilities cover state guarantees on loans issued by nongovernment institutions. Finally, implicit contingent liabilities include hurricane damage, earthquake damage, and so forth.

• Specific proposals for budgetary controls as a means of controlling and managing fiscal risk include: (a) improved reporting of the actual performance of programs under the state guarantees; (b) providing the right incentives by requiring significant risk-sharing—this is similar to reinsurance contracts in which the reinsurer requires the insurance company to take the first layer of damages before insuring a prespecified second layer; and (c) modifying and supplanting the accrual-based accounting procedures to shed light on hidden liabilities.

• Risk management tools that are already prevalent in the private sector can be applied to the public sector, such as prudent provisioning, stress testing, and organizational allocation of risk management responsibilities.

The challenge that remains in risk management is to improve the practical task of risk reporting by more completely tapping into the insights of economic theory that were summarized earlier. This chapter attempts to do precisely that.

Institutional Framework for
Risk Measurement in the Private Sector

One place to look for some guidance on risk measurement and management is the private sector. Any firm wishing to actively manage risk has to pass the hurdle that firms need not manage the risks that are easily diversified by stockholders. The basis for this hurdle arises from capital market theory and asset-pricing models in the finance literature. Unless active risk management results in a higher value to the stockholders, there is no need for a firm to manage risk. Typically, two factors make risk management by a firm value-maximizing. The first is the cost of financial distress: if the firm's risk of financial distress is increased as a consequence of not hedging market risks and the resulting process of financial reorganization or liquidation is costly, then risk management adds value to the firm. Second is the underinvestment problem: if the benefits of a project largely accrue to the bondholders, then the firm may underinvest. This situation can be mitigated by hedging under some circumstances. There also may be tax and regulatory-related incentives for firms to hedge risk.

A fundamental aspect of corporate organization is that there are markets in which the claims issued by corporations are actively traded. Such markets include equity markets such as the New York Stock Exchange as well as bond markets in both exchanges and the dealer community. These claims are exchanged by sets of investors many times in any day. For this process to operate efficiently, considerable information has to be produced daily about the risks assumed by corporations. Thus corporations operate in an economic environment in which information is produced by many independent outside groups. In well-developed economies, the following organizations produce information about corporate risks.

Stock analysts follow the earnings potential of corporations. For big corporations such as Microsoft, thousands of analysts assess the economic future of the company and produce earning forecasts and generate recommendations about whether the stock price of the company (which summarizes the risk-return tradeoff to the stockholders) is "fair."

Credit rating agencies such as Moody's and Standard and Poor's analyze the economic environment faced by the companies that issue debt capital. Such agencies often place some faltering companies under "credit watch" and downgrade companies whose economic standing has deteriorated or is in danger of deteriorating.

Commercial banks monitor the activities of the borrowing corporations actively. Bank loans are typically senior and secured, and banks attempt to anticipate any economic difficulty that the borrower may face.

External auditors certify the financial standing of the borrowing corporation and provide credible reports on the risks faced by the company. By enforcing high accounting and reporting standards, auditing firms are able to issue financial statements (including statements about off–balance sheet liabilities) that provide useful guidelines to stakeholders in the company. Although this is generally the case, from time to time auditors appear to perform their functions poorly.

Finally, *external markets*, which fall into three categories, apply here. The first category of markets is those in which the claims issued by corporations are traded. Perhaps the most important source of information about the risks taken by corporations is these markets themselves. Equity and bond prices respond quickly in an efficient market to "news" about the riskiness of companies. The second category of markets is those for corporate control. A fall in equity prices may reflect in part a company's declining economic fortunes. In such circumstances, the company may become the target of a takeover attempt, hostile or otherwise, in markets for corporate control. The possibility that such a takeover might result in a reorganization of the company gives the right incentives to senior managers of the company to seek the right balance between risk and returns. Finally, there are markets in which corporations can participate to manage their exposure. Examples are those for securitization, derivatives securities, and credit derivatives.

The private sector therefore has several institutions and markets that produce, disseminate, and update information about the risks taken by corporations. Within this rubric of institutional factors, the task of articulating the risks taken by corporations boils down to a determination of which risks the corporation decides to bear (based on its core competence) and which risks it can either hedge or parcel out to players in the capital markets. The actual reporting of risk takes the form of quarterly earnings reports and annual audited financial statements, which provide stakeholders with much information. Independent reports by stock analysts and credit rating agencies also provide a wealth of information. Finally and perhaps most important, markets provide almost continual information on the risks of companies.

The risk management tools used in the private sector include the following:

- *Measuring market risk.* This category includes the methods used to assess the exposure of a company to interest rates, foreign currencies, commodity prices, and macroeconomic factors. The concept of value at risk (VAR) is becoming a popular way to measure and report the risk of financial institutions and even nonfinancial entities.
- *Measuring and provisioning for credit risk.* The credit risk of a borrowing company is summarized in its credit rating reports, the prices of its loans and bonds, and its stock prices. The financial statements of the company also report its credit exposure.
- *Stress testing.* Subjecting the borrowing company to stress testing by simulating extreme economic environments will reveal how well it might perform under adverse circumstances.
- *Contractual tools*: marking position to markets, requiring extensive credit screenings, establishing margins, and arranging for collateral requirements. By requiring that swaps be marked to market on a daily basis, swap dealers reduce their credit exposure to daily losses. In the absence of marking to market, such losses may accumulate to a level that may threaten the survival of one of the counterparties. Often, contractual provisions stipulate that positions must be settled in cash if one of the counterparties is downgraded by a rating agency. Such provisions try to internalize in contractual provisions future increases in credit risk.

Institutional Framework for Governments

In sharp contrast to the private sector, governments have far fewer independent institutions and markets that monitor and produce information about the risk and contingent liabilities assumed by the government. This section begins by identifying the institutions that articulate the risks of government and contrasting them with those in the private sector.

Because governments do not issue stock, there are no *stock analysts* who produce information about the risks assumed by them. The absence of this source of information is a major difference between private sector entities and governments.

Governments do borrow money in public bond markets. The debt issues of government are evaluated by the *credit rating agencies,* such as Moody's and Standard and Poor's, which analyze the economic and political environment faced by the governments. This can be a potentially useful source of information. Over the last decade sovereign bond markets have grown at a much more rapid rate than sovereign loan markets. This means that there are market rates that reflect information about the risks of countries.

Commercial banks and bank syndicates extend loans to countries, as do organizations such as the IMF and World Bank. These institutions monitor the activities of the borrowing countries actively and produce a wealth of information on the risks of governments.

As for *external markets,* the category of markets that contains information about government risk is limited to the sovereign bond and loan markets. Governments do have access to derivatives markets, and they use them to manage some of their market exposure.

Broadly, the risks facing a government arise from the political and economic environments. Such risks are present whether the government in question represents a developed economy such as the United States or a developing economy such as India. The risks that arise from the political climate facing the country include the possibility of war or dealing with large-scale immigration arising from instability in neighboring regions or natural disasters. Such risks inevitably create fiscal problems of considerable significance. Risks that arise from acts of God such as earthquakes or hurricanes also may contribute to major fiscal strains. The rest of this chapter will explore risk management tools that comprise or address the following:

• *The institutional framework for risk management issues that deal with moral hazard issues—that is, the accountability of government actions—and the legal framework for and enforcement of contracts.* Any risk management system is dependent on the underlying institutional framework for its efficient implementation. This chapter will specify the institutional framework needed to effectively measure and manage government risk.

• *The contingent liabilities of government.* Examples of government's many contingent liabilities include various guarantees, pension liabilities, indexed wage contracts, and health insurance. Using some of the existing framework for classifying these liabilities, this chapter will highlight the risk measurement problem in each category.

• *The unique risks of government:* lender of last resort, disaster relief, public health, famines, financing the growth of impoverished sections, and real options in the economy. An example of real options is the tremendous growth and foreign currency earning possibilities that arise from information technology for a developing country. Subsidies such as tax exemption may accelerate use of the Internet in remote villages, which can form the basis for promoting primary education and eventually eradicating illiteracy.

This discussion is prefaced, however, with a brief review of the methods by which corporations measure and manage risks. This is a useful starting point, because many of the risk management tools and techniques have been developed in the context of corporations. The chapter then articulates the differences between the contingent obligations and fiscal risks of corporations and governments. This allows a focus on the key differences between corporate and government risk management practices. The institutional framework that underlies risk management in the corporate sector will be contrasted with the mechanisms in place for monitoring the risks of government.

Risk Management Tools in the Private Sector

There are two distinct approaches to managing and measuring risks in the private sector. The first approach is to identify those risks that the organization believes it is particularly good at managing and earning an attractive return on in the process. Such risks are fully borne by the firm. Risks of the firm that are more efficiently borne by the markets are securitized and parceled out where such markets are well developed. In their absence, such risks are laid off in listed or dealer derivatives markets such as bond futures contracts or swaps. An example should serve to illustrate this point. Mortgage companies extend fixed-rate mortgages (FRMs) and adjustable-rate mortgages (ARMs). To fund such a loan portfolio, such firms issue liabilities that typically are short term in nature. Some of the liabilities may be noncontingent; others may be contingent. Let us first focus on a simple noncontingent liability in the context of the simple balance sheet shown below.

Assets	Liabilities
Fixed-rate mortgages (FRMs), 6 percent, 30-year, $500 million principal amount	Six-month certificates of deposit, $500 million
Adjustable-rate mortgages (ARMs) indexed to one-year Treasury bill yield, $500 million principal amount	One-year certificates of deposit, $500 million

Consideration of the risk assumed by the mortgage company requires a look at the exposure of its liabilities in relation to that of its assets. If the company decides to hold both FRMs and ARMs in its portfolio, then its risk picture turns out to be quite different: FRMs have a long maturity in relation to the short-term certificates of deposit (CDs) that were issued by the company to help fund the FRM portfolio. In other words, there is a maturity gap (or a duration gap). The precise nature of the gap depends on the risk of prepayments, but that is not the principal concern now. On the other hand, the ARMs are reset every year, and their market risk is closer to the market risk of the liability that was issued to create the ARM portfolio. Hypothetically, assume that the gap measure is zero for the ARM portfolio. In this illustration, the mortgage company may decide to securitize the FRM portfolio, sell it in the mortgage-backed securities (MBS) market, and use the proceeds to retire the liabilities and keep the rest as profits. It may decide to maintain the ARM portfolio in which the market risk is relatively low; the remaining exposure is the credit risk that the company may believe it is in a better position to manage and earn an attractive return on. In such a situation, the risk management and reporting boil down to two actions. First, securitize and dispose of the risk that the market is able to bear more effectively. This reduces the size of the balance sheet and puts a lesser burden on the regulatory capital requirements. Second, manage the risk of the remaining liabilities in relation to the remaining assets on the balance sheet to earn a better return.

Although here the balance sheet is illustrated with direct (non-contingent) liabilities, the same argument applies to contingent liabilities. A government agency such as the Government National Mortgage Association (GNMA or Ginnie Mae) in the United States securitizes pools of mortgage loans and sells them to institutional investors. But at any time it may have a "pipeline" of mortgage loans that are yet to be securitized. On this pipeline, Ginnie Mae is exposed to serious risk of prepayments. By issuing callable bonds (a contingent liability), Ginnie Mae can attempt to align the prepayment risk of its pipeline assets—that is, if interest rates fall and there is a prepayment, then Ginnie Mae can use the cash flows from prepayment to call the liability back. To report the value of this contingent liability without simultaneously recognizing the asset it is hedging would be a mistake. Of course, in these examples the market values of contingent liabilities and the assets they help generate are easier to measure than in the case of a government. Herein lies the challenge of government's fiscal risk measurement.

Regulatory agencies also have a major interest in making sure that financial institutions have a prudent risk management practice. In the United States, institutions such as banks are under the guarantee of the Federal Deposit Insurance Corporation (FDIC), and the government has a major interest in ensuring that these institutions remain solvent. In other instances, the government is interested in ensuring that the risks are managed in a way so that in the event of a "financial contagion," markets and institutions do not collapse. With these in mind, central banks have coordinated mechanisms for managing market risk, credit risk, operational risk, and liquidity risk in the world's financial markets.

To summarize, the risk management actions that can be taken by firms in the private sector can be placed in distinct categories:

• Customize the assets and liabilities so that the overall market exposure is kept at a minimum.

• Securitize risks through the use of special-purpose vehicles (SPVs) and sell the cash flows from the assets in the SPV to institutional investors. This will be done by firms that believe that the cost of securitization (which requires credit enhancements, liquidity enhancements, and other legal expenses) is less than the benefits that arise from securitization. Such benefits may include regulatory capital relief from a reduced balance sheet, an ability to manage the firm better because of the reduced balance sheet, and an increased ability to focus on managing those assets in which the firm believes it has a comparative advantage.

• Use derivative markets to manage risk when appropriate. There are two types of markets in which firms hedge their risks. The first is listed markets, where derivative securities such as options and futures contracts are traded in open outcry markets. Examples of such markets in the United States include the Chicago Board of Trade and the Chicago Options Exchange. Listed markets such as these tend to be standardized and offer extensive liquidity. Some Central American and Latin American countries hedge their external floating dollar debt by trading in the eurodollar futures contracts at the Chicago Mercantile Exchange, for example. Second, firms also use dealer markets to manage their risks. Dealer products tend to be more customized and illiquid. Examples of dealer derivatives include interest rate swaps, foreign currency swaps, and interest rate caps.

- Engage in prudent provisioning for "credit events" that may happen to counterparties in the future. Besides provisioning capital for future contingencies, firms may also enter into contractual safeguards. Contractual provisions may include collateral requirements, marking positions to market periodically and on a contingent basis, and optionality to terminate or renegotiate if the credit rating of the counterparties is in jeopardy.

- Explore the growing *credit derivatives* market. In this market firms can obtain full or partial insurance for specified credit events. Credit default swaps, credit-linked notes, collateralized loan obligations (CLOs), and collateralized bond obligations (CBOs) are examples of such derivatives.

Formulating Risk Management Practices for Governments

In formulating the risk management practices of government, it is important to first determine the incentives that will encourage the private sector to assume the risks that the government is ill-equipped to bear. In addition, the government should attempt to mitigate any signaling costs that may inhibit optimal provision of liquidity. For example, as is often the case, suppose that the central bank, as the lender of last resort, provides credit under the discount window. But the borrowings under the discount window may fall because of the perception that other institutions regard discount window borrowing to be a signal of liquidity or credit problems of some significance. Governments can design mechanisms that may result in a better allocation of risks. A few examples will illustrate these points. In all these actions, there are costs and benefits that have to be articulated before such actions are taken.

Often, governments have to face the risks associated with acts of God such as earthquakes or hurricanes. Currently, such risks are insured by insurance companies and reinsurance firms. By helping to create a market for the insurance of such events and securitization of such risks, government is able to transfer at least part of that risk to the capital markets. The development of property and casualty insurance companies, reinsurance companies, catastrophe-based futures contracts, bonds, and so forth in certain markets does in fact suggest that such risks can be managed in the private sector to some degree. The role of such markets has been discussed in Braun, Todd, and Wallace (1998). The growth of catastrophe-linked markets also has complemented the reinsurance markets and helped to change the incentives in the reinsurance markets, which are widely perceived to be noncompetitive.

By issuing guarantees and by supporting loan programs through direct borrowings, the federal government has improved the flow of credit into the housing sector. The development of mortgage-backed securities markets where the risk of prepayments is parceled out to institutional investors such as pension funds and insurance companies has freed the commercial banks from their exposure to this risk. This is an example of a government policy in which the risks are reallocated in the economy so that institutions bear only those risks in which they perceive a comparative advantage. On the other hand, such decisions may prove to be costly to the government. In the 1980s, when the interest rates shot up and the yield curve became inverted, some U.S. federal agencies such as the Federal National Mortgage Association (FNMA, or Fannie Mae) had to be rescued by the government through "regulatory forbearance." In the last decade, agencies such as Fannie Mae have grown so rapidly and have leveraged their equity capital so much that the risk exposure implicitly facing the government could be quite substantial in the event of a failure. Moreover, given the fact that agencies such as Fannie Mae are privately owned companies held by stockholders, it is reasonable for the government to reevaluate whether explicit and implicit subsidies that are currently in place should be continued. For example, Fannie Mae does not pay taxes, it has a direct line of credit with the Treasury, and its securities are exempt from certain regulatory restrictions that make them more attractive to institutional investors.

In response to the potential demand for liquidity during the Y2K period, the central bank of the United States came up with a proactive plan rooted in options pricing. As the lender of last resort, the central bank has a responsibility to extend credit to vulnerable sectors of the economy, but by selling liquidity options the central bank signaled ahead of time that it was ready to extend credit should there be a crisis related to Y2K. Such an action has several effects. First, it signals that the central bank is ready to extend credit. Second, by inviting sealed bids, it protects the identity of the potential buyer of the liquidity options. This is important because there is increasing evidence that borrowing in the "discount window" has reputational costs for the borrower. By specifying the securities that are acceptable as collateral in the options contract, the Federal Reserve Bank lets investors know the terms under which it is offering liquidity.

In addition, the government can follow the practice of the private sector in providing more transparent accounting and reporting of its balance sheet where there is a concerted effort to identify and measure all liabilities (both contingent and noncontingent) and relate them to the asset side of its balance sheet. For example, the guarantees extended by the government to help develop a securitized market for mortgages should show up as a liability. But so must the present value of the benefits that have accrued to the taxpayers as a result of the growth of these markets. The cost of obtaining credit for housing might be considerably higher in the absence of the development of mortgage-backed securities markets that grew because of the government guarantees. This should be stressed along with the cost of government guarantees.

A Framework for Valuing Guarantees

A model for valuing government guarantees is sketched out in the Appendix to this chapter. This section stresses the intuition behind the general approach. Figure 4.1 provides the demand and supply curves for an underlying product or service in the absence of a guarantee. The equilibrium price level is P = 27. Once the government introduces a guarantee to the suppliers, more firms may enter the market, leading to an increased supply and possibly an increased level of risk because some weaker firms may attempt to take advantage of the guarantee to enter the market. Figure 4.2 shows this effect.

As noted, the Appendix to this chapter outlines a model in which one can examine quantitatively the effect of a price guarantee on the welfare of the economy and the allocation.

Figure 4.1. Equilibrium Price

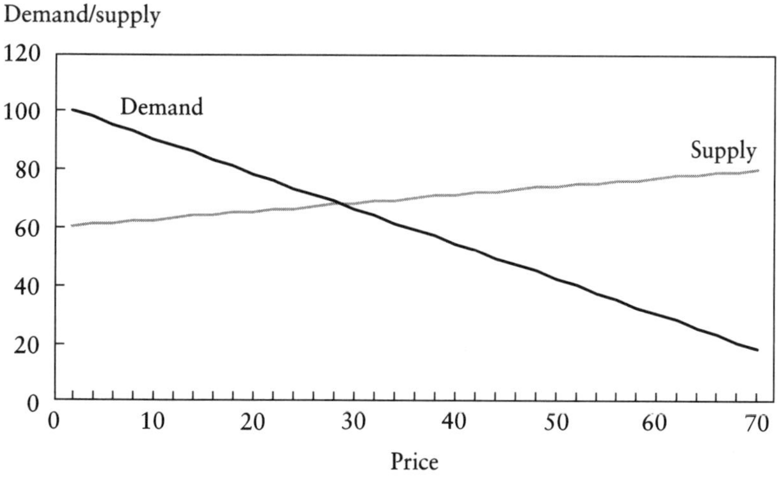

Demand/supply

Price

Source: The author.

Figure 4.2. Equilibrium Price

Demand/supply

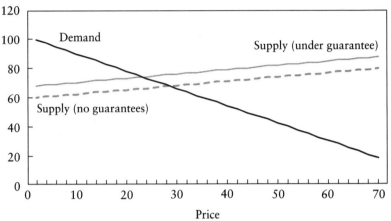

Source: The author.

Conclusion

This chapter has presented an overview of some risk management practices in the private sector and the extent to which they may be useful for managing the fiscal risk of government. Problems that are unique to the risk management in government were identified. They included the potential supply responses to government guarantees and the ability of government to influence significantly the value of any guarantee by its future actions. In recent times, some innovative approaches have been used by governments to manage risk. The use of liquidity options by the central bank of the United States, the selective use of guarantees to promote the development of private markets for securitization, and incentives for the development of risk insurance markets are some examples of innovations in which government has helped develop markets where risks are parceled out to investors who are willing to bear them.

Annex 4.1. A Model of Valuing Government Guarantees

A standard model of valuing contingent liabilities views it as a put option. Consider a simple closed economy in which the price of the output follows an *exogenous* process:

$$dP/P = \alpha dt + \sigma dz$$

where α and σ are positive scalars and $\{z, t > 0\}$ is a Brownian motion process describing the uncertain evolution of the price of the good in the absence of any government contingent liability. Assume that the supply curve in the economy is elastic to the price of the good, so that the supply S is described as the constant elasticity of the supply curve in

$$S = aP^b$$

where

$$b = \frac{\dfrac{dS}{S}}{\dfrac{dP}{P}}$$

is the elasticity of the supply with respect to the output price. If $b = 0$, then $S = a$ and is inelastic. In this economy, with no price guarantees, one can characterize the welfare of the consumer by deriving the value function and the optimal consumption (demand). What happens to this stylized economy when the government introduces a subsidy or a guarantee to the price level? There will be a shift in the optimal consumption (demand) and in the value function of the consumer. Studying these questions requires modeling two things. First, identify the supply response to the guarantees. Second, identify how such supply responses affect the equilibrium price dynamics through the optimal demand of agents in the economy. To study these questions formally, let us investigate the optimal allocation in this economy and measure the value to the economy in the absence of any contingent liability. This will serve as a benchmark for evaluating the effect of such a liability on the price process through (a) a supply response and (b) optimal demand allocation.

Benchmark Allocations

Let the economy be described by a representative agent who maximizes the expected lifetime utility of consumption of the good as

$$\text{Max}_c E \left[\int_t^\infty e^{-\rho s} u(c_s) ds \right]:$$

The wealth of the consumer who also holds all the stock of the goods supplied is simply

$$W = PS = aP^{b+1}$$

The dynamics of the wealth process is

$$dW = W\left[(b+1)\alpha + \frac{1}{2}b(b+1)\sigma^2\right]dt - Pcdt + W(b+1)\sigma dz.$$

The optimal consumption problem of the consumer may be specified in terms of the Hamilton-Jacobi-Bellman (HJB) equation, where J is the value function associated with the optimal consumption allocation:

$$0 = \text{Max}_c \left[\begin{matrix} u(c) - \rho J + J_W\left((b+1)\alpha W + \frac{1}{2}b(b+1)\sigma^2 W - Pc\right) + \\ \frac{1}{2}J_{WW}(b+1)^2W^2\sigma^2 + J_P\alpha P + \frac{1}{2}J_{PP}\sigma^2P^2 + J_{PW}WP(b+1)\sigma^2 \end{matrix}\right].$$

The first order condition for optimality is

$$u_c = PJ_W$$

This problem cannot be solved in closed form in general unless additional restrictions are placed on the problem. To get concrete results, assume that the utility function is of the constant relative risk aversion (CRRA) type, so that

$$u(c) = \frac{c^\gamma}{\gamma}.$$

For this problem one can solve explicitly for the optimal consumption policy and the value function of the economy. This is stated as a proposition below.

The optimal consumption (demand) is linear in wealth and nonlinear in the price level

$$c^* = [\gamma\Phi]^{\frac{1}{\gamma-1}} W$$

where Φ is a function of the price. The function Φ is found by solving the partial differential equation

$$0 = \left[\begin{matrix} \dfrac{[\gamma\Phi]^{\frac{\gamma}{\gamma-1}}}{\gamma} - \rho[\gamma\Phi] + [\gamma\Phi]\left((b+1)\alpha + \frac{1}{2}b(b+1)\sigma^2 - P[\gamma\Phi]^{\frac{1}{\gamma-1}}\right) \\ + \frac{1}{2}[\gamma\Phi](b+1)^2\sigma^2 + [\Phi p\alpha P] + \frac{1}{2}\Phi_{PP}\sigma^2P^2 + \Phi_{P\gamma}P(b+1)\sigma^2 \end{matrix}\right].$$

The value function of the economy is

$$J = W^\gamma\Phi(P).$$

The function $\Phi(P)$ is given by

$$\Phi(P) = a_1 P^{-\gamma}$$

and

$$a_1 = \left[\frac{1 - \gamma}{\rho - \gamma b\alpha - \frac{1}{2}b(b + 1)\gamma\sigma^2 + (\gamma + 1)\gamma\sigma^2 + \gamma^2\sigma^2(b + 1)} \right]^{1 - \gamma}.$$

Note that combining the expressions for J and $\Phi(P)$ yields

$$J = a_1 \left[\frac{W}{P} \right]^\gamma.$$

Allocation with a Guarantee

Consider a simple guarantee scheme that is specified as follows: the government will pay the amount $\bar{P} - P$ whenever $P < \bar{P}$. In such a situation, there is the following supply and consumption response. The supply function will be

$$S = aP^b \text{ for } P > \bar{P}$$

and

$$S = a\bar{P}^b \text{ for } P \leq \bar{P}.$$

This supply response is consistent with the expectations of producers that the government will compensate them in states of the world where the actual price of the good is less than the guaranteed price. As the price goes below the guaranteed level, the supply stays fixed and the only uncertainty that faces the consumer is the wealth level. Corresponding to these two regions, the wealth dynamics evolves as follows:

$$dW = W[(b + 1)\alpha + \tfrac{1}{2}b(b + 1)\sigma^2]dt - Pcdt + W(b + 1)\sigma dz, \text{ when } P > \bar{P}$$

and

$$dW = W\alpha dt - Pcdt + W\sigma dz, \text{ when } P \leq \bar{P}.$$

The optimization problem facing the consumer now can be stated as

$$0 = \text{Max}_c \left[\begin{array}{l} u(c) - \rho J + J_W \left((b + 1)\alpha W + \tfrac{1}{2}b(b + 1)\sigma^2 W - Pc \right) + J_P \alpha P \\ + \tfrac{1}{2}J_{WW} (b + 1)^2 W^2\sigma^2 + \tfrac{1}{2}J_{PP} \sigma^2 P^2 + J_{PW} WP(b + 1)\sigma^2 \end{array} \right],$$

when $P > \bar{P}$ and

$$0 = \text{Max}_c [u(c) - \rho\hat{J} + \hat{J}_W (\alpha W - Pc) + \tfrac{1}{2}\hat{J}_{WW} W^2\sigma^2], \text{ when } P \leq \bar{P}.$$

It turns out that the value function can be written as $J = W^\gamma \Phi(P)$ and $\hat{J} = a_2 W^\gamma$.

Enforcing the conditions of value matching and smooth pasting conditions yields

$$J(\bar{P}, W) = \hat{J}(\bar{P}) \Rightarrow \Phi(\bar{P}) = a_2$$

and

$$J_W(\bar{P}, W) = \hat{J}_W(\bar{P}) \Rightarrow \Phi(\bar{P}) = a_2.$$

This framework, using the value function and the optimal consumption rule, provides a guideline for a numerical solution.

References

Abel, Andrew, and Douglas Bernheim. 1991. "Fiscal Policy with Impure Intergenerational Altruism." *Econometrica* 59: 1687–1711.

Bardsley, Peter. 1994. "The Collapse of the Australian Wool Reserve Price Schemes." *Economic Journal* 104: 1087–1105.

Barro, Robert, J. 1974. "Are Government Bonds Net Wealth?" *Journal of Political Economy* 82: 1095–1117.

———. 1979. "On the Determination of the Public Debt." *Journal of Political Economy* 87: 940–71.

———. 1989. "The Ricardian Approach to Budget Deficits." *Journal of Economic Perspectives* 3 (spring): 37–54.

Bean, Charles, and William Buiter. 1987. "The Plain Man's Guide to Fiscal and Financial Policy." Employment Institute, London, October.

Bernheim, Douglas. 1987. "Ricardian Equivalence: An Evaluation of Theory and Evidence." In Stanley Fischer, ed., *NBER Macroeconomics Annual* (National Bureau of Economic Research). Cambridge: MIT Press.

Bernheim, Douglas, and Kyle Bagwell. 1988. "Is Everything Neutral?" *Journal of Political Economy* 96: 308–38.

Blejer, Mario, and Adrienne Cheasty. 1991. "The Measurement of Fiscal Deficits: Analytical and Methodological Issues." *Journal of Economic Literature* 29: 1644–78.

Borensztein, E., and G. Pennacchi. 1990. "Valuation of Interest Payment Guarantees on Developing Country Debt." *IMF Staff Papers* 37 (December): 806–24, International Monetary Fund, Washington, D.C.

Braun, Anton, Richard Todd, and Neil Wallace. 1998. "The Role of Damage-Contingent Contracts in Allocating the Risks of Natural Catastrophes." Research Department, Federal Reserve Bank of Minneapolis, April.

Brixi, Hana Polackova, and Leila Zlaoui. 1999. "Managing Fiscal Risk in Bulgaria," Draft paper. World Bank, Washington, D.C., November.

Brock, Philip. 1992. "External Shocks and Financial Collapse: Foreign Loan Guarantees and Intertemporal Substitution of Investment in Texas and Chile." *American Economic Review* 82 (2): 168–73.

Buiter, Willem. 1983. "Measurement of the Public Sector Deficit and Its Implications for Policy Evaluation and Design." *IMF Staff Papers* (June): 306–49, International Monetary Fund, Washington, D.C.

Eisner, Robert. 1984. "Which Budget Deficit? Some Issues of Measurement and Their Implications." *American Economic Review* 74 (2): 138–43.

Eisner, Robert, and Paul Pieper. 1984. "A New View of the Federal Debt and Budget Deficits." *American Economic Review* 74 (2): 11–29.

Kryzanowski, L., and G. S. Roberts. 1993. "Canadian Banking Solvency." *Journal of Money Credit and Banking* 25 (3): 361–76.

Merton, Robert C. 1977. "An Analytical Derivation of the Cost of Deposit Insurance and Loan Guarantees." *Journal of Banking and Finance* 1: 3–11.

———. 1978. "On the Cost of Deposit Insurance When There Are Surveillance Costs." *Journal of Business* 51 (July): 439–52.

Polackova, Hana. 1998. "Contingent Government Liabilities: A Hidden Risk for Fiscal Stability." Policy Research Working Paper 1989. World Bank, Washington, D.C.

Salant, S. W. 1983. "The Vulnerability of Price Stabilization Schemes to Speculative Attack." *Journal of Political Economy* 91: 1–38.

Townsend, R. M. 1977. "The Eventual Failure of Price Fixing Schemes." *Journal of Economic Theory* 14: 190–9.

Wu, Yuan-Li. 1950. "Government Guarantees and Private Foreign Investment." *American Economic Review* 40 (1): 61–73.

CHAPTER 5

Analytical Techniques Applicable to Government Management of Fiscal Risk

Krishna Ramaswamy
The Wharton School, University of Pennsylvania

INSTITUTIONS, CONTRACTS BETWEEN institutions, and entire market-places have developed to facilitate the transfer of risks from those unwilling or unable to bear them to those who are both willing and able to do so.

A privately owned corporation typically has a portfolio of projects or activities, each of which contributes a random amount per period to its overall profits. It will, in general, finance these projects with forms of debt or equity capital or with both. In deciding between alternative investment projects, the privately owned corporation looks to add value, net of the cost of the investment. The computation of that value involves discounting the risky stream of cash flows from the project at a rate that is adjusted to account for the risk of the project.

In deciding between alternative ways of financing its portfolio of projects (for example, with short-term or long-term debt, or convertible debt, or preferred stock), the corporation seeks to maximize the value of its shareholder ownership. The shareholders have limited liability—a feature that permits shareholder-appointed managers to take greater risks in search of profitable opportunities. The celebrated Modigliani-Miller theorem offers assurance that, under certain conditions, the total value of the projects undertaken is unaffected by the way in which the firm's activities are financed. This result ensures that the manner in which the risk of the aggregate cash flows from all the projects is partitioned does not affect the firm's current market value.

Absent bankruptcy costs, the use of derivatives to "hedge" the cash flows from the activities does not in itself add value.

A government, or state-owned enterprise, also has a portfolio of activities, although the scale of some of these may be dictated and thus better recognized as *commitments*. These activities will most often be paid for with general tax revenues, and in some cases, the entity might float a public debt issue with a guarantee from another source. It is in comparison with its counterpart in the private sector that several important differences emerge. First, the choice between alternative activities as expenditures or "investments" is generally not made actively—rather, it is set exogenously by law or by a political process. Second, where the private corporation can avail itself of market prices in imputing (current) values to lines of activity or even entire divisions, the state-owned entity cannot perform valuations of equal reliability. Indeed, the notion of "valuing" departments or activities within a government budget—by computing the present value of future net outlays or receipts, thereby acknowledging the intertemporal nature of these activities—runs at odds with the conventional cash flow-based budgeting that forms the basis of decisions in the public sector. Third, where the private corporation's shareholders can seek protection from its creditors, the public entity cannot avoid its explicit and implicit commitments in the event of a crisis. Here I have highlighted the three major differences that an academic finance theorist would see; readers with experience in these contexts will recognize other differences.

The purpose of this chapter is to describe the analytical techniques that can *reasonably* apply to the measurement of risks within a fiscal budgeting context and to discuss, in conceptual terms, the analytical methods that enable a decisionmaker to analyze them.

What are the main analytical tools for measuring fiscal risk that can be brought to bear from financial theory? A popular paradigm in finance employs mean-variance analysis, in which undesirable fluctuations in wealth or cash flow, as measured statistically by the variance (or equivalently by the standard deviation), are balanced against the desirable characteristic of the mean or expected value. Researchers have developed models of risk measurement in this context—known as *factor models*—in which the randomness in the fluctuations in the value of an investment is related to some basic economic variables such as the gross national product (GNP) or industrial production. This class of models enables computation of the risk (standard deviation) of an asset or a cash flow as it derives from more basic and fundamental influences; it also enables identification of those influences that are more important than others. This chapter explores an application of factor models within a mean-variance framework and applies it to a budgeting context in which random (cash flow) expenditures from several distinct units (departments or subnationals, say) create the fiscal risk for a national body.

What are the main tools for controlling fiscal risk? This question is not easily answered for the following reasons. First, fiscal risk is an outcome of commitments that are either explicit or implicit, and the immediate control measure, to scale back these commitments or to "deleverage" them, may not be a realistic alternative in many cases. Second, the normal prescription—to purchase insurance and effect the transfer of the risk to those who are willing and able to bear the risk—may require the use of markets that are not yet developed and that in many cases remain closed for fundamental reasons. That said, forms of risk transfer in the public sector, such as loan guarantees and insurance coverage, do constitute valid methods.

For the application of the relevant analytical methods (such as option pricing), some conditions must be met.[1] In order to provide a useful treatment, I will

- Stay (as much as an academic can) within the practical context in which most government decisionmakers find themselves.
- Take the basic situation to be one in which a parent government unit (a federal or national authority) oversees the budgets of several state-owned enterprises, or subnational units, or even departments.
- Take as given a common period for which the parent and subunits are assessing the fiscal risks.
- Take the typical budget process to be one in which each subunit prepares its budget for the future time period with a common set of forecasts—of, for example, the expected rate of growth in per capita income, an average exchange rate or interest rate, or expected fuel prices—that are determined by the parent government unit or that are agreed on in preparing the budget.
- Assume that the parent government takes up the *net deficits* that occur at the level of the subunits. This means that surpluses and deficits at the subunit levels are passed through to the parent unit.

It is possible to relax most of these assumptions and employ the ideas in other contexts as well. The final assumption, however, is more critical. I have taken as a working assumption (because it simplifies the analysis considerably) that the parent government receives the surpluses and is responsible for the deficits. Such a symmetrical pass-through of surpluses and deficits might make the analysis more suitable for a parent unit that oversees several subunits or departments that have little or no autonomy. In the conclusion of this chapter, I have a few remarks about the one-sided case in which only the (gross) aggregate deficits (perhaps exceeding some level) are borne by the parent unit and what methods can be applied in this case.

Risk Measurement in a Fiscal Context

Contributors to this book (see Chapter 1 by Brixi and Mody and Chapter 18 by Ma) and others (see, for example, Polackova 1998 and Lewis and Mody 1997) have discussed the classifications of risk in a fiscal context and recommendations about its measurement and control. In this section, I add to this practical discussion by describing the analytical tools that can be applied from the field of finance. To do so, I introduce some symbols to simplify the nature of the analysis, but I surround them with their definitions and explain in words the important concept to be retained.

It is useful discipline for every government unit to recognize all its activities and departments nominally as sources and users of funds. Because some units may be both, it is recognized that in making a quantitative tally one might equally rely on the *net* source of funds to describe a department's contribution to the overall fiscal surplus or deficit. Within a government unit i, I denote the net cash flow amounts in a budget period t as $\tilde{C}_{it}$, which can be thought of as the period's net expenditure. I treat positive numbers as a use of funds (as is typical of most expenditure-oriented activities) and negative numbers as a source of funds (as would be normal for a surplus unit or a revenue authority). The squiggle above the letter C serves as a reminder that the projected cash flow amount is a random variable. Like any random quantity, it has an anticipated component—the expected value—which is almost always the basis for the departmental budget allocation. In what follows I use the terms *anticipated budget* or *expected cash flow* interchangeably to apply to the expected value, denoted by $E(\tilde{C}_{it})$.

The realized cash flow in period t can take values that are higher or lower than expected, and the unanticipated component is denoted as $\tilde{u}_{it}$ and is the difference between the realized and expected values:

$$\tilde{u}_{it} = \tilde{C}_{it} - E(\tilde{C}_{it})$$

Note that ex ante—at the beginning of period t—the value of $\tilde{u}_{it}$ is random, but when it is revealed that the i-th activity has a larger (or smaller) deficit than had been budgeted, $\tilde{u}_{it}$ is positive and is an unpleasant (or negative and a pleasant) surprise, ex post.

I characterize the fluctuations in the unanticipated shocks $\tilde{u}_{it}$ as the fiscal risk contributed by the i-th government unit. By its definition, the average value of these shocks is zero.

An individual unit might further recognize that there are some dominant sources that drive the fluctuations in the values of $\tilde{u}_{it}$. For example, the costs of operating a network of schools will involve energy use and related transportation costs, where both the amount used and its price are weather-dependent and outside the control of the overseeing department. In other contexts, the demand for government relief services might be related inversely to the aggregate output and employment, or heavily dependent on the international price of a locally produced and exported commodity. A classification of the underlying influences that affect the unanticipated component of the i-th unit's net expenditure is valuable not only in helping design systems to monitor and control those risks, but also in permitting the supranational or overseeing entity to assess its exposure to those influences.

A risk model of this type is conventionally called a *factor model*. For example, in assessing the risk of a portfolio of common stocks, a financial theorist would assess the stocks' individual risks (standard deviations) as well as the correlations between every pair of stocks in the portfolio. A more parsimonious description of the risk structure of the stocks in this portfolio is a model that assumes there are a few common factors that affect each stock's returns and that a given stock has an elasticity or a sensitivity to each of these factors. The fluctuations in a given stock's returns depend on the sum of the influences contributed by each of these factors, plus a risk that is unique or idiosyncratic to that stock and uncorrelated to the returns of the other stocks. Anyone summarizing a factor model for a useful representation of the risks in stock market portfolios would need for a given stock a list of the elasticities to each of the K common factors and a measure (standard deviation) of the risk of its unique component. In practice, such a model can be statistically estimated from historical data using the technique of *factor analysis* in which the data reveal what the common influences are, or it can be conducted with a prespecified list of factors that are imposed a priori (for a clear and useful exposition of such a procedure, see Sharpe 1981).

In the context of the application here, the lack of adequate historical data related to budget expenditures (especially in a government context in which departments and activities are being added over time) will not permit the statistical estimation of such a factor model. However, the very procedure of constructing a periodic budget will point up the factors (such as fuel prices or exchange rates) that are influential and lead to the estimation of the elasticities.

The Measurement of Risk at the Level of the Unit

The probability distribution of the unanticipated shock $\tilde{u}_{it}$ to the i-th department's budget in period t associates with each (possible) level of the random shock an assessment of the likelihood of its occurrence. The standard measure of risk in this context is the *variance* of the related quantity, the standard deviation. When the likely shocks are symmetrical around their average value of zero, the standard deviation measure reveals that approximately two-thirds of the realized outcomes will lie in an interval of one standard deviation on either side of zero. The graph that follows shows such a distribution; it encompasses extreme values that are more than two standard deviations away and thus occur with lower probability (likelihood), but the bulk of the outcomes occur in the middle.

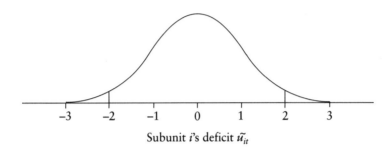

Subunit i's deficit $\tilde{u}_{it}$

Arriving at a forecast of the standard deviation of $\tilde{u}_{it}$ is a difficult but necessary step. It can draw on historical experience, or it can be derived from a subjective forecast of, say, three or more scenarios for the most significant influences on the department's activity.

One could expect that the larger the department, the larger would be its expected cash flow $E(\tilde{C}_{it})$ and the larger would be the standard deviation of its unanticipated component. There is no reason to expect, however, that there is a special relationship—proportional or linear—between the expected values and the risks of a departmental cash flow when viewing these quantities across departments. One could (reasonably) expect that the risk or standard deviation of a particular department is related positively to the *growth* rate in the department's budget—the year-on-year growth in the anticipated budget item $E(\tilde{C}_{it})$. Note, however, that the *level* of the anticipated budget $E(\tilde{C}_{it})$ may be a policy-driven variable that can be taken as exogenously given or as a forecast, and its growth rate might also reflect an active decision coming from a political process.

The Aggregation of Cash Flows of Constituent Units

At the supradepartmental or governmental level, the aggregation of the cash flows requires adding up the contribution from the N constituent units:

$$\text{Aggregate Cash Flow} = \tilde{C}_{1t} + \tilde{C}_{2t} + \tilde{C}_{3t} + \ldots + \tilde{C}_{Nt}.$$

Within the period, and working with a cash flow–based budget process, one can anticipate the fiscal deficit at the governmental level to be the expected value of

$$E(\text{Aggregate Cash Flow}) = E(\tilde{C}_{1t}) + E(\tilde{C}_{2t}) + E(\tilde{C}_{3t}) + \ldots + E(\tilde{C}_{Nt}),$$

which works out to the sum of the anticipated budgets of the N constituent units. If this aggregate number is positive, then the government anticipates and plans for a deficit, given that I chose to use positive numbers to represent net expenditures or uses of funds.

What can be said about the risk at the level of the parental government unit? Typically, it is committed to meeting the needs of unanticipated net expenditures at each department level, and I shall assume that it does. It might have the ability to draw on the unanticipated surplus from those units that has come in with lower-than-expected net expenditures, or higher-than-expected net revenues, perhaps with a lag. In other, perhaps more realistic situations, the ability to use the cash flow from surplus units might be limited. I proceed here with the assumption that the government can draw on these resources fully. This assumption enables me to write that the unanticipated component of the government deficit labeled in period t is $\tilde{U}_t$, which is the sum of the unanticipated components at all the departmental levels

$$\tilde{U}_t = \tilde{u}_{1t} + \tilde{u}_{2t} + \tilde{u}_{3t} + \ldots + \tilde{u}_{Nt}.$$

If each departmental unit stayed just at its anticipated budget level, then the realized value of each unanticipated component would be zero, and, as a result, the government deficit also would be right on target. However, this is an unlikely outcome; in practice, some units would show net expenditures higher than targeted and others might come in at below-target levels.

In this scheme is a diversification effect. The risk (or standard deviation) of the aggregate unanticipated deficit is not equal to the sum of the risks (or standard deviations) of the individual unanticipated components. The standard textbook analysis would point up that if the unanticipated components were less than perfectly correlated—assuming for the sake of argument that some pairs were negatively correlated—the aggregate component would show a lower level of fluctuation than the sum of component unit risks would lead one to believe.

But a more useful analysis can be brought to bear conceptually. Suppose, as was argued earlier, that for the i-th unit the unanticipated net expenditure $\tilde{u}_{it}$—the deviation of actual expenditures from those that were anticipated and budgeted—is weakly and positively influenced by the realized growth rate in per capita income, but strongly and positively related to the deviation of fuel prices from the values that were used in planning the anticipated budget. These driving "factors" are the sources of risk, and the sensitivities of the net excess expenditures over the anticipated budget to these factors will be large in relation to fuel prices but small in relation to the income growth rate.

Other budget units might face exposures to these two "factors"—the growth in incomes and fuel prices, factor sensitivities of different magnitudes—and they also might be exposed to an additional and different group of factors altogether. The exposure of the supranational government to these factors is the sum of the exposures of the individual units to each of the separately identified factors. The presence of common and pervasive factors—including aggregate demand levels, exchange rates, interest rates, international commodity price levels, and so on—in each departmental unit means that the variances and covariances of the unanticipated net expenditures across departments will display a "factor" structure. The Appendix to this chapter shows the computation of the aggregate risk in the case in which one can identify a few common and pervasive factors that affect the net expenditures of the constituent units; a stylized numerical example with two common factors is provided.

The computation of the aggregate risk reveals the following properties, in each of the following conditions:

• *Case 1.* The individual units are exposed to diverse and unrelated risk factors, so that there is little commonality among them. In this, the risk reduction achieved depends on the levels of the relative planned expenditures (the anticipated budgets) within the units.

• *Case 2.* The separate units are exposed to the same common factors in the same way; the sensitivities to these factors across the units are all of the same sign but of different magnitudes. In this case, the exposure at the government level to the factors is the sum of the exposures across the units. Here the magnitudes of the budgets remain relevant, but the important point is that the exposure to the factor—oil prices or interest rates—is averaged across the units.

• *Case 3.* There is commonality among the factors to which the individual units are exposed, but the sensitivities to these factors are of opposing signs, so that, for example, one unit has a positive exposure to fuel price rises while others have negative exposures. It is in this case that the maximum reduction in exposures to the factors can be anticipated, but it would be an atypical occurrence.

What can be said of the risks that are unique to the subunits, the realizations of $\tilde{\varepsilon}$? If the sums have been done right and all the common factors have been considered, these risks should be unrelated. However, it can be anticipated that some departments' expenditures would be hit by "acts of God"—earthquakes or unforeseen emergencies, and so on—and that the incidence of such "catastrophic" risks might be modeled further, perhaps in a Monte Carlo simulation context.

Is it possible to compute a figure to serve as a barometer of future fiscal shocks? Given a distribution for the aggregate fiscal risk, it is natural to ask what is the likelihood of an unanticipated shock of a given size to the deficit? This calculation would be similar in spirit to the daily evaluations of the prospective risk exposure of the portfolio of a large financial institution. In these organizations, there is a daily calculation of the value at risk (VAR), or of a related number, which indicates the level of loss one can expect over the next day or week with a prespecified probability level. For example, a 10-day, 95 percent VAR of $45 million would indicate that a loss of more than $45 million could be expected over the next 10 days with 5 percent probability. In the context here such a calculation is possible, not on a short-term basis—which would not really be relevant—but over the future interval for which the budgets are prepared.[2]

To summarize, the nature of fiscal risks that derive from an aggregate exposure to several subunit budgets can be assessed quantitatively by employing a factor structure in which the factors as economic influences are imposed from prior knowledge of the subunits' activities. An estimation of such risks is a first step to computing the exposures and the overall liability of the parent unit.

The Control of Fiscal Risks

A shareholder-managed corporation in the private sector can exploit the diversification of the cash flows from the aggregation of the component cash flows from all the projects and divisions on its balance sheet in precisely the same way as described here for the government. However, the corporation in the private sector can alter the allocation of its investments across its divisions, thereby controlling the risk (and the expected profitability) of the overall enterprise to its current shareholders as owners. But such changes in the allocation of budgets to the underlying departments are not generally feasible for the government unit.

This brings us squarely to the issue of how the risk at the aggregate governmental level *can* be controlled. It is by now well recognized (and it has been stressed repeatedly elsewhere in the chapters in this volume) that budgeting for government fiscal risks is made more difficult when the subunits under the government's direction exploit the fact that excess unanticipated expenditures will be financed by the parent unit. An explicit (or implicit) coverage of this type provides the wrong incentives for the subunits: they may no longer take pains to prepare accurate budgets and forecasts, and they may not monitor expenditures and control risks to the extent that they would if they were residual claimants as are the shareholders of a private sector corporation. When a subunit has the ability to affect the level of the net expenditures, any coverage of the excess net expenditures over the anticipated budget will raise issues related to moral hazard. In this sense, the assessment of the probability distribution of each unit's $\tilde{u}_{it}$ is made doubly difficult.

In an individual's risk asset portfolio, the most immediate and direct way to reduce risk is to allocate part of the portfolio wealth to the risk-free asset.[3] That way, the overall risk is reduced. When an insurer (the example here is of the government unit) assesses the actuarial or expected value of any future liabilities arising from unanticipated expenditures, and it incurs and provisions for it, it effectively invests in a risk-free asset to reduce its risk. In practical terms, this is equivalent to limiting the size of its activities.

As we shall see in the rest of this chapter, in cases in which the liability incurred is related to an economic quantity that is effectively a traded asset, it is possible to actively control the liability.

Market-Based Vehicles for Controlling Risk

What are the other ways in which a privately held corporation can control its risks? Exchange-traded and over-the-counter methods for risk control undertaken by corporations take myriad forms, but their diversity (and complexity) can be reduced to one or more of the following:

- *Forward and futures contracts*. These are methods that enable the user to lock in a fixed price or fixed rate at a future date.
- *Options contracts*. These are essentially the same in this context as acquiring insurance. They enable the user to purchase protection against unfavorable outcomes. The purchase of put options would insure against unfavorably low prices for an asset or commodity that one wishes to sell. The purchase of call options would provide insurance against unfavorably high prices for an asset or commodity that one is preparing to buy.
- *Swaps*. These are methods that provide protection against risk over several periods, being in essence a portfolio of forward positions.

Note that these contracts can apply to risks related to economic quantities such as exchange rates, interest rates, equity values, commodity prices, including energy prices, and default premiums. (Other mechanisms for risk management, such as securitization and sale of related securities, are discussed elsewhere in this volume.) Often the risk that a particular company faces might not be identical to a traded underlying asset—but this "basis risk" poses only occasional difficulties to most risk managers' operations.

A conventional question in this context posed to the risk manager is related to the cost of risk reduction or hedging. The fact that no outlay is needed to engage in forward contracts, or for that matter in closely related swap contracts, cannot be taken to imply that there is no *cost* to hedging. By locking in, via a forward contract, a fixed price for the acquisition of heating oil in the future, the consumer reduces the fluctuations in expenditures, but knows that the fixed price that was quoted is adjusted for the risk of the fluctuations that someone else is now bearing. In the case of options contracts, the up-front fee for the option is the actuarially fair price for insuring against unfavorable future prices.[4]

In looking at the risk inherent in its fiscal deficit, a government typically sees the risk of low growth as the most important factor. It would be impractical for the government to hedge against this "factor."[5] But there are other factors that drive at least part of the fiscal deficit against which the government can hedge, such as fuel prices, commodity prices, and interest rates.

One contingent liability that is discussed repeatedly in this volume relates to a loan guarantee, or an insurance guarantee such as that given for deposits at financial institutions. It is well known that these guarantees are isomorphic to (typically) put options. The celebrated Black-Scholes model provides the analytical basis for the valuation of these guarantees; it is based on the assumption of the tradability of the underlying risk and the feasibility of a dynamic hedging strategy. When these assumptions do not hold (as they may not in the context of many developing countries' guarantee provisions), it does not mean that the valuation cannot proceed; in these cases, one can reasonably use the technique of computing the discounted expected value.[6]

Here I must stress that the recognition of the liability and the computation of its "fair value" take on the usefulness of an amulet, because these actions in themselves do not limit the liability or even help to control it. A government that provides guarantees is in the same position as an individual investor who has written a put option—and that investor typically will not remain sanguine in the knowledge that he has carefully recorded the option's Black-Scholes value as a liability. It is only in the constructive act of taking offsetting positions that the risk is reduced.

The Factor Model and Contingent Liabilities

The factor model described earlier highlighted the fact that a parent government unit faced the sum of the exposures to the common economic influences that affected the subunit budgets. Some of these common influences may be traded economic quantities, a fact that the parent unit can exploit in one of two ways.

The parent unit can sell explicit guarantees to the subunits against unfavorable outcomes in these quantities. Such guarantees could be hedged by the explicit purchase of marketed insurance contracts at the level of the parent. Under this scheme, the parent serves as a warehouse that manages a book of these liabilities. Incentives at the subunit level are maintained—they would still need monitoring—because the economic quantity that is the basis of the guarantee is observable to both parties, so long as the parent is not also the guarantor of the deficit from all sources of risk.

An alternative scheme is for the parent to take up the exposures to the factors from the subunit levels, but purchase insurance against the resulting aggregate factor exposures to traded underlying risks directly from the market. Consider the following example: a state government oversees the expenditures of several units, including the Department of Highways, the Department of Prisons, the Department of Unemployment Relief, and the Department of Public Education. Each submits a budget and prepares estimates of the quantity of fuel and heating oil it would need, using projections for the demands for its services and using forecasts of forward prices. A severe winter would lead to higher consumption of heating oil at both the schools and the prisons, perhaps at higher-than-expected prices. Extremely severe winters would require increased use of fuel to clear the highways, but savings in heating oil at the schools. A prolonged bout of bad weather can hurt agricultural output and affect future unemployment levels. Both heating oil and gasoline are traded commodities, and it is possible to structure risk management of the unanticipated expenditures in relation to a fuel-related factor. Weather derivatives are available, as are insurance contracts against severe weather. An assessment of the exposures of the separate departments to fuel price fluctuations and to extreme weather scenarios would permit the parent state government to either hedge the unanticipated demands on its resources or provide explicit insurance where it is feasible to do so.

Conclusion

Analytical techniques for risk measurement and risk management that have been developed in finance are applicable to the management of government fiscal risks; the most well-known example among these is the provision of guarantees or insurance in the context of pension benefits, deposit insurance, and protection against default by a public or private corporation.

In this chapter I have highlighted the role of risk measurement in the fiscal context by employing a factor model, which forms the basis of risk measurement in portfolio analysis. The model can be adapted to the fiscal context where a parent government oversees the expenditures of several subunits with separate budgets; the risk factors in this context may be recognized by examining the economic influences within these budgets. Whereas the typical application of the factor model in a portfolio context leads to the allocation of investments, in the context of fiscal risks the application is confined to measuring and monitoring risks. However, this is an important first step in the use of techniques to control for these risks. The factor model is particularly suited to the aggregation of risks and the recognition of the net exposure of the parent unit to latent risks in the departmental or subunit budgets.

Annex 5.1

This Appendix spells out the technical details of the analytical model. The model corresponds to a K-factor model of the net expenditures of N separate entities, which were described as departments or subunits earlier in this chapter. The parent government unit aggregates the cash flows across these subunits and is assumed to be responsible for the aggregate net expenditures that are unanticipated, implying that at the end of the period the parent government will meet the net demands for aid from each of the subunits.

Let $\tilde{C}_{it}$ represent the cash flow of the i-th subunit, which is first written as

$$\tilde{C}_{it} = E(\tilde{C}_{it}) + \tilde{u}_{it}.$$

This equation says that the random cash flow from the i-th unit in period t is (tautologically) decomposed into its expected value plus a mean zero error, $\tilde{u}_{it}$. The expected value corresponds to the anticipated budget or forecast budget for department i; the error term $\tilde{u}_{it}$ corresponds to the surprise or what earlier in the chapter I called the *unanticipated* net expenditure.

Factor Structure

Now I shall impose a linear factor structure on the unanticipated net expenditure; K pervasive common factors will affect the i-th department's budget expenditures:

$$\tilde{u}_{it} = \sum_{k=1}^{K} \{b_{ik}\tilde{f}_k\} + \tilde{\varepsilon}_{it}.$$

This relation says that the K separate factors are underlying sources of risk that drive the risk at the department's budget level. The sensitivity of the budget to the particular factor k—say, the fuel price, representing the *deviation* of the realized fuel price from the value that was used in designing the department's budgeted expenditure for fuel—is captured by b_{ik}. Large positive values for b_{ik} would imply that the department's net expenditures amplify the fluctuations in fuel prices around their forecast values; small and positive values indicate a lower sensitivity, while a negative value indicates that the effect on the department's budget is to promote a surplus (deficit) relative to budget estimates of total net expenditures when fuel prices are higher (lower) than expected. Note that some factor sensitivities may be zero—the subunit may have no exposure to exchange rates or interest rates. The final term, $\tilde{\varepsilon}_{it}$, represents the risk that is unique to the i-th subunit and unrelated to any of the chosen factors; it is the idiosyncratic risk whose variation will be the only source of variation in the subunit's realized budget figures if *each* of the factors takes on the value zero (which would mean, for the example of the k-th fuel price-related factor, that the realized fuel price was equal to its expected value, used in preparing the anticipated budget).

The following remarks apply to the choice of the factors and the factor sensitivities:

• The factors should be chosen to represent the major common influences to which the subunits are exposed. The examples I give: fuel prices, foreign exchange rates, interest rates, aggregate economic activity-related variables such as employment or per capita income, the international price of a locally produced or imported item or raw material, and so on.

• The factor sensitivities can actually be traced through the budget process as a budgeting variance. By tracing the effect of a 1 percent change in the forecast fuel price, one can ask what the effect on the overall budget would be, keeping other things constant.

• One assumption I place on the model says that the expectation of the unique or idiosyncratic shock at the department level, conditional on the factor realizations, is zero—that is,

$$E\left(\tilde{\varepsilon}_{it} \mid f_1, f_2, f_3, \ldots, f_K\right) = 0.$$

This relation says that the unique or idiosyncratic term is just that: unpredictable noise that is unrelated to the factors.

• Note that I do *not* make the assumption that the factors are uncorrelated to each other. In fact, I expect that several assumptions about the factors have been used in devising the budget items, including assumptions about average fuel prices, unemployment levels, and exchange rates. And I expect that these economic quantities are related.

• Now consider the factor structure for the net unanticipated expenditures for two separate subunits, i and j. If I have extracted all the common factors between the net random expenditures of the subunits, then I can conclude that the correlation (equivalently, covariance) between the residual or idiosyncratic risks, $\tilde{\varepsilon}_{it}$ and $\tilde{\varepsilon}_{jt}$, is zero.

In typical finance applications, the factors are extracted from the data, and the usefulness of the factor model comes from the properties of the correlation between these "residual" risk terms. There, it is usually argued that the correlations between the idiosyncratic risks are weak, or zero.

In the application that is the focus here, the factor model is being employed to capture commonalities in net unanticipated budget expenditures. Here I do not have the luxury of a sample of past data from which to extract common factors: rather, I will impose such factors and attempt to capture as many important economic influences that can make the subunit's actual expenditures depart from budgeted expenditures. Of course, one outcome of this is that if my specification of these factors is partial or incomplete, then the residual risks can be correlated across the subunits.

The variance of the unanticipated net expenditures at the level of the subunit is then

$$\mathrm{Var}(\tilde{C}_{it}) = \mathrm{Var}(\tilde{u}_{it}) = \mathrm{Var}\left\{\sum_{k=1}^{K} b_{ik}\tilde{f}_k\right\} + \mathrm{Var}(\tilde{\varepsilon}_{it}) .$$

Notice that a degree of "diversification" is taking place within the subunit itself: the net budget shortfall or surplus will be driven by the aggregate influence of K factors. The ratio of the variance due to the factors to the total variance captures how much of the variation in the budget expenditures is captured by the K chosen factors in the decomposition.

Aggregation to the Government Level

The parent unit serves to absorb the sum of the unanticipated net expenditures at the level of the subunits, so let us look to find the properties of

$$\tilde{U}_t = \sum_{i=1}^{N} \tilde{u}_{it}.$$

Using the factor decomposition that was developed for $\tilde{u}_{it}$ yields

$$\tilde{U}_t = \left\{\left(\sum_{i=1}^{N} b_{i1}\right)\tilde{f}_1\right\} + \left\{\left(\sum_{i=1}^{N} b_{i2}\right)\tilde{f}_2\right\} + \cdots + \left\{\left(\sum_{i=1}^{N} b_{iK}\right)\tilde{f}_K\right\} + \left(\sum_{i=1}^{N} \tilde{\varepsilon}_{it}\right)$$

which shows that the unanticipated demand on the parent's deficit coverage (a) depends on the same K factors, and (b) is also exposed to the sum of the idiosyncratic shocks to each department's budget that is unrelated to the K factors.

Defining the K separate sensitivities at the parent level as

$$B_k = \left\{ \sum_{i=1}^{N} b_{ik} \right\} \quad k = 1, 2, \ldots, K$$

reveals that the sensitivity to the k-th factor at the aggregate level is the sum of the sensitivities at all the subunit levels. The aggregate unanticipated deficit can then be written as

$$\tilde{U}_t = \sum_{k=1}^{K} B_k \tilde{f}_k + \left(\sum_{i=1}^{N} \tilde{\varepsilon}_{it} \right).$$

The following observations regarding $\tilde{U}_t$, the unanticipated budget expenditures at the aggregate level, are now in order:

• Summing the exposures across each of the K factors would reveal that for some cases the risk exposures are reduced in the aggregate.
• Assuming the residual risks $\tilde{\varepsilon}_{it}$ at the subunit levels are not correlated across subunits, one finds that the risk unrelated to the factors at the aggregate level has a smaller effect on the aggregate risk.
• What are the properties of the distribution of the aggregate budget risk? Earlier in the chapter, I define in broad terms a number (by analogy to value at risk, VAR) that applies to a percentile of the distribution of $\tilde{U}_t$. Unlike the corresponding VAR measures, which are applied to the potential cash flow gains and losses over the next day or week, the fiscal risk measures described here apply to the risk levels faced by the government unit over the next budget period.

Aggregate Budget Deficit (Positive) or Surplus (Negative)

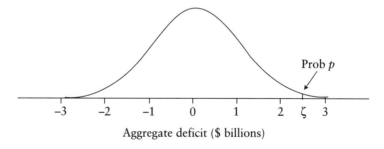

Aggregate deficit ($ billions)

In the graph, an aggregate deficit figure larger than ζ = $2.5B is seen with probability p. I have used the distribution of the aggregate deficit as a bell-shaped curve only as an example.

This measure is best suited to time periods and situations in which the risks do not change—that is, the VAR number is likely to be accurate only for short periods and for portfolios whose risk characteristics do not change during the periods. If the portfolio has options positions, or nonlinear characteristics, then these assumptions can be violated. In the context of government budgets and fiscal risks, the budget periods are typically annual (at best quarterly), and there may be contingent liabilities that have option-like characteristics. For these reasons, the at-risk figure computed as described above will not be accurate and should only be taken as an approximation.

- Some of the K factors (say the first m factors, k = 1, 2, . . . , m) may be related to traded assets, and the remaining factors (k = m + 1, m + 2, . . . , K) may be important economic influences that are not traded. In that case, what would be the risk levels if the decision were made to hedge some of the traded risks—perhaps with the use of derivatives for which there is a market?

The Factor Model: A Numerical Example

A simple numerical example will illustrate the workings of a factor model. Assume that there are four government units or state-owned enterprises (SOEs), and that two common economic factors affect the cash flows of these units—GNP growth ($\tilde{f}_1$) and the average level of energy prices ($\tilde{f}_2$). Each government unit prepares a budget for the coming year, and each unit's budget process builds in certain baseline assumptions about GNP growth and the expected energy price level. The realized GNP growth rate and the actual energy prices will constitute departures from these baseline assumptions and will therefore lead to surpluses and deficits *relative to the budget amounts* in each unit's planned cash flow. These baseline assumptions are provided by a central forecasting service, and, for the sake of argument, suppose that these assumptions include a forecast of the standard deviation of the forecast percentage of GNP growth (σ_1 = 0.5%) and the standard deviation of forecast error in baseline energy prices (σ_2 = 0.7%), and that these factors are uncorrelated.

Suppose now that the expected budget amount for Unit 1, say, is $50 million, in accordance with the baseline assumptions. An analysis of the budget process of this unit reveals that the effect of a 1 percent departure of GNP growth rate from the baseline expected growth rate corresponds to an unanticipated $5 million in expenditures, and a 1 percent departure from assumed baseline energy prices gives rise to an unanticipated $1.2 million in expenditures. These numbers are derived by tracing their effect through the budget planning process. In the notation of the previous section, $b_{i1} = 5$ and $b_{i2} = 1.2$ for Unit $i = 1$. In addition, other idiosyncratic factors affect the cash flows of Unit 1 that are unrelated to the two common factors. Assume that the standard deviation of the idiosyncratic risk in the budget for Unit 1 is \$2 million. In the notation established above, the idiosyncratic risk in Unit 1's budget is $\sqrt{\mathrm{Var}(\tilde{\varepsilon}_{1t})} = \sigma(\tilde{\varepsilon}_{1t}) = \$2M$.

These three quantities—the sensitivities b_{i1}, b_{i2} to the two factors, plus the idiosyncratic standard deviation $\sigma(\tilde{\varepsilon}_{it})$—constitute the numbers that must be assessed for each unit, from the information embedded in the budget process. Listed in the table below are the numbers for the numerical example.

Item	GNP sensitivity b_{i1}	Energy sensitivity b_{i2}	Idiosyncratic risk $\sigma(\varepsilon_{it})$	Budget level $E(C_i)$
Unit 1	5	1.2	2.0	−25
Unit 2	1	0.5	0.5	10
Unit 3	0	1.5	2.5	15
Unit 4	−12	0.1	4.0	30
Total	−6	3.3	Not applicable	30

An explanation of the entries in the table follows:

• The last column of the table contains the expected budget level of the unit, in millions of dollars. Only the first unit is revenue-producing; the others expect to incur deficits. However, the factor model applies to the unanticipated component—the risk in the aggregate deficit—which is the departure from the expected levels. The total (aggregate) expected budget deficit is \$30 million, as shown in the last row.

• Unit 4 has a negative elasticity to the GNP growth rate; if the economy grows faster than expected, by 1 percent, then the budget deficit actually *declines* in that unit by \$12 million. But the forecast also acknowledges that the idiosyncratic risk in that unit's cash flows is also highest, while it is least sensitive to energy prices. This unit might have responsibilities that devolve, for example, on health or education, or welfare, so that its expenditures might be reduced if the economy does well.

• Unit 4 has no exposure to GNP; its risk draws entirely from energy-related and idiosyncratic risks.

• The last row provides the total aggregate exposure to the two common factors. Note that the aggregate exposure to the energy price factor simply adds up and that no unit provides a diversifying exposure to energy prices. In contrast, Unit 4 has a large negative exposure to GNP, so that the aggregate exposure is actually negative. In the notation of the section above, $B_1 = -6$ and $B_2 = 3.3$.

• Finally, note that the standard deviations of the idiosyncratic risks do not add up, so it makes no sense to sum them.

To compute the budget risks for each of the units and for the parent unit, take the numbers corresponding to the standard deviations of the two factors provided by the central forecasting service, $\sigma_1 = 0.5\%$ and $\sigma_2 = 0.7\%$. Then the variance of Unit 1's budget can be computed as

$$\text{Var}(\tilde{C}_{1t}) = b^2_{11}\sigma^2_1 + b^2_{12}\sigma^2_2 + \sigma^2(\tilde{\varepsilon}_{it}),$$

which computes to

$$\text{Var}(\tilde{C}_{1t}) = (5^2 \times 0.5^2) + (1.2^2 \times 0.7^2) + 2^2 = 10.96,$$

implying that Unit 1's budget on a stand-alone basis (its own total risk) has a standard deviation of $\sqrt{10.96} = \$3.31M$. It can be verified using the numbers in the table that the stand-alone risks of Units 2, 3, and 4 are given by the standard deviation levels of $0.79 million, $2.71 million, and $7.21 million, respectively. As expected, Unit 4 shows the highest overall risk level.

Thus the expected budget expenditure for Unit 1 is *revenue* of $25 million, which translates into the statement that the realized revenue is forecast to fluctuate in the region $25M \pm 3.31M = \$21.69M$ to $\$28.31M$ two-thirds of the time, assuming a normal distribution of factor and idiosyncratic influences. Similarly, Unit 4's budget will show a deficit ranging from $22.79 million to $37.21 million in two out of three years.

But the common factor exposures at the individual unit level aggregate to provide total exposures as shown in the last row of the table. The aggregate deficit can now be computed as

$$\text{Var(Aggr Def.)} = B^2_1\sigma^2_1 + B^2_2\sigma^2_2 + \sum_{i=1}^{i=4} \sigma^2(\varepsilon_{it}),$$

which when we use the numbers yields

$$40.84 = ((-6)^2 \times 0.5^2) + ((3.3)^2 \times 0.7^2) + \{2^2 + 0.5^2 + 2.5^2 + 4^2\}.$$

The standard deviation at the aggregate level works out to $\sqrt{40.84} = \$6.39M$, implying that the parent will feel a deficit in the range of $30M \pm 6.39M = \$23.31M$ to $\$36.39M$ in two out of three years. As this stylized example shows, an averaging of factor exposures reduces the exposure to GNP fluctuations, and the diversification of idiosyncratic influences occurs as well. Indeed, the risk at the parent level is less than the total stand-alone risk felt by the managers at Unit 4.

Notes

1. See, for example, Chapter 4 by Suresh M. Sundaresan and Chapter 13 by George Pennacchi in this volume. I will restrict the discussion in this chapter to analytical methods that follow up on the factor model just introduced.

2. There is a close correspondence between the practice of stress testing the budgets and this effective VAR number.

3. The most immediate way to increase risk is to leverage the portfolio by borrowing.

4. In some arrangements, the contract for insuring the risk buries the cost of hedging in a net payment that occurs later—that is, the cost of insurance is paid at the end, in favorable outcome states, so no up-front fee is needed. But in those cases, the insurance is not free and must still be budgeted for in a fiscal context.

5. It would require the government to take a "short" position in the market—to enable it to receive cash when aggregate output is below expectations—and in any case this would require a reliable positive correlation between output and market values, which is not typically observed.

6. In the event that the no-arbitrage assumptions are met, one can compute the expectation of the payoff under the guarantee in a risk-neutral economy and discount it at the risk-free rate.

References

Arrow, K. J. 1971. *Essays in the Theory of Risk Bearing.* Chicago: Markham.

Arrow, K. J., and R. C. Lind. 1970."Uncertainty and the Evaluation of Public Investments." *American Economic Review* 60: 364–78.

Lewis, Christopher, and Ashoka Mody. 1997. "The Management of Contingent Liabilities: A Risk Management Framework for National Governments." In Timothy Irwin, Michael Klein, Guillermo Perry, and Mateen Thobani, eds., *Dealing with Public Risk in Private Infrastructure.* World Bank Latin American and Caribbean Studies. Washington, D.C.: World Bank.

Merton, R. C. 1990. *Continuous Time Finance.* Cambridge, Mass.: Blackwell.

Polackova, Hana. 1998. "Contingent Government Liabilities: A Hidden Risk for Fiscal Stability." Policy Research Working Paper 1989. World Bank, Washington, D.C.

Sharpe, W. F. 1981. "Some Factors in NYSE Security Returns: 1931–79." *Journal of Portfolio Management* 8 (4): 5–19.

CHAPTER 6

Fiscal Sustainability and a Contingency Trust Fund

Daniel Cohen

Université de Paris, École normale supérieure

THIS CHAPTER SETS UP A simple framework to analyze the consequences of contingent liabilities for the management of public finances. From this framework, it suggests the design of an institutional solution to the problem of fiscal opportunism in government when dealing with contingent liabilities.[1]

The idea developed here is that government should handle contingent liabilities by setting up an independent trust fund that itself will have limited liabilities. The government is expected to be the key, but not necessarily the only, shareholder of the fund. When the fund is established, it is endowed with capital that corresponds to the overall size of the government commitment. A government would finance this endowment by raising correspondingly its debt. This first stage has the merit of imposing on government decisionmaking a one-to-one relationship between the government's commitments to the private sector and its own liabilities to the financial market. As a shareholder of the trust fund, on the other hand, the government can expect to receive dividends. The dividends should be set so that they keep constant (say, in real terms) the resources that are managed by the trust fund—in effect, maintaining a constant level of guarantees that the fund is entitled to offer. Under these circumstances, the government needs only to raise taxes by an amount that corresponds to the difference between the debt it has issued and the "market value" of the trust fund. The market value of the trust fund corresponds in theory to the difference between the resources with which it has been endowed and the cost it is expected to cover. Raising taxes to the difference between the initial endowment of the trust fund and what it should be expected, on average, to pay is exactly what the theory of optimal taxation suggests.

There are two merits to and two critical questions about this scheme. The first merit is that it forces the government to internalize immediately the cost of the scheme it wants to implement. The second merit is that the limited liability nature of the trust fund puts an explicit ceiling on government involvement. If risks are initially underreported, this would not represent an additional burden to the government, unless it willingly accepts the idea of sharing the extra burden with the private sector. This leads to the first question. How can the government appropriately assess the market value of its commitments? This question can be partially answered by dragging in the private sector. If shares of the trust fund were to be marketed, the information revealed by the market could then be channeled to the government, allowing it to finance adequately the net burden that this commitment adds to those of its other commitments. The second question is associated with the nature of the risks involved. Should the government set up one trust fund for all contingent liabilities, or one for each category of risk? In principle, it is optimal to set up one trust fund for each category of risk. As I will argue, however, pooling risks tends to lower the cost to the government and is therefore bad from an allocative perspective, but good from a financial perspective.

The chapter proceeds as follows. I first briefly summarize the framework of the theory of government solvency. I then examine how it should be extended to encompass contingent liabilities. Finally, I analyze the merits (and the limits) of the institutional framework I have sketched.

The Basic Analytical Framework

An Intertemporal Approach to Government Solvency

The simplest framework for analyzing fiscal sustainability is to follow the law of motion of government debt over time (all technical details are given in the Appendix to this chapter). The debt buildup of the government stems from the primary deficit (which is simply the difference between government expenditures other than interest payments and government revenues) and the interest bill itself. While the former can, in principle, be changed at will, the latter is the legacy of the past and can only be changed with time. This explains how a profligate government can exhaust the solvency of its successors by leaving out a stock of debt that might turn out to be "unsustainable" (on these issues, see, for example, Buiter 1985 and Cohen 1991).

A direct way to assess whether a government is solvent is to write, in present value terms, all items that will contribute to the buildup or to the reduction of the debt in the future. (The present value terms simply weight any item forthcoming at a time in the future by the inverse of the compounded interest that applies up to that time.) The increase in the present value of the debt between any initial time and the future can then be written straightforwardly as the sum of the present values of forthcoming primary surpluses. Solvency thus can be defined as follows: a government is solvent if and only if it is able to generate in the future a stream of primary surpluses that are sufficient to repay (in present value terms) the stock of outstanding debt that it has inherited from its predecessors. It is a straightforward analytical exercise to demonstrate that such a condition will hold if and only if the present discounted value of the debt will itself converge toward zero in the long run. Indeed, if this is the case this condition implies that the debt is "repaid" asymptotically and that there will always be a chain of investors willing to refinance the government (so long as they are certain that the government will continue to implement the set of primary surpluses that generate such an outcome).

Incorporating Contingent Liabilities

The above principles address the case in which a government can commit itself to a stream of primary surpluses that can handle the debt it has inherited. Let us now see how these principles should be amended to encompass the case of contingent liabilities. In order to do so, let us assume that the government grants the private sector a guarantee against a one-off event such as an earthquake or a banking crisis. To simplify the presentation, let us assume here that the guarantee will cost, if exercised, a fixed value that is known in advance. Clearly, the cost of the guarantee must take account of the probability that the shock will occur, but also, and most important, the likely timing of the shock itself. Assume that the shock is most likely to occur in 10 years, although it might also occur, with a lower probability, in 2 or 20 years. The government therefore should budget the contingent liabilities based on the present value, mostly for a 10-year horizon, of the expenses that will be involved on average.

So long as interest rates are positive, this present value will be less than the expected value of the cost itself. Clearly, there are only two situations in which the expected cost (guarantee times probability of exercising it) may not be the right measure of the burden involved: when the time horizon over which the contingent liability is expected to be exercised is very short, or when the interest rate is very low. In each of these two extreme cases, the government should simply budget the expected value of the cost (cost times probability of occurrence). In all other intermediate cases, it should budget a lower number.

This simple result is at odds with the conventional idea that any contingent liability should be incorporated in the budget either at face value or at a lower number that is measured simply by the likelihood that the guarantee will be exercised. The basic principles just presented reveal that the expected timing of the event is crucial. Events that are certain to occur sometime in the future may cost less than events that might occur with a probability lower than one, but fairly soon if they do occur. Take the example of a financial crisis affecting the banking sector. It is a sure thing in most developing countries that such crises will occur. No one expects it to happen tomorrow morning, however, which allows the government to take actions progressively in order to meet the expected cost (see below). Imagine instead that the government extends a guarantee against the risk that the Y2K bug will disrupt the payment system. Here the probability is certainly smaller than one, but the timing of the event is very sharp: it might cost the government more to provision the latter risk than the former.

Practical Implications

How should the government handle the financing of contingent liabilities in practical terms? Two different methods come to mind. One option is to wait until the guarantee is exercised. At that point, the debt is increased by an amount corresponding to the guarantee to be exercised. Another option is to raise taxes preventively in order to match the market value of the expenses that are generated by the contingent liability. If government pays any attention to smoothing taxation, as is usually the case when taxation is distortionary, this latter option is bound to dominate the former one. At this point, however, the complexity of the political process plays a critical role. From the perspective of a current government that does not internalize the welfare of its successors, the first scheme is likely to appear preferable, at the expense of social efficiency. (See Polackova 1998 and Kharas and Mishra 2001 for a more detailed discussion of contingent liabilities and their fiscal implications.)

Government Risk and Institutional Designs

The Risk of Government Repudiation

In most developing countries, a state of fiscal crisis is almost a fact of life, making it difficult for the government to guarantee contracts in the future, when its own debt is quite often at risk. In order to give some empirical insights into the extent of such risk, I calculated the primary surpluses of three European countries—Belgium, Italy, and Ireland—that faced deep financial problems in the 1980s but were successfully dragged out of their crises. To summarize, in the 1980s Belgium's government surplus as a fraction of the tax receipts of the high debtors of the Organisation for Economic Co-operation and Development (OECD) was 10 percent. Italy's corresponding surplus was 12 percent and Ireland's 15 percent.

These numbers, which are not far apart, point to the idea that the "financial crisis" of a state originates from a relatively low ratio of government surpluses to tax receipts. Contingent liabilities such as protecting the banking sector or guaranteeing some major environmental damage often involve costs that are typically larger than the immediate financing capacity of the government. In such cases, the government would not be willing to honor its previous commitment and the entire scheme would collapse.

Institutional Designs

If the government's signature is at risk, the guarantee that it granted will not necessarily be honored. Take the extreme case in which the risk that is protected corresponds to the risk of government default (such as a "systemic" risk that threatens the banking sector and simultaneously endangers public finances). The private sector will then never be protected ex post and government guarantees will be pointless. In such a case, there is room for institutional improvements that will protect the private sector against the risk of government default. One simple way to address this issue is to set up an independent trust fund that is endowed by the government by an amount that is explicitly geared toward protecting the private risk. Let us now review how such a scheme should proceed.

In terms of credibility, the easiest way to proceed is to endow the trust fund with an amount that corresponds to the risk that is protected and to make the government the shareholder of the fund. This one-off transfer is financed through an increase in government debt. As long as the risk does not materialize, the fund makes profits that can be captured by the government (essentially in the same way that a central bank's profits are redeemed by the government). Once the risk materializes, the trust fund extends its guarantee to the private sector, regardless of the government's financial situation. The fact that the trust fund capitalizes on its assets as long as the risk has not materialized means that the government receives a transfer every period, as dividends, as long as the risk does not show up. Through such a policy (assumed to be designed in real terms), the fund's resources are kept to the initial level. In present value terms, this strategy corresponds to a net receipt, which can be subtracted from the direct cost originally involved in the transfer. This leaves the government with a net burden that obviously corresponds with the number involved in the first evaluation of the cost, and that must be matched by raising taxes by the corresponding expected amount. Clearly, then, the optimal taxation scheme that I alluded to earlier in this chapter can be readily delivered by this scheme.

Bailing in the Private Sector

There is no reason why the government should be the only shareholder of the trust fund. In particular, when there is uncertainty about the nature of the risk involved it may be critical that the government build on the private sector's knowledge.

Assume, for example, that the risk covered by the government materializes with a probability that is common knowledge among private agents but not shared with government officials. If shares of the trust fund are marketable, the government can immediately observe the full value of the trust fund and needs only to finance the residual. In practice, obviously, the government needs only to trade a few shares in order to capture the information on the value of the risk. This information can be immediately acknowledged in the government's account. In that case, the government simply has to raise taxes to take account of the net burden. Clearly, however, nothing prevents the government from going further and perhaps selling the entire project to the private sector. In such a situation, the net cost is readily measured by the one-off difference between the level of the guarantee and the market value of the trust fund, and the optimal taxation scheme is easy to implement. This situation corresponds to many practical examples such as that of an export credit agency. The government could well help the private sector to create such an agency that insures exporters against the risk of foreign default, and then privatize the agency itself. The government's involvement is limited to a one-off endowment that can be properly financed. The same might be true of a guarantee on the banking sector. The government could set up a version of the U.S. Federal Deposit Insurance Corporation (FDIC) aimed at guaranteeing deposits and then let the banking community manage and sustain the agency later on.

Pay as You Go

The trust fund scheme also can be applied to the cases in which the government is involved in repeated transactions (for example, taking care of pensions) rather than one-off mechanisms only. If the government rolls over every period new guarantees as the old ones are exercised, the nature of the game becomes different. But one can still rely on a trust fund to protect government finance from the risk that the scheme is misconceived. Assume that the government is willing to commit itself up to a given amount and is willing to renew its commitments in order to keep that amount constant over the years. Rather than self-managing this set of guarantees, the government could as well create a fund, endowed appropriately each period, that would monitor the risks. This arrangement would have the virtue of protecting government finances from unwanted shifts in the underlying probabilities. If the projects involved are riskier than initially thought, the private sector will bear the consequences, not the public finances. This may not be an optimal risk-sharing method, but when the government's solvency is threatened by an unwanted increase in public expenditures, it might be the best way to go. Similarly, one could drag in the private sector. Think of a trade credit agency that the government wants to help by granting guarantees against adverse events. The government could endow the trade agency with a given flow of resources and let the private sector bring some additional collateral. If the risk is appropriately measured, then the scheme is neutral to the private sector. If it is underreported, then the collateral brought by the private sector will be lost (at least in part). This could form the basis of a truthful exchange of information. At a minimum, the private sector would not want to underestimate the fundamental risk. In fact, it would want to overestimate that risk, but this would then immediately raise government involvement and would have a deterrence effect.

Merging Risks

Until now, it was implicitly assumed that the government had to deal only with one category of risks. Assume instead that there are two classes of risk (the general case would proceed immediately): good risks and bad risks. Good risks that fall due later (on average) than bad risks are less costly to guarantee. In theory, the optimal strategy for the government would be to pledge these two risks, each with a different trust fund. There is, however, an interesting paradox here: not being able to monitor the two classes of risk *reduces* the cost of operating the trust fund, in a situation in which each class of risk is managed separately. The intuition behind this apparently paradoxical result is that the bad risks disappear more rapidly than the good ones, so that the process by which the risks are reallocated regularly benefits the good ones. It is then a safe strategy, from the government perspective, to pool risk, provided, of course, that the usual adverse selection biases are taken care of.

Conclusion

Whatever the precise institutional setting that one has in mind, it should be clear that the proper management of contingent liabilities imposes two imperative constraints. One is a full reporting of the cost involved. Another is the proper internalization of these costs by the government. The specific mechanism proposed here is one in which the full cost is determined by setting up a limited liability framework that imposes, by fiat, an upper limit to the scope of government intervention. The proper internalization by government proceeds from the fact that the financing should be up-front. Although other, somehow less extreme methods may be possible, it is nonetheless critical that the government acknowledge ex ante the fiscal implications of the guarantees involved. Intervening ex post is not only bad from the point of view of the tax system (which would suffer from the strains of increased expenses), but also bad for the sectors that might feel protected by government guarantees to discover only too late that governments do default repeatedly on earlier commitments.

Annex 6.1
Fiscal Sustainability and Contingent Liabilities

The simplest framework for analyzing fiscal sustainability is one in which all government debt is short term, the interest rate is a constant r, and the economy is deterministic.[2] Before relaxing these assumptions, one by one, let us first investigate how fiscal sustainability can be analyzed in this highly simplified environment.

Call D_t the stock of government debt at time t, G_t government expenditures, and T_t the amount of tax collections. The law of motion of government debt can then be written as

$$(6.1) \qquad D_t = (1 + r)D_{t-1} + G_t - T_t .$$

$(G_t - T_t)$ is simply the primary deficit of the government, and $rD_{t-1} + G_t - T_t$ represents the overall deficit. At this stage, equation 6.1 is nothing but an accounting identity that states that the increase in government debt amounts to the overall deficit. To see how this equation can be turned into a constraint imposed on government finances, let us write (6.1) in present value terms, from the perspective of an initial (and arbitrary) initial time $t = 0$. Dividing both sides of the equation by the discount factor $1/(1 + r)^t$ produces

$$(6.2) \qquad \frac{D_T}{(1 + r)^t} = \frac{D_{t-1}}{(1 + r)^{t-1}} + \frac{G_t - T_t}{(1 + r)^t}$$

which has a straightforward interpretation: in present value terms the increase in debt is worth the present value of the primary deficit. Adding up all such equations 6.2 from the initial time $t = 0$ to an arbitrary time T in the future yields

$$(6.3) \qquad \frac{D_T}{(1 + r)^T} = D_{-1}(1 + r) = \sum_{t = 0}^{T} \frac{G_t - T_t}{(1 + r)^t}.$$

The increase of the debt, in present value terms, is the sum of the present values of the primary deficit. When T is allowed to go to infinity, this yields

$$(6.4) \qquad \lim_{T \to \infty} \frac{D_T}{(1 + r)^T} = D_{-1}(1 + r) = \sum_{t = 0}^{\infty} \frac{D_t - T_t}{(1 + r)^t}.$$

The asymptotic value of the present value of the debt is worth the sum of all past primary deficits and the initial debt.

The straightforward definition of solvency that is then imposed on the government is called the "transversality condition"—namely

$$(6.5) \qquad \lim_{T \to \infty} \frac{D_T}{(1 + r)^T} = 0.$$

This condition states that the government should let the *present value* of its debt go to zero in the long run. Once this condition is granted, one can see from equation 6.4 that the government is solvent in the following sense that

$$(6.6) \qquad \sum_{t = 0}^{\infty} \frac{T_t}{(1 + r)^t} = D_{-1}(1 + r) + \sum_{t = 0}^{\infty} \frac{G_t}{(1 + r)^t}.$$

The sum of all tax collections to come, when written in present value terms, must match the initial value of the debt accumulated by the government and the sum of all present values of future government expenditures. The beauty of the transversality condition is that a simple requirement on long-run debt is equivalent to a complex analysis of the determinant of future tax and expenses.

The Case of a Growing Economy

Consider the simple case of a growing economy in which the tax capability of the government is driven by an exogenous law

$$(6.7) \qquad T_t = T_0(1 + n)^t$$

in which n is the underlying growth rate of the economy. Assume furthermore that the interest rate is larger than the growth rate—that is,

(6.8) $r > n.$

In order to simplify the analysis, also assume that government expenditures grow at the same exogenous rate n—that is,

(6.9) $G_t = G_0(1 + n)^t$

One can then write the present value of the primary deficits as

(6.10) $$\sum_0^\infty \frac{G_t - T_t}{(1 + r)^t} = (G_0 - T_0) \frac{1 + r}{r - n}$$

so that the government is solvent if and only if

(6.11) $$D_{-1} \le \frac{T_0 - G_0}{(r - n)}.$$

Assume that G_0 is lifted up to the limit of what the government can afford. Then the primary surplus of the government must be exactly equal to

(6.12) $T_0 - G_0 = (r - n)D_{-1}.$

One can straightforwardly see that debt is exactly growing at the rate n, so that at any later time one has

(6.13) $T_t - G_t = (r - n)D_{t-1}$

and

(6.14) $D_t = (1 + n)D_{t-1}.$

Clearly, this implies that

(6.15) $$\lim_{t \to \infty} \frac{D_t}{(1 + r)^t} = D_0 \lim_{t \to \infty} \left(\frac{1 + n}{1 + r}\right)^t = 0.$$

The solvency condition does not then imply that debt should be stabilized. Indeed, in this critical example, debt is growing to infinity. It does impose, however, that debt should not be growing faster than tax receipts. In other words, it imposes that the debt-to-tax ratio should be bounded.

Contingent Liabilities

Assume that the guarantee has pledged to insure a risk that is expected to be exercised according to a Poisson process of parameter λ. This means simply that the probability that the guarantee will be called upon at time t is $\lambda/(1 + \lambda)^t$; $t \geq 1$. Call K the value of the government guarantee. From a market perspective, the value of the grant can then be simply written as

$$(6.16) \qquad V = E_T \left\{ \frac{1}{(1 + r)^T} K \right\}$$

in which E_T represents the expected value with respect to the time T at which the government will have to extend its guarantee—that is,

$$(6.17) \qquad V = \sum_1^\infty \frac{\lambda}{(1 + \lambda)^t} \frac{1}{(1 + r)^t} K = \frac{\lambda}{(\lambda + r)} K.$$

The market value V of the guarantee coincides with the amount involved, K, in two limiting cases: when l goes to infinity or when r goes to zero. In the first case, l infinitely large, the guarantee is expected to be delivered very rapidly; in the second case, the fact that it will be granted sooner or later is irrelevant if the market puts no weight on present events compared with later ones. In either of these two extreme cases, the government should fund the guarantee immediately and include it at *face* value as part of government expenses.

In less extreme cases, however, the government should set aside a lower number that takes account of the fact that the guarantee will be exercised at some time in the *future*, thus corresponding to a lower cost than the face value itself.

In that case, taxes must be raised to the point where they solve for the new intertemporal budget constraint

$$(6.18) \qquad \sum_1^\infty \frac{G_t}{(1 + r)^t} + D_0 + \frac{\lambda}{(r + \lambda)} K = \sum_1^\infty \frac{T'_t}{(1 + r)^t}$$

where

$$(6.19) \qquad T'_t = T_t + \frac{r\lambda}{(r + \lambda)} K.$$

Repeated Shocks

Let us now investigate the dynamics that are involved when the government extends continually the set of guarantees that it grants to the private sector. For simplicity, assume here that all the guarantees pertain to the same class of risks, parametrized by λ (this hypothesis is relaxed below). Call K_t the value, at any given time t, of the outstanding stock of guarantees that are granted by the government. In market terms, the value V_t of these commitments can be written simply as

$$(6.20) \qquad V_t = \frac{1}{(1 + r)} \left[\frac{\lambda}{(1 + \lambda)} K_{t+1} + V_{t+1} \right],$$

the sum of the present value of the payments that the government is expected to make in the next period and of the remaining commitments one period later. Furthermore, if X_t is the *flows* of new contingent liabilities that the government extends every period, the outstanding stock of government guarantees can be written as

$$(6.21) \qquad K_{t+1} - K_t = - \frac{\lambda}{(1 + \lambda)} K_t + X_t$$

since a fraction $\lambda/(1 + \lambda)$ is redeemed each period and a new flow X_t is added to the total.

Referring to (6.20) and (6.21), specifically expressing K_{t+1} in the (6.21) and substituting it for K_{t+1} in (6.20), one can write a general formula that measures the cost (in present value terms) to the budget of such a government policy:

$$(6.22) \quad V_0 = \frac{\lambda K_0}{(r + \lambda)} + \lambda \sum_{t=1}^{\infty} \frac{1}{(1 + r)^t (1 + \lambda)^t} \left[\sum_{s=1}^{\infty} \frac{X_{t+s}}{(1 + \lambda)^s} \right].$$

The intuition behind such a formula can be readily conveyed by examining a few relatively simple cases. For example, when $X_t = 0$, the government lets the stock of guarantees be depleted as time passes. This yields the same result obtained in the previous subsection:

$$(6.23) \qquad V = \frac{\lambda}{(r + \lambda)} K.$$

Now consider the case in which the government keeps replenishing the stock of contingent liabilities as they are exercised in order to maintain the stock of long-term liabilities at a given level K. The overall cost of such a policy can be simply written as

$$(6.24) \qquad V = \frac{\lambda}{r(1 + \lambda)} K,$$

which then has a straightforward policy implication: the government has to raise taxes by the amount

$$(6.25) \qquad \Delta T = rV = \frac{\lambda}{(1 + \lambda)} K$$

to be solvent. This is a version of the pay-as-you-go system, because now the government pays the contingent liabilities as they get going.

Two polar cases are thus emerging. When the government is committed to a one-off guarantee, funding its scheme is essential to avoid a one-off increase in taxes when the time comes to exercise the guarantee. But when the government is continually rolling over the amount of its contingent liabilities, then a pay-as-you-go system is fine in theory, provided that an explicit limit is set on the amount of the government's guarantees.

Merging Risks

Assume that there are two classes of risk: good risks that fall due with a Poisson process l_1, and bad risks that fall due with a Poisson process λ_2 with $\lambda_2 > \lambda_1$ (bad risks come earlier on). If K_1 is the amount committed to the good risk and K_2 the amount committed to the bad risk, then the government must endow each fund with

$$(6.26) \qquad F_1 = \frac{\lambda_1 K_1}{r} \ ; \ F_2 = \frac{\lambda_2 K_2}{r}$$

or equivalently pledge to each of the two trust funds annual transfers $Z_1 = rF_1 = \lambda K_1$ and $Z_2 = rF_2 = \lambda K_2$.

Assume, however, that the government cannot differentiate between the two groups, and furthermore assume that the government is maintaining a constant level of commitments, as they were exercised, to the private sector, no matter which one of the two risks is covered. The value of such commitments can be written as

$$(6.27a) \qquad V_t = \frac{1}{(1 + r)} \left[V_{t+1} + \frac{\lambda_1}{(1 + \lambda_1)} K_1 (t + 1) + \frac{\lambda_2}{(1 + \lambda_2)} K_2 (t + 1) \right]$$

$$(6.27b) \qquad K_1 (t + 1) = -\frac{\lambda_1}{(1 + \lambda_1)} K_1(t) + X_1(t + 1)$$

(6.27c) $K_2(t + 1) = -\dfrac{\lambda_2}{(1 + \lambda_2)} K_2(t) + X_2(t + 1)$

(6.27d) $X(t) \equiv X_1(t) + X_2(t) = \lambda_1 K_1(t) + \lambda_2 K_2(t).$

In this model, the outstanding level of government guarantees $K_1(t)$ + $K_2(t) = K(t)$ is maintained at a constant through government decisions, but the internal composition of these guarantees is left to its own dynamics. Call θ the proportion of good risk in the economy and assume that the reallocation of new guarantees is extended accordingly—that is,

(6.28a) $X_1(t) = \theta X(t)$

(6.28b) $X_2(t) = (1 - \theta)X(t)$

in which

(6.29a) $X_1(t) = \theta[\lambda_1 K_1(t) + \lambda_2 K_2(t)]$

(6.29b) $X_2(t) = (1 - \theta)[\lambda_1 K_1(t) + \lambda_2 K_2(t)].$

Asymptotically, the composition of the fund will evolve toward

(6.30a) $K_1(\infty) = \dfrac{\lambda_2 \theta}{\lambda_1(1 - \theta) + \lambda_2 \theta} K$

(6.30b) $K_1(\infty) = \dfrac{\lambda_1(1 - \theta)}{\lambda_1(1 - \theta) + \lambda_2 \theta} K.$

The total asymptotic cost of the fund will then be

(6.31) $F_\infty = \dfrac{1}{r} \left[\dfrac{\lambda_1 \lambda_2}{\lambda_1(1 - \theta) + \lambda_2 \theta} \right] K$

while monitoring the two risks separately would involve the cost

(6.32) $F_\infty^* = \dfrac{1}{r} [\theta \lambda_1 + (1 - \theta)\lambda_2]K.$

The cost of managing the merged trust fund is strictly below the cost of monitoring each of the two funds separately. The intuition is given in the text.

Notes

1. The problem of fiscal opportunism encompasses several aspects. Governments whose time horizon is rarely far beyond the next election usually enjoy extending contingent liabilities because they are not counted as a current cost. The short time horizon also implies that governments tend to underrate the risk of their contingent liabilities and, particularly, make inadequate provisions for future contingent payments. Similarly, contingent liabilities expose the government to a risk of default that is not necessarily a source of concern for financial markets. A government's repudiation of its contingent liabilities does not necessarily imply that it will default on other debts. Therefore, under standard conditions no strong incentives are working against government risk-taking and toward proper provisioning for risk. In this volume, issues of fiscal opportunism are discussed in more detail in the Introduction and in Chapter 1 by Hana Polackova Brixi and Ashoka Mody and Chapter 3 by Allen Schick.

2. I thank Hana Polackova Brixi for very helpful comments on an earlier draft. Errors are mine.

References

Buiter, Willem. 1985. "A Guide to Private Sector Debt and Deficits." *Economic Policy* (November): 14–79.

Cohen, Daniel. 1991. *Private Lending to Sovereign States.* Cambridge, Mass.: MIT Press.

Kharas, Homi, and Deepak Mishra. 2001. "Fiscal Policy, Hidden Deficits, and Currency Crises." In S. Devarajan, F. H. Rogers, and L. Squire, eds. *World Bank Economists' Forum.* Washington, D.C.: World Bank.

Polackova, Hana. 1998. "Contingent Government Liabilities: A Hidden Risk to Fiscal Stability." Policy Research Working Paper 1989. World Bank, Washington, D.C.

CHAPTER 7

A Framework for Assessing Fiscal Vulnerability

Richard Hemming
International Monetary Fund

Murray Petrie
The Economics and Strategy Group

FISCAL VULNERABILITY GOES BEYOND a situation in which a government currently pursues inappropriate fiscal policies, or it lacks the ability to implement better policies.[1] While obviously bad policies and a lack of implementation capacity will almost always signal vulnerability, governments that seem well positioned in relation to both may nonetheless find that they are vulnerable in two respects. First, underlying weaknesses may be present that do not affect fiscal outcomes today but could at some time in the future prevent a government from achieving its fiscal policy objectives. And, second, such weaknesses may limit a government's ability to respond to future fiscal policy challenges, such as the need for fiscal consolidation as part of a coordinated policy response to an external shock.

The focus in this chapter is on fiscal vulnerability from a macroeconomic perspective, and the suggested framework for assessing vulnerability highlights four macrofiscal aspects of vulnerability: (a) incorrect specification of the initial fiscal position; (b) sensitivity of short-term fiscal outcomes to risk; (c) threats to longer-term fiscal sustainability; and (d) structural or institutional weaknesses affecting the design and implementation of fiscal policy. The framework is intended primarily to be a basis for identifying situations in which an anticipatory response to potentially poor macrofiscal outcomes is required. But it also goes beyond this point, because a clear link exists between fiscal vulnerability and economic vulnerability more generally.[2] This being the case, *the importance of assessing fiscal vulnerability also derives from its contribution to effective macroeconomic surveillance.* The framework suggested in this chapter can be viewed as providing guidance that will assist countries in assessing their fiscal vulnerability.

Work on fiscal vulnerability has paralleled work on financial sector vulnerability (see Downes, Marston, and Ötker 1999). Strong links exist between fiscal and financial sector vulnerability, because fiscal vulnerability can manifest itself as a financial sector problem (such as government preemption of bank lending on concessional terms), while addressing a financial sector problem can be a source of fiscal vulnerability (such as government support for bank restructuring). A new financial architecture should pay attention to both fiscal and financial sector vulnerability, although the former has so far attracted much less attention.

Reflecting the fact that a lack of transparency can be a major source of vulnerability, *there is a considerable overlap between assessments of fiscal vulnerability and assessments of fiscal transparency.* For this reason, many of the issues discussed in this chapter are also covered by the IMF's Code of Good Practices on Fiscal Transparency (the transparency code) issued by the International Monetary Fund (IMF) and taken up in more detail in IMF's Manual on Fiscal Transparency (the transparency manual)—see IMF (2001). Indeed, it is inevitable that vulnerability assessments will be informed by fiscal transparency assessments included in Reports on the Observance of Standards and Codes (ROSCs), for those countries where they are available, or undertaken independently of the ROSC process. Transparency is also important, because a prerequisite for a vulnerability assessment is a reasonable degree of transparency. It would be difficult to assess the vulnerability of a totally nontransparent fiscal system. This chapter covers certain parts of the transparency material that are absolutely central to vulnerability assessments, both in the sense of identifying sources of vulnerability and in facilitating assessments.

The chapter is organized as follows. The next section specifies the fiscal policy objectives that provide a benchmark against which vulnerability assessments are made. The third section discusses different macrofiscal aspects of vulnerability and the methodology for vulnerability assessments. That section is followed by one that suggests vulnerability indicators and provides guidance on their interpretation, and then by one that addresses some aspects of vulnerability that are microstructural, as distinct from macrofiscal, in nature. The last section offers concluding comments.

Fiscal Policy Objectives

Fiscal policy can be viewed as operating at three levels. The first is the *aggregate level*, where the concern is with total expenditure and taxation (or the revenue effort more generally), the overall fiscal balance and the associated deficit financing or use of fiscal surpluses, and the fiscal consequences of accumulated liabilities and assets. The second is the *sectoral level*, where there is a strategic focus on the broad structure of spending (across major programs) and revenue (mainly across major tax bases). And the third is the *program level*, where the emphasis is on the microeconomic efficiency of individual spending and tax programs.[3]

Fiscal vulnerability can manifest itself and can therefore be assessed at any of these three levels. *This chapter focuses on fiscal vulnerability in a situation in which a government is exposed to the possibility of failing to achieve its aggregate fiscal policy (or macrofiscal) objectives.* These objectives are:[4]

1. Foremost, a government should *seek to avoid excessive fiscal deficits and debt;* they could directly threaten short-term macroeconomic stability and longer-term fiscal sustainability.

2. A government should *ensure that fiscal policy contributes to effective demand management* by retaining sufficient flexibility to respond in an appropriate and timely way to domestic and external macroeconomic imbalances.

3. A government should *raise revenue in a manner consistent with maintaining reasonable and stable tax rates*, which contribute to an environment that encourages economic activity.[5]

Fiscal vulnerability could reflect a possible inability to meet any or all of these macrofiscal objectives. Certainly each is important in its own right. Thus a fiscal vulnerability assessment might suggest that, given a government's expenditure plans: the money creation necessary to finance the fiscal deficit may lead to inflation or a debt sustainability problem may emerge; fiscal policy will have to be undesirably tight, and maybe pro-cyclical, during an economic downturn; or tax rates will have to increase over time to levels that are likely to have significant disincentive effects. Any one of these possible macrofiscal outcomes would be a source of concern. However, in most circumstances such outcomes will not be independent. So if deficits and debt are a concern, providing a fiscal stimulus during a recession will usually be costly given the high interest rate premia that are imposed when the fiscal position is weak. And if the need instead is to contain a boom, the scope to do so may be limited if the room for tax increases has been exhausted before deficits and debt become a concern.

There are also clear interactions between macrofiscal objectives and what might be called (to distinguish them from macrofiscal objectives) the microstructural objectives of fiscal policy—that is, objectives set at the sectoral and program levels. The causality can run both ways. Weaknesses in the design and operation of spending and tax programs can and do contribute directly to poor macrofiscal outcomes. At the same time, if poor macrofiscal outcomes are possible, then it is likely that some of a government's microstructural objectives will go unmet as a consequence. There is also the possibility that the aggregate fiscal policy approach could indicate that a country is not especially vulnerable, yet at the same time the country is falling short of meeting, for example, a high-priority poverty alleviation target. Clearly, such an outcome can create vulnerability in the obvious sense that a government that fails to meet such a critical equity goal may have to respond in a manner that either compromises its macrofiscal objectives (if it has to spend more on poverty alleviation programs and raise already high taxes or borrow excessively to pay for the additional spending), or, if there is little unproductive spending, it will have to cut some other high-priority programs or shift some spending off-budget (which simply shifts the source of vulnerability). If a government does neither of these things, its political survival may be threatened.

Macrofiscal Aspects of Vulnerability

The starting point for meaningful analysis and discussion of fiscal vulnerability from an aggregate fiscal policy perspective is a clear view of the initial fiscal position, both in terms of whether macrofiscal objectives are initially being met and in terms of the quality of the information that is available about the initial fiscal position. In particular, it is important that the initial fiscal position describes the full range of fiscal activity in the economy. The next step is to develop an understanding of the range of possible short-term macrofiscal outcomes by assessing their sensitivity to underlying risk. The focus should then shift to government exposure to medium- and longer-term adverse trends or influences that may affect fiscal sustainability. Finally, attention should be paid to vulnerabilities that arise from weaknesses in the structure of public finances, the institutional capacity for fiscal management, and the broader effectiveness of government. These four aspects of fiscal vulnerability provide the organizational structure of the framework for assessing vulnerability that is suggested in this chapter.

Because assessing vulnerability is a forward-looking endeavor, it necessarily requires that a view is formed about future economic developments in general and future fiscal developments in particular. In this connection, the position taken in this chapter is that *fiscal vulner-*

ability assessments need to be prudent, in the sense that they should be prepared using a framework that has a bias toward downside risks. A prudent approach can be justified by asymmetries in the economic implications of unfavorable versus favorable outcomes, especially given the weak initial fiscal positions or deficit bias in many countries.[6] It is also necessary to lean against a systematic tendency toward optimism arising from elements of the political environment, such as the short time horizon of elected officials.

The Initial Fiscal Position

The initial fiscal position is clearly a source of vulnerability to the extent that the macrofiscal objectives described above are initially not met. Thus if the starting position is characterized by high deficits and debt, an inability to respond to macroeconomic imbalances (for example, because automatic stabilizers are small and discretionary fiscal policies take time to formulate and implement), or very high tax rates, then there would usually be a presumption of vulnerability. However, the concern here is more with the possibility that the available fiscal information may not relate to the full range of fiscal activity that is undertaken by or on behalf of the government.

It would typically be the case that *a description of the initial fiscal position takes the latest central government budget as its starting point,* and this is reasonable if the budget is realistic. If the budget is not realistic, the estimated outturn for the preceding year should be the starting point. If a vulnerability assessment is being made some time after the budget has been formulated, it would be appropriate to begin with an estimate of the budget outturn rather than the budget or the preceding year's outturn. This would allow several factors to be taken into account, including: new data for the outturn for the preceding year that render a budget based on an earlier estimate unrealistic; revised macroeconomic forecasts affecting the assumptions underlying the budget; and other fiscal policy developments (new programs, official statements about budgetary policy, and so forth).

From such a starting point, it is crucial to go beyond the budget, because it is most unusual that the budget captures all fiscal activity:

- Where lower levels of government are large, *focus on the general government.*[7]
- *Include extrabudgetary activities of the central government and lower levels of government.*
- *Cover quasi-fiscal activities undertaken outside government.* The central bank, public financial institutions, and nonfinancial public enterprises to varying degrees are all involved in such activities, which tend to generate implicit or explicit obligations for the government. In

many cases, precise quantification may be difficult. A qualitative statement about quasi-fiscal activities would in the first instance suffice, but rough orders of magnitude should be provided for the main quasi-fiscal activities and the need for better information should be emphasized. Where quasi-fiscal activities are significant, *the focus should shift to the public sector.*

Another problem is that fiscal activity is often measured in an unreliable or incomplete manner because of weak accounting and control systems. With poor fiscal data, there will often be large discrepancies in the fiscal accounts, for example between above-the-line and below-the-line fiscal balances. The cash accounting traditionally used by governments, while having a number of advantages, also has inherent weaknesses as a measure of fiscal activity. Most notably, it fails to reflect activities that give rise to arrears and noncash-based provisions to clear arrears (for example, netting of expenditure arrears and tax offsets).

It is important to take into account changes in the stock of government liabilities and assets. Knowing a government's gross debt is a minimum requirement for longer-term sustainability analysis, while information on the structure of debt (that is, maturity, fixed versus variable interest rates, and currency composition) is needed to assess short-term fiscal risk. If a government has sizable financial assets, its net financial debt is more relevant than its gross debt to longer-term sustainability. And where available, even partial information on other asset transactions (most usefully on privatization and government investment in productive assets) would provide some basis for determining whether the effects of fiscal policy actions that show up as changes in aggregate revenue and expenditure, and the resulting changes in the fiscal deficit, are being accompanied by changes on the government's balance sheet that might undo their impact.[8]

Explicit and implicit contingent liabilities also should be covered. The Fiscal Risk Matrix in Chapter 1 of this volume outlines the classification and examples of such government obligations. Where there is provisioning against contingent liabilities—for example, a deposit insurance scheme—the level of provisioning should be noted and the focus should be on the uncovered contingent liability. Again, the quantification of contingent liabilities may be difficult. If so, they should be handled in the same way as quasi-fiscal activities.

Finally, the difficulty in interpreting fiscal balances can be a source of vulnerability. This difficulty derives in part from the extent of fiscal activity to which the fiscal balance refers. But it also relates to the way in which the fiscal balance is measured. Because assessing vulnerability will necessarily become a comparative exercise—assessments for some countries will inform assessments for other countries—there are advantages to using an internationally comparable measure of the fiscal balance (and other fiscal aggregates) in all countries. The overall balance, appropriately adjusted in response to its most obvious shortcomings (for example, to reflect expenditure arrears, the use of privatization proceeds), is best suited to this purpose. However, *the overall balance should be supplemented by other fiscal balance measures where they provide a better indicator of the stance of fiscal policy from a macroeconomic perspective.*[9]

Short-term Risks

Fiscal outcomes are exposed to variations in key underlying assumptions and other factors. (Chapter 5 by Ramaswamy in this volume addresses this fact by applying a factor model.) To assess the sensitivity of fiscal outcomes, it is necessary to move beyond the initial fiscal position, because the one-year time horizon of a budget, and by implication of the initial fiscal position, does not do justice to the full extent of the short-term risks to which fiscal outcomes are exposed. For this reason, the initial fiscal position should be accompanied by a short-term forecast that looks at least two years ahead. The short-term forecast should be based on unchanged policies, in the sense that policy intentions that have been announced but not implemented should be excluded, and it should be purged of temporary measures affecting the initial fiscal position. This forecast should be fairly detailed, but possibly less so than the description of the initial fiscal position. Both the initial fiscal position, which typically itself has a forward-looking component, and the short-term forecast should then be subjected to sensitivity analysis.

The principal short-term risks that need to be addressed are the following:[10]

• *The initial fiscal position and the short-term forecast are sensitive to changes in macroeconomic variables and other sources of economic risk.* Unanticipated changes in growth of the gross domestic product (GDP), unemployment, inflation, interest rates, external trade, capital flows, the exchange rate, and other macroeconomic variables affecting macrofiscal outcomes give rise to forecasting risk affecting revenue, expenditure, and financing. The structure of debt is important in this regard, because it affects the fiscal risk associated with short-term movements in interest rates and the exchange rate. Revenue and expenditure are also subject to other risks affecting the tax base (such as corporate profitability), nontax revenue (such as mineral prices), and spending programs (such as government wage increases).
• *It is possible that contingent liabilities will be called when no budget provision has been made to meet them.* The appropriate way

to provide for contingent liabilities, and the practicalities of doing so, raise issues that have resulted in limited provisioning (see Chapter 2 by Petrie in this volume for further discussion). Implicit liabilities will always entail more substantial risk, since provisioning is usually judged inappropriate because of moral hazard problems.

• *There may be a lack of clarity about the size of specific expenditure commitments* in that provision may be made in the budget for spending on an activity (such as bank restructuring), but there is less than the usual precision about the cost implications of that activity.

• Finally, *some fiscal policies may be defined imprecisely.* This would be the case where a government announces a policy intention (such as providing incentives for saving and investment) but either the details of the way in which the policy is to be implemented are not well developed or the implications of an announced method of implementation are unclear.

Fiscal analysis should therefore involve an examination of the range of possible short-term macrofiscal outcomes, with a focus on variations in underlying assumptions and other parameters to which a probability or likelihood of different events can be attached, albeit in some cases only approximately. However, while the realization of a typical risk might signal the need for policy adjustment, it would not necessarily imply vulnerability because the consequences may be easily accommodated. This being the case, there is merit in subjecting a short-term forecast to more aggressive stress testing, especially when there are reasonable grounds to consider that a substantial shock to the economy, be it global, regional, or country-specific, is more than a remote short-term possibility. This situation is addressed in the next section in the context of stress testing a baseline medium-term projection.[11]

Longer-term Fiscal Sustainability

Even if fiscal outcomes are not exposed to significant short-term risks, running persistent fiscal deficits may result in debt levels that become a source of fiscal and broader macroeconomic difficulties over the medium term. The standard debt dynamics analysis is the usual basis for identifying the impact of deficits on indebtedness, and more generally for assessing the implications of past and current fiscal policies for longer-term sustainability. Where available, market-based indicators (for example, a government debt rating or interest rate premia) can supplement debt dynamics analysis.[12]

The starting point for an assessment of longer-term sustainability is a baseline, medium-term fiscal projection, which typically would look at least five years ahead. It should assume a continuation of current policies, which will often require difficult judgments as to what is and what is not a current policy.[13] Although it encompasses the initial fiscal position and the short-term forecast, such a baseline does not need to be as detailed. To assess vulnerability, *the baseline medium-term projection should be supplemented by alternative scenarios*. These scenarios should illustrate the responsiveness of the medium-term fiscal outlook to different specifications of the initial fiscal position and short-term forecasts. In particular, it should be recognized that short-term risks may persist, and some could be greater, in the medium term. For example, certain contingent liabilities, such as pension guarantees, are probably a bigger source of medium-term risk than of short-term risk.

Stress testing would then be used to assess the impact of short-term and medium-term shocks (for example, a global interest rate or business cycle shock, a regional or country-specific reversal of market sentiment, or a sharp deterioration in the terms of trade). Stress testing should identify how the fiscal outlook would change under circumstances ranging up to the fairly extreme and shed light on why the outlook changes in the way it does.[14] It is therefore important to identify the key transmission mechanisms through which the main fiscal aggregates are affected. Moreover, the likely correlation between different transmission mechanisms should be recognized. For example, a major macroeconomic shock such as an output collapse may cause revenue to fall, expenditure to increase (for example, on the social safety net), and contingent liabilities to come home to roost, all at the same time. A downside scenario should envisage some of the worst things that can happen (for example, full-blown crises).[15] In this way, stress testing, in combination with identification of the policy responses that reduce vulnerability, provides the basis for systematic fiscal contingency planning, which has to be a key outcome of effective surveillance.

Long-term projections and scenarios are a natural extension of medium-term analysis. However, they can be even less detailed given their more speculative nature. It is particularly important to take into account long-term expenditure pressures. The impact of demographic developments on pensions and health spending is an obvious source of such pressure in many countries. The possible exhaustion of a natural resource that generates substantial revenue, and any associated environmental degradation, will also be relevant to long-term fiscal sustainability in some countries.

Structural Weaknesses

The composition of expenditure and revenue is important in assessing vulnerability. A *principal source of vulnerability is a high proportion of nondiscretionary spending to total spending*, which limits a government's flexibility to adjust spending levels downward when it needs to do so. Nondiscretionary spending is that for which a government is under a legal or other strong obligation to meet. The most notable examples are interest payments, formula-based transfers to lower levels of government, and public pensions.[16] However, the components will vary from country to country, and classifying all spending as either nondiscretionary or discretionary may require difficult judgments. In many countries, the distinction may boil down to that between spending on transfers (broadly defined) and spending on goods and services.

Some large expenditure items are a source of vulnerability, because they are resistant to adjustment given the powerful interest groups they serve. Military spending is a case in point, although a large government wage bill may be every bit as entrenched where public sector unions are strong or the government is an employer of last resort. *There also may be latent expenditure needs that do not manifest themselves until triggered by a shock or discontinuity of some kind.* Any significant gap in expenditure, compared with established norms, could be exposed in this way. For example, the need for a social safety net may become apparent only after an economic crisis, but once in place it will almost certainly become permanent.

A good tax structure is one in which revenue derives from a range of taxes with broad bases, ideally large macroeconomic aggregates (that is, wages, profits, and consumption, including imports of consumables). Not only will such a structure tend to result in reasonable tax rates, but it also will ensure a moderately elastic tax system, which is desirable from the point of view of facilitating countercyclical fiscal policy through the operation of automatic stabilizers. *A revenue composition dominated by just one or two taxes, especially if they have narrow bases, is a source of vulnerability*, both in terms of increasing a government's exposure to unexpected fiscal developments because revenue from just a few taxes is likely to be volatile (for example, trade tax revenue is highly sensitive to exchange rate changes), and in terms of limiting its capacity to respond when the need arises because tax rates probably have to be very high. Frequent tax law changes, especially when they result in more exemptions, tax holidays, and other relief, as is often the case, can add to vulnerability by progressively undermining the tax base. A government's capacity to respond is also constrained by extensive earmarking, which limits the scope for discretionary tax changes. Finally, a heavy reliance on nontax revenue, the main sources of which (grants, royalties, privatization proceeds, central bank profits) may not be stable or particularly responsive to policy intervention, also can contribute to vulnerability.

The institutional capacity for fiscal management is a major determinant of fiscal vulnerability. Numerous aspects of the institutional capacity for fiscal management could be relevant to fiscal vulnerability—most notably, the administrative capability for expenditure management and revenue collection, the roles and responsibilities of government and within government, the public availability of information, the budget process, and the integrity of fiscal information collection. The emphasis should be on particular weaknesses that can signal that poor macrofiscal outcomes are possible (for example, expenditure and tax arrears, ineffective audit procedures).

Finally, *a government that has a general reputation for being ineffective will usually be vulnerable.* Thus a government that gets involved in too many activities that should be left to the private sector, whose agents (that is, public servants, public enterprise managers) have a relationship with politicians that is inconsistent with the arm's-length principle, or that is characterized by extensive nontransparency and corruption, cannot be expected to meet its macrofiscal objectives on a consistent basis.

Clearly, the four aspects of vulnerability just highlighted are closely related. Obviously, an incorrect specification of the initial fiscal position makes it difficult to assess both short-term risks and longer-term sustainability. Moreover, a chronic misspecification of the initial fiscal position is likely to be a manifestation of weak institutional capacity for fiscal management. But some of the interactions are subtler. For example, weak fiscal institutions can act to amplify rather than dampen macroeconomic volatility, as would be the case when a country pursues pro-cyclical fiscal policy because an inability to save fiscal resources generated by a buoyant economy—reflecting political pressures for such savings to be spent—leads to a pattern of tax cuts during expansions and tax increases during recessions.[17]

Vulnerability Indicators

There are clear gains in convenience if the results of the analysis of the initial fiscal position, short-term risks, longer-term sustainability, and structural weaknesses could be summarized in a few key vulnerability indicators, and the preceding discussion suggests some obvious candidates. However, selecting a set of vulnerability indicators involves trade-offs. While the inclusion of a large number of indicators increases the probability that fiscal vulnerability will be identified, they may make it difficult to identify the main sources of vulnerability. A large number of indicators also will tend to increase the information requirements of vulnerability assessments, which would create difficulty in ensuring comparability across countries and generally make assessments less manageable. In the end, then, *a set of vulnerability indicators that is fairly parsimonious is needed.*

The set of indicators described in general terms in Box 7.1 and in more detail in the Appendix focuses on the aspects of vulnerability

---

Box 7.1 A Possible Set of Fiscal Vulnerability Indicators

- *Fiscal position indicators*—weak initial fiscal position; incomplete coverage of government fiscal activity; poor accounting and control; insufficient balance sheet information; sizable uncovered contingent liabilities; and significant quasi-fiscal activities.
- *Short-term risk indicators*—high sensitivity of short-term fiscal outcomes to changes in key macroeconomic variables; inappropriate debt structure; variable revenue sources and expenditure programs; calling of uncovered contingent liabilities; and other expenditure risks.
- *Longer-term sustainability indicators*—unfavorable debt dynamics; low government debt rating or high interest rate premia; adverse demographic trends; and rapid natural resource depletion or serious environmental degradation.
- *Expenditure indicators*—large share of nondiscretionary spending or transfers; excessive military spending; and significant gaps in expenditures (for example, social security, safety net, health and education, infrastructure).
- *Revenue indicators*—inelastic revenue system; highly concentrated tax revenue; frequent tax law changes; extensive earmarking; and reliance on grants and other major nontax revenue sources.
- *Fiscal management indicators*—large expenditure arrears and use of netting arrangements; marked deviation between the original budget and the budget outturn; nonexistent or weak medium-term budget planning; long delays in preparing and auditing final accounts; large tax arrears and use of tax offsets; a large stock of tax refunds, especially for the value added tax (VAT); an out-of-date taxpayer register; and an ineffective tax audit program.
- *Government effectiveness indicators*—poor results from surveys of public sector performance, corruption, and so forth.

---

discussed in this chapter and avoids reference to features of the fiscal system that are unrelated to vulnerability at the aggregate level. Even so, for a number of reasons these indicators should still be regarded as provisional. First, the acid test of their suitability will come only when they are implemented in the context of actual vulnerability assessments. *Country experience may suggest that there are more useful alternatives to the suggested indicators.* Second, *country experience may also suggest a need for additional indicators.* Political factors, for example, are not included, despite the fact that a specific political event, such as an approaching election, may generate an unusual amount of uncertainty about short-term fiscal policy in many countries. There also may be a case for looking at characteristics of the fiscal management system that give rise to vulnerabilities beyond those directly related to aggregate fiscal policy, because indirect effects (for example, where macrofiscal outcomes are affected by the need to meet microstructural objectives) will often be important. Finally, the scope for greater use of survey-based indicators that capture important supplementary information bearing on fiscal vulnerability should be explored.[18]

The fiscal vulnerability indicators can be used in a range of ways. At the least demanding extreme, they can be viewed as no more than a checklist that someone assessing fiscal vulnerability could use to keep track of whether he or she has covered all the relevant aspects of vulnerability. At the other much more demanding extreme, it is easy to envisage them as a stepping-stone on the way to the type of systematic assessment that could ultimately produce an index of vulnerability. In the first instance, the indicators should probably be used more as a checklist, albeit an evolving one as the indicators are modified in response to experience with their use. But once a final set of indicators begins to emerge, they can be used in a more ambitious way, perhaps with the objective of developing a small number of broad categories of vulnerability. In this connection, however, *it will be necessary to assign the indicators priority*, to take account of differences in fiscal institutions across countries, and perhaps to develop indicators relevant to particular groups of countries (or weight indicators differently across groups of countries).[19]

In whatever form they are used, *fiscal vulnerability indicators have to be interpreted with caution.* It has already been noted that indicators of short-term fiscal risk may point to the need for a relatively small fiscal correction within the context of an otherwise strong underlying fiscal position. It is important to distinguish this from a situation in which the underlying position is also weak.[20] Although it will often be the case that a high level of exposure to short-term fiscal risk will be a leading indicator of longer-term vulnerability, it is important that fiscal vulnerability assessments avoid judgments based only on a few indicators.

The policy significance of a similar level of fiscal vulnerability also will vary across countries, depending on the broader economic context in which fiscal policy is placed. For example, evidence of short-term risk may be a serious concern in a country with a currency board or a fixed exchange rate, where the scope for discretionary monetary policy is limited. Government deficits and debt also may be more of a concern in a country with relatively low national savings and a high external debt, or with high inflation and an underdeveloped financial sector. And fiscal vulnerability in a country where an external crisis could have contagion effects should warrant particular attention. Finally, a given level of fiscal vulnerability also may be a cause for greater concern if combined with a low level of adherence to a broader set of standards related to government performance.

Microstructural Aspects of Vulnerability

This chapter has focused so far on a government's aggregate fiscal policy objectives. As noted, however, a government has to pursue other microstructural objectives, and failure to meet such objectives can create vulnerability just as surely as failure to meet macrofiscal objectives. A government can have a wide range of microstructural objectives. Abedian (2000) focuses on those microstructural objectives that are most closely linked to a government's socioeconomic legitimacy. Equity goals related to poverty alleviation, income redistribution, and improvements in other indicators of human development fit into this category. So too do many of the efficiency goals that traditionally (that is, in a welfare economics sense) justify government intervention in the economy, such as providing public goods and merit goods, taking account of the external costs and benefits associated with private decisions, and addressing other aspects of market failure.

Two microstructural aspects of vulnerability are discussed in Abedian (2000). The first aspect is those undesirable features of the environment supporting government activity that can lead to government (or bureaucratic) failure. This failure in turn manifests itself in the pursuit of inappropriate equity and efficiency goals. Weaknesses in this area extend beyond those noted above as relevant to macrofiscal vulnerability and cover such things as the political process, the public sector culture or ethos, and the general approach to governance. The second aspect is the fiscal management system, where weaknesses that again extend beyond those noted above result in delivery failure, that is a large gap between a government's equity and efficiency goals and what it actually achieves.[21]

Concluding Comments

The aim of fiscal vulnerability assessments is to identify those features of a country's fiscal system that compromise the ability of the government to meet its aggregate fiscal policy objectives. They also provide a basis for managing vulnerability in order to limit the government's exposure to possible adverse outcomes, in particular by enhancing its ability to respond to fiscal and broader economic developments. Managing vulnerability requires a preemptive effort to address potential problems revealed by vulnerability assessments.

It is primarily the organizational framework that vulnerability assessments provide that is new. However, the true value added will not become clear until the framework is implemented. In particular, the vulnerability indicators will almost definitely need fine-tuning and possibly more extensive reconsideration.

Finally, although this chapter has discussed government liabilities and assets in terms of the importance of having information on their levels and structure as indicators of vulnerability, it has not discussed a government strategy for their management. Yet, as Chapter 1 by Hana Polackova Brixi and Ashoka Mody indicated, government liabilities and assets can be managed in a way to contain vulnerability by reducing government risk exposure. The sophistication of a government's risk management strategy may not be done justice by the indicators suggested above. More work is needed to offer practical guidance on optimal risk-reduction strategies.[22]

Annex 7.1:
Measurement of Fiscal Vulnerability Indicators

Indicators	Measures
Fiscal position indicators	
Weak initial fiscal position	Overall fiscal balance as a share of GDP
	Other fiscal balance measures as a share of GDP (where relevant)
	Net financial debt as a share of GDP
	Size of automatic stabilizers (small/average/large)
	Average and maximum rates of tax (for each main tax)
Incomplete coverage of government fiscal activity	Revenue covered in fiscal data as a share of general government revenue
	Expenditure covered by fiscal data as a share of general government expenditure
Poor accounting and control	Fiscal balance measured from above-the-line relative to the fiscal balance measured from below-the-line
Insufficient balance sheet information	Gross debt
	Net financial debt
	Other balance sheet data
Sizable uncovered contingent liabilities	Gross contingent liabilities as a share of total revenue
	Net contingent liabilities as a share of total revenue
	Or
	Description of main contingent liabilities and quantification of largest net contingent liabilities
Significant quasi-fiscal activities	Quasi-fiscal activities as a share of total revenue
	Or
	Description of main quasi-fiscal activities and quantification of largest quasi-fiscal activities

(Table continues on the following pages.)

Indicators	Measures
Short-term fiscal risk indicators	
High sensitivity of short-term fiscal outcomes to changes in key macro-economic variables	Impact of variations in forecasted GDP growth, inflation, balance of payments, exchange rate, and interest rates on the fiscal balance
Inappropriate debt structure	Maturity (short, medium, and long term), interest rate structure (fixed versus variable rates), and currency composition of debt
Variable revenue sources and expenditure programs	Impact of variations in other economic and noneconomic determinants of revenue and expenditure on the fiscal balance
Calling of uncovered contingent liabilities	Net contingent liabilities as a share of GDP; expected payments in connection with guarantees and other contingent liabilities
Other expenditure risks	Description of programs and policies that give rise to risks
Longer-term sustainability indicators	
Unfavorable debt dynamics	5–10 year projection of gross or net debt as a share of GDP, and change in the primary balance as a share of GDP required to stabilize the debt ratio at the current level or at a specific target level
Low government debt rating and/or high interest rate premia	The Bloomberg website *<www.bloomberg.com>* provides information on how to calculate interest rate premia.
Adverse demographic trends	Long-term projection of retirement age and school-age population relative to total and working population; impact on expenditure as a share of GDP and on tax rates
Rapid resource depletion	Years of usable reserves at current exploitation rate; resource-related revenue as a share of total revenue; resource-related financial assets as a share of GDP; serious environmental degradation
Expenditure indicators	
Large share of nondiscretionary spending and/or transfers	Nondiscretionary spending and transfers as a share of GDP
Excessive military spending	Military spending as a share of GDP
Significant gaps in expenditure	Programs for which spending as a share of GDP is significantly below the average for comparable countries

Indicators	*Measures*
Revenue indicators	
Inelastic revenue system	Tax elasticity or buoyancy
Highly concentrated tax revenue	Revenue composition, particularly trade tax revenue as a share of total tax revenue
Frequent tax law changes	Major tax changes, especially new exemptions and other reliefs, every year or every two years
Extensive earmarking	Revenue from earmarked taxes as a share of total revenue
Reliance on grants and other unstable nontax revenue sources	Nontax revenue as a share of total revenue; composition of nontax revenue
Fiscal management indicators	
Large expenditure arrears and use of netting arrangements	Expenditure arrears as a share of total revenue; significant netting of arrears; inability to report on sizeable arrears
Marked deviation between the original budget and the budget outturn	Expenditure outturn relative to original expenditure; resort to large supplementary budgets
Nonexistent or weak medium-term budget planning	Effective medium-term budget planning
Long delays in preparing and auditing final accounts	Length of time between end of fiscal year and (a) preparation of final accounts and (b) release of audited accounts
Large tax arrears and use of tax offsets	Tax arrears as a share of total revenue; sharp increase in tax arrears; significant tax offsets
A large stock of tax refunds, especially for value added tax (VAT)	Stock of tax/VAT refunds as a share of tax/VAT revenue
Out-of-date taxpayer register	Currentness of taxpayer register by main tax
An ineffective tax audit program	Coverage of tax audit; targeting of tax audit
Government effectiveness indicators	
Poor results from surveys of public sector performance, corruption, and so forth	Information available from the Institute for Management Development's *World Competitiveness Yearbook;* the Transparency International's Corruption Perceptions Index

Notes

1. This chaper was originally issued as IMF Working Paper WP/00/52 by the International Monetary Fund (IMF), Washington, D.C. It draws on a companion paper by Iraj Abedian and has been prepared with significant input from William Allan, John Crotty, and Steve Symansky. It also has benefited from comments made by many colleagues in the Fiscal Affairs Department at the IMF and by seminar participants at the European Central Bank and the World Bank.

2. This is illustrated by recent work that points to variables related to fiscal imbalance—for example, high domestic credit growth and large current account deficits—as being among the strongest predictors of an external crisis (IMF 1999).

3. The World Bank (1998) refers to these as the level-1, level-2, and level-3 operations of fiscal policy.

4. In addition to these general objectives, a country may have specific fiscal policy objectives that the government has set for itself (for example, as reflected in a fiscal rule) or that may have been agreed on with others (for example, as part of IMF conditionality).

5. Stability of tax rates is also justified by the fact that the distortionary cost of taxation is reduced by smoothing tax rates over time. Tax smoothing is also consistent with countercyclical fiscal policy.

6. Prudence is consistent with the usual approach in accounting, where financial statements consistently err on the side of caution in recording events or transactions that are likely to have a favorable impact, while being less cautious when the results are likely to be unfavorable.

7. Although lower levels of government that set their own objectives and are subject to market discipline can be viewed as independent of central government from an economic perspective, from a vulnerability perspective consolidation is desirable (although vulnerability could be assessed independently for lower levels of government).

8. Easterly (1999) finds evidence from an analysis of countries borrowing from the IMF and the World Bank and of European countries covered by the Maastricht Treaty that fiscal adjustment often takes the form of privatization and cuts in government investment, so that changes in reported fiscal deficits represent illusory rather than real adjustment because there is an offsetting balance sheet transaction.

9. Depending on a country's circumstances, other such measures might include the structural balance, the operational balance, the primary balance, or the augmented balance.

10. These risks are the same as those discussed in the fiscal transparency manual, because a requirement of the fiscal transparency code is that all governments should publish a fiscal risk statement with the annual budget.

11. However, if the focus of a vulnerability assessment is on short-term fiscal outcomes alone, stress testing should be part of such an assessment.

12. They cannot, however, substitute for such analysis, or for vulnerability assessments more generally, because there is little evidence that either debt ratings or interest rate premia adequately reflect fiscal sustainability. They are in-

fluenced more by external sustainability, level of development, and the depth of the market for a country's debt.

13. The difficulty is illustrated by the discussion of fiscal policy in Asia in IMF's *World Economic Outlook, October 1998* (IMF 1998), where, in distinguishing discretionary from nondiscretionary fiscal measures, it had to be decided whether holding nominal spending constant when spending had in the past increased represents changed or unchanged policy.

14. Stress testing clearly goes beyond the usual scenario analysis, which in the fiscal area tends to involve producing higher-growth and lower-growth scenarios to illustrate the benefits of stronger fiscal policies and the costs of weaker fiscal policies than in the baseline.

15. There is a parallel here with risk assessment in the private sector. Standard value-at-risk methodologies used in financial analysis show how much a bank or firm could potentially lose over a specified time period for likely market movements. Stress testing is used to assess and manage extreme risks.

16. Not all nondiscretionary spending is necessarily a problem. For example, spending on unemployment compensation is cyclically sensitive. It therefore acts as an automatic stabilizer during a cyclical downturn, reducing the need for discretionary fiscal policy.

17. Talvi and Végh (2000) find that fiscal policy in developing countries is for such a reason highly pro-cyclical. They suggest that attention be paid to designing fiscal arrangements (such as stabilization funds) aimed at ensuring that fiscal savings generated during good times is saved for bad times.

18. The weakness of survey-based indicators is that surveys fail to reflect the strength with which views are held and thus the weight of opinion. However, they can incorporate information from a wider range of sources.

19. In this connection, Bird and Banta (1999) suggest indicators for transition economies that take account of their special circumstances.

20. This is analogous to the differentiation often applied to companies to distinguish those with short-term cash flow problems but positive net worth from those with negative net worth.

21. These sources of microstructural vulnerability also affect what Tanzi (2000) refers to as the quality of the public sector.

22. For some discussion of the issues in this area, see Skilling (1999).

References

The word *processed* describes informally reproduced works that may not be commonly available through libraries.

Abedian, Iraj. 2000. "Micro-Structural Aspects of Fiscal Vulnerability." International Monetary Fund, Washington, D.C. Processed.
Bird, Richard M., and Susan M. Banta. 1999. "Fiscal Sustainability and Fiscal Indicators in Transitional Countries." Paper presented at the USAID Conference on Fiscal Reform and Sustainability, Istanbul, June.

Downes, Patrick T., Dewitt D. Marston, and Inci Ötker. 1999. "Mapping Financial Sector Vulnerability in a Non-Crisis Country." IMF Policy Discussion Paper PDP/99/4. International Monetary Fund, Washington, D.C.

Easterly, William. 1999. "When Is Fiscal Adjustment an Illusion?" *Economic Policy* 28 (April): 57–86.

IMF (International Monetary Fund). 1998. *World Economic Outlook, October 1998*. World Economic and Financial Surveys. Washington, D.C.

———. 1999. *World Economic Outlook, October 1999*. World Economic and Financial Surveys. Washington, D.C.

IMF (International Monetary Fund), Fiscal Affairs Department. 2001. "Code of Good Practices on Fiscal Transparency" and "Manual on Fiscal Transparency" *<www.imf.org/external/np/fad/trans/index.htm>*.

Skilling, David. 1999. "How Should Governments Invest Financial Assets and Manage Debt?" Paper presented at the 20th Annual Meeting of Senior Budget Officers, Organisation for Economic Co-operation and Development, Paris.

Talvi, Ernesto, and Carlos A. Végh. 2000. "Tax Base Variability and Procyclical Fiscal Policy." NBER Working Paper 7499. National Bureau of Economic Research, Cambridge, Mass.

Tanzi, V. 2000. "The Quality of the Public Sector." International Monetary Fund, Washington, D.C. Processed.

World Bank. 1998. *Public Expenditure Management Handbook*. Washington, D.C.

Country Examples

CHAPTER 8

Evaluating Government Net Worth in Colombia and República Bolivariana de Venezuela

William Easterly
and David Yuravlivker
World Bank

ONE OF THE MOST IMPORTANT questions to ask about public finance in any given country is: Does the government's balance sheet contain assets (treasures), such as oil or valuable public enterprises, that can help the government meet its long-run budget constraints? Or does the government's balance sheet contain large implicit liabilities (time bombs), such as a pension system temporarily in surplus but headed for big future deficits? Even if the government's balance sheet contains treasures, are those treasures being depleted to finance current consumption, at the expense of future generations?

The conventional approach to assessing the sustainability of a given fiscal deficit is to compare it with the deficit necessary to keep the public debt-to-GDP (gross domestic product) ratio constant. This is justified by the reasoning that if a country is not already in a debt crisis, then keeping the public debt ratio constant will be sufficient to avoid a debt crisis in the future.[1]

The main objectives of this chapter are: (a) to present the assets/liabilities/net worth approach to evaluating the true financial position of the public sector in order to achieve a better assessment of longer-term fiscal sustainability; and (b) to present applications of this approach to the cases of Colombia and República Bolivariana de Venezuela in order to illustrate its use and to help their authorities in the process of fiscal adjustment. In particular, this study could help ensure that the fiscal measures that governments are implementing to address present fiscal gaps are coherent and consistent with achieving longer-term fiscal sustainability. In addition, the conceptual framework developed here and its application to these two country cases could be useful in analyzing similar problems in other countries.

The next section of this chapter presents the assets/liabilities/net worth conceptual framework and methodology. The final section summarizes the main findings of the chapter and offers some concluding remarks.

Assets/Liabilities/Net Worth Approach

Conceptual Framework

The limitations of conventional sustainability analysis call for broadening the sustainability analysis to consider the evolution of the government's complete balance sheet (Table 8.1).[2]

Which components of the government's fiscal policy package improve the government's net financial position and which ones worsen it?

Anyone considering the longer-term sustainability of a government's finances would find it helpful to think first about the balance sheet that the government must manage.[3] Although one cannot always measure all of the items in this balance sheet, the balance sheet approach is a useful way to think of which government actions imply progress or regress toward sustainability.[4] Investing in a project with an economic rate of return higher than the discount rate, for example, improves the government's net financial position. (The government has to devise a way to capture the revenues that accrue to the society from this project, however.) Forward-looking individuals and firms (and credit rating agencies) will react more favorably to a fiscal adjustment that preserves high rate of return activities while cutting consumption than to a myopic package that cuts projects with high returns just to improve this year's fiscal balance.

Note that in Table 8.1 the present values of government consumption or government tax revenue do not appear in the balance sheet. *The government's intertemporal budget constraint is that the present value of government consumption minus government revenues be less than or equal to the government's net worth* (more on the daunting task of implementing this in a moment). If the government's intertemporal budget constraint is violated under current revenue and expenditure plans, then fiscal sustainability does not hold. The future fiscal adjustment required to satisfy the intertemporal budget constraint is a measure of the distance from sustainability in government finances. A more sophisticated analysis would refer to a *desired* net worth level,

Table 8.1 Government Balance Sheet for Fiscal Sustainability Assessment

Assets	Liabilities
Government-owned public goods (such as infrastructure, schools, and health clinics that generate an adequate economic rate of return and an indirect financial rate of return through tax collection)	Public external debt
Government-owned capital that is financially profitable (anything for which government can charge user fees to generate an adequate financial rate of return)	Public domestic debt
Value of government-owned natural resource stocks (such as oil and minerals)	Contingent liabilities (for example, bank deposit guarantees, net present value of pension scheme, guarantees of private debt)
Expected net present value of loans to private sector and other financial assets	Government's net worth

Source: The authors.

but that would depend on the social preferences of each particular society, and it goes beyond the scope of this chapter.

Methodology: Applying the Concept

Sustainability can be evaluated using the balance sheet approach in two ways. The first is to estimate the stocks in the government's balance sheet and assess whether the public sector net worth is positive or negative. If it is negative, then sustainability will require that the present value of tax revenues minus government consumption be sufficient to cover the negative net worth.

The second approach would look at sustainability in flow terms. The criterion for sustainability would then be to maintain a constant ratio of net worth to GDP. The idea is that if there is no payments crisis today, then keeping the net worth-to-GDP ratio constant will avoid a payments crisis in the future. So fiscal sustainability would require keeping government net worth to GDP constant. If there is a payments crisis today, then the rule would imply increasing the ratio of net worth to GDP.

If one cannot measure government net worth directly, a pragmatic approach would be to first measure all balance sheet items that can be measured to calculate the net debt of the government and then evaluate individual government actions for their effect on fiscal and external sustainability.

Note that analyzing this broader notion of fiscal sustainability requires many assumptions to calculate concepts such as the implicit pension debt and the value of oil reserves. This kind of exercise should be thought of as illustrative of how the government's long-run finances will evolve if certain assumptions hold.

What about balance sheet items that cannot be measured? All we can say is that sustainability is worsened by any action that reduces government assets or increases contingent liabilities. For example, a cut in operations and maintenance (O&M) spending that lowers the value of government-owned highways will worsen sustainability, even though this spending cut improves the conventional measure of the fiscal deficit. (If the proceeds from cutting O&M are used to repay foreign debt, and if the rate of return on O&M is the same as the interest rate on foreign debt, the spending cut would have a neutral effect on fiscal sustainability. However, estimates of returns to O&M are usually well above the interest rate on foreign debt.) A cut in profitable public investments will worsen fiscal sustainability, even though this cut improves the conventional measure of the fiscal deficit. Expansion of deposit insurance increases the government's contingent liabilities and so worsens fiscal sustainability, even though it does not show up in conventional deficit measures. Deposit insurance may bring benefits such as increased deposits in the banking system, but the contingent liability of the government should still be accounted correctly. Consuming the revenues from extraction of a nonrenewable resource or from privatization worsens sustainability.

In summary, balance sheet accounting can produce a better long-run perspective on fiscal sustainability than can be obtained from conventional deficit measures. Although the task of measuring government assets and liabilities is always difficult and sometimes impossible, the balance sheet approach still encourages clear thinking about what actions will improve or worsen the government's long-run finances. That is particularly important when governments need to implement urgent stabilization measures, to ensure that the measures are consistent with longer-term fiscal sustainability.

Results from Colombia and República Bolivariana de Venezuela

This section reviews the application of the assets/liabilities/net worth approach to Colombia and República Bolivariana de Venezuela. These are summaries of two very thorough studies conducted in both countries by local teams that had a unique access to the data required to carry out such a task. The Colombian study expands the traditional government balance sheet by calculating other assets as well as contingent and implicit liabilities of the public sector such as pension liabilities and the potential costs of a peace agreement with the guerrillas. The Venezuelan study, rather than looking at stocks, calculates the changes in the main public sector assets and liabilities since 1970, and then looks forward and calculates the net present value of the key assets and liabilities of the public sector. Both studies conclude that fiscal adjustment measures are needed to ensure longer-term fiscal sustainability.

Colombia

Echeverry and others (1999) perform a comprehensive estimate of public sector stocks, including contingent assets and liabilities (Table 8.2). Because their estimates are fraught with uncertainty and require many special assumptions, one should think of this exercise as mainly illustrative.

Table 8.2 estimates that the Colombian public sector has 162 percent of GDP in assets. The most important assets are investments, plant and equipment, and natural resources. (The estimate does not include the value of national infrastructure because of the difficulties of valuation.) However, the Colombian public sector has liabilities amounting to 232 percent of GDP, implying a negative net worth of 70 percent of GDP. The most important liability by far is the implicit pension debt, which amounts to 156 percent of GDP. In contrast, the total public debt, which is usually the focus of sustainability analyses, amounts to only 20 percent of GDP. The advantage of the balance sheet approach is that it identifies a "hole" in the intertemporal public finances that would not have been apparent using conventional deficit or debt measures.

How could Colombia's finances be made sustainable if the public sector's net worth is negative? To cover the negative net worth, the public sector could run a perpetual primary surplus (government revenues minus government noninterest spending). Here is a rough idea of the amount of surplus necessary: the present value of a perpetual surplus of x percent of GDP at a discount rate of r and a GDP growth rate of g would simply be $x/(r - g)$. If $r = 0.10$ and $g = 0.04$, for example, this would imply a required perpetual primary current surplus of 4.2 percent of GDP to cover negative net worth of 70 percent of GDP.

Given the importance of the implicit pension liability in the overall picture, it is worthwhile to look at it in more detail. Table 8.3 breaks down the pension liability into its components.

The most striking finding is that the central government's pension obligations are more important than the obligations of the general social security system (although the latter are far from trivial). Another

Table 8.2 Comprehensive Public Sector Balance Sheet, Colombia, 1997
(percent of GDP)

	National level		Territorial level		Total
	Decentralized	Central	Decentralized	Central	Public sector
Assets	**48.4**	**42.5**	**25.9**	**23.6**	**162.3**
Current assets	15.8	5.6	4.5	3.6	29.5
Cash	1.7	1.3	0.5	1.0	4.4
Investments	3.5	2.2	1.6	0.7	8.1
Rents	0.0	0.8	0.0	0.6	1.4
Accounts payable	9.0	1.2	1.9	0.8	12.9
Inventories	0.9	0.0	0.4	0.0	1.3
Other	0.6	0.0	0.3	0.4	1.3
Fixed assets	32.6	36.9	21.4	20.1	132.8
Investments	1.4	17.5	2.0	6.9	27.8
Rents	0.0	0.0	0.0	0.2	0.2
Loans	6.3	1.9	2.6	0.2	11.0
Plant and equipment	13.8	2.4	10.8	5.6	32.5
Public goods	3.3	0.1	0.4	3.3	7.1
Natural resources	1.0	14.4	0.0	1.1	38.4
Other (mostly electromagnetic spectrum)	6.9	0.5	5.6	2.8	15.8

Liabilities				
Liabilities	**34.9**	**20.8**	**15.4**	**7.1**	**232.3**
Current liabilities	14.4	5.3	3.4	3.1	26.1
Required deposits	5.2	0.0	0.1	0.0	5.3
Public debt	0.1	2.8	0.3	0.4	3.6
Financial obligations	2.4	0.0	0.2	0.3	3.0
Suppliers' credits	3.7	1.1	1.2	1.5	7.6
Labor obligations	1.1	0.2	0.8	0.7	2.8
Bonds	1.2	0.3	0.0	0.0	1.5
Other	0.5	0.9	0.7	0.2	2.4
Long-term liabilities	20.4	15.5	11.9	4.0	205.9
Public debt	1.2	14.2	1.8	2.6	19.8
Financial obligations	3.1	0.0	2.5	0.2	5.7
Suppliers' credits	0.8	1.0	1.2	0.1	3.1
Labor obligations	0.0	0.0	0.1	0.1	0.2
Bonds	2.4	0.1	0.2	0.1	2.7
Other	12.9	0.2	6.1	1.0	20.2
Contingent liabilities					154.1
Pension liability					156.5
Net other contingent liabilities					-2.4
Other	0.1	0.0	0.1	0.0	0.2
Public sector net worth	**13.5**	**21.7**	**10.6**	**16.5**	**-69.9**
Public Treasury	0.0	23.9	0.2	16.2	-92.0
Institutional	13.0	0.0	9.8	0.0	22.8
Other	0.5	-2.2	0.6	0.3	-0.7
Total liabilities, including net worth	**48.4**	**42.5**	**25.9**	**23.6**	**162.3**

Sources: Echeverry and others (1999) and the authors of this chapter.

Table 8.3 Estimates of the Implicit Pension Liability,
Colombia, 1997
(percent of GDP)

Entity	Pension liability
National central government[a]	69.76
Teachers[b]	30.10
Armed forces[c]	15.92
Rest of central government[c]	23.74
National decentralized government[d]	5.76
Caprecom[c]	2.99
Ecopetrol[c]	2.28
Ecocarbón[c]	0.03
Caja Agraria[c]	0.46
Territorial[e]	32.54
Social security[c]	48.48
Total	156.54

a. Liabilities assumed directly by the national government.
b. Based on actuarial estimates done for Echeverry and others (1999).
c. Based on actuarial estimates done in 1997.
d. Liabilities assumed by state enterprises and decentralized agencies.
e. Based on actuarial estimates done in 1998.
Sources: Ministerio de Hacienda y Crédito Público, Colombia, and calculations of
Echeverry and others (1999).

way to reach sustainability would be to reform the government's pension system in order to raise contributions, postpone retirement, or
take other measures to lower the net present value of pension obligations. The same reforms to the general social security system could
also help reach sustainability.

Other contingent liabilities do not place a very heavy strain on public sector finances. Table 8.4 shows that nonpension contingent liabilities only sum to 14.5 percent of GDP. Among the most important of
the other contingent liabilities are the fiscal guarantees to the metros
(urban subway systems), the cost of achieving peace with the domestic
guerilla movements, and the expected present value of the bailout of
the financial system.

It is important to note that the public sector also has assets of conditional value. The Colombian government has partial claim to oil, gas,
and coal reserves, whose value is contingent on world prices. (The price
assumptions are US$10 per barrel for oil, $30 per ton for coal, and
$1.30 per cubic foot for gas.) Note that these asset calculations subtract
off the unit costs of exploration and extraction. The public sector also
owns the electromagnetic spectrum, which it sells to cell phone compa-

Table 8.4 Other Contingent Liabilities of Public Sector
(Excluding Pensions), Colombia, 1997

Contingent liabilities	Percentage of GDP
Natural disasters	1.10
Earthquakes	1.09
Floods	0.01
Bailing out financial system	2.18
Infrastructure guarantees	5.89
Roads	0.10
Airports	0.70
Electricity	0.50
Telecommunications	0.23
Metros	4.36
External debt guarantees	0.69
Judicial findings against public sector	0.16
Guarantees of municipal and provincial debt	0.48
Cost of reaching peace agreement	4.04
Total	14.54

Sources: Echeverry and others (1999) and the authors of this chapter.

nies. As of 1997, these contingent sources of future government revenues were: petroleum reserves, 14.6 percent of GDP; natural gas reserves, 9.0 percent; coal reserves, 11.9 percent; and electromagnetic
spectrum, 18.3 percent. They totaled 53.9 percent of GDP.

Note that the value of the stock of natural resources is not that high
relative to GDP, only amounting to 36 percent of GDP. Later it is
revealed that the value of natural resources in République Bolivariana
de Venezuela is much larger.

In summary, the Colombia experience illustrates the value of the
balance sheet approach to public sector finances. This approach finds
negative net worth of the public sector, requiring a fiscal adjustment
whose need would not have been apparent from conventional deficit
measures.

République Bolivariana de Venezuela

For République Bolivariana de Venezuela, Garcia, Balza, and Villasmil
(1999) use a more dynamic approach to look at longer-term fiscal
sustainability. They calculate the annual change in the net worth of
the public sector during the past 30 years. That change was used to
finance public consumption and to subsidize domestic consumption of

oil products. They also calculate the implicit and contingent liabilities of the public sector and project the evolution of public assets, liabilities, and net worth into the future in order to estimate the maximum nonoil fiscal deficit that would be consistent with longer-term fiscal sustainability. Furthermore, these projections are done under a range of assumptions to test for their sensitivity to various domestic and external conditions. Finally, Garcia, Balza, and Villasmil discuss key policy measures that would help the fiscal accounts move in the right direction to achieve a solid financial position on a sustainable basis.

The Evolution of Public Assets, Liabilities, and Net Worth, 1970-98. Garcia, Balza, and Villasmil (1999) describe five major developments that affected the financial position of the Venezuelan public sector in this century:

• 1930–70—the discovery of oil and use of its revenues to finance investment in infrastructure and the provision of public services;
• 1973–83—the decision to invest heavily in public enterprises by means of growing external indebtedness;
• 1983–88—the decision to reduce investment in social sectors and public infrastructure in order to maintain a high level of investment in public enterprises and to service external debt;
• 1989–95—the use of privatization revenues to finance recurrent public deficits; and
• 1996–98—the decision to increase investment and production in the oil sector, financed by cuts in expenditure and investment in other areas.

The sharp increases in oil prices in 1973–74 and in 1978–79, and the expectation that prices would continue their upward trend, led to a growing reliance on external debt to finance public expenditure and advance ambitious investment projects. At the same time, the availability of huge oil revenues and foreign credit delayed implementation of the structural reforms that were necessary to improve the efficiency and competitiveness of the economy. Eventually, the volatility of oil prices led to large ups and downs in the Venezuelan economy in general and in the fiscal accounts in particular.

Estimating the evolution of public assets and liabilities is a very difficult exercise. Garcia, Balza, and Villasmil (1999) focus on four main sources that add liabilities or reduce assets: changes in the external debt, changes in the domestic debt, privatization revenues, and the value of oil production, net of production and investment costs. They also identify three main uses that add assets or reduce liabilities: investment in nonfinancial public enterprises, other public investment, and changes in international reserves. The difference between variations in uses and sources would then reveal the changes in the net worth of the public sector. Tables 8.5 and 8.6 show the evolution of these variables from 1970 to 1998.

According to Table 8.5, the net worth of the public sector (in net present value terms using a discount rate of 5 percent) declined by nearly US$300 billion (287 percent of 1999 GDP) over the period 1970–98. It should be noted, however, that this estimation does not include the discovery of 50 billion barrels of new oil reserves during those years, which brought the total level of proved reserves to 76 billion barrels. Depending on the price of oil, these new discoveries would represent $60–$180 billion in net present value terms. The decline in the net worth of the public sector shows the drop in assets, or increase in liabilities, used to: (a) finance current public consumption (net of nonoil revenues) amounting to $177 billion and (b) subsidize the domestic consumption of oil products (which were sold not only at below-border prices but even below their production costs for most of the period) by $86 billion in net present value terms. The remainder, nearly $32 billion, is classified as errors and omissions, which reflect measurement errors in public expenditure accounts and transfers to the private sector that were not properly accounted for.

The loss of public net worth could be overstated, because current public expenditures include the provision of education and health services, which are in fact an investment in human capital. From that point of view, there was an increase in private assets that compensates for the decline in public assets. However, the magnitude of the drop in net public worth is well beyond the fraction of current public expenditure that could be accounted for as investment in human capital. Furthermore, the drop in the quality of public services during the period as well as the decline in real per capita GDP of over 10 percent suggest that the public sector "jewelry" was not used in the most efficient way. That calls for an evaluation of the use of public resources to ensure that they do not undermine the financial position of the public sector and that they contribute efficiently to the development of the physical and human capital base of the country.

The loss of public net worth also could be understated because many of the public investments turned out to be unprofitable. For example, the heavy investment in steel production in the 1970s and 1980s, at a time of overcapacity in the world steel market, almost surely did not increase the value of public capital very much.

Contingent and Implicit Liabilities. The calculation described above does not take into account the existence and evolution of contingent or implicit public sector liabilities. Therefore, after discussing short-term fiscal stabilization measures for 1999–2000, Garcia, Balza, and Villasmil (1999) identify and estimate the net present value of the public sector liabilities embodied in: (a) the social security system; (b) the

Table 8.5 Net Worth of the Public Sector, Républica Bolivariana de Venezuela, 1970–98
(millions of U.S. dollars)

	Change in net external debt	Change in net domestic debt	Privati- zation income	Value of oil prod- uction (net investment and oper- ational expenses)	Investment by non- financial public enter- prises	Other public investment	Change in inter- national reserves	Change in public net worth $(8) = (5) + (6) + (7) - (1) - (2) - (3) - (4)$	Net current expenses (nonoil)	Subsidies to domestic oil con- sumption	Errors and omissions $(11) = -(8) - (9) - (10)$
	(1)	(2)	(3)	(4)	(5)	(6)	(7)	(8)	(9)	(10)	(11)
1970	152	81		940	225	573	85	−289	−16	75	230
1971	270	31		1,569	442	610	444	−375	180	87	108
1972	1,084	43		1,701	867	605	218	−1,138	339	100	699
1973	135	99		2,665	859	782	724	−534	389	114	31
1974	−112	502		9,204	816	1,932	3,842	−3,004	−707	132	3,579
1975	−301	331		7,843	1,534	3,028	2,613	−698	−196	151	742
1976	2,667	342		6,127	1,566	3,702	−286	−4,154	1,436	174	2,544
1977	5,322	1,446		8,256	3,985	3,494	−425	−7,970	2,328	635	5,008
1978	4,779	803		6,668	3,927	3,172	−1,707	−6,858	1,836	253	4,768
1979	6,721	308		11,485	3,457	2,977	1,302	−10,778	3,184	917	6,677
1980	4,656	1		16,083	3,762	3,529	−715	−14,164	5,040	1,976	7,148

Year											
1981	2,331	1,535		16,099	4,681	3,460	1,594	-10,231	6,526	2,814	890
1982	-1,281	1,090		11,175	5,564	4,830	1,420	830	5,846	1,984	-8,660
1983	2,167	975		12,245	4,964	4,781	1,110	-4,531	4,418	2,749	-2,635
1984	-1,127	-2,032		16,130	1,971	3,756	1,320	-5,924	3,050	3,363	-488
1985	-1,470	1,704		15,303	2,152	3,933	1,281	-8,171	2,462	3,838	1,871
1986	293	1,565		5,780	3,241	3,880	-3,892	-4,409	2,211	898	1,300
1987	2,313	-3,840		9,864	2,407	2,311	-483	-4,102	3,484	2,586	-1,968
1988	645	128		7,142	2,843	3,933	-2,705	-3,844	4,111	1,748	-2,015
1989	-1,321	-1,960		11,176	2,121	1,499	740	-3,535	4,282	2,883	-3,630
1990	1,746	-323	10	15,018	1,993	2,162	4,348	-7,948	6,455	3,592	-2,100
1991	874	1,497	2,278	11,340	1,515	4,118	2,346	-8,010	5,842	2,447	-280
1992	3,306	-272	30	8,566	1,679	2,261	-1,104	-8,793	5,749	2,315	729
1993	-7,571	1,309	32	8,238	1,068	1,788	-345	503	4,101	2,070	-6,674
1994	174	2,058	18	8,603	644	1,391	-1,149	-9,967	11,770	2,413	-4,216
1995	-2,365	1,299	20	9,400	962	2,390	-1,784	-6,785	5,797	3,002	-2,015
1996	-988	-3,996	1,159	15,120	854	1,731	5,506	-3,205	3,397	3,504	-3,696
1997	212	-843	2,425	12,538	1,154	3,332	2,589	-7,256	4,547	2,896	-187
1998	-666	-1,338	110	271	1,135	3,313	-2,969	3,102	1,672	-1,573	-3,202
Total	22,645	2,543	6,082	266,549	62,388	79,273	13,919	-142,238	99,533	48,143	-5,443
NPV[a]	71,586	12,948	7,643	546,088	132,279	168,260	35,527	-295,199	177,181	86,365	31,653

a. In 1999 net present value, at a 5 percent discount rate.

Sources: Garcia, Balza, and Villasmil (1999) and the authors of this chapter.

Table 8.6 Net Worth of the Public Sector, Républica Bolivariana de Venezuela, 1970–98 (percent of GDP)

	Change in net external debt	Change in net domestic debt	Privatization income	Value of oil production (net investment and operational expenses)	Investment by nonfinancial public enterprises	Other public investment	Change in international reserves	Change in public net worth $(8) = (5) + (6) + (7) - (1) - (2) - (3) - (4)$	Net current expenses (nonoil)	Subsidies to domestic oil consumption	Errors and omissions $(11) = -(8) - (9) - (10)$
	(1)	(2)	(3)	(4)	(5)	(6)	(7)	(8)	(9)	(10)	(11)
1970	1.1	0.6		7.0	1.7	4.3	0.6	-2.2	-0.1	0.6	1.7
1971	1.8	0.2		10.3	2.9	4.0	2.9	-2.5	1.2	0.6	0.7
1972	6.5	0.3		10.2	5.2	3.6	1.3	-6.8	2.0	0.6	4.2
1973	0.7	0.5		13.2	4.3	3.9	3.6	-2.6	1.9	0.6	0.1
1974	-0.4	1.7		30.6	2.7	6.4	12.8	-10.0	-2.4	0.4	11.9
1975	-0.9	1.0		24.2	4.7	9.3	8.0	-2.2	-0.6	0.5	2.3
1976	7.1	0.9		16.4	4.2	9.9	-0.8	-11.1	3.8	0.5	6.8
1977	12.2	3.3		18.9	9.1	8.0	-1.0	-18.2	5.3	1.5	11.4
1978	9.9	1.7		13.9	8.2	6.6	-3.6	-14.3	3.8	0.5	9.9
1979	11.7	0.5		19.9	6.0	5.2	2.3	-18.7	5.5	1.6	11.6
1980	6.7	0.0		23.2	5.4	5.1	-1.0	-20.4	7.3	2.8	10.3

Year											
1981	3.0	2.0		20.6	6.0	4.4	2.0	−13.1	8.4	3.6	1.1
1982	−1.6	1.4		14.1	7.0	6.1	1.8	1.0	7.4	2.5	−10.9
1983	2.7	1.2		15.1	6.1	5.9	1.4	−5.6	5.4	3.4	−3.2
1984	−1.9	−3.4		26.9	3.3	6.3	2.2	−9.9	5.1	5.6	−0.8
1985	−2.4	2.8		24.7	3.5	6.3	2.1	−13.2	4.0	6.2	3.0
1986	0.5	2.6		9.6	5.4	6.4	−6.4	−7.3	3.7	1.5	2.1
1987	4.8	−8.0		20.5	5.0	4.8	−1.0	−8.5	7.3	5.4	−4.1
1988	1.1	0.2		11.9	4.7	6.5	−4.5	−6.4	6.8	2.9	−3.3
1989	−3.0	−4.5		25.7	4.9	3.4	1.7	−8.1	9.8	6.6	−8.3
1990	3.6	−0.7		30.9	4.1	4.4	8.9	−16.4	13.3	7.4	−4.3
1991	1.6	2.8	4.3	21.2	2.8	7.7	4.4	−15.0	10.9	4.6	−0.5
1992	5.4	−0.4	0.0	14.1	2.8	3.7	−1.8	−14.5	9.5	3.8	1.2
1993	−12.6	2.2	0.1	13.7	1.8	3.0	−0.6	0.8	6.8	3.4	−11.1
1994	0.3	3.5	0.0	14.7	1.1	2.4	−2.0	−17.1	20.2	4.1	−7.2
1995	−3.1	1.7	0.0	12.2	1.2	3.1	−2.3	−8.8	7.5	3.9	−2.6
1996	−1.4	−5.7	1.6	21.5	1.2	2.5	7.8	−4.6	4.8	5.0	−5.3
1997	0.2	−1.0	2.7	14.2	1.3	3.8	2.9	−8.2	5.1	3.3	−0.2
1998	−0.7	−1.4	0.1	0.3	1.2	3.5	−3.1	3.3	1.8	−1.7	−3.4
NPV[a]	69.7	12.6	7.4	531.3	128.7	163.7	34.6	287.2	172.4	84.0	30.8

a. In 1999 net present value, at a 5 percent discount rate.
Sources: Garcia, Balza, and Villasmil (1999) and the authors of this chapter.

guaranteed minimum pension for public sector employees; (c) the labor liabilities of the public sector; and (d) the public guarantee of bank deposits. Those estimations are later used to assess the long-term fiscal sustainability of the public sector in República Bolivariana de Venezuela.

The pay-as-you-go social security system that was in place until 1998 collapsed because of various factors, including a growing informal sector that currently accounts for 53 percent of employment, evasion of payment of contributions to the system, and the use of social security funds to cover the deficits of the health care system. Had it not been reformed, that system would have gone bankrupt, affecting over a half-million people and costing the public sector the equivalent of 77 percent of GDP in present value terms. The 1998 reform created a mixed system of personal accumulation funds and a solidarity pension fund administered by the state. The retirement age of women was raised to 60 years (as it is for men), contribution rates were doubled to 12–13 percent, and the minimum contribution period was raised from 15 to 20 years.

The fiscal cost of the reform has three components: (a) the existing retirees and those retiring in 1999 under the old system; (b) the "recognition bond" to people who contributed to the old system but who have not yet reached retirement age; and (c) the solidarity pension fund. Under certain assumptions, the total fiscal impact of the new system was estimated, in present value terms, at nearly US$60 billion, equivalent to 65 percent of GDP at the end of 1998.

There are special pension regimes in the public sector that are not contributive, including those of the central government, the local governments, most public enterprises, autonomous agencies, the judicial system, the national universities, and the armed forces. These regimes are financed directly from the budgets of these agencies, whose statistical and financial information base is in many cases quite deficient. At the end of 1998, these regimes had nearly 250,000 retirees and nearly 1 million current public sector employees under their umbrella. A conservative estimate of this public liability is US$12.4 billion in present value terms, equivalent to 13.5 percent of GDP at the end of 1998.

The labor liabilities of the public sector include the accumulated benefits of one month's salary per year of work per employee. The 1997 reform of the Organic Labor Law abolished the indexation of those benefits to the last salary and the doubling of the benefits when the employee was laid off for "unjustified reasons," but extended the benefit to two months per year. The new law also called for payment of the arrears of this benefit, which were accumulated under the old law, over a period of five years, including an additional bond for the transfer from the old to the new system. By the end of 1998, the total public debt on this account amounted to US$7 billion, equivalent to 7.6 percent of GDP.

República Bolivariana de Venezuela had two systemic banking crisis in 1961–63 and 1994–95 and three large bank bankruptcies in between. In all cases, the central bank (and the deposit insurance guarantee agency, or FOGADE, in 1994–95) stepped in to cover all deposits, and in the last crisis it extended that coverage up to a limit of VEB10 million, two and a half times higher than the VEB4 million established in the original deposit insurance scheme. At the end of 1998, the total deposits in the banking system amounted to US$16.3 billion, or 17.7 percent of GDP. Of those, $7.5 billion consisted of deposits under VEB4 million, which are guaranteed by FOGADE, and $9.8 billion of deposits under VEB10 million, which was the actual coverage limit after the last banking crisis. FOGADE, on the other hand, had assets of only $760 million. Therefore, the implicit public guarantee amounts to about $9 billion, equivalent to nearly 10 percent of GDP. The estimate of the contingent liability would be lower, depending on the probability of banking losses.

Table 8.7 shows the assets, liabilities, and net worth of the Venezuelan public sector in terms of net present value (US$ millions). Assets include reserves of oil, gas, and coal and international reserves, leaving out other mineral reserves as well as the value of public utilities and public enterprises because of estimating difficulties. Liabilities include external and domestic debt, social security, the labor and pension liabilities of the public sector, and bank deposit guarantees. The calculations assume a growth rate of 4 percent and a discount rate of 9 percent.

As Table 8.7 shows, the difference between assets and liabilities results in a public sector net worth of US$43.5 billion, equivalent to 45 percent of GDP. This net worth could be consumed by allowing the public sector to have primary nonoil deficits on the order of 2 percent of GDP on a permanent basis.

Table 8.7 Net Worth of the Public Sector in República Bolivariana de Venezuela
(net present value, millions of U.S. dollars)

Assets		Liabilities	
Oil[a]	120,000	External debt	23,613
Gas	16,000	Domestic debt	3,980
Coal	2,300	Deposit insurance	10,961
International reserves	14,849	Labor debt and public pensions	20,032
Seigniorage	10,834	Social security debt	61,921
Total	163,983	Total	120,507
		Net worth	43,476

a. Assuming a price of oil of US$16 per barrel.
Sources: Garcia, Balza, and Villasmil (1999) and the authors of this chapter.

This analysis has certain limitations, because the implicit assumption is that the public sector has perfect access to international credit markets and can borrow on the basis of the net present value of its net worth. However, as recent history has shown, access to international credit is anything but perfect, and it depends on changing global conditions. Furthermore, the volatility in oil prices introduces a lot of uncertainty into any calculation of the value of that asset. At the same time, these calculations show that continuing the trend of the past 29 years, when the nonoil primary deficit averaged 12.8 percent of GDP, is clearly unsustainable. Even nonoil primary deficits on the order of 7 percent of GDP, the average of the 1990s, would require an average oil price of nearly US$20 per barrel. Thus Garcia, Balza, and Villasmil (1999) concluded that, even under relatively optimistic assumptions, the Venezuelan public sector could not maintain, on a permanent basis, nonoil primary deficits of over 6 percent of GDP.

Overdependence on future oil revenues is risky, because within 30 years or so there could be a technological change that would bring about a sharp decline in the demand for oil. Furthermore, exploiting and consuming an exhaustible resource raise the issue of intergenerational appropriation of the national wealth. In that respect, there are two approaches to oil revenues: one is to treat them as any other source of revenue; the second is to treat them as an asset being depleted, making sure that the proceeds of oil are invested and generate other income in the future, resulting in a constant rent over time.

Apart from the principle of equal rights to the national wealth by all generations of Venezuelans, the second approach also would prevent a major adjustment in the future, whenever the production of oil goes down. To implement this approach, the government could invest part of the oil revenues abroad, to cushion the county from permanent oil shocks (temporary shocks are addressed by the oil stabilization fund). Keeping these resources abroad also would reduce overvaluation pressures, which have negative effects both on the fiscal accounts and on the real sector of the economy. However, the country would have to balance these considerations with the need to expand infrastructure investment and human capital accumulation within the country itself, which means that the economic rate of return on oil revenues could well be, at least in the next few years, higher when invested internally than when kept abroad.

Finally, it should be noted that the results are sensitive to the assumptions about GDP growth and the discount rate. Robust, sustainable growth is essential for long-term fiscal sustainability, and reducing the volatility of economic activity (by limiting the impact of oil price shocks, for example) would have a positive effect in terms of a lower country risk and the risk premium that República Bolivariana de Venezuela pays on its external borrowing. Also, the quality of fiscal adjustment is very important in order not to undermine the infrastructure development of the country. Thus, apart from improving the efficiency and effectiveness of public investment and expenditures, there is a need to increase nonoil revenues and to reduce the contingent and implicit liabilities of the public sector. In terms of levels, the nonoil fiscal deficit should on average be below 4 percent of GDP in order to ensure longer-term fiscal sustainability.

Summary and Conclusions

This chapter describes two ways to evaluate sustainability using the balance sheet approach. The first is to estimate the stocks in the government's balance sheet and assess whether public sector net worth is positive or negative. If it is negative, then sustainability will require that the present value of tax revenues minus government consumption be sufficient to cover the negative net worth.

The second approach is to look at sustainability in flow terms. The criterion for sustainability would then be to maintain a constant ratio of net worth to GDP or, if a desired level of net worth can be determined, to maintain that ratio above the desired level. The basic idea is that if there is no payments crisis today, then keeping the net worth-to-GDP ratio constant will avoid a payments crisis in the future. Thus fiscal sustainability would require keeping the government net worth-to-GDP ratio constant, or above a minimum desired level. If there is a payments crisis today, then the rule would imply increasing the ratio of net worth to GDP.

This chapter presents the conclusions of two country studies, for Colombia and República Bolivariana de Venezuela. The first study uses the first approach, calculating stocks of assets and liabilities, and the second study illustrates the second approach, focusing mostly on changes of assets and liabilities over time. Both, however, have clear-cut conclusions about the actions needed to achieve longer-term fiscal sustainability.

For Colombia, Echeverry and others (1999) estimate that the public sector has 162 percent of GDP in assets. However, the Colombian public sector has liabilities amounting to 232 percent of GDP (the most important by far is the implicit pension debt, which amounts to 156 percent of GDP), implying a negative net worth of 70 percent of GDP. In contrast, the total public debt, which is usually the focus of sustainability analyses, amounts to only 20 percent of GDP. Given this estimate of net worth, achieving longer-term fiscal sustainability would require a perpetual primary current surplus of 4.2 percent of GDP.

For República Bolivariana de Venezuela, Garcia, Balza, and Villasmil (1999) reveal that in 1970–98 the net worth of the public sector declined by nearly US$300 billion, the equivalent of 287 percent of 1999 GDP. This decline shows the drop in assets, or rise in liabilities, used to: (a) finance current public consumption (net of nonoil revenues) amounting to $177 billion, and (b) subsidize the domestic consumption of oil products (which were sold not only at below-border prices but even below their production costs for most of the period) by $86 billion in net present value terms.

The difference between Venezuelan assets and liabilities results in a public sector net worth of US$43.5 billion, equivalent to 45 percent of GDP. That would allow the public sector to have nonoil deficits on the order of 2–6 percent of GDP on a permanent basis, depending on the assumed future oil price.

These calculations show that continuing the trend of the past 29 years, when the nonoil primary deficit averaged 12.8 percent of GDP, is clearly unsustainable. Even nonoil primary deficits on the order of 7 percent of GDP, the average of the 1990s, would require an average oil price of nearly US$20 per barrel. Thus Garcia, Balza, and Villasmil concluded that, even under relatively optimistic assumptions, the Venezuelan public sector cannot maintain, on a permanent basis, nonoil primary deficits of over 6 percent of GDP.

In conclusion, our picture of public finance in two test cases, Colombia and República Bolivariana de Venezuela, was dramatically altered by using the balance sheet approach to public finances. We found both treasures and time bombs in the governments' balance sheets.

Notes

1. This approach is used as well to assess the consistency between a budget deficit and inflation targets, where not only the debt ratio is presumed constant but also the money-to-GDP ratio. Revenues from money creation are calculated as the sum of the inflation rate times the money-to-GDP ratio (the inflation tax) and the growth rate times the money-to-GDP ratio (seigniorage). Economists have used these calculations on many occasions to assess the consistency of the fiscal stance with avoiding a debt crisis and excessive inflation. The classic references are Buiter (1983, 1985) and Anand and van Wijnbergen (1989). Other examples of references are Marshall and Schmidt-Hebbel (1994) for Chile, Haque and Montiel (1994) for Pakistan, and Morandé and Schmidt-Hebbel (1994) for Zimbabwe.

2. For an illustration of the shortcomings of conventional sustainability analysis, see Blejer and Cheasty (1991), Polackova (1998), and Easterly (1999).

3. Buiter (1983, 1985) pioneered the use of the balance sheet approach to fiscal accounts. The government of New Zealand has pioneered the use of the balance sheet approach in its fiscal accounting (Scott 1996).

4. Some assets are omitted because they are impossible to measure, such as the value of the human capital embodied in the government's work force.

References

The word *processed* describes informally reproduced works that may not be commonly available through libraries.

Anand, Ritu, and Sweder van Wijnbergen. 1989. "Inflation and the Financing of Government Expenditure: An Introductory Analysis with an Application to Turkey." *World Bank Economic Review* 3 (January): 17–38.

Blejer, Mario I., and Andrienne Cheasty. 1991. "The Measurement of Fiscal Deficits: Analytical and Methodological Issues." *Journal of Economic Literature* 29: 1644–78.

Buiter, W. 1983. "Measurement of the Public Sector and Its Implications for Policy Evaluation and Design." *IMF Staff Papers*. (Updated and reprinted in Mario I. Blejer and Andrienne Cheasty, eds. 1993. *How to Measure the Public Deficit: Analytical and Methodological Issues*. Washington, D.C.: International Monetary Fund.)

———. 1985. "A Guide to Public Sector Debt and Deficits." *Economic Policy* (November): 14–79.

Easterly, William. 1999. "When Is Fiscal Adjustment an Illusion?" *Economic Policy* (April): 57–86.

Echeverry, Juan Carlos, Maria Victoria Angulo, Gustavo Hernandez, Israel Fainboim, Cielo Numpaque, Gabriel Piraquive, Carlos Rodriguez, and Natalia Salazar. 1999. "El Balance del Sector Público y la Sostenibilidad Fiscal de Colombia." *Archivos de Macroeconomía*. No. 115. National Planning Department, Bogota.

Garcia Osio, Gustavo, Rafael Rodriguez Balza, and Ricardo Villasmil. 1999. "Ajuste y Sostenibilidad Fiscal de Largo Plazo—El Caso de Venezuela." Oficina de Asesoria Economica y Financiera del Congreso de la Republica, Caracas. Processed.

Haque, Nadeem Ul, and Peter Montiel. 1994. "Pakistan: Fiscal Sustainability and Macroeconomic Policy." In William Easterly, Carlos Alfredo Rodriguez, and Klaus Schmidt-Hebbel, eds., *Public Sector Deficits and Macroeconomic Performance*. Washington, D.C.: World Bank.

Marshall, Jorge, and Klaus Schmidt-Hebbel. 1994. "Chile: Fiscal Adjustment and Successful Performance." In William Easterly, Carlos Alfredo Rodriguez, and Klaus Schmidt-Hebbel, eds., *Public Sector Deficits and Macroeconomic Performance*. Washington, D.C.: World Bank.

Morandé, Felipe, and Klaus Schmidt-Hebbel. 1994. "Zimbabwe: Fiscal Disequilibria and Low Growth." In William Easterly, Carlos Alfredo Rodriguez, and Klaus Schmidt-Hebbel, eds., *Public Sector Deficits and Macroeconomic Performance*. Washington, D.C.: World Bank.

Polackova, H. 1998. "Contingent Liabilities: A Threat to Fiscal Stability." *World Bank PREM Notes*. No. 9. Washington, D.C.

Scott, G. 1996. "Government Reform in New Zealand." IMF Occasional Paper 140. International Monetary Fund, Washington, D.C.

CHAPTER 9

The Challenges of Fiscal Risks in Transition: Czech Republic, Hungary, and Bulgaria

Hana Polackova Brixi
World Bank

Allen Schick
University of Maryland

Leila Zlaoui
World Bank

AN ESSENTIAL STEP IN controlling the expansion of government contingent liabilities and reducing fiscal risk is being able to identify and measure them. In this chapter we discuss how this may be done, and we demonstrate how an assessment of fiscal adjustment may change substantially when a broader picture of government obligations is included. The chapter is based on a 1999 analysis of fiscal adjustment in the Czech Republic, Hungary, and Bulgaria.

The Czech case provides an example of officially balanced government budgets and of the extensive use of guarantees and other forms of off-budget support. The case study shows how to deal with some difficult conceptual and measurement issues when estimating government contingent liabilities and the unreported portion of fiscal deficit. In contrast to the Czech Republic, Hungary internalized most fiscal risks in the government debt and constrained off-budget fiscal activities. While the Czech Republic enjoyed "budget balance," Hungary faced high budget deficit and debt levels. Less-visible aspects of fiscal adjustment, however, pull the comparison of the fiscal performance of the two countries in the opposite direction. Somewhat like Hungary, Bulgaria maintained low, transparent government exposure to fiscal risk. And somewhat like the Czech Republic, Bulgaria has been committed to low budget deficits and macroeconomic stability—since 1997 at least, after having introduced a currency board arrangement. In contrast to both the Czech Republic and Hungary, however, Bulgaria has been slow in the transition process and has yet to meet the fiscal challenges of the needed enterprise restructuring and investment in infrastructure and environment.

Although each of the three countries has taken a different path to fiscal adjustment, economic realities and opportunities may lead to more similar behavior in the future. As the Czech Republic's hidden liabilities came to light in 1998, the government faced pressure to impose discipline in resolving old and taking on new fiscal risks. As for Hungary, the favorable fiscal performance in the second half of the 1990s emboldened the government to take on greater liabilities than it had been able to handle during the adjustment period. With the Czech government taking a tougher stand on contingent liabilities and the Hungarian government showing signs of loosening its established controls, a comparison of the two countries in the future may show a different pattern than that evident at the end of the 1990s. Bulgaria's recent favorable fiscal performance has yet to be tested by the tradeoff of fiscal prudence versus a more aggressive strategy toward the country's development and accession to the European Union (EU). All three countries consider their accession to the European Union a key policy priority, and their motivation to meet the EU accession requirements (including requirements on the quality of infrastructure and environment) is high.

The three sections that follow apply the Fiscal Risk Matrix (presented in Chapter 1 of this volume) and analyze the "true" fiscal position of the Czech Republic, Hungary, and Bulgaria. The main conclusions and suggestions for future work are summarized in the final section.

Measuring the True Fiscal Deficit
of the Czech Republic

The Czech Republic has been known for its balanced government budgets. In contrast to most countries, however, fiscal performance in the Czech Republic encompasses a significant number of government activities financed outside the budgetary system. These activities generate fiscal risks. Recently, these off-budget fiscal risks have become more visible, because state guarantees and agencies that are either explicitly or implicitly guaranteed by the government have generated significant claims on the budget (see Table 9.1).

Given the magnitude of off-budget activities, fiscal analysis in the Czech Republic should identify all the main activities of a fiscal nature

Table 9.1 Fiscal Risk Matrix, Czech Republic

Sources of obligations	Direct liabilities (obligation in any event)	Contingent liabilities (obligation if a particular event occurs)
Explicit Government liability as recognized by a law or contract	• Foreign and domestic sovereign debt • Budget expenditures • Future legally binding expenditures	• State guarantees • Liabilities and other obligations of Konsolidacni Banka • Obligations of Ceska Exportni, EGAP (an export guarantee fund), and Deposit Insurance Fund
Implicit A "moral" obligation of government that reflects public and interest group pressures	• Future investment expenditures to meet EU accession requirements • Future recurrent expenditures related to public investment projects • Military expenditures as required by North Atlantic Treaty Organization (NATO)	• Obligations of National Property Fund (own debt, guarantees, and obligations to Ceska Inkasni, Land Fund, and similar entities) • Liabilities of Ceska Financni and Czech National Bank (result of the central bank's nonstandard operations) • Liabilities of banks (Komercni Banka, Ceska Sporitelna) • Further losses and defaults of large enterprises (Czech Railways) • Obligations of PGRLF (an agricultural credit and guarantee fund) • Liabilities and other obligations of subnational governments • Liabilities of credit unions (Kampelicka) and private pension funds

Note: The liabilities listed refer to the fiscal authorities of the central government. Because the government is legally obliged to pay future public pensions (a public pay-as-you-go pension scheme), future pensions constitute a direct (expected with certainty) explicit (legal) liability. The expected investment expenditures that are needed to meet EU accession requirements are the major direct implicit liability. State guarantees and financing through state-guaranteed institutions are key examples of explicit contingent liabilities. And, like that of many other countries, the financial system represents the most serious source of implicit contingent liabilities for the Czech government.

Source: The authors.

in order to determine the "true fiscal deficit." Excluding the quasi-
fiscal activities of the central bank, the Czech National Bank, the "hidden" part of the fiscal deficit comprises two main components: (a) net
spending on programs of a fiscal nature by special off-budget institutions—Konsolidacni Banka (KOB), Ceska Inkasni (CI), Ceska Financni
(CF),[1] and the National Property Fund (NPF); and (b) implied subsidies extended through state guarantees. For the financial relationships
of the special institutions, see Figure 9.1 (developed by the Ministry of
Finance of the Czech Republic).

For any given year, net public spending by these institutions includes cash outlays on new programs in the form of directed credits
and asset purchases,[2] and interest expenditures. This spending is adjusted for debt collection, interest revenue, and other revenue from
programs. Table 9.2 shows the components of the "hidden" deficit. In
the remainder of this section, we explain each row of this table in
detail.

Figure 9.1. Financial Relationships of Special, Off-Budget
Institutions, Czech Republic

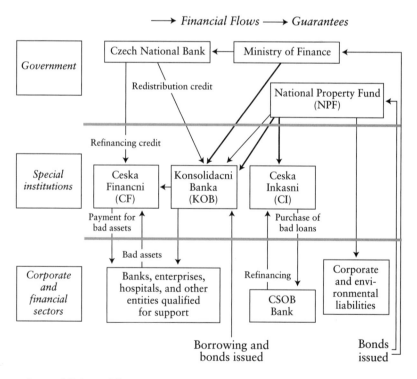

Source: Ministry of Finance.

Table 9.2 Sources of "Hidden" Deficit in the Czech Republic, 1993–98

(billions of Czech koruny)

	1993	1994	1995	1996	1997	1998
Konsolidacni Banka (KOB)[a] (net public expenditures)	7.7	7.3	4.5	0.9	10.6	28.8
Ceska Inkasni (CI) (net public expenditures)	20.1	6.6	4.9	4.8	3.1	2.7
Ceska Financni (CF) (net public expenditures)	n.a.	n.a.	n.a.	n.a.	0.6[b]	1.8[b]
National Property Fund (NPF) (net public expenditures, excluding KOB and CI)	4.2	8.2	4.3	1.9	2.0	2.6
State guarantees ("hidden" subsidy, risk-adjusted)	0.1	–0.4	1.3	14.9	51.5	26.7
Total (% of GDP)	3.2	1.9	1.1	1.5	4.1	3.5

n.a. Not applicable.

a. Activities of KOB include a credit to finance stabilization program of CF. Therefore, table includes only interest payments by CF (which are reported as interest income of KOB).

b. These figures are interest payments to KOB on credit taken by CF from KOB to finance stabilization program. In addition, CF paid interest to CZK0.8 billion and CZK2.8 billion in 1997 and 1998, respectively, to Czech National Bank on its credit from Czech National Bank to finance consolidation program.

Sources: Ministry of Finance, Konsolidacni Banka, Ceska Financni, National Property Fund, and calculations by the authors.

Until 1993, off-budget programs dealt mainly with pretransition problems inherited by the banking sector. These programs had been financed through Konsolidacni Banka. This bank was capitalized by the National Property Fund (the privatization agency whose revenues are derived from asset sales and borrowing on domestic markets) and borrowing from the Czech National Bank.[3] In 1995 the Ministry of Finance established Ceska Inkasni, a nonbank financial institution with the mandate of cleaning up the portfolio of a state-owned bank, the CSOB. Covered by a guarantee issued by the National Property Fund, Ceska Inkasni obtained a credit from the CSOB and used this credit to purchase CSOB's bad assets at face value.

During 1996–98, a new bank consolidation and stabilization program was launched to deal with newly emerging problems in the banking sector. In order to implement these programs, the Czech National Bank established Ceska Financni, another nonbank financial institution. In 1998 Ceska Financni had in its portfolio nonperforming assets purchased at face value from small and medium-size banks (in the amount of about CZK50 billion, or 3 percent of GDP). It financed the purchase through borrowing (one-third) from Konsolidacni Banka and (two-thirds) from the Czech National Bank.

The Czech National Bank also financed other bank rescue operations, which became the source of a further addition (CZK161 billion, over 9 percent of GDP) to its portfolio of substandard assets in 1998. Of the total amount of substandard assets held by Czech National Bank, the government covered the risk for 12 percent of the assets. A further 22 percent of these assets were in the form of a credit from the Czech National Bank to Konsolidacni Banka and thus were indirectly also covered by government.

Aside from the bank rescue operations, Konsolidacni Banka and, less directly, the National Property Fund financed government programs to support troubled health insurance companies, public hospitals, and the Czech Railways, to build infrastructure, and to clean up industrial enterprises for privatization (see Table 9.3). The National Property Fund financed these programs partly from privatization revenues but also partly from its debt issuance. The contributions to the "true" fiscal deficit by the National Property Fund exclude principal repayments and thus do not reflect the ongoing financing of pre-1993 programs by the National Property Fund. In addition, both Konsolidacni Banka and the National Property Fund accumulated their own contingent liabilities in the form of various guarantees on environmental liabilities.[4]

The impact of guarantees on the hidden deficit is estimated as the net implicit subsidy provided through guarantees in a given year from the portfolio of guarantees issued in that year. This estimate is the potential fiscal cost of government obligations, which will emerge from the guarantees in the future. If the amount of this subsidy had been transferred to a guarantee reserve fund the same year the guarantee was issued, it would have covered potential future claims emerging from the guarantee. The cost of default would be paid from the guarantee reserve fund and thus would not affect the budget and the deficit.

Our assessment of each guarantee and its underlying project provided the basis for estimating their future fiscal costs. Projects were ranked according to their risk. Accordingly, the default risk of each guarantee was estimated. The probability of default was determined by careful consideration of each loan. Table 9.4 shows the amounts of

Table 9.3 Programs Covered by National Property Fund,
Czech Republic, 1993–98
(billions of Czech koruny)

	1993	1994	1995	1996	1997	1998
Financing environment-						
al rehabilitation	..	0.1	0.8	1.0	1.4	2.1
Financing development						
of railway route	n.a.	n.a.	n.a.	0.1	..	0.2
Support to state-owned						
enterprises	2.1	0.5	0.9	0.3	0.2	0.3
Support to agricultural						
businesses	n.a.	6.1	1.0	n.a.	n.a.	n.a.
Bond interest	2.1	1.5	1.6	0.5	0.4	0.5
National Property Fund's						
"hidden" fiscal deficit[a]	4.2	8.2	4.3	1.9	2.0	2.9
Others, already included						
in hidden deficit cal-						
culation:						
Health insurance						
companies						
(through KOB)[b]	n.a.	n.a.	n.a.	0.8	0.4	0.4
Support to aviation						
companies						
(through KOB)[b]	n.a.	n.a.	n.a.	n.a.	0.1	..
Provisions to Ceska						
Inkasni (CI)[b]	n.a.	n.a.	3.4	10.3	5.5	6.0
Stabilization pro-						
gram of CF						
(through KOB)[b]	n.a.	n.a.	n.a.	n.a.	0.6	1.8
Others, included in						
reported budget						
deficit:						
Transfers accord-						
ing to state						
budget law[b]	9.5	19.4	10.7	n.a.	n.a.	n.a.

n.a. Not applicable.
.. Negligible.
Note: KOB = Konsolidacni Banka; CF = Ceska Financni.
    a. Excluding transfers to KOB, CI, and CF and transfers according to state budget law.
    b. These items are excluded from the "true" deficit calculation. National Property Fund's expenditures related to KOB, CI, and CF are accounted for as financing items of these institutions.
    Sources: National Property Fund's annual reports and calculations by the authors.

Table 9.4 Risk of Guarantees Issued, Czech Republic,
1993–98

(face values, billions of Czech koruny)

Risk	1993	1994	1995	1996	1997	1998
Very high (90%)	0.0	0.0	0.0	10.8	51.7	31.0
High (30%)	0.0	0.0	0.0	16.2	20.3	0.0
Medium (15%)	5.0	0.0	13.3	3.0	5.8	7.8
Low (5%)	3.7	0.0	1.8	0.0	0.0	87.0
Total	8.7	0.0	15.1	30.0	77.8	125.8

Sources: Ministry of Finance and calculations by the authors.

guarantees issued according to their risk ranking. The implicit subsidy
(risk-adjusted) imbedded in state guarantees is calculated by multiplying the loan amount for which a guarantee was issued by the default
risk. To avoid double counting, the net implicit subsidy, or the net
contribution to the hidden deficit in a given year, is defined as the total
implicit subsidy provided in a given year minus guarantee claims paid
from the budget and reported in the budget that year. Table 9.5 provides the risk-adjusted amounts of guarantees issued each year and the
claims paid from the budget on guarantee defaults each year.

Estimates of the "true" fiscal deficit in the Czech Republic (Table
9.6) indicate that, contrary to the widely accepted view, the Czech
Republic's fiscal performance has not been noteworthy for its fiscal
restraint. Moreover, demands on new guarantees and programs to be
financed through various off-budget agencies have been growing. If
left to grow as in the past, the off-budget risk to future fiscal stability

Table 9.5 Contribution of Guarantees to "Hidden" Deficit,
Czech Republic, 1993–98

(billions of Czech koruny)

Risk	1993	1994	1995	1996	1997	1998
Very high (90%)	0.0	0.0	0.0	9.7	46.5	27.9
High (30%)	0.0	0.0	0.0	4.9	6.1	0.0
Medium (15%)	0.7	0.0	2.0	0.4	0.9	1.2
Low (5%)	0.2	0.0	0.1	0.0	0.0	4.4
Subtotal	0.9	0.0	2.1	15.0	53.5	33.4
Budget paid out (–)	–0.8	–0.4	–0.8	–0.1	–2.0	-6.7
Total	0.1	–0.4	1.3	14.9	51.5	26.7
(as % of GDP)	*0.0*	*–0.0*	*0.1*	*1.0*	*3.1*	*1.5*

Sources: Ministry of Finance and calculations of the authors.

Table 9.6 Czech Republic "True" Fiscal Deficit, 1993–98
(percent of GDP)

	1993	1994	1995	1996	1997	1998
Reported fiscal deficit	–0.5	–1.3	0.3	0.5	1.1	1.4
"Hidden" fiscal deficit in the special institutions (KOB, CI, CF, and NPF)	3.2	1.9	1.0	0.5	1.0	2.0
"Hidden" fiscal deficit in guarantees (net hidden subsidy, risk-adjusted)	0	0	0.1	1.0	3.1	1.5
"True" fiscal deficit	2.7	0.6	1.4	2.0	5.2	4.9

Source: Calculations of the author.

would increase significantly. By mid-1999, the government had only begun to develop an institutional mechanism to keep a check on its off-budget obligations and the ensuing fiscal risk.

The sharp increase in the amount and risk of guarantees issued by the state is troubling. The bulk of the increase has emerged from the government's support of the banks and the Czech Railways. In 1997 and 1998 the government issued a CZK22 billion (1.4 percent of GDP) guarantee to Czech National Bank on some of its very risky lending for bank restructuring and a CZK31 billion (nearly 2 percent of GDP) guarantee to a bank (CSOB) on its claim against a Slovak financial institution (Slovenska Inkasni). To support the Czech Railways, the government issued two guarantees, each over CZK20 billion with a very high default risk in 1996 and 1997 on railway modernization. The hidden cost of the guarantees has already started to show as a growing claim on the budget emerging from guarantee defaults. Claims on the budget increased from about CZK1 billion annually during 1993–96 to CZK2 billion in 1997 and almost CZK7 billion in 1998.[5]

Another related, troubling fact is the *rapidly increasing level of hidden public liabilities.* Stocks of these liabilities have been accumulating outside the budgetary system as a result of the hidden deficits (annual flows), mainly in the form of borrowing by the special institutions to finance their government programs.[6] Table 9.7 shows the approximate levels of hidden public liabilities, excluding the nonguaranteed quasi-fiscal operations of the Czech National Bank. Comparison of the figures of hidden deficits in Table 9.2 with the resulting hidden liabilities in Table 9.7 illustrates the extent of cross-financing among the special institutions and of the use of privatization revenues to partly cover the cost of off-budget programs.

Off-budget programs, such as guarantees and support extended through Konsolidacni Banka, the National Property Fund, PGRLF (an

Table 9.7 Hidden Public Liabilities, Czech Republic, 1993–98
(billions of Czech koruny)

	1993	1994	1995	1996	1997	1998
Konsolidacni Banka[a]	79	81	79	70	86	98
Ceska Inkasni[a]	20	27	25	17	8	7
National Property Fund[a]	29	33	40	22	17	15
State guarantees[b]	3	3	6	28	74	107
Hidden public liabilities[a]	**131**	**144**	**150**	**137**	**185**	**226**
Hidden public liabilities						
(% of GDP)[a]	*13.1*	*12.1*	*10.8*	*8.7*	*10.9*	*12.4*
Reported gross government						
debt	159	162	154	155	173	194
Reported gross government						
debt (% of GDP)	*15.8*	*13.7*	*11.2*	*11.2*	*10.3*	*10.6*

a. Activities of Konsolidacni Banka include financing of the stabilization program of Ceska Financni. Therefore, the table does not include Ceska Financni as a separate entity. All figures are net of provisions and reserves.

b. Guarantees outstanding at the end of each year adjusted for risk.

Sources: Konsolidacni Banka, Ceska Inkasni, National Property Fund, and calculations of the authors.

agricultural credit and guarantee fund), and other, possibly new agencies and guarantee funds, *impose costs on taxpayers with a delay but with no discount.* As has already begun to happen, past hidden deficits and servicing of the hidden government debt outside the budgetary system generate claims on the government budget.

State guarantees generate significant budget claims. Assuming that no new state guarantees are issued, the budget may need to cover about CZK4 billion annually in future years and CZK33 billion in 2002 if the debt of Slovenska Inkasni to CSOB is not resolved. Table 9.8 builds on Table 9.5, and, taking into account individual guaranteed debt repayment schedules, it shows the expected guarantee claims on future budgets. Figures in Table 9.8 are obtained by multiplying the default risk by the annual scheduled payments. More conservative assumptions of default risk would increase the estimated claims on budget resources.

Another source of future claims on the budget is Konsolidacni Banka. It experienced a loss of about CZK14.4 billion in 1998 that later was covered by a state bond issue. New programs, however, have required further borrowing and continue to generate losses. Claims on the state budget reached CZK80 billion during 1999–2000.

Without further privatization revenues, the National Property Fund will need to borrow further to meet its commitment for Ceska Financni, Ceska Inkasni, environmental recovery, and railway development, and to cover principal repayments for its obligations.[7] Analy-

Table 9.8 Estimated Guarantee Claims on the Budget,
Czech Republic, 1999–2030
(billions of Czech koruny)

Guaran- tees out- standing in 1998	Average default risk	Expect- ed total claims	1999	2000	2001	2002	2003	1999– 2003	1999– 2030
284.8	38%	107.4ᵃ	3.3	4.9	5.4	33.3	3.7	50.5	97.8

a. The government guarantees both interest and principle repayments. The figure shown
is the net present value of guarantee claims on future budgets.
Sources: Ministry of Finance and calculations of the authors.

sis of the National Property Fund's commitments, excluding those
for Konsolidacni Banka, suggests that, to meet its obligations, the
fund will need about CZK15 billion a year during 1999–2003 and
about CZK33 billion in 2004.

In the medium to long term, off-budget financing of government
activities, guarantees, and other contingent liabilities surfaces as increases in government debt. In the Czech Republic, the expected increase in the public debt by the amount of hidden public liabilities
(estimated in 1999 at around 12.4 percent of 1998 GDP as shown in
Table 9.7) is significant but not disastrous. What appears as disastrous
is the dynamic in the rise of the hidden public liabilities. Clearly, the
levels of new guarantees issued and the new government programs
entrusted for financing to Konsolidacni Banka are not sustainable. Their
continued growth at the current pace would in a few years endanger
fiscal stability and thus play against the country's objective of EU accession. The situation will appear more serious if "implicit" government liabilities are included in the deficit and debt calculations.

Finally, it remains questionable to what extent off-budget programs
contributed to achieving the main policy objectives of the government.
In some instances, these programs substituted for structural reforms.
For example, instead of preventing problems in the banking sector from
recurring, bailouts of banks and enterprises paid for failures likely to
occur again. Sometimes programs that did not qualify for budgetary
support (for example, an additional subsidy to the Czech Railways) did
qualify for assistance outside the budget (such as a very risky guarantee
extended to the railways). Moreover, often these programs implied that
government would help again in the event of future failures, and thus
may have generated moral hazard among market agents, reducing their
incentives to improve productivity and competitiveness.

Because EU accession and integration with European markets are
the highest policy priority, the government has a powerful incentive to
enhance its fiscal management. Recent moves in this direction include

periodic reporting on contingent liabilities and fiscal risks, new laws on budget management and state asset management, consolidation of the assets and liabilities of Ceska Financni and Ceska Inkasni in a single portfolio under Konsolidacni Banka, a law restricting the functions of Konsolidacni Banka, privatization of the large state-owned banks, the planned introduction of a medium-term expenditure framework that would reflect off-budget fiscal risks, and a new capacity in the Ministry of Finance to analyze and manage fiscal risks. If implemented, these initiatives should significantly narrow the gap between the reported and true budget deficit and improve the overall effectiveness and efficiency of the use of public resources.

Transparency and Containment of Fiscal Risk in Hungary

Compared with the Czech Republic, Hungary emerged in 1990 with a much larger government debt and a higher expenditure-to-GDP ratio. But Hungary has been more determined and successful in managing fiscal risk. In liquidating old contingent obligations and undertaking new ones, the government has been guided by two principles: explicit risks should be identified, and new risks should be undertaken within the approved budget framework. These principles—transparency and containment—have not always been applied consistently, but they have put the government in a better position to withstand economic setbacks.

Transparency has been achieved as the risks and costs of past policies have been made explicit and, where appropriate, funds have been set aside to pay for them. The pension system is an example. Restructuring the pension system compelled the government to recognize costs that had long been concealed and make provisions in the budget for them.

Containment has proceeded along two tracks: liquidating preexisting risks through pension reform, bank consolidation, and enterprise consolidation, and regulating the volume of new risks through the rules and procedures discussed in the previous section of this chapter. Although these controls are on a cash basis and do not use sophisticated risk assessment techniques, they may nevertheless be effective.

Recent fiscal performance attests to the prudent management of risk. The amount set aside in the budget for calls on individual and institutional guarantees is less than 1 percent of total budgeted expenditures. The amount paid out in actual calls has consistently been less than the budgeted amount. The contingent liabilities of state institutions are barely half of the authorized level. Conservative estimates of calls from outstanding guarantees of all types are less than 2 percent of budgeted expenditures. Government and state institutions have established several reserve funds to cover fiscal risks, including a deposit insurance fund, the private pension guarantee fund, and funds provisioned by various institutions to pay for calls on the risks they hold. The draw on these funds has been very small thus far. Risk in the financial sector has been diversified and transferred (in most cases) to foreign investors. Financial markets have given Hungary a much more favorable rating than in the past, as reflected by the government's success in floating longer-term bonds.

Like in the Czech Republic, early in the transition, fiscal stability in Hungary was undermined by the *banking system* and its large volume of nonperforming loans. To finance bank restructuring and encourage privatization, the government issued bonds and guarantees (Table 9.9). Because they bypassed the budget, bonds and guarantees created "hidden deficits." Only guarantees, however, in a very small amount, generated a hidden debt.

Table 9.9 Fiscal Cost of Banking Problems, Hungary, 1991–98
(billions of Hungarian forints)

	1991	1992	1993	1994	1995	1996	1997	1998
Bonds issued[a]	0.0	0.0	285.6	47.0	6.0	9.0	0.0	182.0
Guarantees issued	10.4	0.0	0.0	0.0	0.0	16.5	27.8	44.0
Total "hidden" deficit	10.4	0.0	285.6	47.0	6.0	25.5	27.8	226.0
Amortization of bonds from budget	0.0	0.0	0.0	0.0	0.0	0.0	85.9	0.0
Interest paid on bank consolidation bonds	0.0	0.0	0.0	54.5	96.6	102.7	86.5	50.5
Guarantees called	0.0	2.3	0.4	0.0	6.8	2.9	11.8	6.2
Guarantees recovered	0.0	0.0	0.0	0.0	–0.2	–0.1	0.0	–1.1
Total realized fiscal cost	0.0	2.3	0.4	54.5	103.2	105.5	184.2	55.6
Total realized fiscal cost[b] *(% of GDP)*	*0.00*	*0.08*	*0.01*	*1.25*	*1.85*	*1.53*	*2.16*	*0.58*

a. Bank consolidation was largely financed directly from new debt issues, bypassing the budget. Bonds issued in 1993 to finance bank consolidation (over 8 percent of GDP) partly also served debtor (enterprise) consolidation.

b. The total realized fiscal cost, as shown through the government budget, is calculated on a cash basis as payments on bond amortization and interest plus payments on guarantees called, minus revenues from guarantees recovered. The amounts of bonds and guarantees issued suggest how the fiscal cost of bank consolidation will affect future budgets.

Sources: Ministry of Finance and Government Debt Management Agency.

In its first stage, reform of the banking sector did not contain fiscal risk nor was its fiscal cost transparent. The first stage involved government acquisition of a substantial portion of the bad debt held by banks. The loan strategy transferred risk from the banks to the government, but the true cost was concealed by treating the transactions as asset purchases rather than as subsidies. Although some of the acquired loans were sold or restructured, most were transferred to state agencies (such as the Hungarian Development Bank) or written off. The second stage of reforms entailed risk-sharing, with assisted banks required to sign consolidation agreements spelling out the measures they would take to improve their financial condition. This strategy was mainly financed from 20-year bonds. In the 1994–96 period, annual interest payments on these loans averaged approximately 1.5 percent of GDP. Successful consolidation set the stage for privatization of most banks,[8] allowing the government to transfer most of the risk into foreign hands.

However, the government violated its transparency rule in the case of Postabanka. A run on the bank in 1997 prompted the government to provide new equity capital and loan guarantees. The government channeled most of the assistance through the Hungarian Development Bank and the State Privatization and Holding Agency, thereby creating not only a "hidden" fiscal deficit but also a hidden debt (liabilities accumulated in these two agencies in exchange for low-quality assets). In late 1998 the government was compelled to recapitalize Postabanka by injecting HUF150 billion (1.5 percent of GDP) from government bonds and to compensate the Hungarian Development Bank in the amount of HUF40 billion for Postabanka-related losses.

Compared with the Czech Republic, Hungary chose a more transparent approach to *enterprise privatization and to the use of privatization revenues*. Most of privatization proceeds were used to repay foreign debt (see Table 9.10). As for the privatization process itself, Hungary proceeded slowly, company by company, restructuring and managing them before selling them, and insisted on cash sales rather than on vouchers and other noncash transactions implemented in the Czech Republic. The State Property Agency has not warranted the future financial condition or performance of privatized enterprises, nor has it indemnified the new owners for the cost of meeting new environmental standards. It has issued several types of guarantees in the privatization process, but maintains a reserve fund, which appears sufficient to cover expected claims.

Hungary's *pension reform* of 1997 reduced the government's largest implicit liability and made it explicit.[9] The reform required new workers to enroll in a fully funded, privately managed, defined-contribution system and gave most existing workers the option of remaining in the government-operated, defined-benefit program or migrating to the new system. The reform significantly reduced the government's

Table 9.10 Use of Privatization Revenues, Hungary, 1990–98
(billions of Hungarian forints)

	1990	1991	1992	1993	1994	1995	1996	1997	1998
Government debt repayment	0.5	22.4	51.5	57.5	151.7	218.4	22.9	254.8	39.0
Transfers to state budget	0.0	0.0	0.0	0.0	0.0	150.0	100.0	0.0	0.0
Municipalities	0.0	2.3	4.8	3.4	6.0	6.1	21.6	26.4	0.0
Direct privati- zation costs	0.0	1.1	6.2	7.6	25.3	33.6	33.0	36.1	46.3
Reorganization costs	0.0	0.0	8.7	49.5	8.0	9.8	16.8	12.1	13.5
Guarantees	0.0	0.0	5.8	7.8	7.0	3.7	33.2	16.0	51.6
Total	0.5	25.8	77.0	125.8	198.0	421.6	227.5	345.4	150.4
Total (% of GDP)	0.02	1.1	2.6	3.6	4.5	7.5	3.3	4.1	1.5

Sources: Ministry of Finance and State Property Agency.

.

future fiscal exposure, but it raised the short-term budget deficit by requiring the government to make up shortfalls in the old pension fund. The more workers who switched, the greater the reduction in future liabilities, but the greater the loss of income in the old fund, the greater the reported budget deficit.

To build public support for pension reform, the government guaranteed that each participant in the new, privately managed pension funds would receive benefits equal to at least 93 percent of the pension that would have been paid by the old system. Because only workers below the age of 47 had the option of joining the new pension system, the government will not face any call on this guarantee for at least 15 years, when the first cohort of participants in the defined-contribution plan retire. If the guarantees are called in the future, payments will be made by the new Private Pensions Guarantee Fund, which accumulates reserves for this purpose by charging privately managed pension funds fees for various services. There is some risk that these guarantees may spur participants to enroll in funds that promise the highest yields, without concern about whether the funds will have sufficient resources to cover their promises. To guard against undue risk-taking, the government has introduced various regulatory measures to oversee the privately managed funds.

Throughout the transition process, Hungary also has taken *new fiscal risks* by guaranteeing loans, indemnifying importers and exporters, and taking other steps to promote investment and entrepreneurial behavior. Moreover, Hungary has authorized a number of quasi-independent institutions to issue guarantees, including Eximbank, MEHIB (Hungarian Export Credit Insurance Ltd.), the Credit Guarantee Company, the Rural Credit Guarantee Foundation, and the Hungarian Development Bank, and thus has accumulated contingent liabilities (see Table 9.11).

Overall, Hungary's government has been prudent in issuing guarantees directly or through state-established institutions. Compared with the Czech Republic, Hungary has maintained a set of strict controls that limit the volume of guarantees, making provision in the budget, and require assessment of risks prior to the execution of guarantee contracts and timely reporting on the risks of outstanding guarantees (see Box 9.1). The controls are cash-based; they limit the volume of new guarantees or the total outstanding amount and set aside cash in

Table 9.11 Contingent Liabilities Outstanding and Expected Claims, Hungary, as of 1998–99
(billions of Hungarian forints)

Type	Ceiling	Out-standing	Average risk (%)	Expected claims
Individual guarantees				
Individual guarantees (within the limit)	28[a]	120	30	36
Individual guarantees (beyond the limit)	158[b]	125	5	6
Guarantees to activities of specific institutions				
Hungarian Development Bank	80	32	5	2
Eximbank	75	52	7	3
MEHIB—Hungarian Export Credit Insurance Ltd.	185	76	8	6
Credit Guarantee Co.	49	42	5	2
Rural Credit Guarantee Foundation	23	10	5	1
Total	n.a.	457	n.a.	56[c]

n.a. Not applicable.
Note: The table excludes guaranteed loans from international financial institutions.
a. The 1998 ceiling on the issue of new guarantees.
b. Total amount of individual guarantees beyond the percentage limit.
c. Because the government guarantees both interest and principal repayments, this figure roughly represents the net present value of future claims. The 1998 budget appropriated HUF11.8 billion for guarantee calls and actually paid HUF7.9 billion. The 1999 budget set aside HUF12 billion for calls on individual guarantees and another HUF9.5 billion to cover guarantees issued by state institutions.
Sources: Ministry of Finance and calculations of the authors.

Box 9.1 Hungarian Public Finance Institutions Designed to Constrain the Accumulation of Contingent Liabilities

Hungary's Public Finance Act is the legal basis for issuing and budgeting for guarantees. It provides that the annual budget limit the volume of guarantees undertaken during the fiscal year. It also requires that funds be set aside in the budget for calls expected during the year. And it requires the government to publish information on borrowers, the reasons for issuing specific guarantees and the amounts, and the risk and the conditions pertaining to the guarantees. The government must report each guarantee to the State Audit Office, and the closing accounts for each fiscal year must include all guarantees undertaken and payments made.

The next link in the control process is the annual budget, which limits the volume of guarantees to be issued (or outstanding) during the year and sets aside funds for guarantees that may be called. At present, the budget limits the total of new guarantees to 1 percent of budgeted expenditures. The government generally has stayed within the limit, but for several reasons it issues guarantees or incurs related obligations well in excess of the limit. The limit applies only to individual guarantees issued directly by the government; it does not cover guarantees issued by state institutions. Guarantees for various strategic purposes (such as for oil and gas imports) and for loans contracted with international finance institutions are exempt from the limit. The limit may be exceeded during the year by a decision of the parliament.

The budget contains numerous provisions regulating the issuance of guarantees by the government and state institutions. The following are among the most important. The government may charge an origination fee of up to 0.5 percent of the value of its commitment. The budget limits the amount of guarantees that each state institution may have outstanding at any time during the year. (In some cases, the limit is adjusted annually to accommodate increased credit activity. For example, the 1999 budget raised the ceiling for the Hungarian Export Credit Insurance Ltd. to HUF250 billion from the HUF185 billion designated the previous year.) The government may reinsure up to a specified percentage of the obligations of various state institutions (for example, it reinsures 70 percent of the obligations of the Credit Guarantee Company and the Rural Credit Guarantee Foundation). The budget provides for guarantee programs such as new student loan guarantees, and it appropriates a fixed amount to cover potential calls during the year.

The third link in the control chain is a decree prescribing the procedures to be used in undertaking individual guarantees. The decree currently in effect designates the minister of finance as guarantor on behalf of the state and specifies the form and content in which proposed guarantees should be presented to the government for decision. The proposal

(Box continues on the following page.)

Box 9.1 (continued)

should include an explanation of the reasons for the guarantee, information on any previous guarantees issued to the same borrower, and an assessment of the probability that the guarantee will be called. The government is required to publish decisions on individual guarantees in the official *Hungarian Gazette*. It maintains an up-to-date database on outstanding guarantees, including information on the purpose of each transaction, the amount guaranteed, the date the guarantee was contracted, and when the government obligation will expire. During 1998, official records showed that the government entered into 34 individual guarantee contracts within the 1 percent limit, two guarantees outside the limit, and several dozen guarantees on foreign loans by banks and enterprises.

A guarantee becomes effective only when a properly executed contract has been signed. The Ministry of Finance has prepared several standard contracts for various types of arrangements. Each contract includes provisions protecting the government's interest in case of default and procedures for recovering payments made pursuant to calls.

the budget to cover possible calls during the fiscal year. The controls are not self-enforcing, however. Their effectiveness depends on the extent to which the rules are followed.

Despite its generally prudent record, the government still holds significant risks. First, the budget constraints are not as constrictive as they appear to be. Guarantees tendered outside the 1 percent budget limit exceed those within the limit. Second, state institutions have become active risk-takers, and (as occurred in the use of the Hungarian Development Bank as a conduit for bailing out Postabanka) sometimes at the request of the government. Third, in view of the country's high public expenditure and debt ratios the government may have little margin in financing contingent obligations that come due. Fourth, Hungary, like other countries, still faces some implicit liabilities in the financial sector, in privatized enterprises, and in privately financed infrastructure. Fifth, there is pressure on government to undo some reforms because previously unrecorded liabilities now burden the budget. So far, the government has not succumbed to the temptation to show a more favorable budget posture by, for example, reverting to the old pension system and hiding future pension liabilities.

The favorable fiscal posture may, however, lull the government into taking risks that it may have avoided during the adjustment years. In 1999, it increased the ceilings on contingent liabilities of various institutions and has boosted the ceiling on new individual state guarantees

from 1 percent to 1.5 percent of state revenues. Moreover, it has proposed new, large highway construction programs, to be implemented
through the Hungarian Development Bank. Using such an off-budget
channel to finance a huge public investment program may open the
door to other schemes in the future.

Fiscal Risks of Transition under the Currency Board Arrangement in Bulgaria

After the introduction of a currency board arrangement in 1997–2000,
Bulgaria's government achieved major success in fiscal adjustment.
The tight macroeconomic constraint introduced by the currency board,
however, also reduces the government's capacity to absorb risks and
respond to future possible shocks by increasing its borrowing. Thus
Bulgaria's fiscal performance is more vulnerable to risks than those of
the Czech Republic and Hungary, where government borrowing is less
constrained. Applying the Fiscal Risk Matrix, Bulgaria's government
has identified the main sources of its risk exposure (see Table 9.12).

Sovereign Debt

The size and structure of Bulgaria's public debt are somewhat worrisome. After the 1992–94 successful restructuring, the government reduced its external debt to 82 percent of GDP and domestic debt to 4
percent of GDP by the end of 1999 (Figure 9.2). It also announced
further reductions for the future. Prudent debt management allowed
Bulgaria to reclaim investors' confidence. Over 1998–2000, the average maturity of domestic Treasury bills doubled, reaching almost two
years, and the sovereign credit rating on foreign debt stabilized at B2/
B+ with a positive outlook. In spite of continued debt reduction, however, Bulgaria remains one of the most heavily indebted countries of
Central and Eastern Europe.
    The current structure of government debt may give rise to increases
in the cost of future debt service and new borrowing (Figure 9.3). The
reason is that several risks are at play. *Refinancing risk,* as measured
by the maturity structure of public debt and its volatility, appears limited, but so are the refinancing options. For external debt, the average
portfolio maturity is long—over 13 years—which limits refinancing
risk. However, neither restructured Paris and London Club obligations nor the debt to international financial institutions can be rolled
over easily. Similarly, the government will find it difficult to refinance
its long-term foreign currency-denominated domestic debt. Refinancing risk thus remains important as long as the domestic bond market

Table 9.12 Fiscal Risk Matrix, Bulgaria

Sources of obligations	Direct liabilities (obligation in any event)	Contingent liabilities (obligation if a particular event occurs)
Explicit Government liability as recognized by a law or contract	• Foreign and domestic sovereign debt (size and structure) [H] • Future pension expenditures required by law [M] • Health expenditures required by law [M]	• Individual state guarantees for nonsovereign borrowing and obligations [L] • Obligation to recover past environmental damages assumed in enterprise privatization and other environmental liabilities [M] • Obligations of business promotion bank [L] • Obligations of export insurance agency (insurance policies to cover political and medium-term commercial risks) [L] • Obligations of state fund for agriculture [L]
Implicit A "moral" obligation of government that reflects public and interest group pressures	• Accumulated and expected public investment needs to sustain delivery of public services and meet key requirements for accession to the EU [H] • Future recurrent costs of public investment projects	• Environmental commitments for still unknown damages and nuclear and toxic waste [U] • Cleanup of enterprise arrears and liabilities [M] • Default of municipalities on own nonguaranteed debt, own guarantees, or own obligations to provide critical public services [M] • Support to the banking sector in case of crisis [L]

Note: Risk level: H = high; M = medium; L = low; U = unknown. Obligations listed refer to the fiscal authorities, not the central bank.
Source: The authors.

remains shallow and unimpressed by government bonds of three-year and higher maturities.

Currency risk is less important. The currency board arrangement pegging the Bulgarian leva to the euro appears credible and thus removes foreign exchange risk. Cross-currency risk remains a fiscal risk, particularly with respect to the appreciation of the dollar vis-à-vis the euro.[10]

Most problematic appears the *interest rate risk*. At the end of 1999, three-quarters of government debt had a floating interest rate. During

Figure 9.2. Bulgaria's Public Debt, 1993–99

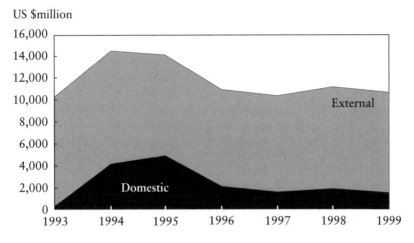

Source: The authors.

Figure 9.3. Structure of Bulgaria's Public Debt
as of December 31, 1999

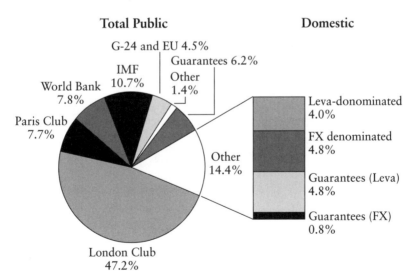

Note: IMF = International Monetary Fund; FX = foreign exchange.
Source: The authors.

1997–98, the exceptionally low LIBOR (London interbank offered rate) allowed the government to keep debt service at about 10 percent of central government revenues. Any increases in the LIBOR, however, will increase the government's debt burden significantly.

In the short run, given its financing constraints, the government can do little to alleviate the interest rate risk. As much as possible, however, it will need to issue new debt at a fixed interest rate.

Pension and Health Care Expenditures

By the late 1990s, the pension and health care systems in Bulgaria had become highly inefficient and financially unsustainable. The pension system suffered from adverse demographics, generous entitlements, a low retirement age, and declining revenues despite high contribution rates. The universal and nominally free health care system was characterized by low investment, declining quality of health services, and increasing costs to the patients in terms of side payments (such as user fees and bribes). To strengthen its fiscal outlook and the quality of services provided, the government launched ambitious pension and health care reforms in 1999. The pension reform aims to restore the long-term viability of the traditional pay-as-you-go scheme by reducing entitlements and completing it with fully funded voluntary and compulsory pillars (Figure 9.4). Under the health care reform, a Health Insurance Fund

Figure 9.4. Projected Deficit of Pillar I with and without the Reform, Bulgaria, 1999–2047

Percent of GDP

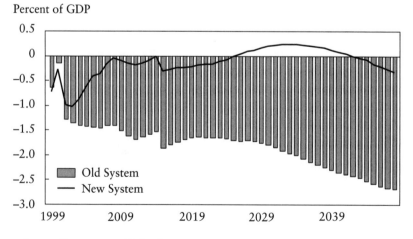

Source: Government of Bulgaria.

created in 1999 is expected to gradually contract out health care provision to competing public and private providers. The reforms temporarily increase government spending in both sectors. The health care reform involves up-front costs to build institutional capacity and gradually recapitalize Bulgaria's health care facilities. Transition to the new, funded components of the pension system while maintaining a pay-as-you-go scheme entails up-front revenue losses for the government in 1999–2001 before delivering financial improvement.

The Financial Sector

In the financial sector, the 1996–97 hyperinflation, crisis, and subsequent policy actions by the Bulgarian National Bank effectively cleaned up the banking sector. The ensuing reform successfully capped both explicit and implicit government obligations for lost deposits and failed banks. Since then, improved supervision has controlled the exposure of banks to liquidity and interest rate risks. The quality of banks' loan portfolios and their foreign exchange exposure are not a significant fiscal risk so far.

State Guarantees and Guarantee Funds

Bulgaria's explicit contingent liabilities are modest. The government has applied prudent limits and regulations to state guarantees. The government entered the year 2000 reporting guaranteed debt (face value) of about 17 percent of GDP. Of this amount, 9 percent of GDP was in the form of the central bank's debt to the International Monetary Fund (IMF) and a further 4 percent of GDP was in the form of a deposit guarantee that expired in April 2000. Calls on the remaining guarantees (about 4 percent of GDP outstanding in 2000) would have limited fiscal cost (Figure 9.5). In addition, the government guarantees obligations of agencies such as the State Fund for Agriculture, the Export Insurance Agency, and the Business Promotion Bank. These guarantees also are small so far, but, as we discuss in the next section, the government is likely to face increasing pressure to provide guarantees and other forms of off-budget support in the near future.

Economic Restructuring and Investment Requirements

Compared with the Czech Republic, Hungary, and several other more advanced EU accession countries, Bulgaria has delayed most structural reforms and investment. Only in 1997 did Bulgaria stabilize its macroeconomic conditions and embark on a comprehensive program of reforms to lay the foundations of a market-based economy. To support these reforms, and particularly to introduce financial discipline in

Figure 9.5. Fiscal Impact of Called Guarantees, Bulgaria,
1999–2004

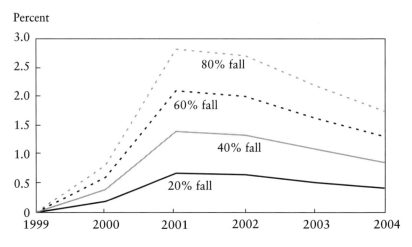

Source: The authors.

banks, enterprises, and government agencies, the government established the currency board arrangement. In addition, the government
needs to support the reforms financially. The reform program required
expenditure on protecting the poor, modernizing public administration, reforming the judicial system, renewing infrastructure, and addressing environmental problems. Low levels of public investment
(averaging about 1–2 percent of GDP during 1993–98) and deferred
maintenance during most of the 1990s only sharpened the challenge of
transition and of meeting the requirements of EU accession in the early
2000s. Under its 2000–2004 public investment program, the government plans to spend 3–3.5 percent of GDP annually. The objectives of
economic growth and EU accession, however, call for significantly more
new investment as well as for low budget deficits. Thus the government will need to encourage private sector initiatives. As long as commercial banks are opposed to providing long-term credits and foreign
creditors lack confidence, this in turn will require government guarantees through the various existing and possibly new state-guaranteed
agencies. Box 9.2 illustrates the fiscal risks that have arisen in Bulgaria
from private participation in the energy sector.

Fiscal Vulnerability

Bulgaria's current fiscal position appears solid. In the late 1990s, revenue performance was strong and resilient to the economic shocks

Box 9.2 Fiscal Risks Associated with Bulgaria's
Energy Sector

In the energy sector, fiscal risks arise mainly from (a) explicit state guarantee contracts for loans to state-owned energy enterprises and (b) explicit and implicit state guarantees of long-term take-or-pay contracts. Contracts of both types are likely to increase rapidly if investments to modernize energy infrastructure and to meet European Union accession requirements are not carefully selected or properly structured.

The years 1999–2000 witnessed a high demand for state guarantees on energy projects. The government considered credit guarantees on energy investments in the amount of about US$850 million to be implemented during 2000–2004. These include investments in nuclear plant safety, waste disposal, and plant upgrades ($380 million); electricity transmission and dispatch ($150 million); district heating ($120 million); and expansion of gas transit capacity to Turkey ($47 million).

Take-or-pay guarantees also are demanded, and the one such guarantee already provided is expected to be called. In 1998 the government provided a long-term take-or-pay guarantee on a gas contract between Bulgargaz and Gazprom. This guarantee requires Bulgaria to take or pay for predetermined annual volumes of gas until 2010. The contracted volume of 4 billion cubic meters for 1999 was valued at US$320 million. A slightly higher volume was contracted for 2000 and onward. In Bulgaria, however, the demand for gas has been declining and the government is expected to pay for the contracted volume that is not taken.

Expected power purchase agreements between the state-owned National Electricity Company and privatized power producers also call for long-term take-or-pay state guarantees. A state guarantee is sought on the electric company's obligation to purchase electricity for about US$180 million a year for 15 years upon completion of a $400 million, 840-megawatt rehabilitation project, and for about $175 million a year for 10–15 years upon completion of a new $1.0 billion, 600-megawatt plant. (Source: Brixi, Shatalov, and Zlaoui 2000.)

caused by, for example, the Russian crisis and the Kosovo war.[11] General government revenues increased from 31.4 percent of GDP in 1997 to 36.8 percent of GDP in 1998 and exceeded 40 percent of GDP in 1999, providing adequate coverage for expenditures that rose from 35.8 percent of GDP in 1998 to 41.2 percent of GDP in 1999, mainly driven by the social sectors.

Room to accommodate fiscal risks, however, is limited. First, although the currency board arrangement is effective in achieving fiscal stability, it does by definition reduce the range of options otherwise available for deficit financing and therefore the scope for fiscal expansion or for accommodating sudden financing pressures. Out of the four possibilities that are available to most countries in financing their public sector deficit (printing money, reducing foreign reserves, and foreign and domestic government borrowing), the currency board arrangement inhibits the former two. Foreign and domestic borrowing, along with exceptional proceeds such as privatization revenues, thus remains the only means of deficit financing and of raising money to face sudden shocks.

Following adoption of the currency board arrangement, the main source of deficit financing shifted from the domestic banking system (on a net basis) to privatization revenues[12] (Figure 9.6), followed by external borrowing from official creditors. As the privatization process nears an end, revenues from the sale of state-owned enterprises will subside. The largest and most profitable state-owned enterprises were already privatized. Further sizable revenues could be expected from the privatization of BTC (Bulgaria telecommunications company), Bulgartabac (tobacco company), Bulbank (the largest state-owned bank), and several power distribution companies in 2000–01, after which the scope for raising substantial revenues from privatization shrinks. This may raise questions about the availability of resources for debt payment and investment financing.

Second, similar to other EU accession countries, Bulgaria's government faces a constraint on both the revenue side and the expenditure

Figure 9.6. General Government Overall Balance
and Its Financing, Bulgaria, 1996–99

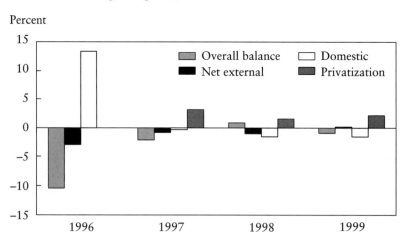

Percent

Source: The authors.

side. With revenues at about 40 percent of GDP in 1999 and a bias toward a payroll tax, a further increase in tax rates would damage investment and growth. In this respect, the government's main objective is to broaden the tax base and strengthen tax collection in order to lower tax rates on labor and income. The structure of government spending is rigid, with a large share of nondiscretionary expenditures. In 1999 spending was dominated by social security, debt service, operations and maintenance, and wages. Pensions and other social outlays accounted for 12 percent of GDP, wages for over 5 percent of GDP, and interest payments for 4 percent of GDP. The operations and maintenance expenditure amounted to 8 percent of GDP, while capital and defense expenditures each accounted for 4 percent of GDP.

Fiscal Risk Management

In line with the requirements of a currency board arrangement, Bulgaria has maintained comfortable levels of both external and fiscal reserves. In its fiscal reserves account, which consists of the balances of all government budgetary and extrabudgetary accounts in the banking sector, the government maintains a certain floor throughout the fiscal year. This floor was around 11 percent of GDP at the end of 1999 and is expected to rise to accommodate contingent expenditures on structural reforms, interest payments above the baseline projection, or a shortfall of official financing relative to program projections. In addition, the government allocates resources within the budget for contingent expenditures. About 1 percent of GDP in 1999 and 1.2 percent of GDP in 2000 were allocated for possible calls on guarantees and implementation problems of pension and health care reforms. Large reserves, however, impose opportunity costs of investment and growth. Therefore, the government has sought to improve its capacity to analyze, mitigate, and manage risk; reflect risks in its medium-term fiscal strategy; and combine its reserve requirement with public-private risk-sharing mechanisms and with a good hedging strategy.

In building its risk management capacity, the government achieved some success in managing its debt. After rescheduling the stock of Paris Club and London Club obligations, the government successfully bought back debt owed to the former Comecon banks at deep discounts, eliminating over US$1 billion of external debt in nominal terms. In its new debt management strategy, the government set as its main goals to minimize the volatility of debt servicing cost, foster the deepening of the domestic capital market, enhance investor confidence by increasing fiscal transparency, attain an investment grade rating for sovereign debt instruments, and reduce the debt level below the Maastricht threshold criteria of 60 percent.

To achieve its debt management goals, the government announced a plan to actively manage its refinancing, exchange rate, and interest risk exposures through quantitative benchmarks that would preset the ratio of domestic versus foreign debt and the ratio of the fixed versus floating interest rate and would gradually raise the duration of domestic and foreign debt. The government also seeks to establish a special performance benchmark against which to evaluate the actual results of debt management and to introduce a cost-at-risk framework to measure the variability of its future debt service. Finally, the government has explored derivative instruments to contain interest risk. Given Bulgaria's sub-investment grade credit rating, which makes derivatives, such as the needed fixed-for-floating interest rate swaps, pricey, World Bank hedging products appear attractive.[13]

Similar to the situation in Hungary, the government's institutional arrangements for managing fiscal risks have been strong in many aspects but not totally reassuring. The government established a simple framework for dealing with guarantees. In particular, it developed a comprehensive register of guarantees and introduced regular publication of the aggregate amounts of guarantees outstanding along with the government debt figures. The register covers all external and domestic guarantees, indicating the beneficiary, creditor, project title, amount, currency, and debt repayment schedule. The government also centralized the issuance of new guarantees and subjected each new guarantee to the executive and legislative scrutiny associated with the regular budget process.

In terms of nominal limits, Decree 482 of 1997 set the annual limit on guarantees (face value) issued at 20 percent of expected budget revenues. A recent amendment to this decree, however, dropped the complementary ceiling of 20 percent of GDP on the total amount of guaranteed debt outstanding, replacing it with a flexible ceiling to be set in the budget process each year. This change significantly expanded the legal room for the government to issue new guarantees.

Furthermore, under state guarantee contracts the government always covers the full amount of the debtor's obligation and all risks, without analyzing their determinants. Such coverage was largely required in the 1990s, because official creditors, providing concessional resources for development projects and balance-of-payments support, dominated the list of creditors under state guarantees. The government understands, however, that, if extended to commercial creditors, this practice would negatively affect market behavior, creating moral hazard for both debtors and creditors.

Municipal borrowing is subject to a legal limit of 10 percent of the annual revenues of the respective municipality. Of this amount, as much as 10 percent of the preceding month's revenues can be in the form of a short-term, interest-free credit from the central budget. Municipalities are allowed to seek the remaining credit from commercial banks and from other municipalities and request state guarantees for them. Subject to the approval of the Securities and Exchange Commission, municipalities are allowed to issue bonds. In 1999 the city of Sofia successfully placed EUR50 million in Luxembourg. Bond issues are not covered by explicit state guarantees, but chances are that the central government would face pressures to intervene should a city or municipality become insolvent. Municipal guarantees and other contingent municipal obligations and municipal ownership of enterprises and financial institutions are not regulated under any existing law.

The Risk versus Investment Dilemma

Bulgaria finds itself in a complex and challenging situation. Macroeconomic stabilization was more painful and required more drastic measures than in most other EU accession countries. Because the stabilization succeeded, fiscal management has been prudent and transparent but has yet to be tested by the risks of transition and investment requirements of recovery and EU accession. With an already high level of indebtedness, Bulgaria faces a difficult tradeoff. Should the country adhere to a very conservative stance toward debt and fiscal risk, or should it accept a slower pace of debt reduction and promote to a larger extent investment, economic restructuring, and programs to protect the poor and vulnerable?

Concluding Remarks

Our work in the Czech Republic, Hungary, and Bulgaria demonstrates the importance of including contingent liabilities when assessing the magnitude of a true fiscal adjustment and when analyzing fiscal sustainability. To the extent that explicit expenditures are shifted off-budget or replaced by the issuance of guarantees, the achieved improvement in fiscal balances is overstated. For the Czech Republic, we find that the adjustment may have been overstated by some 3–4 percent of GDP annually. The accumulation of contingent liabilities today is a threat to future fiscal stability. Thus a stabilization program that is accompanied by a buildup of contingent liabilities may not be sustainable. In Hungary, on the other hand, transparency and containment of fiscal risks, rather than low budget deficits, have been the guiding principles of fiscal policy and management. Although government-reported debt in Hungary has been about five times higher than in the Czech Republic, Hungary's future fiscal performance is likely to suffer less from pressures of guarantee claims and hidden liabilities. Since 1997, Bulgaria has tried to achieve both transparency and low exposure to fiscal risks as well as low budget deficits. Many of the challenges of transition that already have been overcome in the Czech Republic and Hungary, however, have yet to test the Bulgarian government's commitment to fiscal prudence.

There never is a final ending to a country's management of fiscal risk. One country overwhelmed with the accumulated cost of past hidden liabilities takes steps to constrain new risks and to liquidate old claims in a transparent manner; another country does a good job of regulating contingent liabilities, but then is lured into hiding new liabilities by the promise that the costs will be covered by the dividends of future economic growth. In comparing the Czech Republic and Hungary, countries like Bulgaria can learn much from both the failures and the successes.

Notes

1. Ceska Financni has financed two blocks of programs geared toward bank revitalization. One block, in the total amount of approximately CZK35 billion, is financed and guaranteed by the Czech National Bank. The other, called the stabilization program, in the amount of about CZK12 billion, is financed through Konsolidacni Banka and thus is guaranteed by the government. It is only the latter block that is considered in the "true" deficit calculation. It is included as an activity of Konsolidacni Banka.

2. The assets purchased through off-budget programs are of extremely low quality. Therefore, the analysis considers asset purchases as a spending program rather than as a financial transaction.

3. The debt to the Czech National Bank still constitutes about half of Konsolidacni Banka's total debt.

4. Risk assessment of guarantees issued by the National Property Fund and Konsolidacni Banka is not available. Therefore, calculation of the "true" fiscal deficit includes only the implicit subsidy extended through net spending by the special institutions and through guarantees issued directly by the state, but not guarantees issued by special institutions.

5. Because the guarantee claims paid from the budget have contributed to the reported deficit, the "hidden" deficit that emerges from guarantees only includes the difference between the hidden subsidy extended by the government through new guarantees and the claims mostly on guarantees issued in previous years. Unadjusted for guarantee claims, the hidden subsidy through guarantees actually reached CZK55 billion and CZK32 billion in 1997 and 1998, respectively.

6. Hidden public liabilities are calculated on a gross basis. The analysis focuses on gross liabilities, because the quality of directed loans extended and assets purchased through off-budget programs is so extremely low and their potential value is on average estimated at about 10 percent (3 percent for CI, less than 10 percent for CF, and under 20 percent for KOB).

7. The initial bond issue by the National Property Fund was used mainly to capitalize Konsolidacni Banka.

8. During 1994–97, state ownership fell from 67 to 22 percent, while foreign ownership rose from 15 to 61 percent.

9. Hungary inherited a mandatory retirement scheme that promised future benefits but did not put aside sufficient money in the pension fund to pay for them. Because it is on a cash basis, the budget does not disclose unfunded pension liabilities, including those that are direct, explicit obligations of the government. But projections showed that as the population aged over the next half-century, the cash deficit in the pension fund would widen to 6 percent of GDP.

10. From the balance-of-payments perspective, this risk is partly neutralized by euro-denominated foreign reserves and dollar-denominated net exports.

11. Investors' confidence as well as renewed growth and macroeconomic stability emerged from the introduction of the currency board arrangement and sound policies. Economic growth recovered in 1998, recording a 3.5 percent positive growth rate, and continued in 1999 with 2.5 percent growth despite the unfavorable external environment marked by turmoil in the region and emerging international markets. Inflation was confined to the single-digit level.

12. In Bulgaria, privatization receipts cannot be used for current budgetary expenditures. They enter the fiscal reserve account and can be used for debt repayments and investment financing. The privatization receipts of the municipalities can be used for ecological projects, investment debt repayments, or writing off nonperforming loans of municipality-owned enterprises.

13. For example, fixed-spread loans allow borrowers to flexibly fix the interest rate on disbursed amounts at any time during the life of the loan, to create a cap or collar (a floor and cap simultaneously), to unfix or change the rate on disbursed amounts, and to adjust the currency and loan repayment terms if needed. This way, the loan maturity and currency structure may be set to smooth an uneven and sensitive future debt servicing profile. World Bank hedging products such as interest rate swaps, caps and collars, currency swaps, and commodity swaps allow reductions in the risk exposure arising from old World Bank loans and, possibly in the future, from the country's overall debt portfolio. By dealing with some of these instruments, countries also gain experience that is useful later in accessing the international derivatives markets.

Bibliography

Blejer, Mario, and Adrienne Cheasty. 1991. "The Measurement of Fiscal Deficits: Analytical and Methodological Issues." *Journal of Economic Literature* 29: 1644–78.

Bokros, Lajos, and Jean-Jacques Dethier, eds, 1998. *Public Finance Reform during the Transition: The Experience of Hungary.* New York: Oxford University Press.

Brixi, Hana Polackova, Hafez Ghanem, and Roumeen Islam. 1999. "Fiscal Adjustment and Contingent Government Liabilities: Case Studies of the Czech Republic and Macedonia." Policy Research Working Paper 2177. World Bank, Washington, D.C.

Brixi, Hana Polackova, Anita Papp, and Allen Schick. 1999. "Fiscal Risks and the Quality of Fiscal Adjustment in Hungary." Policy Research Working Paper 2176. World Bank, Washington, D.C.

Brixi, Hana Polackova, Sergei Shatalov, and Leila Zlaoui. 2000. "Managing Fiscal Risk in Bulgaria." Policy Research Working Paper 2282. World Bank, Washington, D.C.

Buiter, Willem. 1983. "Measurement of the Public Sector and Its Implications for Policy Evaluation and Design." IMF Staff Papers 30: 306–49, International Monetary Fund, Washington, D.C.

———. 1985. "A Guide to Public Sector Debt and Deficits." Economic Policy (November): 14–79.

Easterly, William. 1999. "When Is Fiscal Adjustment an Illusion?" Economic Policy (April): 57–86.

Glatzel, Dieter. 1998. "The Measurement of Deficit and Debt under the Maastricht Treaty: Some Statistical Considerations." In The Challenges for Public Liability Management in Central Europe. Washington, D.C.: World Bank.

Honohan, Patrick. 1999. "Fiscal Contingency Planning for Financial Crises." Policy Research Working Paper 2228. World Bank, Washington, D.C.

Kharas, Homi, and Deepak Mishra. 2001. "Fiscal Policy, Hidden Deficits, and Currency Crises." In S. Devarajan, F. H. Rogers, and L.. Squire, eds., World Bank Economists' Forum. Washington, D.C.: World Bank.

Kotlikoff, Laurence. 1993. Generational Accounting. New York: Free Press.

Polackova, Hana. 1998. "Contingent Government Liabilities: A Hidden Risk for Fiscal Stability." Policy Research Working Paper 1989. World Bank, Washington, D.C.

Rubin, Irene. 1997. The Politics of Public Budgeting: Getting and Spending, Borrowing and Balancing. Chatham, N.J.: Chatham House.

Selowsky, Marcelo. 1998. "Fiscal Deficits and the Quality of Fiscal Adjustment." In The Challenges for Public Liability Management in Central Europe. Washington, D.C.: World Bank.

World Bank. 1999. "Czech Republic: Dealing with Contingent Liabilities." In Czech Republic toward EU Accession, A World Bank Country Study. Washington, D.C.

CHAPTER 10

Analyzing Government Fiscal Risk Exposure in China

Kathie L. Krumm
World Bank

Christine P. Wong
University of Washington

THREE RECENT DEVELOPMENTS have brought the fiscal risk of contingent liabilities into the center of policy debates in China.[1] First, in response to the economic slowdown in 1997–98, which was compounded by the East Asian financial crisis, the government implemented a fiscal stimulus program in 1998 that continued through 2001. In a country that has managed a conservative fiscal stance that has kept budget deficits within the range of 1.5–2.5 percent of the gross domestic product (GDP) throughout the past two decades of transition to a market economy, this deficit spending raised immediate questions about the sustainability of such stimulus. China's fiscal deficit by official definitions was 2.8 percent of GDP in 2000.[2] Second, as China prepares to implement measures to clean up the portfolios of large state-owned commercial banks, the design of asset management companies and other measures for resolving bad debts have raised questions about the appropriate fiscal contribution, highlighting the large hidden liabilities inherited from the planned economy. And, third, to strengthen the social safety nets in order to support an accelerated program of restructuring state-owned enterprises (SOEs) and the economic slowdown, the central government made special appropriations in 1998 and 1999 to bail out local social security schemes, focusing attention on the contingent liabilities associated with these schemes.

The focus on fiscal risks is long overdue in China. Like other transition economies, the budget in China is not comprehensive, and the government undertakes substantial activity off-budget, such as directing bank loans to favored enterprises and investment projects. Some of these activities have produced significant off-budget liabilities for the government, to which must be added past contingent liabilities that generate claims on future budgets. Moreover, even though China's explicit public debt is relatively modest—with about 22 percent of GDP in domestic debt and 4 percent of GDP in medium- and long-term external debt in 2000[3]—the government's revenue capacity is also small; the budget is only 15 percent of GDP (as of 2000), and the portion under the central government is only half.

This chapter begins by assessing the fiscal risk of contingent liabilities in China. It then relates them to fiscal stability and identifies major measures critical to managing fiscal risks. Finally, it discusses the institutional context in which contingent liabilities are created and need to be managed.

An Assessment

Sources of Risk

China is faced with several potential obligations that could pose a significant fiscal risk: banking and nonbanking financial sector contingent liabilities; pension liabilities; foreign public and publicly guaranteed debt; and liabilities from private participation in infrastructure.

Financial Sector. The contingent liabilities in the banking sector represent *implicit* liabilities.[4] However, within the banking sector the nature of the implicit obligation differs. The largest category applies to the four large commercial banks owned by the central government. These big four are major deposit-takers whose likely loan losses far exceed any provisioning. Because they are state-owned, the implicit guarantee for depositors and other creditors is strong. Risks include some exposure to weak real estate markets, but they mainly reflect quasi-fiscal lending and financial weakness in the domestic corporate sector. The state-owned enterprise reforms to date have failed to stem losses sufficiently. Unfavorable global and domestic economic developments are putting further pressure on the financial performance of enterprises, including foreign-invested and nonstate firms. To date, the central government has taken on the task of covering the losses. A recapitalization exercise for the four large state-owned banks was carried out in 1998 through the injection of the proceeds from the issuance of special Treasury bonds. But this exercise was not based on loan classification, interest accrual, and loss provisioning standards that meet international best practices. Further in 1999, the central

government announced plans to establish asset management companies to remove part of the bad loans from these four large banks, with
the first pilot established in April. The state also has an implicit liability with respect to the financial performance of the state-owned policy
banks established in 1994. For example, the agricultural banks have
"grain debts," accumulated losses in grain procurement and distribution as well as diversion to nongrain businesses, which are not backed
by grain stocks or covered by sufficient budgetary allocations. The
China Development Bank's largely infrastructure portfolio is not subject to adequate risk analysis and provisioning. However, these banks'
portfolios are dwarfed by those of the commercial banks.

In addition to those in the state-owned banking sector, implicit liabilities are associated with weaknesses in regional and city commercial banks. Other parts of the financial system also have a high
proportion of nonperforming assets. Many nonbank financial intermediaries that have developed alongside the traditional banking sector since the mid-1980s have taken high risks; trust and investment
companies (which account for 3 percent of China's financial assets)
are one example. Two-thirds of rural credit cooperatives (which account for 10 percent of China's financial assets) are reportedly in very
weak financial positions.

The stated principle is that the central government is fiscally responsible for state financial institution failures, and local governments
are fiscally responsible for failures of local ones. In practice, though,
this principle has worked only in certain circumstances. In some cases,
the central bank or the state-owned banks take on the obligations to
small depositors in the absence of matching performing assets. In the
closures of small troubled financial institutions over the last couple of
years, the Chinese authorities have de facto protected depositors, even
where deposit-taking was technically illegal. Indirectly, the central
government, which owns the central bank and the state-owned banks,
has incurred fiscal costs. Yet there is clearly a difference in perception
among depositors as to the strength of the implicit central government
guarantee, as reflected in a spate of localized runs on rural credit cooperatives and a decline in the share of bank deposits held by the non-
state-owned banks. The complex policy question likely to emerge
increasingly will be how to allocate the fiscal burden when there is
significant overlap or the decisions by one part of the government
affect outcomes in the rest of the economy because of financial sector
contagion or social stability concerns. In addition, almost all local,
non-state-owned banks were licensed by either the head or local offices of the central bank (before the reorganization that reduced the
control of local governments over the central bank's branches), raising
the question of the responsibility of the central government, because
central bank branches were party to the licensing and inadequate

supervision of weak local financial institutions. Thus, in an assessment of fiscal risk, this situation implies that the central government cannot rule out an additional fiscal burden associated with such local government financial institutions.

Pension Liabilities. In China, the pension system constitutes an implicit contingent liability for the government or enterprise running the pay-as-you-go (PAYG) pension scheme. Pension liabilities are included in this analysis of contingent liabilities, however, because there are risks of additional fiscal costs to the government if it ultimately must pay the pensions out of other revenue streams, depending on the nature and extent of the reforms to the pension scheme. Faced with a rapidly aging population, the government has recognized the current system as nonviable, has made significant progress in moving from an enterprise-based system to a pooled system, and is planning to make a transition from the present PAYG system to a funded, multipillar one.[5]

In principle, the responsibility for contingencies associated with pension liabilities is that of local governments (municipal and provincial). A complex issue arises, however, when national concerns about mitigating inequity or maintaining social stability are threatened. For example, the central government provided support to the provinces in both 1998 and 1999 to cover those whose collections were less than disbursements, and the provinces extended similar support to localities strapped for financing. At the same time, the central government rightly is unwilling to extend an explicit guarantee so long as it has no control over its potential exposure. With administration decentralized to a municipal and often corporate level, special early retirements discretionary, and benefit levels still subject to decentralized wage calculations, the possibilities for abuse are obvious. Strengthening mechanisms for control will be essential to clarifying the nature of government responsibility.

Foreign Public and Publicly Guaranteed Debt. Total public and publicly guaranteed debt as recorded by the State Administration for Foreign Exchange exceeds the external debts of government. This represents an explicit contingent liability in addition to the direct liability. Moreover, additional foreign debt with the explicit or implicit guarantee of local governments but without official registration at the State Administration for Foreign Exchange has come to light over the past year, in particular as part of the clampdown on the financial activities of the troubled international trust and investment corporations. The authorities have issued several statements in recent years warning investors that unauthorized external borrowings would not be guaranteed by the central government. Nevertheless, the closure and bankruptcy in late 1998 of the Guangdong International Trust and Investment

Corporation, the second largest foreign debt-issuing international trust and investment company in China, sent a strong signal to markets that the Chinese government was not implicitly guaranteeing all external obligations of Chinese entities. However, the experience of other countries indicates that the fiscal authorities may be called upon to honor short-term debts in the event of a short-term loss of confidence in order to circumvent a more prolonged crisis.

Private Participation in Infrastructure Projects. China has followed the global trend of growing private investment in infrastructure, particularly in power plants and highways. Regulatory constraints, however, have so far limited private investment in power distribution and transmission and in water distribution and sanitation systems. The fact that large projects require approval by the State Development Planning Commission (SDPC) probably has held contingent liabilities associated with foreign investment to a minimum, because the SDPC has taken a cautious approach to government assumption of risk. Most projects with private participation are at the provincial and municipal levels. Anecdotal evidence suggests that these projects are being broken down into units of less than $30 million to avoid the regulatory gaze of the SDPC. At these local levels, it is more common to have guaranteed rates of return on investment in power and transport, which represent contingent liabilities for those levels of government. While a few of the provincial power projects are 100 percent foreign–owned, the majority are jointly owned by foreign and Chinese interests, with the latter holding the majority of shares in most cases. The situation is similar in transport and water.

Size of Risks Associated with Contingent Liabilities

The size of China's contingent liabilities is likely to be significant. Incorporating them into calculations of fiscal debt would imply multiples of government debt as currently narrowly defined and reported. Illustrative estimates have been carried out for the following significant sources of risk: state-owned banks, the pension system, and foreign borrowings. Roughly measured more comprehensively, World Bank estimates of the Chinese government's debt rise from the comparatively low level of about 11 percent of GDP to levels comparable with the narrow government debt ratios of middle- and higher-income countries. The impact of contingencies on debt levels should give pause to those evaluating fiscal risk based on the narrow fiscal position.

Illustrative Estimates of Contingent Liabilities Associated with State-owned Commercial Banks. Regardless of the measures taken to prevent future contingent liabilities associated with state-owned commercial banks, a major fiscal burden cannot be avoided. For one thing, policies and institutional measures clearly are critical to reducing the flow of increased bad loans, but the estimates made here refer to inherited bad loans. These illustrative estimates assume that any contribution of fiscal resources is conditioned on thorough and credible financial, operational, and managerial restructuring and efforts to stem the flow of additional quasi-fiscal loans that are deemed impaired. Otherwise, this sector could well represent an even greater eventual drain on fiscal resources. Second, there is probably only limited scope for spreading the burden of bad loans across other agents. For example, the initial burden is usually taken by the bank owners through loss of equity, but in China's case the large banks are state-owned.

An illustrative range for the contingent liabilities is measured by estimating the magnitude of nonperforming loans in the banking system, the recovery rate on loans, and the size of the banking system, as shown in Table 10.1.

A previous official estimate of nonperforming loans in the banking system of about 25 percent of GDP was based on the standardized classification system prevailing in 1995. The actual level is probably significantly higher than this, not only because of the introduction of a new classification system that conforms more closely to international standards but also because other countries' experience indicates that banking crises reveal higher losses than supervisory estimates.[6]

An earlier official estimate (in 2000) of 6 percent of loan losses implies an official assumption of a 70 percent recovery rate, or a 30 percent loan loss rate. However, based on experience in other countries, a more likely range is 10–40 percent recovery, or a 60–90 percent loan loss rate. Experience with collateral foreclosure and liquidation indicates that, even in those cases with economies of scale and a framework for asset sales, such as selling bundles of loans (Resolution Trust Corporation in the United States) or encouraging overseas

Table 10.1 Illustrative Loan Losses, China
(percent of GDP)

Recovery rate	70	40	20	10
Loan loss rate (100 = recovery rate)	30	60	80	90
Nonperforming loan level				
25	6 (official)	13	17	
40	10	20	27	31
60	15	31	40	46
80	20	41	54	

Note: Table is based on the loans of the four large state-owned banks, representing 85 percent of GDP.

investors willing to take risks in a particular industry or enterprise (Thai Financial Restructuring Authority's auction of hire-purchase car loans), recovery rates were about 70 percent and 50 percent, respectively. Experience with recovery on unsecured corporate lending is more elusive, let alone in those transition economies where the private sector is less developed. For example, Mexico's asset management company, in a very unsuccessful case, had to take assets from banks that continued to operate, and it has sold less than 1 percent of the assets transferred. The asset management company in the Philippines, set up in 1987 to deal with a diverse range of assets, including restructuring large state enterprises, is still in operation today and has disposed of only 50 percent of the transferred assets. In Central European banking reforms, recovery rates have been in the 34–40 percent range.

Finally, the loans of the four large state-owned commercial banks account for 85 percent of GDP. The loans of all deposit money banks, including medium-size banks and urban and rural credit cooperatives, account for 111 percent of GDP.

Although these are speculative estimates that make a number of assumptions, they indicate the importance of this contingency's fiscal implications. For example, if 40 percent of state bank commercial loans were nonperforming and only 40 percent of the original value can be recovered, the loss would be about 20 percent of GDP. If this same condition holds for all money center banks, the loss would be about 25 percent of GDP. If 60 percent of the state bank commercial loans were nonperforming and only 20 percent of the original value can be recovered, the loss would be about 40 percent of GDP. The loss would be the same magnitude if, for example, 40 percent were nonperforming with only 10 percent recovery.

Given the uncertain nature of the central government's liability for contingent liabilities in other parts of the financial system, there has been no attempt to provide illustrative estimates for these.

Illustrative Estimates of Implicit Pension Liabilities. These estimates draw on simulations carried out in an earlier World Bank study (World Bank 1997a). One estimate is based on a cash flow approach, which indicates transition costs to the budget of anywhere from zero to 1.5 percent of GDP during the period of time under consideration.

Another estimate is based on the net present value of the fraction of implicit pension debt (IPD) that is not envisaged under current policy to be financed through pension sector reform options. The size of the implicit pension debt—that is, the present value of benefits that have to be paid to current pensioners plus the present value of pension rights that current workers have already earned and would have to be paid if the system were stopped today—was estimated at about 40 percent of GDP as of 1995.[7] If one assumes additional coverage of workers under the scheme, a portion of whose contributions would be to the mandatory basic scheme, the estimate would be reduced to about 15 percent of GDP (World Bank 1997a: Table 3.9). Because the analysis was carried out in 1995, these estimates may well underrepresent the liability, which likely continued to grow faster than GDP during the decade. This analysis also assumes that the necessary steps are taken in terms of retirement age, benefit levels, collection enforcement, and returns on investments of pension surplus funds to ensure the financial viability of the first (basic benefit from social pool) and second (supplemental benefit from funded individual account) pillars going forward. This option is only illustrative of the kinds of adjustments that would affect the contingent liability. However, it reflects the importance of the pension system contingency to longer-term fiscal risk.

Illustrative Estimates of Contingent Liabilities Associated with Foreign Public and Publicly Guaranteed Debt. At year-end 1997 the external debts of the Chinese government as reported by the Ministry of Finance stood at US$72.5 billion. However, the total public and publicly guaranteed long-term and short-term debt registered with the State Administration for Foreign Exchange stood at $117 billion, so that the government has an explicit contingent liability of $44.5 billion in addition to its direct liability, or about 5 percent of GDP. There may be unregistered debt that is guaranteed by local governments, which could turn into implicit liabilities for the central government (for example, see the discussion of international trust and investment corporations below).

Illustrative Estimates of Contingent Liabilities Associated with Private Participation in Infrastructure Projects. As a reference, total foreign investment in power, transport, and water is under US$30 billion, or well under 5 percent of GDP.[8] Because contingent liabilities are only a small fraction of the investments in those sectors where there has been some private participation, the aggregate potential liability is relatively modest at present. However, it may pose concentrated risks in certain localities. Anecdotal evidence suggests that some problems are already beginning to surface. For example, slow growth in 1999 caused in some instances a default in guarantees of the minimum offtake of electricity.

Risk Analysis

To analyze the fiscal risk implied by these contingent liabilities, we used a fiscal rules approach augmented by inclusion of the liability estimates. The balance sheet method was considered, because it encompasses not only liabilities but also assets. This is attractive in the case of China given that—in addition to contingent liabilities—the government has at its disposal significant real assets that could be liquidated—for example, in the form of divestiture to the private sector. However, in the China case, the balance sheet method was found too informationally demanding to be applied.

The fiscal rules approach is captured in a debt dynamics analysis.[9] The estimates of the size of contingent liabilities are summarized into one of two variables, stock of debt or annual cash flow expenditure supplements. Debt dynamics analysis is then carried out based on narrowly defined fiscal numbers, and again based on more comprehensive definitions of stock of debt or annual expenditures incorporating contingent liabilities. This enables a comparison, and thus an analysis, of the implications for fiscal risk of considering contingent liabilities.

Conclusion

This analysis leads to four conclusions about risk management in China. First, the implied level of public liabilities taking contingent liabilities into account is multiples of the narrowly defined stock of public debt without taking these into account, which is the shorter bar at the far right of Figure 10.1.

Second, these levels of public liabilities taking contingencies into account are not that out of line with comparators in medium- and high-income countries because of the low level of explicit debt and debt servicing. Based on a narrow definition of public debt (thereby excluding contingent liabilities in those countries), the average debt-to-GDP ratio for middle- and high-income countries in 1995 was 39.9 percent and 60.7 percent, respectively (World Bank 1997b, 1998).

Third, the central government revenue-generating capacity is out of line with the comparators. This makes a strong case, from the perspective of macromanagement, for some *recentralization* of fiscal management in China in contrast to worldwide trends. These points are illustrated in Figure 10.2.

Fourth, progress on structural reforms is key to managing fiscal risks. Three major areas are the banking system, the pension system, and budget management. Banking reform aimed at stemming the further accumulation of bad debts is essential. Reform of the pension system should aim at financing the implicit pension debt and strengthening the financial viability of the system going forward. Strengthening the capacity of government to manage public resources, including mobilizing central revenues, making the budget more comprehensive, as well as rationalizing the balance of central and local responsibilities and resources, is essential to meeting the government's huge contingent liabilities in the future.

Figure 10.1. Stock of Debt as Percent of GDP, China, Illustrative Estimates for Year-End 1997

Percent of GDP

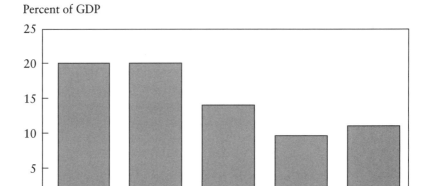

Source: World Bank staff estimates.

Figure 10.2. Stock of Debt and Central Government Revenue, China and Middle-Income and High-Income Countries

Percent of GDP

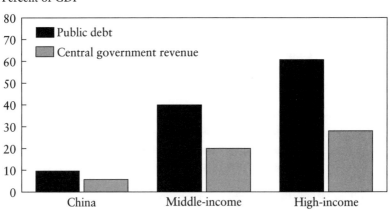

Source: World Bank staff estimates.

Various scenarios using the debt dynamics framework can be used to illustrate these points. For example, illustrative scenarios suggest that without reducing the accumulation of bad debts in the banking system, debt ratios could explode.[10] Three alternative assumptions are: the continued accumulation of bad loans at the past rate; at the other extreme, immediate cessation of quasi-fiscal lending through the banking system and no further accumulation; or a feasible reform option of gradual adjustment in quasi-fiscal lending with a steady decline and eventual elimination. Under the first scenario, the stock of debt continues to grow in an unbounded way. Under the second scenario, the debt-to-GDP ratios fall off quickly as does the share of central government revenue taken to cover interest costs. Under the third "baseline" scenario assumptions, the stock of debt continues to climb but peaks in a few years, declining thereafter, with primary balances turning positive. Note, however, that although declining, the share of interest in central government revenue would remain high throughout this period (35–50 percent). Also, a number of downside factors may be highly correlated. China could face lower growth, less robustness of revenues, high loan losses in state-owned banks, and additional depositor guarantee obligations from other worsening financial institutions. These possibilities further suggest the urgency of tackling the enterprise performance problems and banking sector transformation underlying financial sector weakness.[11]

Institutional Setting for Creating and Managing Fiscal Risks

Information and Accountability

The minister of finance is responsible for preparing and presenting the budget to the legislature, the National People's Congress (NPC), each year. At present, the budget does not include any information on contingent liabilities. However, the government is accountable to the legislature in explaining any sudden increases in debt. Because of historical experiences, political leaders are acutely aware of the inflationary risks associated with a large fiscal imbalance, and thus any proposed adjustments are heavily debated and scrutinized.

An apt example is related to the recapitalization of the four large state-owned commercial banks, which was a decision that reflected in part the contingent liabilities embedded in the financial sector. In the interim between the annual budget exercises, the Ministry of Finance consulted with the NPC's economic and finance committee and then made a special submission to seek the NPC's approval before issuance of the special Treasury bonds used to carry out this transaction.

Awareness of the costs of hidden and contingent liabilities has already led to some demands for change in China. For example, responding in part to recent concerns about fiscal sustainability and in part to the auditor-general's harsh criticisms of budget implementation, in June 1999 the National People's Congress ordered the Ministry of Finance to strengthen budget processes, increase the transparency and accountability of public spending, and disclose publicly all intergovernmental transfers by province. The Ministry of Finance has taken this as an opening to introduce some planned reforms to the budget system, the first step of which was to require government ministries and departments to report all resources and spending, including budgetary and extrabudgetary accounts. More reforms are planned over the next few years to improve information flows and strengthen accountability. They include: introducing Treasury management, revising the system of budget classification, strengthening budget forecasting, changing the budget cycle and consultation processes, and strengthening monitoring and audit procedures.

Policy Practice and Risk Management Capabilities

Policy practice and risk management capabilities are still quite limited in China as in many other developing countries. A further complication is that the transition process from a centrally planned to a socialist market economy results in explicit and implicit involvement of the government—and the party—throughout the economy, thereby further blurring lines of responsibility. However, there is a growing awareness of the importance, and the complexities, of managing certain components of fiscal risk associated with contingent liabilities.

One recent change in the government's policy practice was a clarification of the rules of the game for sovereign responsibility for semiofficial financial activities. As mentioned above, the cleanup effort among nonbank financial intermediaries accelerated in 1998 with the closure of several prominent ones. This move began to establish limits on sovereign responsibility and challenged previously held assumptions about the extent of liabilities of the state. Meanwhile, the central government had to withstand considerable pressure from local governments, foreign financiers, and others. The difficulties of the international trust and investment corporations have prompted markets to increasingly differentiate between sovereign and nonsovereign entities in China. In light of the complexities revealed during this experience, the government is continuing to examine its policies in this area.

Regarding pension liabilities, in designing measures to address the immediate and urgent problem of funding pensions for employees of distressed state-owned enterprises, the government is cognizant of the moral hazard issues. As noted, the government has recognized the importance of improving administration in order to enhance internal controls before extending an explicit guarantee. It consolidated responsibility for social insurance in March 1998 under the Ministry of Labor and Social Security.

As for private participation in infrastructure, the central government, as noted, has been quite prudent about the risks it will assume and is working with the World Bank (and others) to modify its practices in light of experiences emerging from the East Asian financial crisis. However, the government still faces the challenge of strengthening the legal and regulatory framework that guides infrastructure developments at all levels of government, with adoption of competitive procedures for the award of concessions, so that investors will be less likely to demand guarantees.

In conclusion, China faces high fiscal risks associated with contingent liabilities of the financial sector, the fiscal obligations arising from reform of state-owned enterprises and the social security system, and the problematic fiscal relations between the central and local governments. Clearly, the government's ability to manage these fiscal risks depends largely on how it addresses these problems. Expanding on conventional fiscal analysis and putting these problems into a broader fiscal context may help reinforce the importance of addressing them. One legacy of the planned economy is that the Ministry of Finance is a relatively weak institution: it is not in charge of formulating a comprehensive budget; it is not empowered by law to be the sole manager of public funds and assets; and the budget process is not well-designed to ensure efficiency of public spending. A comprehensive reform of the budget system is essential for strengthening the institutional arrangements for managing fiscal risks. Given that the necessary reforms will redistribute power and resources across ministries and departments, however, the process will likely be protracted and difficult and will require commitment from the highest levels of China's political structure.

Notes

1. This chapter represents the views of the authors and not necessarily those of the World Bank. The authors are grateful to Li Xiaoshi, Xie Ping, Li Keping, Guo Xiangjun, Peng Longyun, Bill Easterly, Hana Polackova Brixi, and Estelle James for their invaluable comments during seminars held in Beijing and consultations held in Washington, D.C., and to Wei Ding, E. C. Hwa, Tom Richardson, Richard Scurfield, and JoAnn Paulson for their contributions to the work. We also are indebted to Luo Guangqin and Liu Li-gang for invaluable administrative support and research assistance.

248   KRUMM AND WONG

This chapter is based on work carried out by the World Bank China program in collaboration with the Ministry of Finance of the People's Republic of China in late 1998 through mid-1999, as summarized in World Bank (1999). The International Monetary Fund also participated in the work.

2. In addition to the budgeted fiscal deficit, a supplementary fiscal package was announced in late 2000 for western region development.

3. See World Bank (2001). The figure for the domestic public sector debt includes Treasury bonds, as well as policy financial bonds and other financial bonds (end-period outstanding).

4. In the early 2000s, liquidity has not been the issue. The core of the state-owned banking sector remains liquid even if nonperforming loans are substantial and growing. Deposits have continued to grow, with substantial excess reserves held with the central bank. The domestic savings rate is high, and there are few alternative saving vehicles to banking institutions. In the current environment of deflationary concerns, the policy concern is the reverse—namely, that households are reluctant to consume. Liquidity is also stronger than it otherwise would be because banks have been hesitant to lend.

5. A State Council decision of August 1998 sets out the basic parameters—namely, (a) provide a mandatory basic public benefit for a redistributive role, with pooling to be extended from the municipal to the provincial and ultimately to the national level; (b) establish mandatory individual accounts, though these accounts are largely unfunded currently; and (c) encourage establishment of supplementary, voluntary individual accounts.

6. In 2001 the chairman of the Bank of China, one of the four state-owned commercial banks, revealed a higher estimate of nonperforming loans, and the level in the other banks likely exceeds that of the Bank of China.

7. The IPD estimates were based on the current features of the system (retirement ages of 55 for women and 60 for men, replacement rates of 80 percent for retirement and 40 percent for disability, and real wage indexation of 50 percent). Additional assumptions include projected wage increases at an annual rate of 5 percent during 2000–2010 and 4 percent during 2011–2030; discount rates at 5 percent during 2000–2010 and 4 percent during 2011–2030. The IPD is even larger if pension contributions are lost through mismanagement or fraud, which appears to be a significant problem in the current fragmented, locally managed systems.

8. Estimates of foreign investment are on the order of US$15 billion in the power sector, $11.5 billion in transport, and probably less than $0.5 billion in water treatment facilities.

9. The International Monetary Fund participated in the World Bank work on this issue. The debt dynamics framework draws substantially from Tsibouris, 1998/99).

10. These scenarios make a number of assumptions, including a two-percentage-point improvement in revenue capacity; no change in the central-local government share of those revenues; real GDP growth in the 6–8 percent

range; and loan losses in the state banking sector ranging from 20 to 40 percent of GDP.

11. In this regard, the policy guidelines announced by the Party Central Committee in September 1999 focused heavily on SOE reform.

References

Tsibouris, George. 1998/99. "Fiscal Sustainability in China." IMF Working Paper. International Monetary Fund, Washington, D.C.

World Bank. 1997a. *China 2020: Old Age Security.* Washington, D.C.

———. 1997b. *World Development Report.* Washington, D.C.

———. 1998. *World Development Indicators.* Washington, D.C.

———. 1999. "China: Weathering the Storm and Learning the Lessons." Country Economic Memorandum. Washington, D.C.

———. 2001. "China Update." Beijing, March.

CHAPTER 11

Dealing with Contingent Liabilities in Indonesia and Thailand

Hana Polackova Brixi and Sudarshan Gooptu
World Bank

AMONG THE EAST ASIAN COUNTRIES, Indonesia and Thailand belong to those most heavily hit by the 1997 financial crisis. Their experience has only confirmed how rapidly government contingent liabilities can turn into actual liabilities, how dearly they have to be paid for, and what serious consequences they have for the fiscal and overall economic performance of a country for many years into the future.

In both Indonesia and Thailand, government debt as a share of the gross domestic product (GDP) more than tripled during 1997–2000 (the situation was similar in Korea and, to a lesser degree, in Malaysia). Most of the increase came from implicit government guarantees to the financial sector (as a cost of recapitalizing the banking sector), from explicit government guarantees in power and road sectors (in the form of government outlays to honor "take-or-pay" contracts), and from government credit guarantees to enterprises that had been called.

Although the governments dealt with obligations that came due after the 1997 shake-up, new fiscal risks emerged as a consequence. This chapter focuses on the risks facing the governments of Indonesia and Thailand at the end of 2000, builds an illustrative stress scenario for Indonesia, analyzes the largest risks facing the government of Thailand, and describes the strategies that have been adopted by these governments to prevent and deal with fiscal risks in the future.[1]

Analyzing the Overall Government
Risk Exposure in Indonesia

As a result of the 1997 crisis, Indonesia's government entered the new millennium facing two major sources of fiscal risks. One was related to the large portfolio of government debt; the other was related to government programs, some in the form of contingent support, whose cost may suddenly rise.

Government debt increased from US$53 billion (23 percent of GDP) before the crisis to about $134 billion (83 percent of GDP) in early 2000. Almost three-quarters of the increase in debt is new domestic debt arising from the financial crisis—$72 billion in bonds issued to recapitalize banks and to compensate Bank Indonesia for liquidity credits. This rise in debt is the combined result of past policy mistakes and the economic crisis, not new spending. Debt service obligations (interest and amortization) are projected at over 40 percent of government revenue for several years. Moreover, the government's debt service is subject to serious risks, because about one-half of the government debt portfolio is denominated in foreign currency, and a majority of the domestic debt had interest payments flexibly linked to the domestic interest rates and inflation (see Table 11.1). Thus an increase in the domestic interest rates, depreciation of the rupiah, and inflation, as well as new debt needed to account for past or new policy mistakes, would significantly increase the cost of the government's future debt service.

As for the unexpected spending pressures, these may arise from possible social or political pressures and from off-budget obligations associated with financial institutions, state-owned enterprises, independent government agencies, and subnational governments. The like-

Table 11.1 Domestic Government Debt, Indonesia,
December 1998–June 2000
(cumulative, trillions of rupiah)

	Variable-rate bonds	Fixed-rate bonds	Inflation indexed bonds	Hedge bonds	Total
Dec. 1998	0	0	100	0	20
March 1999	0	0	165	0	165
June 1999	95	9	218	0	322
Sept. 1999	95	9	218	0	322
Dec. 1999	204	51	218	27	500
March 2000	204	53	218	25	500
June 2000	330	59	218–253	29	636–671

Sources: Ministry of Finance and World Bank estimates.

lihood of these pressures actually resulting in additional government expenditures would depend heavily on the government's commitment to prudent and transparent fiscal management.

The Portfolio of Government Fiscal Risks

The Fiscal Risk Matrix in Table 11.2 illustrates the sources of future possible pressures on government finances in Indonesia. The largest contingent liabilities relate to the banking sector (the government's explicit guarantee on interbank claims and an implicit commitment to recapitalize large state-owned banks and maintain a stable financial system). Sources of fiscal risk also include the power sector (concerns about excess power generation capacity and the unsolicited, long-term take-or-pay contracts signed with some of the 26 independent power producers before the crisis),[2] the pension system,[3] and credit programs and guarantees vis-à-vis the private sector.[4]

The Fiscal Hedge Matrix in Table 11.3 summarizes potential sources of government financial security—that is, sources of future revenues that may become available to the government to meet its obligations. Among these, the largest is the value of assets collected by the Indonesian Bank Restructuring Agency (IBRA), an asset management company established by the government after the 1997 crisis.

Both obligations and sources of financial safety are sensitive to various factors. Recovery of IBRA assets, for example, requires the workout and sale of nonperforming loans and sale of equity, some of which was previously owned by powerful individuals. Thus the recovery rate would depend on the extent of investor confidence and government commitment.[5]

Overall, the leading factors affecting the potential fiscal costs arising from the government's obligations and its capacity to meet them in the future can be summarized as follows. First, *investor confidence* is vital for the government to successfully recover an estimated IDR207 trillion from asset sales by IBRA and raise revenues from privatizing state-owned enterprises. It is also critical for renewed growth, keeping interest rates down, achieving government tax revenue targets, and establishing a successful domestic bond market. Investor confidence, in turn, will depend on prudent fiscal and monetary policies, sound market institutions, and transparency in government decisionmaking.

Second, *domestic interest rates* in Indonesia strongly affect the cost of debt service and the size of likely off-budget losses. A one-percentage-point increase in the SBI (Bank Indonesia certificate) rate would increase the cost of servicing the domestic debt by about 0.3 percent of GDP annually (IDR4 trillion). An increase in domestic interest rates would weaken government credit programs[6] and increase likely

Table 11.2 Fiscal Risk Matrix, Indonesia

Sources of obligations	Direct liabilities (obligation in any event)	Contingent liabilities (obligation if a particular event occurs)
Explicit Government liability as recognized by a law or contract	• Sovereign debt (domestic and external, loans contracted and securities issued by government) • Expenditures—nondiscretionary and legally binding in the long term (salaries and pensions of civil servants, minimum benefits under the pay-as-you-go pension scheme Taspen)	• Blanket guarantee on bank depositors (cost IDR600 trillion during 1997–99) • Guarantee on interbank claims • Umbrella government guarantees for nonsovereign borrowing by small and medium-size enterprises, farmers, BULOG (government rice procurement company), and other entities • Trade and exchange rate guarantees via the Export Bank, INDRA (Indonesian Debt Restructuring Agency), and other entities
Implicit A moral obligation of government that reflects public and interest group pressures	• Future recurrent costs of public investment projects and other discretionary expenditures	• Losses associated with take-or-pay contracts of public utility companies • Support to enterprises (government possibly covering losses and assuming nonguaranteed obligations of state-owned or private enterprises) • Subsidies related to the pricing of rice and regulated oil products via BULOG and PERTAMINA (state oil company) • Possible need for further recapitalization of any banks that fail to reach the 8 percent capital asset ratio by year-end 2001 • Possible need for further recapitalization of Bank Indonesia • Possible spillover of subnational government obligations to the central government

Note: Estimates of the future potential revenues are reflected in the stress scenario depicted in Figure 11.1.

Source: World Bank staff.

Table 11.3 Fiscal Hedge Matrix, Indonesia

Sources of financial safety	Direct sources of safety (based on the stock of existing assets)	Contingent sources of safety (dependent on future events, such as value generated in the future)
Explicit Based on government legal powers (ownership and the right to raise revenues)	• IBRA (asset management company) assets recovery (workout and sales of nonperforming loans and sales of equity) • Privatization of state-owned enterprises and other public resources	• Government revenues from oil and gas • Tax revenues less revenue committed to subnational governments • Savings from cuts of discretionary expenditures, such as subsidies • Hedging instruments and (re-)insurance policies purchased by the government from financial institutions • Recovery of loans made by government to public enterprises
Implicit Based on government indirect control	• Bank Indonesia's reserves to the extent of positive net worth (adjusted for their liquidity and currency risk)	• Future profits of state-owned enterprises and agencies under government control

Source: World Bank staff.

corporate and banking sector losses that could in turn increase government obligations.

Third, *political actions* can significantly alter the size of off-budget obligations and the revenues from asset sales. For example, a soft stance vis-à-vis large banks or enterprises could result in further bank recapitalization costs and reduce IBRA revenues. Indirectly, any perceptions among market participants that there is a lack of political will in dealing with the complex issues emerging from the ongoing process of corporate and financial restructuring may tend to undermine the return of investor confidence.

Furthermore, *policy actions* directly affect government revenues (for example, through tax exemptions), current expenditures (such as subsidies on petroleum products, electricity, and rice), and potential future expenditures (such as potential liabilities arising from credit programs; the operations of BULOG, the government rice procurement company;

and power projects). A failure to maintain fiscal discipline, which could happen with the implementation of fiscal decentralization, would increase government debt.

Fourth, *operational risks* pervade fiscal and debt management arrangements. A shortage of trained staff in many aspects of fiscal risk and debt management, together with inadequate information and institutional arrangements within government, gives rise to the likelihood of making misjudgments and poor implementation decisions. For example, an audit of Bank Indonesia in 2000 revealed that the bank did not correctly implement the bank recapitalization scheme and as a result actually had negative net worth. Subsequently, the government had to recapitalize Bank Indonesia.

Fifth, *changes in the rupiah* affect external debt service payments, exchange rate guarantees provided by the Export Bank and the Indonesian Debt Restructuring Agency (INDRA), and liquidity and solvency problems of banks with large foreign debts. This effect on expenditures is partly offset by changes in oil revenues and the market value of export companies under IBRA control. Deregulation of domestic fuel prices would increase the offsetting effect that oil price has on fiscal balances. Cross-currency risk, particularly the risk of yen appreciation, is significant, because 39 percent of government foreign debt is denominated in yen and Indonesia has a large (US$1 billion) deficit in yen-denominated trade. A 10 percent appreciation of the yen would increase government debt by nearly $2.3 billion.

Sixth, *commodity price changes*, particularly for oil and rice, affect government finances. The budget deficit falls by about 0.1 percent of GDP for every US$1 rise in the oil price (World Bank 1999). An increase in the price of rice affects the government budget through BULOG losses.[7]

The baseline scenario for Indonesia for 2000 appeared to be that of relative stability and gradual overcoming of the government debt burden. This scenario, however, assumed that the government takes the actions needed to have investor confidence return and to achieve renewed economic growth. Should the government fail to take the needed actions, or should other factors negatively affect, for example, investor confidence, a different scenario would become reality in consequence. To illustrate such a possible scenario, the interplay of its underlying factors and its potential fiscal cost, a hypothetical stress scenario is built below.

A Stress Scenario

By simulating the possible impact of a sudden decline in investor confidence, Figure 11.1 illustrates the importance of containing off-budget losses and counteracting fiscal risks. This stress scenario assumes that

Figure 11.1. Fiscal Risk Stress Scenario, Indonesia, as of May 2000

Government debt/GDP (percent)

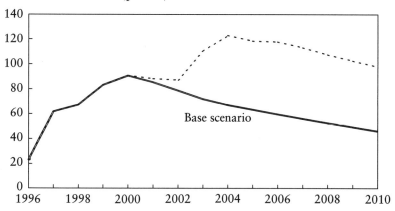

investor confidence declines again in 2003, which is followed by a sudden decline in demand for rupiah and other Indonesian assets. This decline would generate a temporary sharp depreciation of the rupiah (say, 12,000 rupiah per U.S. dollar during 2003–04) and an increase in the domestic interest rate (up to 40 percent in 2003 and 28 percent in 2004). The decline in the value of the rupiah would make imports more expensive and thus generate inflation (up to 30 percent in 2003 and 10 percent in 2004). This loss of confidence and the associated rise in uncertainty would negatively affect overall economic performance (reducing GDP growth from 6 to –2 percent in 2003 and 0 percent in 2004), lead to renewed primary fiscal deficits (5 percent of GDP in 2003 and 2004), generate new off-budget losses through bank recapitalization and other contingent liabilities (up by about IDR100 trillion in 2003 and 2004), and erode revenues from government asset sales. Following this 2003–04 stress, all assumptions are assumed to return to the baseline. The scenario illustrates that a temporary loss of confidence not only would slow down the repayment of government debt, but also could actually result in a further increase in government debt as a share of GDP and thus create an even more difficult debt burden.

Measuring Selected Fiscal Risks in Thailand

Since the 1997 Asian financial crisis, the government of Thailand has faced increasing fiscal risks, particularly in the form of contingent liabilities emerging from the banking and enterprise sectors (Box 11.1).[8] Some of these obligations are of a legal nature (for example, state-guaranteed debt; others reflect policy commitments (for example, the nonguaranteed obligations of state-owned enterprises and revolving funds to sustain price controls). So far, when the state budget has been unable to cover claims arising from these obligations, state-owned enterprises (such as the Royal State Railway of Thailand and state rubber plantation) and extrabudgetary funds (namely, the Sugar Cane Fund) have borrowed further instead. If enterprises and funds incur continued losses, however, this practice of allowing their further borrowings (often with explicit government guarantees) only postpones

---

Box 11.1 Categories of Contingent Liabilities in Thailand

The *explicit contingent liabilities* of the Thai government are commitments that are based on law and contracts (they primarily include guaranteed debt and other liabilities of state-owned enterprises) and the financing needs under price support programs. The Act Empowering the Ministry of Finance to Guarantee, B.E. 2510 (1967), provides the Ministry of Finance with the mandate to issue sovereign guarantees on domestic and external borrowings by government agencies, limited companies that are partly owned by the state, and specialized financial institutions in Thailand, subject to the approval of the cabinet.

Government *implicit contingent liabilities* are commitments that are based on political announcements, public expectations, and possible interest group pressures. In Thailand, these mainly include:

• Obligations of the Financial Institutions Development Fund (FIDF), an agency established by the Bank of Thailand to issue bonds and recapitalize financial institutions, provide liquidity support, and cover deposit insurance claims. (In 2000 the Ministry of Finance asked the Bank of Thailand to refinance THB20 billion of FIDF bonds. The first tranche of these new government bonds with maturity of six years and an 8 percent coupon rate was auctioned in September 2000. This was followed by another tranche of THB14.8 billion with maturity of 11 years and a 7.5 percent coupon rate.)
• Liabilities of extrabudgetary funds.
• Possible negative net worth of Bank of Thailand.
• Losses, nonguaranteed obligations, arrears, and deferred maintenance of state-owned enterprises (including concession agreements of state-owned utilities, arrears of State Railways on fuel bills, and deferred railway track rehabilitation).
• Future possible commitments and obligations of subnational governments (for example, via losses of provincial enterprises).

the need for government direct financing and increases the size of government off-budget obligations.

Given the nature of its contingent liabilities, the government of Thailand has often found it unimportant to distinguish whether the obligations are explicit or implicit. Most explicit and implicit government contingent liabilities directly relate to losses in state banks, specialized financial institutions, and banks in which the government has intervened. Because these institutions already have problems of capitalization, any additional losses will have to be fiscalized in the future. The recapitalization needs of banks will rise further if state-owned enterprises and funds default on their nonguaranteed debt. For example, should the Sugar Cane Fund default on its nonguaranteed debt to the Bank for Agriculture and Agricultural Cooperatives, a new nonperforming loan in the portfolio of this already undercapitalized financial institution would only increase its recapitalization needs. With respect to the financial sector, should the fiscal authorities fail to cover the obligations of the Financial Institutions Development Fund (FIDF, an asset management company that issued bonds to pay for the bad assets of Thai banks) or any future bank recapitalization needs, the Bank of Thailand would do so ex post, thereby running down its net worth. But there does not appear to be an adequate cushion in the Bank of Thailand's net worth to meet this contingency, and eventually public resources would be required to maintain its solvency and credibility. In addition, many enterprises and funds are critical for delivery of public services, such as cheap passenger transport. Therefore, unless policy priorities change the government will eventually pay for the nonguaranteed as well as guaranteed liabilities, arrears, and deferred maintenance of such enterprises and funds.

Obligations vis-à-vis the Banking Sector

In early 2000 it became clear that the cost of past recapitalization programs, largely reflected in the liability portfolio of the FIDF, and the further recapitalization needs of the Thai banking sector would significantly affect the amounts of future government borrowing. The FIDF estimated that the fiscal authorities would need to provide about THB1.1 trillion to cover its liabilities and operating costs. This amount is expected to be paid from new government borrowing during 2000–2005. Other available estimates range from THB1.1 trillion to THB1.4 trillion (World Bank 2000d). This cost would increase with lower recovery rates on nonperforming loans in state banks and intervened banks, higher domestic interest rates, and a lower market value for the four joint venture banks expected to be sold by the government.

On top of the FIDF's financial institution rescue and depositor/creditor protection program, the government is expected to support the recapitalization and subsidy needs of the specialized financial institutions, such as the Government Housing Bank and the Bank for Agriculture and Agricultural Cooperatives. Furthermore, any future costs of protecting depositor funds in private banks, net of insurance and bank fees, would have to be fiscalized. Finally, fiscal risks also have emanated from the structure of the FIDF debt portfolio and the bond issuance strategy.

Debts of State Enterprises

The government has provided guarantees on domestic and external borrowing to most nonfinancial enterprises and to selected financial institutions. At the end of 1999, the stock of guaranteed debt surpassed THB1 trillion (see Figure 11.2). The stock of nonguaranteed debt by nonfinancial state-owned enterprises amounts to nearly THB500 billion (World Bank 2000d). In addition to these reported amounts, several large enterprises have accumulated arrears (for example, on the fuel cost and for deferred maintenance on the State Railway and Bangkok Mass Transit Authority).

In Thailand, the Public Debt Management Office was entrusted with the task of estimating the likely future demands of state-owned enterprises on the government budget. Its approach was to focus on the recent and expected financial and economic performance of enterprises that represent an explicit or implicit fiscal risk for the government. In its analysis, state-owned enterprises were divided into four mutually exclusive risk categories: a risk level of 5 percent for best performers, 25 percent for enterprises likely to make profits, 50 percent for enterprises with fluctuating profit and investment performance, and 90 percent for enterprises that have been showing continued losses or have embarked on very risky projects.[9] For each category, the outstanding liabilities of enterprises were adjusted by their respective risk weights (outstanding liabilities that are either explicitly or implicitly guaranteed by the government were multiplied by the risk level of the respective enterprise).

By aggregating the risk-adjusted amounts of guaranteed liabilities of enterprises, the Public Debt Management Office obtained the total risk-adjusted level of its explicitly and implicitly guaranteed debt. The risk-adjusted amount of guaranteed debt can be interpreted as the net present value of the future expected fiscal cost of government guarantees, or as an amount of reserves the government should have accumulated by the end of 1999 to cover future calls on the budget.[10] To assess likely future increases in the enterprise pressure on the government's budget, we have assigned the respective risk levels also to the repayment schedule of guaranteed debt. Figure 11.2 compares the guaranteed

Figure 11.2. Guaranteed Debt Outstanding and
Its Repayment, Thailand, 1999

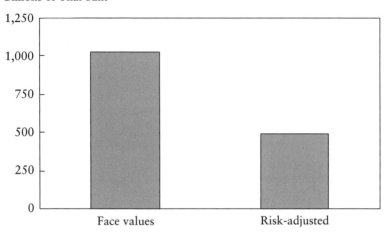

Guaranteed Debt Outstanding

Billions of Thai baht

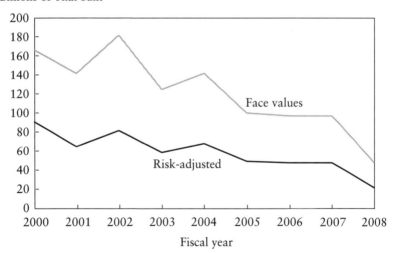

Guaranteed Debt Repayment Schedule

Billions of Thai baht

Note: Includes scheduled principal repayment on domestic and external guaranteed debt and interest payments on external guaranteed debt.

Source: Calculations by the authors based on information provided by Thailand's Public Debt Maintenance Office and Arthur Andersen (2000).

debt repayment schedule in face values with the risk-adjusted amounts. Because many enterprises have relied on short-term borrowing and have held unhedged foreign exposures, government risk exposure rises with increasing interest rates and with depreciation of the baht.[11]

Fiscal risks from state-owned enterprise operations also may emerge from government policy actions (such as price controls that may give rise to operating losses) and their own investment decisions (such as ambitious and risky projects). The State Railway, for example, was actually bankrupt in mid-2000 and required over THB60 billion in public resources just to cover its existing obligations—on top of planned government subsidies to cover its future operating losses and new investments. To a large degree, however, its operating losses and the amount of further possible government obligations depend on the third-class passenger fare, which is regulated by the government.[12] Tables 11.4 and 11.5 illustrate the extent to which the growing bills of the State Railway have necessitated government subsidies, short-term borrowing (mainly overdrafts on bank accounts), arrears (in payments for fuel and payroll), and deferrals (in maintenance and investment). Given the policy commitment of the government, if the State Railway is not able to roll over its credits, obtain new credit and supplies for a promise to pay in the future, and further defer maintenance, government subsidies and credit guarantees will increase.

Table 11.4 Financial Performance and Outlook,
State Railway of Thailand (SRT), 1994–2000
(billions of Thai baht)

	1994	1995	1996	1997	1998	1999[a]	2000[a]
Operating loss	0.51	1.54	1.49	1.64	2.84	6.56	4.77
Reported liabilities	25.63	18.50	21.69	27.36	29.45	35.48[b]	41.52
out of which short-							
term debt	3.49	2.51	4.66	4.90	4.05	6.03	6.04
Deferred main-							
tenance	—	—	—	—	—	32.54[c]	20.08
Arrears	—	—	—	—	2.02[c]	2.16[d]	0

— Not available.

a. Projections.

b. SRT's reported liabilities are almost entirely covered by state guarantees.

c. Track rehabilitation needed to sustain, not expand or upgrade, the existing train traffic. The 2000 budget committed THB12.46 billion.

d. Mainly unpaid fuel cost. The cabinet passed a resolution on November 23, 1999, to pay off the arrears.

Source: Information provided to the authors by SRT and Thailand Development Research Institute.

Table 11.5 Government Cash Flow to State Railway
of Thailand (RT), 1994–2000
(billions of Thai bahts)

	1994	1995	1996	1997	1998	1999[a]	2000[a]
Operating loss compensation	1.16	1.26	1.17	1.16	1.36	1.77	2.78
Loan repayment	0.70	0.74	0.96	0.85	1.04	0.75	1.67
Capital investment	1.65	2.18	0.82	1.45	3.70	2.61	4.26

a. Projections.
Source: Information provided to the authors by SRT and Thailand Development Research Institute.

Developing a Government Risk Management Strategy

During 2000–2001 in Indonesia, any progress in dealing with the existing government fiscal risks was complicated by emerging political and economic imbalances. Furthermore, a clear authority for dealing with fiscal risk had yet to be assigned. Because the responsibility for government debt management was split among several directorates of the Ministry of Finance and Bank Indonesia, even the task of collecting and synthesizing information about the government debt service profile proved difficult to accomplish. Acknowledging the problems, the government considered establishing a single debt management office in the Ministry of Finance and entrusting this office with the management of government direct and contingent liabilities.

To build its strategy and capacity in the management of government debt and fiscal risks, the Indonesian government considered the following three principles. First, the cabinet, in consultation with the parliament, would set the priorities among competing debt management objectives. For example, should the government focus on minimizing the immediate cost of debt service or on minimizing its risk exposure? The debt management office would focus on implementing these government priorities. Given the potentially catastrophic consequences of further increases in debt, the government proposed to place a high priority on reducing the government's risk exposure, ensuring a steady and predictable debt service profile, and enhancing the government's access to debt markets. Specifically, this meant reducing the volatility of debt servicing arising from refinancing risk, currency risk, and interest rate risk and issuing domestic bonds of specific maturities to set a benchmark for the domestic bond market.

Second, the debt management office would develop a capacity to analyze debt management options and their likely consequences. The office was expected to analyze future debt service costs and the debt profile under alternative assumptions, the risks emerging from the government's debt portfolio (refinancing risk, currency risk, interest rate risk), the risks of government contingent liabilities (off-budget pressure emerging from the obligations of state-owned enterprises, banks, independent government agencies, and subnational governments), and the impact of alternative borrowing strategies on the cost and volatility of future debt service.

Third, the debt management office would advise policymakers on the pros and cons of alternative policy choices. As part of this, the office would build awareness of the expected cost of debt service, existing contingent liabilities, and proposed budgetary and off-budget commitments. This would also cover the borrowing and risk exposure of subnational (provincial- and district-level) governments, independent government agencies, and state-owned enterprises.

Progress on this agenda in Indonesia has been slow. Meanwhile, Thailand has embarked on an ambitious program of building government risk management capacity in its Public Debt Management Office, established at the Ministry of Finance in 1999. New legislation entrusted the Debt Office with the primary responsibility for analyzing and actively managing the government's obligations, including its direct and contingent liabilities. Underlying responsibilities included debt service forecasting, cash management, risk management (to address currency, interest rate, funding and refinancing, credit and operational risks, among other things), implementing transactions related to project finance, and monitoring and advising the government on how to deal with its contingent liabilities. In close collaboration with the Bank of Thailand, the Debt Office began to develop a comprehensive, medium-term financial and debt management and risk management strategy for the government to approve and, then, for the Debt Office to implement. The risk management strategy was expected to specify to what extent the government is prepared to take on risks in the form of contingent liabilities and similar obligations and to face associated volatility in its future financing requirement. To take on such new responsibilities, the Debt Office began to build a whole range of systems (including a database for direct and contingent liabilities, risk management models, and cash management systems) and recruit and train staff.

Beyond the improvements at the Thai Public Debt Management Office, broader institutional changes have been launched to support government risk management. For example, in dealing with contingent government liabilities, the Debt Office would need to rely on the close cooperation of several agencies and units of the government and of the Bank of Thailand. It also would need to rely on data collected and information processed by the comptroller general's department and to cooperate with the Fiscal Planning Office and Budget Office. With respect to government contingent liabilities arising in the financial sector, the Debt Office would need to rely on analytical inputs from the Bank of Thailand and the FIDF. In this context, the responsibilities of the Debt Office, Comptroller General's Department, Fiscal Planning Office, and Budget Office in dealing with contingent liabilities would have to be clearly specified. Furthermore, to ensure that the Comptroller General's Department and Debt Office obtain information that is relevant for analyzing and monitoring the risk of contingent liabilities, the minister of finance has sought to update the existing reporting requirements for state-owned enterprises, extrabudgetary funds, and other public sector entities and government agencies. Similarly, the Bank of Thailand was asked to consider enhancing reporting requirements for financial institutions. Finally, the Ministry of Finance called for government guidelines for risk exposure and financial and risk management of state-owned enterprises and other public sector entities. Such guidelines would help the government to better pursue its shareholder interests in state-owned enterprises and would be enforced through government representatives sitting on the boards of directors of enterprises and in the State Audit Office. Interestingly, these guidelines would be quite an innovative approach to dealing with risk-taking in the public sector and possibly would be of interest to other countries.

Notes

1. This chapter draws on several World Bank studies (2000a, 2000b, 2000c, 2000d).

2. Toll roads are mainly financed by domestic banks and, unless generating expected revenues, they deteriorate bank performance. To the extent that they were already part of a bank's nonperforming portfolio during bank recapitalization, they do not represent an additional contingent liability.

3. In 1995 just 12 million workers (less than a fifth of the work force) were enrolled in pension plans. Pension enrollments, however, grew rapidly after the 1997 financial crisis without a corresponding increase in their funding and asset base. The government is legally responsible for financing the civil service employees' pension scheme (Taspen) and does so from its general revenues. Government responsibility for the public pay-as-you-go pension scheme (Jamsostek) is only implicit. Jamsostek has repeatedly reported zero return on its assets (earlier because of the financial crisis, later mainly because of its high administrative cost), making the level of future public pension benefits questionable.

4. For example, in the case of Garuda Indonesia, the state-owned airline, the government decided to take over the repayment of Garuda Indonesia's external debt totaling about US$1.8 billion for the lease of 11 Boeing 737s. This arrangement implied a fiscal cost of $62 million a year, on average, for eight years. Of particular concern can be the off-balance sheet obligations of public sector corporations, which ultimately are the obligations of the government.

5. This relationship has already surfaced through asset management companies in a number of countries, including Mexico and the Philippines. IBRA reported a significant drop in debt collection rates following the Bank Bali scandal in 1999. The book value of IBRA assets is reported to be IDR533 trillion. The average expected recovery rate is about 30–35 percent, which is still high in the context of international experience (Klingebiel 2000).

6. In 2000–01, the government is expected to face a contingent liability of about IDR28 trillion on credits outstanding. For most credits, such as KUT (credit for farming undertakings) and KKPA (credit for primary cooperatives members), the government explicitly covers default risk. The average maturity of these credits is 12 months and the average default risk is 40 percent.

7. BULOG procures domestically produced rice at a price fixed by the government and distributes rice to the poor and the army at low prices.

8. No major sources of fiscal risk (that is, of volatility in government financing and borrowing requirements) have been identified in the portfolio of government assets and revenues. The government seems to face a downward trend rather than volatility in the value of its assets and future revenues.

9. See Arthur Andersen (2000) for the details underlying the assignment of a risk level to each enterprise.

10. In all guarantee contracts the government covers the entire principal and interest payments against all risks.

11. Sensitivity analysis would be needed to determine the extent of the change in government risk exposure with respect to the underlying variables. Unlike in Indonesia, as of 2001 a stress scenario to illustrate the maximum likely fiscal cost of contingent liabilities had not been developed in Thailand.

12. The Thailand Development Research Institute calculated that a gradual increase in the third-class passenger fare by 40 percent would yield nearly THB300 million in 2000 and over THB500 million in 2001. Sixty percent of operations by the State Railway of Thailand is in passenger transport, the fare of which is regulated by the state. The third-class fare, which applies to about 90 percent of passenger transport, has been fixed since 1974. The railway reports about a THB20 billion positive net worth, thanks mainly to the reported value of its net properties of THB43 billion. For details, see Thailand Development Research Institute (1999).

References

The word *processed* describes informally reproduced works that may not be commonly available through libraries.

Arthur Andersen. 2000. "Thailand—The Fiscal Costs of State Enterprises and Private Participation in Infrastructure." Processed.
Klingebiel, Daniela. 2000. "The Use of Asset Management Companies in the Resolution of Banking Crises: Cross-Country Experiences." Policy Research Working Paper 2284. World Bank, Washington, D.C.

Thailand Development Research Institute. 1999. *State Railway of Thailand Short-term Financial Strategy Development Project*. Final Report. Bangkok, June.

World Bank. 1999. "Republic of Indonesia: Second Policy Reform Support Loan." Report No. P-7308-IND. Washington, D.C.

———. 2000a. "Public Spending in a Time of Change." Poverty Reduction and Economic Management Sector Unit, East Asia and Pacific Region. Washington, D.C., April.

———. 2000b. "Thailand: Social and Structural Review." Report No. 19732-TH. Washington, D.C., January 25.

———. 2000c. "Indonesia: Managing Government Debt and Its Risks." Report No. 20436-IND. Washington, D.C.

———. 2000d. "Thailand: Building Government Capacity to Manage Its Debt and Fiscal Risks." Washington, D.C. Processed.

CHAPTER 12

Dealing with Contingent Liabilities in Colombia

Juan Carlos Echeverry,
Verónica Navas, Juan Camilo Gutierrez,
Jorge Enrique Cardona
Government of Colombia

COMPARED WITH THAT OF most South American countries, Colombia's fiscal management was prudent until the mid-1950s.[1] Since then, however, the decentralization of public sector contracts, including those between the government and labor unions, has loosened budget constraints and given rise to large contingent liabilities.

Traditionally, the Colombian government has based its fiscal analysis on the study of deficit dynamics and has explained an unsustainable fiscal stance in terms of growing and persistent deficits. As a consequence, the pursuit of short-term goals, such as immediate deficit reductions, has led to short-sighted fiscal policy decisions, delivering many of the classic examples of fiscal illusion described by Easterly (1999).

In view of the shortcomings and negative consequences of the conventional focus on budget deficits and the benefits to be gained from analyzing a comprehensive balance sheet of the government, the Colombian National Planning Department decided in 1997 to improve the official government balance sheet produced by the National Accounts Office. In order to present a more accurate picture of the increasing fiscal imbalance, officials called for the new government balance sheet to include both implicit and contingent, as well as explicit and direct, assets and liabilities. In the process, the value of all these items had to be estimated and reestimated (Echeverry and others 1999). Unexpectedly to some, the process of identifying and quantifying government obligations revealed major cracks in the institutional mechanism in Colombia's public finance management—cracks that had given rise to large government contingent liabilities, many of which had been poorly designed and were exposing the government to excessive risk.

Quantifying Government Contingent Liabilities

In its wide-ranging attempt to identify and then quantify all major sources of government fiscal risk, the government focused on the biggest items: pension liabilities, a guerrilla peace "buyout," natural disasters, the financial sector, credit guarantees to the public sector, and concessions on private financing of infrastructure.

Pension liabilities, mainly in the form of government-guaranteed pensions to social security beneficiaries and teachers, surfaced as the biggest source of fiscal risk for the government (for an analysis of Colombia's comprehensive balance sheet, see Chapter 8 by Easterly and Yuravlivker in this volume). The net present value of future pension outlays (an implicit direct liability for the government) was estimated at about 159 percent of the gross domestic product (GDP), of which almost half was designated for social security beneficiaries and one-third for teachers.

In its analysis, the government also included seemingly unquantifiable contingent liabilities such as the cost of possible peace negotiations. For example, to determine the cost of the contingent liability of dealing with Colombia's guerrillas, analysts evaluated the guerrillas' business and calculated the sum required to purchase such a business. Based on their calculation of the profitability of guerrilla violence, analysts concluded that guerrilla groups in Colombia expect a profit of US$430 million per year (Echeverry and others 1999:17–20). Therefore, assuming that a guerrilla is risk-averse and taking into account a dollar interest rate of 6 percent a year, they estimated that an investment of approximately $7 billion was required to eliminate a business with such high levels of profitability in the long term. Taking into account efficiency gained from restructuring the army and from acquiring superior military hardware, analysts were able to estimate the cost of reaching peace with the guerrillas at about 4 percent of GDP (in net present value terms in 1997).

Natural disasters, particularly earthquakes and floods, constitute another major implicit contingent liability in Colombia. After disasters, the government has had to provide resources for the reconstruction and rehabilitation of affected areas and for future damage prevention. Aided by evaluations of the cost of the most recent earthquake in Colombia (January 1999), analysts were able to estimate the value of natural disasters as a government contingent liability. They estimated a net present value of about 1.1 percent of GDP for earthquake contingency and about 0.04 percent of GDP for flood contingency.

Government analysts also estimated the implicit contingent liability arising from the financial sector. Again, previous experience with a financial crisis and its fiscal implications were analyzed. Based on an analysis of historical cost and a rough assessment of the present health of financial institutions, analysts estimated that the future liquidation of insolvent institutions and the recapitalization of others represent a contingent liability of between 1.2 percent and 1.7 percent of GDP in net present value terms.

Guarantees on public sector debt, forms of hidden subsidies in Colombia, are another major item. These liabilities are subject to subnational government borrowing regulations, which traditionally have been inefficient, allowing rapid growth of regional debt. Since 1997, borrowing has been limited to the payment capacity of the regional entity concerned and thus associated with the generation of operational savings. The bailout cost of current regional debt was calculated to be 0.5 percent of GDP. Another source of contingent liabilities is judicial rulings against the state, which increased over the past decade from 0.02 percent of GDP in 1990 to 0.3 percent of GDP in 1998.

Significant contingent liabilities in Colombia result from private sector concessions in infrastructure. The state has transformed its role from that of direct service provider to guarantor of minimum sales to private sector service provider. Initially, contracts involved fixed terms within which the government guaranteed a level of profitability. After some adjustments, current contracts are flexible in length, which allows low profitability to be compensated over time. Both types of government guarantees, however, involve uncertainty over whether, when, and how much public financing will be required in the future. Across the guarantees issued, the net present value of contingent liabilities in the infrastructure sector was estimated at about 6 percent of GDP.

In the transport sector, guarantees covered traffic volume and road construction costs. The guarantees on traffic volume are invoked if the anticipated income falls below an agreed-on minimal level related to predicted traffic volume. However, if income rises above an allowed maximum, it becomes a contingent asset and the excess is returned to the state. The calculated net present value of the contingent liability associated with traffic volume is 0.1 percent of GDP. On road construction a large guarantee was issued on the second runway at Bogota's El Dorado International Airport. In addition to the requirement to maintain both runways, the guarantee also covers minimum income conditions. The net present value of this contingency for the duration of the airport project (20 years) was estimated to be about 0.7 percent of GDP.

In the energy sector, the contracts for energy providers have been issued under onerous conditions. The government has had to assume the difference between the actual market price and the price agreed on with investors. The net present value of this contingency was estimated to be about 0.5 percent of GDP.

In the telecommunications sector, the government has provided minimum income guarantees (contained in four-year joint venture contracts), covering a certain number of conversation minutes. The net present value of these guarantees is about 0.2 percent of GDP.

Other contingent liabilities were expected to emerge from the construction of the Bogota Metro. Here the contingency is related to the probability of liabilities being larger than predicted, and is partly a consequence of regulatory ambiguities. The law that authorized the construction of the Bogota Metro states that if excess costs imputable to the public sector are generated, the national government is obliged to cover 70 percent of excess costs. In addition, the government covers currency risks related to external financing as well as the cost of construction delays and of required public services (such as laying pipes for the waterworks).

Most of the contingent liabilities just described emerged from the 1991 constitution, which deepened the decentralization process (the transfer of responsibilities and resources to lower levels of government) and promoted private participation in the provision of public services and infrastructure. On the positive side, private investment in infrastructure increased rapidly, nearly doubling in the 1990s to surpass 5 percent of GDP by 1998. Additional benefits were, among other things, more efficient use of resources and an increase in the quality of these services. In 1997 the future fiscal cost of these projects was estimated to be about 1.5 percent of GDP (which was about a quarter of the underlying investments). The government acknowledged that it could have achieved the same policy outcomes through direct subsidies that would have been less expensive than guarantees. Meanwhile, the government was facing increasing pressure to issue further guarantees.

The Institutional Underpinnings

The 1997 assessment made it clear that often nonpriority or poorly designed projects were undertaken thanks only to the loopholes in government fiscal management that made it possible for such projects to obtain government guarantees. Making matters worse, the government was assuming most if not all of the risk associated with the programs and projects benefiting from guarantees. The inefficient risk allocation mainly reflected the fact that contracting government entities were not clearly liable for their guarantees. Overall, the government had only a few rules in place to guide the issuance and oversight of guarantees and other contingent liabilities (until 1998, the government also lacked a legal framework for private participation in the provision of public services). Furthermore, accounting rules required that outlays on contingent liabilities that fell due be acknowledged as investment overruns. In the budget, however, investments were already squeezed. Lack of budgetary funds thus meant that payments due to the guarantee beneficiaries grew at high penalty interest rates for up to 18 months at a time.

When the size and unpredictability of payments grew beyond the handling capacity of some public entities, budgetary adjustments (most notably in the so-called *vigencias futuras*, or future expenditure commitments) and structuring adjustments (in the mechanisms that insure liquidity for the project) were made. These adjustments gave the government greater ability to honor its guarantees in a more timely fashion. Fundamental problems continued, however. The government did not have the capability to value its obligations, and, more important, it did not have adequate assets to offset its obligations or the cash to provide for them.

Handling contingent liabilities through *vigencias futuras* implied that future budgetary expenditures could be earmarked, ensuring budgeting while explicitly recognizing the obligations. Even though this mechanism ensured the availability of funds to support the liabilities, it introduced severe rigidities for future government budgets and was based on crude valuation methodologies for contingent liabilities. The liquidity mechanisms have taken the form of trusts or standby loan facilities, which imply important costs because they call for greater than necessary budget provisions. In addition, this system has proven inefficient in providing the liquidity required by private investors. Therefore, recent projects have relied on the participation of financial intermediaries that manage the resources allocated to cover these liabilities when they emerge.

Under the initiative of the Ministry of Finance and the General Directorate of Public Credit, the government has sought to correct most of these difficulties, while improving its fiscal discipline and generating the appropriate conditions in the real sectors in order to, for example, attract private capital into the provision of public services without the need for new guarantees. Measures were taken from a normative perspective, such as Law 448 (1998) and Decree 423 (2001), with the purpose of both providing liquidity as contingencies became effective and minimizing the inconveniences that resulted from the reduction in investment resources, or other items, in that event. Law 448 regulated the valuation, budgeting, and control of contingent liabilities; created a contingency fund; and defined the resources to be devoted to financing such liabilities.

Law 448 (1998) and Decree 423 (2001)

The principal elements of Law 448 are that it:

• establishes the obligation for public entities to budget contingent liabilities as debt service, implying that they must make the appropriate provisions to face such liabilities (in this way, the government can assure liquidity for contract guarantees);
• creates the State Entities' Contingency Fund to tackle liabilities generated under specific conditions that are defined by the government;
• regulates the approval and control of contingent liabilities;
• establishes methodologies and procedures for the valuation, budgeting, and control of contingent liabilities;
• grants regulatory powers to the General Directorate of Public Credit (the debt office of the Ministry of Finance) and to each state entity's planning office; and
• establishes the requirement that contingent liabilities be explicitly included in contracts.

Decree 423

• assigns the National Council of Economic and Social Policy (CONPES) responsibility for establishing the guidelines for contractual relationships between public entities and the private sector for the development of infrastructure—thus CONPES is to direct the state's contractual risk policy "based upon the principle, that public entities should assume those risks which are proper to their public character and their social objective, while the private parties should confront those risks which are determined by their profitable nature" (Article 16, Decree 423); and
• creates the State Policy for Contractual Risks, which determines the type of risks each sector is allowed to undertake, while unifying the economic policy on risk management. A recent document issued by CONPES (No. 3107) provides the general guidelines on the types of risks that may be undertaken by the various sectors, and it compiles the individual strategies that should be developed by the specific infrastructure sectors to tackle such risks.

Valuation Methodologies

The General Directorate of Public Credit together with international consultants produced risk quantification methodologies—one general methodology and four sector-specific ones associated with the road infrastructure, energy, basic sanitation, and drinking water sectors. Contingent liabilities deriving from public credit operations also may be regulated in the near future. The methodologies aim to determine the magnitude of the expected present value of contingent liabilities, breaking them down by risk source, and the distribution of payments over time. This should facilitate the construction of an expanded balance sheet, an explicit recognition of contingent liabilities, and the incorporation of cost-of-assumption measures in the contract structuring.

Budgeting for Contingent Liabilities

Government entities are to define their guarantee policy, based on a valuation of the contingent liabilities using the respective methodology, and to quantify the financial and budgetary costs of assuming such obligations. Subsequently, they are to include in their budgets the contribution to the State Entities' Contingency Fund that corresponds to the current year as opposed to the full present value of the liability. Such a contribution is to be budgeted as debt service, not investment. Therefore, the transition from the previous system for existing contracts may result, from a budgetary perspective, in the perception of a reduction in investment.

Overall, the national government policy aims to make contingent liabilities in infrastructure projects evident through their proper valuation and give their inclusion in the budget the same priority as debt service.

Deposit Plan

A deposit plan approved by the General Directorate of Public Credit determines the amount and timing of deposits to be made to the Contingency Fund. These series of payments are meant to distribute through time the building of an asset to offset the generated contingent liability. This arrangement should ensure liquidity and thereby guarantee the availability of resources to cover the contingencies emerging in the next year or two.

State Entities' Contingency Fund

The Contingency Fund is meant to ensure a close relation between the value and liquidity of the guarantee and the explicitly agreed on obligations in contracts for infrastructure projects. Under this arrangement, the guarantee's credibility is improved, because deposits in the fund constitute the offsetting asset required to cover the contingency, and the resources' value is maintained over time as earned interests are reinvested. The funds will be obtained from contributions made by those public entities that participate in projects involving guarantees to the private sector. The fund acts as an account in the sense that it is only held responsible for an amount equivalent to the contribution of the respective entity. Deposits within the fund are broken down by both project and individual risk level. Therefore, the deposits made by different entities are not pooled together. In the event that contingent liabilities do not arise, the entities' payments may be either reimbursed or transferred to other projects.

Contingent Liability Appraisal

Because the individual risk profiles of contingent liabilities can vary over time, the General Directorate of Public Credit will produce a yearly revaluation in order to introduce the appropriate changes in the entities' deposit plan, releasing resources when risk expires. This process increases the probability that the entity's yearly deposits will cover at least the contingency's current year value, therefore allowing a homogenization in magnitude and distribution over time of both the liability and the offsetting asset.

Overall, Law 448 and Decree 423 represent important steps toward attaining fiscal discipline through proper budgeting, adequate and objective accounting through new valuation methodologies that grant greater transparency to the contract system, and the assurance of liquidity to offset assumed liabilities through the new fund. All of the above enhance the achievement of a dynamic fiscal balance through efficient intertemporal risk allocation.

Structural Adjustment

The analysis of fiscal imbalances in Colombia within an intertemporal perspective reveals that the public sector does not have a short- or medium-term liquidity problem, but rather one of long-term insolvency, which is stressed mainly due to the high value of pension liabilities. This problem emphasizes the importance of decreasing contingent liabilities in order to achieve a dynamic fiscal balance. The main problems faced by authorities are the size of the adjustment needed and the institutional constraints to be overcome in order to pursue an efficient allocation of savings to confront flow and stock imbalances.

Among the most important structural reforms directed toward fiscal adjustment are those that tackle the unsustainability problem associated with pension liabilities and subnational entities:

• *Subnational Government Income and Expenditure Reform.* The main reform measures are centered on reducing expenditures. In addition to a reduction in regional pressures on the central government via further decentralization, policies are directed toward more efficient expenditures: the rationalization of the size of the payroll and funding of regional and teacher pension funds. Reductions in the expenditures of the central government refer essentially to public investment, with an emphasis on shifting infrastructure investment to the private sector through a concession system.

• *Reform of Regional Transfers from the Central Government (Constitutional Amendment).* Currently, national government transfers to the regions are the budget item with the greatest relative importance; they are equivalent to 39 percent of the total national expenditure. Additionally, they have recorded a high growth rate, rising from 2.8 percent of GDP in 1990 to 5.3 percent in 1999.

The proposed reform will reduce the pressure that these transfers place on the central government by allowing the transfers to grow in real terms at a rate equivalent to that of the population (1.5 percent) once they reach their maximum value as a percentage of national current income.

• *Creation of a Regional Pension Fund.* Regional pension liabilities have reached a level equivalent to 39 percent of GDP, which already represents a threat to fiscal stability; the lack of regional government savings has resulted in serious payment delays. The objective of the reform policy is therefore to direct resources toward the creation of reserves with the purpose of covering pension liabilities for a maximum period of 30 years. The necessary resources will be obtained from the joint participation of the regional and central governments. Regional funding will be derived from an increasing share of transfers to municipalities.

• *Rationalization of the Social Security System.* One of the most important factors in the current worsening of Colombia's fiscal situation is transfers to the social security fund. These transfers represent 30.4 percent of those at the central government level, of which 17 percent is related to severance payments. Not only do these transfers represent a major burden for the central government, but the design of the social security system implies the rapid growth of these liabilities. Under the current system, severance payments suffer geometric growth, which resulted in the doubling of this liability between 1996 and 1999. This geometric growth is the result of the drawing of severance payments discounted by the nominal value at the moment at which the contribution took place as opposed to the moment of the last contribution. The elimination of the retroactivity of severance payments has been proposed. In addition, the proposed reform of social security contemplates a five-year extension of the age of eligibility for receiving pensions, for both male and female workers, and a 300-week extension of the minimum contribution period (previously 1,000 weeks). In the same sense, reformers contemplate a reduction in the rate at which the pension value increases as a percentage of a determined salary, according to the time of contribution. Moreover, calculation of the pension salary is meant to be transformed so that it is based on a 20-year income reference period rather than the last 10 working years. Further measures imply the elimination of special pension regimes, which entails introducing teachers and armed forces, among others, in the common regime (Law 100); accelerating the transition to a new system in terms of the increase in the retirement age and reduction in the pension salary; and increasing the requirements for the guarantee of a minimum pension and the restrictions associated with the transfer within pension funds in order to avoid speculation and savings mismanagement.

Once the fiscal package has been designed, the government has to confront two independent bodies when seeking approval of the reforms: Congress and the Constitutional Court, both of which can either hinder or promote government efforts to impose long-term fiscal adjustments. Therefore, intertemporal budgeting and financing are a necessary, but not sufficient, condition for long-term sustainability. The commitment of these two arms of public power to harmonizing their policies with fiscal adjustment strategies, by assimilating understanding and assuming the intertemporal consequences of their decisions with the dynamic structure of budget constraint, has become as crucial as the executive strategy itself (Echeverry and Navas 2000).

Note

1. This paper benefited from the collaboration of the Macroeconomic Analysis Unit in the National Planning Department and the Analysis Division in the Ministry of Finance.

References

Easterly, William. 1999. "When Is Fiscal Adjustment an Illusion?" *Economic Policy* (April): 57–86.

Echeverry, Juan Carlos, and Verónica Navas. 2000. "Confronting Fiscal Imbalances via Intertemporal Economics, Politics and Justice: The Case of Colombia." *Archivos de Macroeconomía*. No. 129. National Planning Department, Bogota. (Forthcoming, *Economic Review*, Federal Reserve Bank of Atlanta).

Echeverry, Juan Carlos, Maria Victoria Angulo, Gustavo Hernandez, Israel Fainboim, Cielo Numpaque, Gabriel Piraquive, Carlos Rodriguez, and Natalia Salazar. 1999. "El Balance del Sector Público y la Sostenibilidad Fiscal de Colombia." *Archivos de Macroeconomía*. No. 115. National Planning Department, Bogota.

PART II

Dealing with Specific Sources of Government Fiscal Risk

Analytical and Managerial Tools

CHAPTER 13

Pension Guarantees: A Methodology for Assessing Fiscal Risk

George G. Pennacchi
University of Illinois

TRADITIONALLY, MOST COUNTRIES THAT have provided social security to the elderly have chosen unfunded, defined-benefit pension systems. Many of these pay-as-you-go (PAYG) systems have come under stress because of demographic trends, mismanagement, and economic downturns.[1] Some countries have responded by increasing worker contribution rates, cutting retirement benefits, or making other fiscal adjustments to improve the financial viability of their systems. However, these types of reforms have been politically difficult and have moved pension systems only partway toward long-term solvency.[2] Uncertainty about the sustainability of PAYG systems and their perceived inequities also can lead to worker dissatisfaction and evasion.[3]

An approach that holds greater promise of long-term pension reform is to allow part of an individual's pension to take the form of a fully funded, defined-contribution plan. Combined with a defined-benefit component, such a system represents a dual-pillar approach. The first pillar can take the form of a guaranteed minimum pension for those who contribute over a sufficiently long period to the defined-contribution plan, such as in Chile's current pension system. Alternatively, the first pillar can be a separate defined-benefit PAYG program, but of a more limited size than that of traditional single-pillar systems. The defined-contribution second pillar would be funded by payroll deductions and could be privately or publicly managed.

By reducing the defined-benefit component of an individual's pension, a dual-pillar system decreases the exposure of pension benefits to political manipulation. Potential distortions of an individual's work and savings behavior are mitigated, because the defined-contribution component links at least a part of payroll contributions to an individual's pension benefits. Yet by maintaining a defined-benefit portion, the system provides insurance to workers who experience low lifetime wage incomes or realize low investment returns on their defined-contribution accounts. In this sense, a dual-pillar system provides diversification against political, income, and investment risks.[4]

Because pension systems that include a defined-contribution component expose individuals to investment risks, governments typically find it necessary to provide some type of guarantee on individuals' pension returns. Such guarantees, however, create a government contingent liability that can be difficult to value—that is, the government creates an obligation when it commits to providing the guarantee, but the actual payments required to fulfill it are often far into the future and difficult to predict. Also, the guarantee payments may depend not only on the returns earned on financial market investments but also on the future levels of workers' wages and other macroeconomic and demographic factors.

Although it can be a complex task, estimating the value of these government guarantees is important for gauging the complete fiscal cost of pension reform. Guarantees represent an implicit subsidy to participants in pension plans that, in principle, should be included in government budget statistics. Moreover, it may be possible for the government to recover the cost of its guarantees by charging an initial fair insurance premium to the beneficiaries of the guarantees. In some cases, such a risk-based premium, equal to the government's liability, can reduce the economic distortions associated with the provision of the guarantee.

This chapter describes a methodology for assessing the cost to a government of providing pension guarantees. The approach is alternatively referred to as contingent claims analysis, arbitrage-pricing theory, or option-pricing theory. This framework was first applied to valuing financial options, but it has since been extended to value different types of guarantees, such as government deposit insurance and loan guarantees. The chapter also discusses the economic assumptions underlying this valuation technique. And it describes particular types of pension guarantees provided by different country governments and how a government's risk associated with these guarantees can be managed.

Four main types of government pension guarantees are analyzed. They share a common characteristic in that their values depend, at least in part, on the risk from investments in financial securities. The first two types are associated with a defined-contribution pension plan. They are a guarantee on the periodic rates of return earned by a defined-contribution pension fund and a guarantee of a minimum pension benefit for an individual participant in a defined-contribution plan. The second two types of guarantees relate to defined-benefit plans. Because many countries' pension systems include a voluntary third pillar in the form of an employer-sponsored pension plan, this chapter considers a government guarantee of employee benefits promised by an employer-sponsored defined-benefit plan. It also analyzes a guarantee of benefits paid by a mandatory, partially prefunded, single-pillar, defined-benefit pension system in which payroll tax rates are linked to the investment performance of the plan's trust fund. Although it is not covered in this chapter, Goss (1999) discusses how the solvency of an unfunded, defined-benefit PAYG plan can be assessed.[5]

The chapter is structured as follows. The next section discusses the basic economic assumptions on which the contingent claims valuation framework rests. It considers the financial market conditions necessary for such assumptions to be valid. The example of valuing a simple pension guarantee that follows illustrates the basic technique used to compute the value of guarantees. The next section then analyzes the types of guarantees provided by different country governments. It points out the factors that influence the value and risk of such guarantees and how a guarantee might be structured in order to control the government's exposure and risk. The final section offers concluding comments.

The Methodology Used to Value Pension Guarantees

Guarantees and insurance are examples of contingent claims or derivatives. Other examples include financial options, futures, and swap contracts—securities whose payments are tied to the value of an underlying security or asset. Guarantees are similar to options.

Option contracts fall into two categories. A *call option* is a contract that gives its holder the right to *buy* a particular underlying asset at a prespecified price at some future date. A *put option* gives its holder the right to *sell* a particular underlying asset at a prespecified price at some future date. This prespecified price is referred to as the option's exercise price or strike price. Of the two types of options, put options are the most similar to pension guarantees. Consider a government guarantee of a minimum value for an individual's pension account. In the future, if the value of the individual's pension account (corresponding to the value of an underlying asset) is lower than the prespecified minimum pension level (corresponding to an exercise price), then the individual can "sell" the pension account to the government and receive the minimum pension. In this case, the government realizes a future expense equal to the difference between the minimum pension and the value of the individual's account balance. If, instead, the future value of the individual's pension account exceeds the value of the minimum pension, the individual maintains the account (chooses not to exercise the option to sell it to the government) and the government's realized expense is zero. Thus as the provider of the guarantee (put option), the government realizes a future expense equal to the difference between the guarantee value (exercise price) and the pension account balance (underlying asset) if and only if this difference is positive.

Fortunately, important advances in valuing contingent claims, including government guarantees and insurance, have been made over the past few decades. Since the theoretical work on option pricing by Black and Scholes (1973) and Merton (1973), financial economists have developed and refined a general valuation technique. This research is probably the most significant contribution of modern finance theory. It has led to rigorous, yet practical, valuation models that have stimulated the development of new financial securities and markets. In addition to pricing options, this work has been applied to valuing many nonstandard contingent claims, including government deposit insurance, loan guarantees, and pension guarantees.[6]

This option-pricing framework is attractive because it requires relatively few assumptions and the assumptions are often realistic. The approach starts by noting that a contingent claim or derivative inherits the same risk as its underlying security or asset. In particular, because a pension guarantee provides insurance against low security returns, its payoff is tied to the value of the underlying securities held by the pension fund. For example, an annual rate of return guarantee on a defined-contribution pension fund requires the government to make a payment to participants if their pension fund's annual return is below a prespecified level. Another example is a government guarantee of a minimum pension for a participant in a mandatory, defined-contribution pension plan. The participant's pension account balance at retirement is partly determined by the returns earned by his or her pension fund's securities. If this account balance is below the prespecified minimum pension, then the government is obligated to make a payment equal to the difference between the minimum pension and the account balance. In both of these cases, the guarantee payment depends on particular security returns. Thus the guarantee's value inherits a risk similar to that of the pension fund's securities.

The key insight of option-pricing theory is that, under particular conditions, the risk from providing a contingent claim can be hedged by appropriate trading in its underlying securities. The cost of purchasing this hedge portfolio, which eliminates the liability from providing the contingent claim, must then equal the value of the contingent claim. In other words, it may be possible to create a hedge portfolio, involving positions in the underlying securities, whose cash flows exactly replicate the cash flows of the contingent claim.[7] Such a hedging portfolio represents an asset whose value perfectly offsets the liability of providing the contingent claim, so that the net liability of the provider always equals zero. If it is possible to create this hedging portfolio, then its value must equal that of the contingent claim since their future cash flows will be identical. If their values differed, then arbitrage would exist.

Arbitrage refers to a situation in which an investor can make a riskless profit without investing any of his or her own wealth. More informally, arbitrage can be described as a "free lunch." In highly competitive security markets, arbitrage is extremely rare, because it implies that investors can make riskless profits while putting none of their personal wealth at stake. In the context of a contingent claim and a hedging portfolio that replicates the claim's payoff, if the prices of these two assets were not identical, arbitrage would result from selling the overvalued asset and buying the undervalued one. The difference in the values of the two assets would then represent a riskless profit. An assumption often made by the option-pricing approach is that there are no transactions costs to buying or selling the contingent claim's underlying securities and that in such a "frictionless" market arbitrage does not exist.

In the context of a government pension guarantee, suppose a government chooses to hedge its risk of making payments to pension fund participants if security returns are low. How might this be done? A successful hedge would be one in which the government makes a profit if security prices decline, offsetting its losses in the form of its payments to pension participants. Such profits could be made if the government had a short position in the underlying securities. This could be accomplished by short-selling the securities. In a short sale of a security, the short-seller (government) borrows a share of a security from its owner and promises to return it at some future date.[8] At the beginning of the short-sale period, the short-seller trades the security to a third party, thereby obtaining proceeds equal to the security's market price. These proceeds can then be invested in a riskless security, such as a short-term government bond.[9] At the end of the short-sale period, the short-seller repurchases a share of the security at its end-of-period market price and returns it to the owner. Therefore, the short-seller's profit at the end of the short-sale period equals the security's beginning-of-period market price plus accrued interest minus its end-of-period market price. Thus the lower the security's return over the period, the greater is the short-seller's profit.

An alternative, though similar, method for establishing a short position in securities is via a futures market. If futures contracts on the securities, or on indices of the securities, are traded, then a short position in a futures contract would provide essentially the same hedge as a short sale. Hedging with a short futures position would result in a profit when the securities underlying the futures contract have a low return. Moreover, an attraction of hedging with futures on the securities is that the transactions costs are often quite low compared with those for hedging with the actual underlying securities.

By either method of hedging, the government would be "privatizing" its risk in the sense that the risk from low security returns is transferred to individuals or institutions willing to bear it. In the case of the short-sale hedge, the risk shifts to the party that purchases the securities during the short-sale period. In the case of a futures contract hedge, the risk is transferred to the party taking the opposing long position in the futures contract. The parties that assume this risk may be domestic or foreign investors wishing to diversify their portfolios.

More specifically, it can be shown that whether the government hedges via a short sale or a short futures contract, the appropriate hedge involves a short position in fewer shares of the underlying pension fund securities than those actually held by the pension funds.[10] In addition, the hedge involves an additional investment in risk-free securities—that is, the government would choose to reduce or repurchase some of its debt.

In practice, governments typically do not attempt to hedge their exposure to guarantees—that is, the risks of guarantees are not privatized. However, the option-pricing approach values these guarantees at what would be the theoretical marginal cost that investors would charge the government to take over its commitments. It is assumed that such investors would require an expected rate of return on providing the guarantee that is consistent with the expected rate of return they require from holding the underlying securities. The Appendix to this chapter details this relationship between the expected rate of return on the government's guarantee and the underlying securities.

In cases in which a perfect hedge is not possible, so that the guarantee's cash flows cannot be replicated exactly, the option-pricing approach might still be useful in deriving, or deriving bounds on, the guarantee's value. For example, if the securities underlying the guarantee are costly to trade, it may be possible to trade using alternative securities that have no transactions costs. With these alternative securities, a government might be able to create an imperfect hedge portfolio whose "tracking error" relative to a perfect hedge represents nonsystematic or diversifiable risk. In such a case, the guarantee can be valued exactly as if a perfect hedge could be created (see Merton 1998 for a derivation of this result). In addition, there may be other situations in which the hedge portfolio's tracking error risk is not fully diversifiable but upper and lower bounds on the cost of the contingent claim can be derived (see Cochrane and Saá-Requejo 2000 and Bernardo and Ledoit 2000). The more closely the guarantee's cash flows can be replicated by the underlying securities, the tighter will be the bounds on its cost.

In some cases, guarantees depend not only on the values of underlying financial securities but also on other sources of uncertainty. A minimum pension guarantee for an individual participant in a mandatory, defined-contribution pension plan is an example. In addition to the returns earned by securities in the individual's pension fund, the guarantee depends on the contribution levels of the individual which, in turn, depend on his or her wages. Thus this guarantee is affected by wage risk. However, it may be possible to hedge wage risk using a portfolio of financial securities in which the portfolio's tracking error represents only nonsystematic risk. In such a case, the value of the pension guarantee can be derived (see Pennacchi 1999a for a discussion of the issues involved in modeling wage risk). A similar technique might be used to handle other types of risks that affect pension guarantees, such as mortality risk.[11]

Valuing a Pension Guarantee: A Simple Example

This section illustrates how option pricing can be used to value a simple pension guarantee. Suppose that a defined-contribution pension fund holds a diversified portfolio of common stocks. The value of the pension fund, and therefore the value of the participants' retirement benefits, will vary with fluctuations in this stock portfolio. The pension fund could insure itself against significant declines in the value of its securities by purchasing a put option on its portfolio. For example, assume that the value of the pension fund's securities currently equals $10 million, and it wishes to insure itself against a drop in the value of the portfolio to below $9 million during the next year. If options on such a stock portfolio were available from an options exchange or from an investment bank derivatives dealer, put options on the portfolio having a one-year maturity and an exercise price of $9 million could be purchased.

The value of the put option contracts when they mature in one year's time can be written as max ($9M $-S_1$, 0), where S_1 is the random value of the pension fund's stock portfolio at the end of the year and max ($9M $-S_1$, 0) means select the maximum of $9 million minus S_1 and 0. Thus the put option, being analogous to a guarantee or insurance contract, has a positive maturity value only if the end-of-year value of the pension fund's stocks, S_1, sinks to less than $9 million. By owning this "portfolio insurance," the pension fund has a combined end-of-year value given by S_1 + max ($9M $-S_1$, 0) = max ($9M, S_1$), which is never less than $9 million.

Rather than obtaining insurance by purchasing put options from an exchange or dealer, a government could provide the equivalent pension insurance. In this case, a government guarantor has an end-of-year liability given by max ($9M − S_1, 0). Figure 13.1 graphs the end-of-year values of the pension fund if it were uninsured (equaling S_1), of the guarantee (equaling max ($9M − S_1, 0)), and of the pension fund if it were insured (equaling max ($9M, S_1)). Clearly, the guarantee places a lower bound on the end-of-year value of the insured pension fund.

The value of the government guarantee is easily determined at the end of the year when S_1 becomes known, but it is more challenging to determine its value (cost) at the beginning of the year. If the guarantee were exactly equivalent to a traded put option contract, then its market value could be inferred from the current market price of the option. However, rarely, if ever, does a pension guarantee have an exact private market counterpart. Thus another method, such as option pricing, is needed for calculating the guarantee's theoretical market price.

Figure 13.1. End-of-Year Values of Stock Portfolio, Pension Fund Guarantee, and Pension Fund

(millions of dollars)

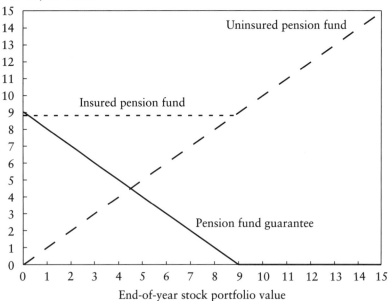

Source: Based on calculations from the author.

As detailed in the Appendix, one useful option-pricing method is the "risk-neutral" valuation technique or, more generally, the martingale-pricing approach. According to this technique, the guarantee's present value equals the risk-neutral expectation of the guarantee's end-of-year value discounted at the risk-free interest rate. The risk-neutral expectation of a random future value is defined as its expected future value under the assumption that the expected rate of return on the underlying assets equals the risk-free interest rate.[12] Thus in using this valuation technique, one would compute the expected value of max ($9M $- S_1$, 0) by setting the expected rate of return on the pension fund's stock portfolio equal to the risk-free rate, even though the "true" expected rate of return on the stock portfolio is really different. The present value of the guarantee then equals this value discounted at the risk-free interest rate.

It should be emphasized that this risk-neutral valuation or martingale-pricing technique *does not* assume that the stocks' expected rates of return truly equal the risk-free rate. The only assumption being made is that the equilibrium values of the guarantee and the underlying stock portfolio are such that investors price the risk inherent in these two assets in a consistent manner. It just turns out that, mathematically, one can arrive at the correct value by computing the guarantee's expected payoff *as if* the stocks' expected rates of return equaled the risk-free rate and then discounting this expected payoff by the risk-free rate.[13]

Intuitively, the risk-neutral technique gives the correct value for the guarantee because of two erroneous assumptions whose effects cancel. One incorrect assumption is that the underlying stock portfolio has an average rate of return equal to the risk-free rate—that is, its expected rate of return contains no risk premium. This implies a risk-neutral expectation of the guarantee's future payoff, max ($9M $- S_1$, 0), that differs from its true expectation, leading to the first error. The other incorrect assumption is that this risky payment should be discounted at the risk-free rate rather than at a rate reflecting the risk premium of the underlying stock portfolio, leading to the second error. Because both the first and second errors fail to account for a risk premium, the first error overstates the expected value of the guarantee's payoff by the risk premium, while the second error understates the discount factor by the risk premium. Mathematically, the two errors cancel, leading to a correct valuation. Importantly, this technique does not require making a tenuous assumption about the true risk premium of the underlying stocks.

To calculate the guarantee value, one needs to specify the variance of the stock portfolio's return, which is a measure of the volatility of the portfolio's value. This variance can be estimated relatively accurately from data on the stocks' historical returns. Then, one can compute the risk-neutral expected value of max ($9M – S_1, 0) using a Monte Carlo technique to simulate the end-of-year values of the portfolio, S_1. This calculation involves applying a random number generator to compute many possible outcomes of S_1, where the portfolio's expected rate of return is set equal to the risk-free rate and its variance of return is set equal to an estimate based on historical returns. Then, for each realized value of S_1, the quantity max ($9M – S_1, 0) is computed and these quantities are averaged over all of the realizations. For a sufficiently large number of random simulations of S_1, the average value of max ($9M – S_1, 0) will be arbitrarily close to its theoretical risk-neutral expected value. The last step is to discount this average using the risk-free rate, which leads to the present value of the guarantee.

Figure 13.2 illustrates this technique in the context of this simple example. Assuming that the beginning-of-year security portfolio value equals $10 million, the risk-free interest rate equals 5.00 percent, and the annual variance of the portfolio's return equals 4.00 percent, the figure shows 200 random realizations of the risk-neutral path of the security portfolio over a 52-week (one-year) period. These simulations

Figure 13.2. Risk-Neutral Paths of Stock Portfolio Values

Portfolio value (millions of dollars)

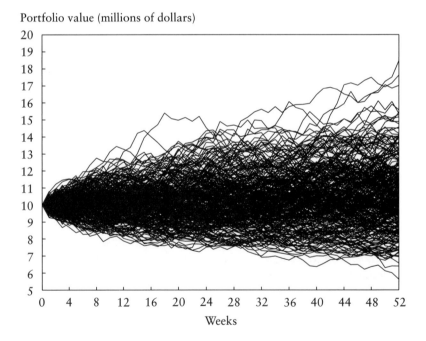

Weeks

Source: Based on calculations from the author.

generate a frequency distribution of values of S_1—that is, a set of real-izations of the end-of-year (week 52) risk-neutral stock portfolio value. For a sufficiently large number of simulations, this frequency distribution takes the shape shown in Figure 13.3.[14]

The risk-neutral value of the government's payment is found by computing the quantity ($9M – S_1) for each realization of S_1 less than $9 million.[15] Summing these quantities and dividing by the total number of simulations (for example, 10,000) results in the risk-neutral expected value. Finally, multiplying this expected value by the risk-free discount factor 1/1.05 results in the present value of the guarantee, which in this example equals $231,000.

This Monte Carlo method for computing the guarantee's value is in the spirit of scenario testing. Each simulated value of S_1 can be viewed as one possible scenario for the pension fund's end-of-year portfolio value. However, the purpose of the technique is not to reveal the various possible ex post future payments the government would be required to make. Rather, it is to find the present value of the contingent guarantee payment.

Figure 13.3. Risk-Neutral Distribution of End-of-Year Portfolio Values

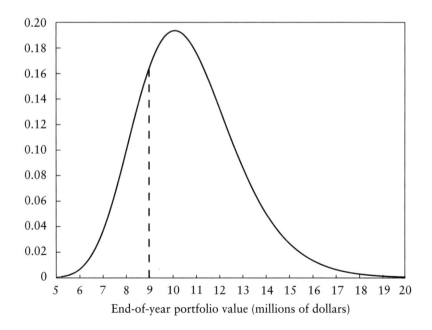

End-of-year portfolio value (millions of dollars)

Source: Based on calculations from the author.

In practice, government guarantees are more complex than the standard put option-type guarantee in the example. In addition to risk from portfolio returns, some guarantees depend on individuals' wage and mortality risk and risk from changes in market interest rates. However, the Monte Carlo simulation technique can be extended to include these other factors (a discussion of how these multiple factors can be modeled is given in the appendix of Pennacchi 1999a).

Analyzing Specific Types of Pension Guarantees

This section considers various types of pension guarantees offered by different countries, discusses how these guarantees can be valued, and analyzes their risk characteristics.

Guarantees on a Pension Fund's Rate of Return

Some countries with pension systems that include a defined-contribution pillar guarantee that pension funds earn a minimum rate of return over given periods of time. These guarantees differ in the way that countries define the minimum return, in the length of the period over which pension fund returns are calculated, and in the actions taken if a pension fund fails to earn the minimum return.

In Uruguay, pension funds are known as *Asociaciones de Fondos de Ahorro Previsional* (AFAPs) and can be publicly or privately managed (see Mitchell 1996 for a discussion of Uruguay's reformed pension system). The government of Uruguay guarantees that public (but not private) pension fund participants earn a minimum annual real rate of return of 2 percent. Thus the government is required to make up the difference between this minimum return and the public pension fund's actual return if, during any year in the future, the actual return turns out to be less than this minimum. Pennacchi (1999a) employs an option-pricing approach to derive an explicit formula for the value of such a fixed real rate of return guarantee.[16] For the general case of a fixed minimum return equal to m, the formula shows that the value of the guarantee increases as $r - m$ declines, where r is the risk-free real interest rate. Also, the greater the variance of the returns earned by the pension fund's portfolio of securities, and the greater the growth rate of participants' net contributions to the pension fund, the higher is the guarantee. Indeed, if the growth rate of net contributions is positive, the present value of the government guarantee can become very large the longer the time horizon over which the government commits to making this guarantee.

The structure of this fixed real rate of return guarantee is somewhat worrisome. Even if pension funds are invested in bonds that pay a real, riskless return, such as the index bonds offered by the Uruguayan government, there is no assurance that their real returns will exceed 2 percent. The real yield on an indexed bond can vary and, in principle, fall below 2 percent or even become negative. This may explain why rate of return guarantees offered by other countries tend to differ from Uruguay's fixed rate of return guarantee. Other countries' guarantees tend to set a minimum rate of return that is linked to a time-varying, market benchmark rate of return.

Chile's mandatory defined-contribution pension system is based on private pension funds known as *Administradoras de Fondos de Pensiones* (AFPs). The minimum annual real rate of return earned by an AFP is linked to a benchmark that equals the average annual real rate of return earned by all Chilean AFPs. Let R_a be the realized average annual rate of return earned by all other AFPs in a given year. Then the requirement is that each AFP earn at least $\min(R_a - \alpha, \beta R_a)$, where $\alpha = 0.02$, $\beta = \frac{1}{2}$, and "$\min(x, y)$" means select the minimum of x and y. This implies that when R_a exceeds 4 percent, each AFP must earn at least $\frac{1}{2}R_a$, and when R_a is below 4 percent, each AFP must earn at least R_a minus 2 percent. Each AFP must hold capital (a guarantee fund) of at least 1 percent of the value of its pension portfolio, invested in the same security portfolio as that of its pension fund. In the event that the fund's return is less than $\min(R_a - \alpha, \beta R_a)$, it must make up the difference from its capital and replenish its capital within 15 days. Failure to do so would lead to a loss of the AFP's license. Thus if an AFP maintains a capital ratio of $c = 0.01$, the government would be exposed to loss when an AFP earns less than $\min(R_a - \alpha, \beta R_a) - c = \min(R_a - \alpha - c, \beta R_a - c)$.

As discussed in Mitchell and Barreto (1997), Peru requires the same minimum return on its second-pillar, private defined-contribution pension funds (*Administradoras Privadas de Fondos de Pensiones*) as does Chile. Argentina has a similar dual-pillar system, but the minimum rate of return required of its private pension funds equals $\min(R_a - \alpha, \beta R_a)$, where $\alpha = 0.02$, but $\beta = 0.7$. As described in Fischer (1998), Colombia sets a minimum rate of return for each of its private pension funds, *Administradoras de Fondos de Pensiones* (AFPs). However, the minimum is linked to a benchmark return that depends not only on the average return earned by other AFPs, but also on a Colombian stock market index and an index of publicly traded debt. Moreover, the benchmark's weights assigned to the stock and debt indices depend on the proportion of Colombian stocks that the individual AFP holds in its portfolio. The stock index's weight in the benchmark increases, up to a limit, with the AFP's portfolio allocation in stocks.

The Eastern European countries that have instituted dual-pillar pension reforms also provide rate of return guarantees. As reported by Palacios and Rocha (1998), Hungary requires that its second-pillar, defined-contribution pension funds earn a return equal to at least 90 percent of the return on a benchmark index of long-term government securities. Thus Hungary has gone a step further than Colombia in that its benchmark depends solely on an index of debt securities. Poland provides still another variation on a rate of return guarantee. As Cholon, Góra, and Rutkowski (1999) describe, Poland requires that its private pension funds earn a rate of return linked to the average return earned by all Polish pension funds, R_a. The formula for the minimum return has a structure similar to those of Chile, Peru, and Argentina. It equals $\min(R_a - \alpha, \beta R_a)$, where $\alpha = 0.04$ and $\beta = \frac{1}{2}$. However, rather than calculate returns on an annual basis, a pension fund's return is compared with this benchmark over a 24-month period.

Both Fischer (1998) and Pennacchi (1999a) use option-pricing approaches to value relative rate of return guarantees. They note that these guarantees are similar to options in that they exchange one asset (the pension fund's portfolio) for another (the benchmark portfolio). Fischer (1998) calculates the value of Colombia's minimum return guarantee, while Pennacchi (1999a) values guarantees of the form offered by Chile, Peru, and Argentina. From their findings, some general conclusions can be drawn about the characteristics of these guarantees. First, as in the case of a fixed minimum return guarantee, the greater the growth rate in net new contributions to the pension fund, the greater is the government's liability. Second, the cost of the government's guarantee increases as the variance in the pension fund's portfolio return rises and as the correlation between the pension fund's portfolio returns and the benchmark returns falls. This latter effect has the potential to create an incentive for pension funds to take excessive risk by increasing their tracking error vis-à-vis the benchmark.

To control this potential moral hazard behavior, governments have established additional regulations. For one thing, governments providing rate of return guarantees regulate the types of securities that a pension fund can hold. Pension funds are limited in the proportions of their portfolios that can be invested in domestic stocks, foreign investments, and high-credit risk debt. This is an obvious attempt to directly limit the pension fund's portfolio variance. Another regulation that works indirectly through incentives is setting minimum capital requirements, c. Because managers of a pension fund will lose their capital if the fund's return falls below its required minimum, but their capital will not increase if the fund posts high returns, the greater a fund's required capital, the smaller is the fund managers' incentive to increase their portfolio's risk. In addition to capital requirements, many governments specify that if the return on a pension fund exceeds a prespecified benchmark, the excess return must be placed in a special reserve fund.[17] This reserve fund is then used, in addition to capital, to make up shortfalls should the fund's return fall below its required minimum in the future. By not rewarding the participants in the fund with excessively high returns, this regulation also reduces risk-taking incentives.

The impact of these regulations appear to have been successful in reducing moral hazard, but, in some sense, they may have been too successful. For example, Chilean AFPs appear to have portfolios that closely resemble each other, giving participants relatively little choice regarding a risk–expected return tradeoff (see the evidence in Diamond and Valdés-Prieto 1994). To avoid such "herding" behavior, Hungary allows wider minimum and maximum returns; Poland allows a longer period (24 rather than 12 months) over which a fund's return is compared with the benchmark; and Mexico requires no minimum or maximum rate of return whatsoever for its private pension funds.

Some countries, such as Colombia, Hungary, and Poland, charge pension funds insurance premiums for their government rate of return guarantee. The pension funds' premiums are then deposited into a guarantee trust fund out of which claims are paid.[18] Although such premiums lower a government's net cost of providing guarantees, the government is still obligated to make good on its guarantee if the guarantee fund becomes insolvent. Using the option-pricing approach, Pennacchi (1999b) shows how a Monte Carlo simulation technique can be used to calculate a government's net liability when it charges premiums and manages a guarantee fund.

Minimum Pension Guarantees

Because a fully funded, defined-contribution plan generally earns risky returns, almost all countries whose social security systems include such a plan offer some type of safety net.[19] Typically, this safety net takes one of three forms: (a) a defined-benefit first pillar; (b) a minimum pension guarantee; or (c) a defined-benefit first pillar together with a minimum pension guarantee. For the first type of safety net, contributors are entitled to certain defined benefits that are only partially earnings-related. As in a single-pillar, defined-benefit system, a minimum pension benefit is implicit in the formula used to specify the relationship between an individual's contributions and retirement benefit, and it is unrelated to the individual's balance in his or her defined-contribution pillar (Argentina's social security system is an example.). The focus of this chapter is, then, on valuing a government's minimum pension guarantee for safety nets of the second and third types, because in these cases the government's payments for a minimum pension depend on the investment risk of the individual's defined-contribution pillar.

A government guarantee of a minimum retirement benefit is one way in which to introduce an element of income redistribution or income insurance into a social security system.[20] Governments set a minimum pension level for qualifying retirees that is often indexed to the country's price level, or its average or minimum wage, or both.[21] If at retirement an individual's accumulated pension fund balance is insufficient to buy an annuity that would pay at least the minimum pension, then the government guarantor can respond in one of two ways. One possibility is that the government makes an immediate payment on behalf of the retiree equal to the difference between the minimum pension annuity and the retiree's fund balance, thereby allowing the individual to purchase the minimum pension annuity.[22] An alternative possibility is that the government allows the retiree to make pension account withdrawals equal to the minimum pension, and, if the individual lives long enough to exhaust the account, the government begins paying the minimum pension directly to the individual. For either possibility, the present value of the government's liability at the time of the individual's retirement depends on the level of real interest rates. The reason is that the level of interest rates affects both the cost of purchasing a minimum pension annuity and the present value of the government's payments after withdrawals deplete the individual's account.

From the preceding discussion, one can identify three random factors that play a key role in determining a government guarantor's liability. First, the real value of wages earned by individuals determines their pension fund contributions, which, in turn, affect the real values of their pension account balances at retirement and the level of the minimum pension set by the government. Second, the real rates of return earned by pension funds affect the workers' pension account balances at retirement, because these rates of return determine how quickly workers' contributions grow. Finally, the level of real interest rates at retirement affects the government's liability by determining the cost of the minimum pension annuity or the present value of the government's payments after depletion of an individual's account balance.

Zarita (1994) uses an option-pricing approach to value Chile's minimum pension guarantee. His model allows pension funds to earn a random rate of return, making a worker's pension account balance at retirement random as well. If the worker's savings at retirement is less than the cost of an annuity providing the minimum pension, the government is assumed to make a payment to cover the difference. The value of this government payment is calculated using a Monte Carlo simulation of the worker's risky pension investment assuming a deterministic level of wage contributions each period and a constant real interest rate.

Pennacchi (1999a) also values Chile's minimum pension guarantee by extending the framework in Zarita (1994). Along with random pension fund returns, a worker's real wage, and thus monthly pension contribution, is assumed to follow a random process.[23] The evolution of real wages also influences the government's minimum pension benefit. In addition, real interest rates are assumed to follow a random process. Another difference from Zarita (1994) is that a retired worker is assumed to select a scheduled withdrawal of funds from his or her pension account rather than purchase an annuity. This is arguably more realistic, because Chile gives retirees the choice between these two actions only if they have a sufficient account balance to purchase a minimum pension annuity.[24]

Pennacchi (1999a) calculates guarantee values using a Monte Carlo simulation based on three random, and possibly correlated, processes: the real rate of return on pension fund assets, the growth in real wages, and the change in the short-term real interest rate. An additional minor source of uncertainty is a person's mortality. The probability of death at each age is assumed to be uncorrelated with economic variables and is taken from Chile's official life table.

The results of Zarita (1994) and Pennacchi (1999a) show that the value of the government's minimum pension guarantee for a particular person is a decreasing, convex function of that person's initial wage. In addition, giving retired workers the option of a scheduled withdraw, rather than mandating the purchase of an annuity, raises the cost of the guarantee. This higher cost stems in part from the Chilean government's withdrawal formula, which allows greater withdrawals for individuals with higher savings, and this arrangement tends to subdue the effect that greater retirement savings has on the age at which pension fund balances are depleted. Other findings from these studies confirm that greater volatility in wage and pension fund returns also increases the value of the minimum pension guarantee.

The Chilean case is an example of a minimum pension guarantee provided solely with a defined-contribution pillar. Countries with similar arrangements include Colombia, El Salvador, Kazakhstan, and Mexico. However, the valuation methodology is readily extended to the case of a minimum pension guarantee provided with both defined-benefit and defined-contribution pillars. Hungary and Poland are examples of such social security systems. Hungarians participating in the defined-contribution second pillar are entitled to a second-pillar retirement annuity of no less than 25 percent of the value of their first pillar (see Brixi, Papp, and Schick 1999 for a discussion of Hungary's pension guarantees). In Poland, the government guarantor incurs an expense if the value of individuals' first- and second-pillar accounts is less than the minimum pension, which equals approximately one-third of the average wage.[25] In both of these cases, the government's cost of providing a minimum pension depends on the retirement balances in both the defined-contribution and defined-benefit accounts. Valuing this guarantee is similar to the case of a guarantee that depends only on a defined-contribution balance, the only difference being that the guarantee's maturity value now depends on the individual's defined-benefit level at retirement, which depends, in turn, on the individual's wage contributions.

Guarantees on Employer-Sponsored, Defined-Benefit Pensions

In many countries, social security is supplemented by voluntary, employer-sponsored pensions. Worldwide, the majority of these employer-sponsored pensions are of the defined-benefit type.[26] Absent a guarantee, employees' promised pension benefits are contingent on their corporate sponsor's ability to make good on these promises, subjecting the employees to default risk. To remove this risk exposure, many governments provide guarantees on these privately sponsored, defined-benefit pension funds.

In analyzing the cost of defined-benefit pension guarantees, it is useful to distinguish between pension plans that are collateralized by pension fund assets and those that are not. In most countries, private, defined-benefit pensions are partially or fully funded by a separate portfolio of assets—that is, a pension trust. However, there are important exceptions, such as France, Germany, and Japan, which do not require corporations to segregate particular assets from other corporate assets for the sole purpose of backing pension benefits. Rather, pension liabilities are combined with other corporate liabilities and backed only by the general assets of the corporation. Thus for these nonsegregated pension plans, pension guarantees can be valued using option-pricing techniques developed to value default risky corporate liabilities. A review of these models for valuing corporate debt is given in Merton (1990: chap. 13.4).

More common are corporate-sponsored, defined-benefit pensions in which a pension fund, segregated from other corporate assets, collateralizes pension liabilities. Such plans can be found in Canada, the Netherlands, the United Kingdom, and the United States. In general, pension funds of this type can be "underfunded," meaning the value of the fund's assets are less than its liabilities, or "overfunded," meaning the value of its assets exceeds the present value of employees' accrued benefits. Should a corporate sponsor become bankrupt at the same time that its insured pension fund is underfunded, then the government guarantor would face a claim.

Several studies have applied option-pricing techniques to value this type of pension guarantee.[27] Because the government experiences a loss only when both the corporate sponsor fails and the sponsor's pension fund is underfunded, the value of such a guarantee must depend on the financial conditions of both the corporate sponsor and its pension fund. Marcus (1987) was the first to use an option-pricing approach to model both financial structures. His model assumes that both the asset/liability ratio of the sponsoring corporation and that of its pension fund evolve randomly. Bankruptcy is assumed to occur when the value of corporate assets first falls below the value of corporate liabilities. If this bankruptcy occurs, it is assumed that the government's payment for providing the guarantee equals the value of pension liabilities less pension assets. However, the Marcus model does not restrict this government payment to being positive. In other words, if the pension fund was overfunded at the time of the bankruptcy, the model assumes that the government guarantor receives a payment equal to the difference between pension fund assets and liabilities.

Because in practice a government does not obtain a positive payment should a firm with an overfunded pension plan fail, Pennacchi and Lewis (1994) revised the Marcus analysis to restrict the government guarantor's payment to being positive. The guarantee is then analogous to a put option on the pension fund's assets, with an exercise price equal to the pension fund's liabilities and a contingent maturity date determined by the sponsoring firm's bankruptcy. Lewis and Pennacchi (1999) extend the model further to allow for random market interest rates. This is an important generalization, because the present value of employees' promised benefits can be highly sensitive to interest rate risk. In addition, their study derives the value of the insurance premiums paid by corporations for pension guarantees assuming the structure of insurance premiums charged by the Pension Benefit Guaranty Corporation (PBGC), the U.S. government guarantor of private pensions. This allows them to calculate the net cost of pension guarantees (the present value of guarantee payments less the present value of insurance premiums) for a sample of U.S. corporate pension funds.

Lewis and Pennacchi's empirical findings indicate that the government's cost of pension guarantees can be significant, even for a financially sound corporation with a currently overfunded pension plan. The reason is that pension guarantees can be very long-term commitments. There is a significant probability that a corporation, especially one in a high-risk industry, could experience financial distress in the future, at which time its pension fund could switch from overfunded to underfunded status. Their results indicate that government regulators should act to help prevent pension underfunding. One policy followed by the PBGC is to charge corporations insurance premiums that rise with the level of pension underfunding. Not only would higher premiums help to reduce the government's net cost of insurance if underfunding rises, but they also would reduce a corporation's incentive to begin pension underfunding.

Guarantees on Social Security Systems Funded with Risky Investments

The U.S. social security system is a traditional single-pillar, PAYG, defined-benefit program. At present, contributions from current work-ing-age individuals exceed payments to currently retired individuals, leading to an increase in the notional reserves of the system's trust fund. However, at current contribution rates and benefit levels this reserve surplus will be dissipated following the retirement of the baby boom generation. One proposal to reduce the system's insolvency is to invest a portion of the trust fund's reserves in private equities (com-mon stocks) rather than continue the current practice of investing all of the reserves in U.S. Treasury bonds.[28] The attraction of such a plan is that because equities tend to earn a higher return than government bonds, future trust fund balances, when invested in equities, would have a higher expected value. It is argued that such a change in trust fund investment policy would improve the solvency of the system. Current contributions need not be raised as much nor do future ben-efits have to be reduced as much in order to cope with the large num-ber of future retirees. Essentially, this proposal would have the government take advantage of the positive risk premium earned by equity securities.

Smetters (1999) uses an option-pricing approach to demonstrate that such a policy represents no free lunch. He considers policies in which future payroll taxes and benefit levels are adjusted, depending on the investment performance, and the resulting size, of the trust fund's future balances. His analysis shows that once the value of the contingent gov-ernment spending on benefits in excess of payroll taxes is taken into account, such a policy change will not, in general, improve the solvency of the social security system. In other words, when one properly values the government's guarantee of a particular future tax and benefit struc-ture, the supposed benefits of the trust fund earning an equity premium are illusory. In large part, this stems from the greater risk introduced into future fiscal policy by such a policy change, and accounting for such risk neutralizes the higher expected net benefits.

Conclusion

Government pension guarantees play a key role in gaining public ac-ceptance of pension reforms. To avoid political meddling and enhance the efficiency of work and savings decisions, reformers often strengthen the link between pension contributions and pension benefits and also give individuals a choice about their pension fund investments. How-ever, such a change can increase an individual's exposure to lower-than-expected retirement benefits because of poor lifetime earnings or poor returns earned on pension contributions. Pension guarantees provide a safety net by reducing an individual's exposure to various sources of downside risk.

Recent advances in option-pricing theory have provided important insights for valuing pension guarantees. Perhaps the most attractive feature of this approach is the relatively few assumptions needed to calculate guarantee values. This chapter illustrates how a Monte Carlo simulation technique can be used to calculate the value of a wide variety of pension guarantees. Such cost calculations, while often complex, are important for gauging the full expense of a pension reform. They also may be the basis for setting fair (risk-related) insurance premiums that could enable the government to recoup its cost of providing guarantees. By setting fair premiums for guarantees, the government may be able to mitigate the moral hazard incentives associated with the guarantees.

Annex 13.1

The Relationship between the Expected Rates of Return on a Pension Guarantee and Its Underlying Securities:

Suppose that the return on a risk-free security equals r, but that investors require an expected rate of return on the underlying securities equal to $r + \theta\sigma_s$, where $\theta\sigma_s$ is defined as the securities' *risk premium*. This risk premium is defined to equal the product of the securities' return volatility, σ_s, and the *market price of risk*, θ. This market price of risk reflects investors' preferences for bearing the type of risk that derives from holding the securities.

The pension guarantee, being a contingent claim on the securities, inherits the same risk as the underlying securities. However, in general, its sensitivity to this risk differs from that of the underlying securities. Thus the contingent claim has a return volatility (standard deviation of return) denoted by σ_c, which is some quantity of risk that differs from σ_s. But because it is affected by the same source of risk, the expected return on the pension guarantee reflects the same market price of this risk, θ. Thus the option-pricing approach implies that the rate of return that investors expect to earn on providing the guarantee equals $r + \theta\sigma_c$. This notion, that the expected returns on the contingent claim and its underlying securities reflect the same market price of risk, is also an implication of there being an absence of arbitrage opportunities if investors incur no transactions costs when trading in the underlying securities.[29] Therefore, the option-pricing approach is also referred to as arbitrage-pricing theory.

Computing the Cost of a Guarantee Using Risk-Neutral Valuation:

Let G_0 denote the present value (cost) of a government guarantee of a minimum end-of-year pension fund value equal to X. Its value can be computed as $G_0 = [1/(1 + r)]\ E^*[\max(X - S_1, 0)]$, where $E^*[\cdot]$ is the risk-neutral expectations operator that takes the expected value of its argument subject to the condition that the expected rate of return on all assets equals the risk-free interest rate, r.

In computing $E^*[\max(X - S_1, 0)]$, a Monte Carlo technique can be used to simulate the end-of-year values of S_1. This involves using a random number generator to compute many possible outcomes of S_1, where the portfolio's expected rate of return is set equal to r and its volatility of return is set equal to an estimate of its true standard deviation, σ_s. For each realized value of S_1, the quantity $\max(X - S_1, 0)$ is computed, and these quantities are averaged over all of the realizations. For a sufficiently large number of random simulations of S_1, the average value of $\max(X - S_1, 0)$ will become arbitrarily close to the theoretical value $E^*[\max(X - S_1, 0)]$.

Notes

1. In most of the world, rising life expectancies and declining fertility rates are increasing the ratio of retirees to working-age people. Along with this rise in the old-age dependency ratio, the tendency for politicians to promise generous future pension benefits also often undermines the long-term viability of PAYG systems.

2. Examples include reforms enacted in the Czech Republic, France, Germany, Japan, and the United States. Implementing a complete reform is difficult; current politicians may be unable to commit to long-term reforms, because changes may be undone by future politicians. Such a lack of commitment can reduce the incentives of competing interest groups to reach a compromise.

3. See Holtzman (2000) for a description of the disadvantages of PAYG systems relative to multipillar pension schemes. A country with a PAYG system may experience lower aggregate savings relative to one with a fully funded retirement system. In addition, because a goal of most pension systems is to redistribute income from higher-income to lower-income workers, in defined-benefit systems this redistribution reduces the correspondence between an individual's contributions and his or her pension benefits. Inefficiencies can result if individuals work less or underreport income in jobs covered by the pension system.

4. Mitchell and Zeldes (1996) and Holtzman (2000) discuss the issues surrounding a country's choice of pension reform, including whether the country's financial markets and financial institutions could support individual defined-

contribution accounts, the country's current fiscal situation, and how accumulated benefits to participants in the old pension system would be treated.

5. Goss (1999) defines solvency for a defined-benefit PAYG system as the condition in which payroll tax revenues and pension reserves are sufficient to pay all expected benefits over a given time period without the need for borrowing by the pension administrator.

6. See the Nobel Prize address of Robert C. Merton (1998) for a discussion of the many applications of contingent claims theory.

7. Such a situation is referred to as a complete market—that is, a market in which it is possible to synthetically construct (replicate the payoffs of) a particular security or contingent claim from other securities or contingent claims.

8. Because security brokers often maintain custody of the securities owned by their clients, short-sellers may borrow securities directly from these brokers rather than the actual owners. For example, the government could borrow (short-sell) the same securities owned by the country's pension funds that are held in the custody of security brokers. Such a transaction would have no effect on the pension funds' operations. Alternatively, another government agency may be holding the appropriate securities for some other purpose, say as part of a defined-contribution pension fund organized for government employees. In this case, the government guarantee provider could short-sell the securities held by the government employee pension fund, a transaction requiring only an accounting entry to transfer the securities.

9. This would be accomplished by the government using the proceeds to buy back some of its debt.

10. For example, if the security holdings of pension funds were $1 billion, the government's hedge would involve a short position in less than $1 billion of the same securities.

11. Mortality risk can be estimated using actuarial data. Often, individual mortality risk is assumed to be fully diversifiable, but that may not be the case if there are unpredictable changes in aggregate life expectancies.

12. The term *risk-neutral* describes a hypothetical economy in which all investors are risk-neutral. In such a situation, the equilibrium rates of return on all assets would equal the risk-free rate.

13. The proof of this result is beyond the scope of this chapter, but mathematical derivations can be found in Duffie (1996) and Kocic (1997).

14. Figure 13.3 gives the theoretical probability (density) of different realizations of S_1. The frequencies generated by the Monte Carlo simulations closely approximate those shown in this graph for a sufficiently large number of simulations.

15. The fraction of all realizations for which S_1 is less than $9 million can be derived from Figure 13.3. It equals the area under the graph that is to the left of $9 million divided by the total area under the graph.

16. Because of the simple nature of this particular guarantee, an explicit formula can be derived by noting the similarity between this guarantee and a

series of "forward start" options. In general, it is not possible to derive a formula for all guarantees. Therefore, one could resort to numerical valuation using the previously discussed Monte Carlo simulation technique.

17. For example, in Chile returns exceeding 2 percent more than the average return on all AFPs are channeled to reserves. For Argentina, returns in excess of $\max(1.3R_a, R_a + 0.02)$ become reserves. In Hungary, returns exceeding 40 percent more than the benchmark are placed in reserves.

18. According to Fischer (1998), Colombian AFPs pay a fixed annual premium equal to 0.17 percent of their assets. Palacios and Rocha (1998) report that the current premium paid by Hungarian pension funds equals 0.4 percent of total contributions. Polish pension funds pay a premium that varies with the level of the guarantee fund, because, by law, the total value of the guarantee fund cannot exceed 0.1 percent of total pension fund assets.

19. The only exception seems to be Peru. See Schwarz and Demirgüç-Kunt (1999) for a comparison of the social security systems of countries that have made major reforms.

20. A "solidarity tax," used in Colombia, is another method. Queisser (1995) reports that Colombian pension participants who earn more than four times the minimum wage are taxed an additional 1 percent of their income. The revenue from this solidarity tax is matched by government budget transfers and used to subsidize the contributions of targeted poor groups in order to extend coverage of the formal social security system.

21. In Chile, the minimum pension is set at the discretion of the government, but it is typically equal to about 25 percent of the average wage. Colombia's minimum pension equals its minimum wage, while in Mexico the minimum pension was set equal to Mexico City's 1997 minimum wage and then indexed to the Consumer Price Index. Argentina's minimum pension is approximately 40 percent of the average wage, and in Poland it is approximately 33 percent, net of contributions.

22. Governments usually require that a new retiree's pension fund balance be used to purchase, from a regulated insurance company, an annuity that pays at least the minimum pension.

23. In Chile, an individual's mandatory pension contribution equals 10 percent of his or her wage.

24. As discussed in Turner and Wantanabe (1995), and Smalhout (1996), a worker who reaches retirement with a pension balance that is slightly above or at the price of a minimum pension annuity will have an incentive not to purchase an annuity but to choose the scheduled withdrawal option. By choosing this scheduled withdrawal, the worker will receive free longevity insurance at the government's expense. Should he or she live longer than expected, the government provides a minimum pension. If, instead, the worker does not live as long as expected, the worker's heirs will inherit the balance of the pension account. Thus in some countries the worker receives a government subsidy that would not have materialized if the worker had purchased an annuity at retirement. For someone reaching retirement with moderate to

small pension savings—that is, the individual most likely to require minimum pension assistance—it is more realistic to assume a scheduled withdrawal of pension funds.

25. The first pillar in Poland is a PAYG notional account in which contributions grow at a specified interest rate. The second pillar is a privately managed, defined-contribution account.

26. In the United States, however, the number of employees covered by defined-contribution plans recently surpassed the number of employees covered by defined-benefit plans.

27. As noted in Cholon, Góra and Rutkowski (1999), this type of pension fund guarantee is quite similar to government guarantees of annuities offered by private insurance companies. Thus these valuation models of guarantees for corporate-sponsored, defined-benefit pensions can be applied to annuity guarantees such as those provided by the government of Poland.

28. For example, in his January 19, 1999, State of the Union speech, President Bill Clinton proposed to invest some of the trust fund reserves in U.S. common stocks. One proposal analyzed by the U.S. Advisory Council on Social Security would also call for investing approximately 40 percent of the trust fund in U.S. equities.

29. The intuition for why an absence of arbitrage implies that the expected return on the contingent claim reflects the same price of risk as its underlying security is as follows. Suppose an investor provides the guarantee and hedges by short-selling the underlying security. When there are no transactions costs, this hedge involves short-selling $C\sigma_c/S\sigma_s$ shares of the underlying security for every guarantee offered, where C is the current value of the guarantee and S is the current share price of the underlying security. Because they are affected by the same source of risk, when there is an unexpected movement in the per share value of the underlying security of $S\sigma_s$, the value of the contingent claim changes by $C\sigma_c$. Thus this hedge provides a riskless position for the provider of the guarantee, because when the guarantee's value increases by $C\sigma_c$ it is negated by a change in the short position in the security of $-(C\sigma_c/S\sigma_s)S\sigma_s = -C\sigma_c$. Now, because the investor receives $\$C$ when agreeing to take over the government's guarantee and obtains $\$(C\sigma_c/S\sigma_s)S$ from short-selling the underlying security, the sum of these proceeds is invested in a riskless security. In the absence of arbitrage, the investor's combined portfolio must earn the risk-free rate. Adding together the return on this riskless security of $[C + (C\sigma_c/S\sigma_s)S]r$ plus an expected return from the short position of $-(C\sigma_c/S\sigma_s)S(r - \theta\sigma_c)$ equals $C(r + \theta\sigma_c)$, the expected return on the contingent claim, which reflects the same market price of risk.

References

The word *processed* describes informally reproduced works that may not be commonly available through libraries.

Bernardo, Antonio E., and Olivier Ledoit. 2000. "Gain, Loss, and Asset Pricing." *Journal of Political Economy* 108: 144–72.

Black, Fischer, and Myron S. Scholes. 1973. "The Pricing of Options and Corporate Liabilities." *Journal of Political Economy* 81: 637–54.

Brixi, Hana Polackova, Anita Papp, and Allen Schick. 1999. "Fiscal Risks and the Quality of Fiscal Adjustment in Hungary." Policy Research Working Paper 2176. World Bank, Washington, D.C.

Cholon, Agnieszka, Marek Góra, and Michal Rutkowski. 1999. "Shaping Pension Reform in Poland: Security through Diversity." World Bank Pension Reform Primer Working Paper. World Bank, Washington, D.C.

Cochrane, John H, and Jesùs Saá-Requejo. 2000. "Beyond Arbitrage: Good-Deal Asset Price Bounds in Incomplete Markets." *Journal of Political Economy* 108: 79–119.

Diamond, Peter, and Salvador Valdés-Prieto. 1994. "Social Security Reforms." In Barry P. Boxworth, Rudiger Dornbusch, and Raul Laban, eds., *The Chilean Economy: Policy Lessons and Challenges*. Washington, D.C.: Brookings Institution.

Duffie, Darrell. 1996. *Dynamic Asset Pricing Theory*. Princeton: Princeton University Press.

Fischer, Klaus P. 1998. "A Discrete Martingale Model of Pension Fund Guarantees in Colombia: Pricing and Market Effects." Working Paper. Université Laval, Quebec.

Goss, Stephen C. 1999. "Measuring Solvency in the Social Security System." In Olivia S. Mitchell, Robert J. Myers, and Howard Young, eds., *Prospects for Social Security Reform*. Philadelphia: University of Pennsylvania Press.

Holtzman, Robert. 2000. "The World Bank Approach to Pension Reform." Processed.

Kocic, Aleksandar. 1997. "Numeraire Invariance and Generalized Risk Neutral Valuation." *Advances in Futures and Options Research* 9: 157–73.

Lewis, Christopher M., and George G. Pennacchi. 1999. "Valuing Insurance for Defined-Benefit Pension Plans." *Advances in Futures and Options Research* (10): 135–67.

Marcus, Alan J. 1987. "Corporate Pension Policy and the Value of PBGC Insurance." In Zvi Bodie, John Shoven, and David Wise, eds., *Issues in Pension Economics*. Chicago: University of Chicago Press.

Merton, Robert C. 1973. "Theory of Rational Option Pricing." *Bell Journal of Economics and Management Science* 4: 141–83.

———. 1990. *Continuous-Time Finance*. Cambridge, Mass.: Blackwell Publishers.

———. 1998. "Applications of Option-Pricing Theory: Twenty-Five Years Later." *American Economic Review* 88: 323–49.

Mitchell, Olivia S. 1996. "Social Security Reform in Uruguay: An Economic Assessment." Pension Research Council Working Paper 96-20. Wharton School, University of Pennsylvania.

Mitchell, Olivia S., and Flavio Ataliba Barreto. 1997. "After Chile, What? Second-Round Pension Reforms in Latin America." *Revista de Análisis Económico* 12: 3–36.

Mitchell, Olivia S., and Stephen P. Zeldes. 1996. "Social Security Privatization: A Structure for Analysis." *American Economic Review* 86: 363–67.

Palacios, Robert, and Roberto Rocha. 1998. "The Hungarian Pension System in Transition." In Lajos Bokros and Jean-Jacques Dethier, eds., *Public Finance Reform during the Transition: The Experience of Hungary*. Washington, D.C.: World Bank.

Pennacchi, George G. 1999a. "The Value of Guarantees on Pension Fund Returns." *Journal of Risk and Insurance* 66: 219–37.

———. 1999b. "The Effects of Setting Deposit Insurance Premiums to Target Insurance Fund Reserves." *Journal of Financial Services Research* 16 (2/3): 153–80.

Pennacchi, George G., and Christopher M. Lewis. 1994. "The Value of Pension Benefit Guaranty Corporation Insurance." *Journal of Money, Credit and Banking* 26: 735–53.

Queisser, Monika. 1995. "Chile and Beyond: The Second-Generation Pension Reforms in Latin America." *International Social Security Review* 48: 23–39.

Schwarz, Anita M., and Asli Demirgüç-Kunt. 1999. "Taking Stock of Pension Reforms around the World." Social Protection Discussion Paper No. SP9917. World Bank, Washington, D.C.

Smalhout, James H. 1996. *The Uncertain Retirement*. Chicago: Irwin Publishing.

Smetters, Kent. 1999. "The Equivalence between State Contingent Tax Policy and Options: An Application to Investing the Social Security Trust Fund in Equities." Working Paper. Wharton School, University of Pennsylvania.

Turner, John A., and Noriyasu Wantanabe. 1995. *Private Pension Policies in Industrialized Countries: A Comparative Analysis*. Kalamazoo: W. E. Upjohn Institute for Employment Research.

Zarita, Salvador. 1994. "Minimum Pension Insurance in the Chilean Pension System." *Revista de Análisis Económico* (9): 105–26.

CHAPTER 14

Measuring and Managing Government Contingent Liabilities in the Banking Sector

Stijn Claessens*
University of Amsterdam

Daniela Klingebiel
World Bank

GOVERNMENT CONTINGENT LIABILITIES in the banking sector arise from explicit government guarantees on banking system liabilities through a public deposit insurance scheme. Public contingent liabilities also can emerge when governments try to limit the loss of confidence in the financial system during periods of financial turbulence by taking over or guaranteeing liabilities that are not formally protected. This "moral' obligation of the government to protect depositors and other creditors reflects public expectations, but it also is influenced by pressures from interest groups, with governments bailing out unprotected creditors instead of imposing losses on them.

Recent experience suggests that the fiscal costs of a banking crisis can be substantial and can, in extreme cases, threaten fiscal stability. As such, an analysis of the causes of and means of limiting these costs has to be an essential component of efforts to limit and manage government contingent liabilities. This chapter analyzes two questions. First, can contingent liabilities arising from the banking system be measured accurately? Second, and more important, what can governments do to control fiscal liabilities arising from the banking sector? The chapter finds

*The author was with the World Bank when he wrote this article; he is currently with the University of Amsterdam.

that existing approaches to measuring contingent liabilities in the banking sector, while representing a good start, are often inadequate. Most are based on static models that focus on the typical causes of a banking crisis, but they fail to recognize the dynamic dimensions of managing contingent liabilities arising from banking distress. The analysis suggests that a substantial portion of the fiscal costs arises from improper crisis management. The chapter also outlines how the probability of banking crises can be reduced through a variety of instruments.

The chapter does not analyze the government's direct or indirect role in the financial system in noncrisis times, a role that may influence the fiscal costs and risks of a financial crisis. This role of the government has at least three aspects. The first concerns the proper role of the government in setting the framework for a country's financial development and in providing deposit insurance and other guarantees. The second aspect relates to the government's ownership of financial institutions. And the third aspect is the short- and long-run costs and benefits of any directed credit programs or other ways in which the government influences, through the financial sector, the allocation of resources in an economy.

The first aspect is a very broad topic (for a recent review, see World Bank 2001a). The consensus is that the general role of the government should be in setting up the institutional, legal, and accounting infrastructure to improve financial development. Proper regulation and supervision are key government roles and crucial to reaping the gains from the deepening of the financial sector. Whether there is a role for deposit insurance and guarantees in enhancing financial sector development is less clear. Properly used, deposit insurance can assist in improving financial stability, and credit guarantees may help institutions attract loans at more reasonable rates. But in many countries a high fiscal cost and an increased risk of financial crises have been associated with deposit insurance and government guarantees (see Demirgüç-Kunt and Detragiache 2000; World Bank 2001a). These costs have arisen because the private sector has reduced its monitoring of financial institutions and moral hazard has increased. When governments are unable to monitor financial institutions effectively, implicit and explicit guarantees can have large costs and retard the longer-term development of a financial sector. Poor financial development can in turn expose the government to additional fiscal risk.

On the second aspect, the general experience with government ownership in the financial sector has been very poor and quite costly in terms of financial sector development. Government-owned financial institutions that borrow for the purpose of lending hurt private sector efforts to do the same and thereby impede financial development. Empirically, government ownership of banks has been found to retard financial sector development and increase the risk of financial crises (for a review, see World Bank 2001a and 2001b). In particular, Barth, Caprio, and Levine (2000) show that for a sample of 66 countries greater state ownership of banks tends to be associated with higher interest rate spreads, less private credit, and less activity on the stock exchange and less nonbank credit, after taking account of real gross domestic product (GDP) per capita, corruption, expropriation risk, bureaucratic efficiency, and the law and order tradition of the country, all of which could influence financial development. This evidence is confirmed for a larger sample of countries in Barth, Caprio, and Levine (2001). A separate study, with data from private industry sources covering the 10 largest commercial and development banks for each of 92 countries for 1970 and 1995, convincingly highlights the causal link (La Porta, Lopez de Silanes, and Shleifer 2000). It finds that greater state ownership of banks in 1970 was associated with lesser financial sector development, lower growth, and lower productivity, and that these effects were larger at lower levels of per capita income, with less initial financial sector development and with weaker property rights protection.

The evidence on the third aspect, the role of directed credit and government involvement in the allocation of resources through the financial sector, is more mixed (for a review, see Caprio and Demirgüç-Kunt 1997). In East Asia throughout the 1980s, for example, directed credit programs were generally considered successful (see World Bank 1993). In weak institutional settings, however, attempts to reach underserviced groups often miss their targets, are captured by special-interest groups, and have large fiscal costs. Thus an immediate cost of directed credit programs may be that funds are directed to uses that might not arise if judgments were based on rational economic criteria. Directed credit programs also can have an impact on financial sector development. The U.S. government loan programs to agriculture, for example, have significantly impeded the development of private sector agriculture finance. Loan guarantees reduce the incentive to develop private credit evaluation systems, which ultimately reduces the allocative efficiency of the financial system. Even if the goals are laudable, such as providing more financial support to small-scale agriculture, better housing for lower-income families, more education benefits (student loans), and help to small businesses, the long-term costs to financial sector development may well offset the benefits. The empirical analysis by Barth, Caprio, and Levine (2001) suggests that, in general, fewer regulatory restrictions and limits on commercial bank activities produce more diverse income streams, encourage greater competition and therefore efficiency, and allow banks to benefit from economies of scale and scope. Directed credit programs, as forms of government restrictions, would thus lead to exactly the opposite results: less financial sector development, greater risk of banking crisis, high ultimate fiscal costs, and lower economic growth.

The rest of this chapter is divided into six sections. The first section details why banking crises matter by reviewing cross-country experience.

The second section, which reviews existing banking crisis prediction models, is followed by one that assesses currently available approaches to measuring contingent liabilities arising from banking system distress. The fourth section analyzes instruments and government tools for controlling fiscal contingencies and the costs of a banking crisis, focusing on the initial phases of a financial crisis. The fifth section presents policy tools to prevent or at least reduce the probability of future systemic banking crises. It is followed by the chapter's conclusions.

Bank Insolvency and Government Liabilities

In recent decades, many developing and developed countries have experienced banking crises requiring major—and expensive—overhauls of their banking systems. By one count, 112 episodes of a systemic banking crisis have occurred in 93 countries since the late 1970s (Caprio and Klingebiel 1999). Banking crises have been very disruptive for two reasons: they tend to be expensive in terms of the fiscal costs that governments, and ultimately the taxpayers, shoulder, and they also can be costly in terms of forgone economic output. By one measure, banking crises have been the most important source of government contingent liabilities (see Kharas and Mishra 2001).

The prevalence of banking system failures has been at least as great in developing and transition countries as in the industrial world. However, financial crises have proved substantially more expensive in developing countries (see Figure 14.1). In a survey of 40 banking crises, Honohan and Klingebiel (2000) found that governments of developing countries spent on average 14.3 percent of GDP to clean up their financial systems, double the amount that governments of industrial countries paid out. Some of the banking crises in developing countries were very expensive. Of those for which there are data, Argentina's crisis in the early 1980s proved to be the most expensive restructuring exercise—about 55 percent of GDP—followed by Indonesia's with a price tag to date of about 50 percent of GDP and Chile's at 41.3 percent. Among industrialized countries, Japan's long and drawn-out banking crisis has been the costliest; authorities already have spent about 20 percent of GDP to restructure the system.

In the past two decades, governments and, thus ultimately taxpayers, have largely shouldered the costs of restructuring banking systems. When governments have not been able to mobilize sufficient resources—through additional taxes, spending cuts, or borrowing—to service the additional debt burden, they have resorted to inflationary financing, passing the losses on to those holding currency, with adverse consequences for growth and income distribution. Although the fiscal costs estimates have often been staggering

Figure 14.1. Fiscal Cost of Banking Crises

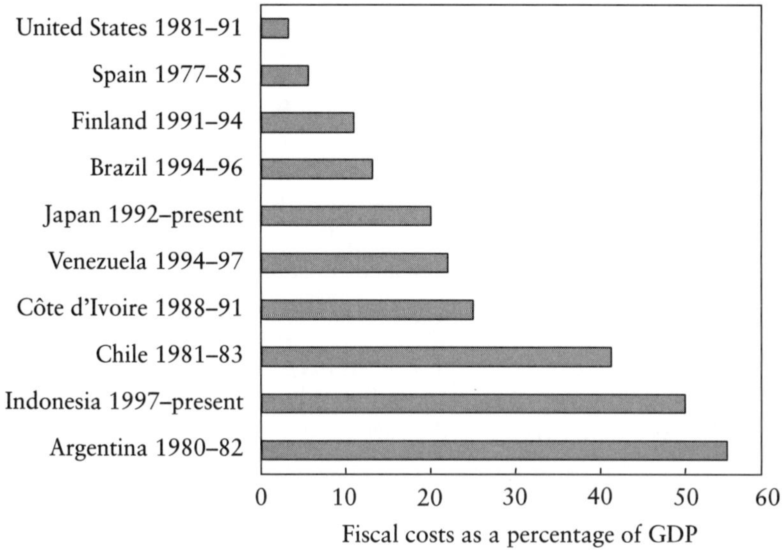

Source: Honohan and Klingebiel (2000).

(see Figure 14.1), the true economic costs of banking crises have been even higher than these estimates suggest. Fiscal costs do not include, for example, the costs borne in some cases by depositors and other creditors of failed banks. They also do not take into account that depositors and borrowers have been often "taxed" in the form of widened spreads to make up for bad loans left on banks' balance sheets. In addition, costs do not reflect the distortions introduced by granting borrowers some monopoly privilege or other means to improve their profits and thereby repay their loans.

The Causes of Banking Crises and Predicting Crises

The large fiscal costs of banking crises raise the question of whether these costs can be avoided, or at least reduced, through specific policy measures. A starting point for answering this question is to identify the exact causes of banking crises. The literature on financial crises is growing (see Kaminsky and Reinhart 1999 and Goldstein, Kaminsky, and Reinhart 2000 for a review of banking crises prediction models). Demirgüç-Kunt and Detriagiache (1998, 2000) employ an econometric model to explain the incidence of banking crises in a large sample of countries. They find that macroeconomic variables—GDP growth; changes in trade, the real interest rate, inflation, growth of credit, fiscal surplus, and reserves cover for money stock; and recent financial liberalization—are important factors in explaining the incidence of financial crises. As such, their model provides important information about the factors contributing to and triggering banking crises. Specifically, they find evidence that large current account and fiscal deficits, rapid credit growth, and financial liberalization in a weak institutional environment increase the probability of a crisis, confirming the earlier results of Caprio and Klingebiel (1997). Other, more recent work has highlighted the role of microeconomic and bank-specific factors (Gonzales-Hermosillo 1999; Laeven 1999; Bongini, Claessens, and Ferri 2001).

Most econometric models, however, have not been able to predict accurately the timing of banking crises. Models typically predict too many crises—type I error—if the threshold probability is kept low, or they miss many crisis episodes—type II error—when the threshold probability is raised. For example, Demirgüç-Kunt and Detragiache (2000) reveal that their model would have missed the recent banking crisis in several of the affected East Asian countries. Indeed, as late as May 1997 the model would not have signaled any problems—for example, it predicted a probability of a banking crisis in Thailand of only 3.3 percent. Overall, they conclude that their model "found the overall image. . . [to have] been a rather reassuring one."

A major limitation of these models as a forecasting tool is that they rely heavily on macrofinancial indicators such as interest rates and exchange rates, whose sudden spikes are hard to forecast. Without these variables—which themselves are often the consequences of financial distress rather than the causes—these models provide little advance warning. Other studies have included longer-term institutional and policy factors that can predispose a country to crises (Hardy and Pazarbasioglu 1998; Keefer 1999). But these factors are often difficult to quantify and therefore do not decrease type I or type II errors significantly.

Although these models may be of limited use as forecasting tools, they consistently point toward areas of policy reform that can be expected to reduce the incidence, and possibly the costs, of financial crisis. The results suggest that governments that pursue relatively sound macroeconomic policies—characterized by low budget deficits, low inflation, and an exchange rate policy that avoids the real appreciation of the exchange rate—can significantly reduce the incidence and costs of banking crises. Preventing rapid credit growth and phasing in financial liberalization properly in a weak institutional environment are two other areas of policy reform that follow from most empirical work.

Approaches to Measuring Contingent Liabilities in the Banking Sector

The banking crises prediction models reviewed earlier in this chapter do not aim to quantify the extent of potential government contingencies arising from a crisis, but just their incidence and timing. This limitation may stem from the fact that market participants are typically more interested in the occurrence of a crisis than in its final costs. Also, contingent liabilities arising from banking crises are difficult to measure. Information on financial institutions' balance sheets and overall risk exposure is often of poor quality and limited value in developing countries. The market values of banks' assets can be volatile in any environment, but even more so in a financial crisis when they are affected by large changes in interest rates and exchange rates, the financial condition of the corporate sector, and economic growth, among other things. Nevertheless, investigators have attempted to quantify the fiscal exposure arising from the banking system. Three major approaches to measuring contingent liabilities in the banking sector can be distinguished: (a) the gross assets-at-risk approach used by Standard and Poor's Sovereign Ratings Service (1999); (b) the value-at-risk (VAR) approach of Blejer and Schumacher (1998), which is also outlined in Chapter 16 by Mario Blejer and Liliana Schumacher in this volume; and (c) the accounting approach to bank losses by Honohan (1999).

Standard and Poor's (S&P) estimates the gross banking assets at risk from a major economic downturn. The framework relies on a quality rating of countries based on perceived vulnerability to asset quality pressure during a recession. The rating, which is subjective, is provided by S&P staffers who also conduct ratings of countries. The model then applies a factor—between zero and one, depending on the rating—to the total assets of the financial system. The figure obtained through this exercise is called the "gross banking assets at risk" from a major economic downturn. The risk of a downturn occurring in the forecast horizon is then assessed in a separate exercise. As the label "gross banking assets at risk" suggests, the S&P approach tries to estimate the gross exposure of the economy to banking system distress. As such, it does not measure the direct fiscal exposure of the government if a banking crisis actually occurs. The method provides an upper limit to contingent fiscal liabilities and as such is closer to the value-at-risk approach, a concept now commonly used in commercial banks to assess risks.

Blejer and Schumacher (1998) employ a value-at-risk approach to appraising a central bank's solvency. They examine the factors from traditional central bank operations and off-balance sheet positions that may affect solvency, including foreign exchange and financial sector guarantees. While a central bank cannot fail commercially, it may behave equivalently if it has to forsake a commitment to an announced nominal regime (such as an exchange or inflation target) because its solvency has been threatened. If indeed the probability of a central bank abandoning its commitments relates to its vulnerability to solvency losses, measures such as VAR could be used as forward-looking indicators of credibility crises. This model might help in identifying the risk of a financial crisis; it does not, however, provide a methodology for estimating the fiscal costs arising from an actual crisis.

Honohan (1999) applies a VAR approach to the whole banking sector. His model assesses the probability and the extent of fiscal contingencies arising from the banking sector because of changes in the macroenvironment. Using accounting data on the size and composition of the balance sheets of the banks, the model simulates several short-term risk factors that can adversely affect bank balance sheets. These risk factors are then used to estimate the amount of contingent fiscal liabilities. The approach is as follows. First, the model specifies and quantifies possible economic shocks, such as changes in the exchange rate, changes in property market values, changes in the terms of trade, or a general economic downturn. Then, using banks' balance sheet information, it classifies various balance sheet items according to whether and to what extent they would be adversely affected by these economic shocks (see Table 14.1).

Table 14.1 Capturing the Effects of Macroshocks
on Individual Bank Balance Sheets

	Primary effects	*Secondary effects*
Exchange rate shocks	Foreign exchange (FX)-denominated loans (affected both directly by currency translation and indirectly by changed loan loss experience)	Other FX-denominated assets (net, affected mainly by currency translation)
Property market shocks	Loans to real estate developers (net worth of borrowers directly affected)	Other loans secured on real estate (value of collateral declines)
General economic shocks	Loan portfolio (net worth of borrowers directly affected)	Marketable investments (market values affected)
Problematic accounting	Government-related loans (unrecognized collection problems due to political influence)	Other loans (evergreening, overly optimistic collateral valuation, and so forth)

Source: Honohan (1999).

The model then applies a multiplier to each group of balance sheet items based on the size of the assumed shock to the affected balance sheet category. In the next step, the capital positions of the various banks are estimated after the effects of each shock and the systemwide capital deficiency are calculated. The latter is assumed to be met by the government. The same exercise is repeated for different sizes of shocks, such as different changes in the exchange rate, with probabilities assigned to each discrete macroshock. Finally, a matrix is constructed for a given macro shock, indicating the potential size of the losses (Table 14.2). For example, in the hypothetical country the potential fiscal liabilities could amount to US$6.9 million if the exchange rate change is greater than 40 percent and loan losses greater than 50 percent. As Honohan notes, this methodology provides an estimate of maximum fiscal liability, because it assumes that banks will be made whole by the fiscal authority. The model would, however, allow for loss absorption by other claimants.

VAR-type approaches are commonly used by financial institutions and are being introduced in estimating government contingent liabilities as well (see Chapters 4 by Sundaresan and 5 by Ramaswamy in this volume). Applying VAR-type approaches to the banking sector can be a good starting point, but it has limitations when estimating potential banking losses and the resulting fiscal costs. VAR-type approaches are essentially backward looking and static, and the results derived from them can be problematic. The fiscal costs of banking crises are determined not only by the size of the macroshock, the initial conditions, and the known risk exposures in the banking sector, but also by government policies in managing the crisis. The cost of a banking system failure is a function of the policies adopted.

Table 14.2 Potential Fiscal Liability Arising from a Depreciation and Loan Losses

US$ million		$V =$				
		0%	14.3%	25%	40%	50%
	0.1	0	0	0	0	0
	0.2	0	0	0	0	0
	0.3	0	0	0	0	1.0
$?(v) =$	0.4	0	0	0.6	2.4	5.8
	0.5	0.5	1.2	2.7	6.9	14.7
	0.6	2.6	4.5	7.5	16.1	26.9
	0.7	6.6	10.2	14.7	28.9	43.2

Note: v is percentage depreciation; $?(v)$ is percentage loan losses. The entries provide the total loss of the joint events.
Source: Honohan (1999).

One way to identify the most important policy measures for containing fiscal costs is to review past crises. In a recent paper, Honohan and Klingebiel (2000) analyzed the determinants of the total fiscal costs for 40 banking crises during the 1980s and 1990s. They found that government policies in the initial containment phase of the crisis are more important explanatory factors of the final fiscal costs, as measured ex post, than the initial macro- and microvulnerabilities. Indeed, according to Honohan and Klingebiel, fiscal costs are systematically associated with a set of crisis management strategies. They found that the explanatory variables employed—mainly policy variables—can explain 60–80 percent of cross-country variation in fiscal costs. Their empirical findings reveal that unlimited deposit guarantees, open-ended liquidity support, repeated recapitalizations, debtor bailouts, and regulatory forbearance add significantly and sizably to costs. Using the regression results to simulate the effects of these policies, they learned that if countries had not extended all these policies, the average fiscal costs in their sample could have been limited to about 1 percent of GDP—that is, a little more than one-tenth of what was actually experienced. On the other hand, policy could have been worse: had countries engaged in all of the above policies, fiscal costs in excess of 60 percent of GDP would have been the result (Figure 14. 2). As Table 14.3 indicates, liquidity support and forbearance measures are the costliest ones. Even if deposit guarantees, forbearance, and repeated recapitalizations are employed, not extending liquidity support could reduce fiscal costs by almost two-thirds.

These results suggest that the contingent liabilities arising from a banking crisis are importantly influenced by government policies rather

Figure 14.2. Size Effect of Crisis Resolution Policies

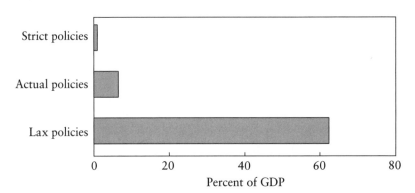

Note: Graph shows the predicted fiscal cost of a banking crisis if countries adopt different kinds of crisis resolution policies.
Source: Honohan and Klingebiel (2000).

Table 14.3 Estimated Individual Impacts of Policy Variables on Fiscal Costs
(percent of base case fiscal cost)

| | Best policy employed in percentage of cases | Estimated saving (percent of base case fiscal cost) by switching one policy tool from: | | |
| | | Strict value | | Lax value |
		A	B	C
LIQSUP	0.421	165.1	50.8	–62.3
FORB-A	0.763	120.6	82.9	–54.6
FORB-B	0.158	118.6	13.1	–54.3
REPCAP	0.763	112.1	77.5	–52.9
GUAR	0.447	55.7	21.9	–35.8
PDRP	0.789	50.7	38.2	–33.6

Note: LIQSUP indicates whether unlimited liquidity support was provided to banks. Two measures of forbearance are: FORB-A, which captures whether insolvent banks were permitted to continue functioning, and FORB-B, which denotes whether other bank prudential regulations were suspended or not fully applied. REPCAP indicates where banks were repeatedly recapitalized. GUAR denotes that either governments issued an explicit guarantee on all bank liabilities or market participants were implicitly protected from any losses if public banks' market share exceeded 75 percent. PDRP indicates that governments implemented across-the-board public debt relief programs.

Columns A and B show the effect of a policy relaxation—that is, switching the value of one policy variable from strict to lax—on the predicted cost of the crisis. Column A assumes all other variables are held at strict values; Column B sets the other policy dummies in the regression at their sample mean (fractional) values. Column C shows the effect of a policy tightening, assuming all other variables are left at their lax values. Thus, for example, a policy of unlimited liquidity support would increase the average crisis cost by 65 percent of the value that would occur if all variables were held at their strict values.

Source: Honohan and Klingebiel (2000).

than only by ex ante weaknesses. Furthermore, the results indicate that the fiscal outlays incurred in resolving banking system distress can to a great extent be attributed to the measures adopted by the government during the first two years of the crisis. They also suggest that governments can control fiscal costs by adequately managing the crisis resolution process. The specific measures most likely to be successful are analyzed in the next section.

Approaches to Controlling the Costs of a Banking Crisis

Cross-country experiences point to several clear processes and principles, which if adopted during the containment phase of a banking crisis, will control the fiscal costs of the crisis (see, for example, Sheng

1996 and Claessens 1999). The empirical results highlight that an adequate government strategy should, during the early or containment phase of a crisis, include the following three main components:

• Governments should not provide liquidity support to weak financial institutions to delay problem recognition but rather should address the problem early on and develop a strategy that deals with the problem comprehensively and credibly.

• Governments should avoid issuing a blanket government guarantee that distorts incentives for both managers and shareholders of banks to behave prudently and for their creditors to monitor the institution closely.

• Governments should not employ forbearance policies—that is, policies involving deviations from prudential standards aimed at allowing institutions to recapitalize from increased earnings, but only in certain limited circumstances.

Cross-country evidence also suggests a set of policies that are important both to control fiscal outlays in the short run and to strengthen over the medium term the incentive framework in which market participants operate.[1] In particular, the following medium-term policies are important:

• Government should not bail out banks, nor is it necessary to bail out depositors in all cases.

• Governments should complement bank restructuring with an adequate framework for corporate restructuring.

• A proper incentive framework for restructuring should be adopted.

The Short-term Containment Phase

Liquidity Support. To contain fiscal costs arising from a banking crisis, government should not provide liquidity on an ongoing basis until it is satisfied that the bank is viable and oversight is adequate. Governments have often used liquidity support to delay crisis recognition and avoid intervening in de facto insolvent institutions. But this strategy is doomed to failure. Managerial and shareholder incentives quickly shift for a financial institution when it becomes insolvent: managers have no incentive to run the institution on a viable basis and their actions often speedily drain away resources—including liquidity support from the central bank. In 1997 this situation was disastrously demonstrated in Thailand, where large-scale liquidity support—10 percent of GDP—was extended to finance companies that turned out to be black holes of insolvency.

Government Guarantees. Governments should not resort to the quick fix of giving guarantees to depositors and creditors to stem the loss of confidence. Such guarantees limit their maneuverability in allocating losses in the future. More important, if guarantees are credible, they reduce (large) creditors' incentives to monitor financial institutions and therefore increase the importance of early intervention in weak institutions to stop managers and shareholders from engaging in the "gamble for resurrection." As a result, the costs of banking crises increase, especially in weak regulatory environments.[2]

Forbearance. Many countries have adopted a policy of forbearance to allow banks to recapitalize from retained earnings. Explicit forbearance policies include lower capital adequacy requirements, more lenient tax treatments, tax breaks, lower reserve or provisioning requirements, more lenient accounting standards and practices, guarantees on bank assets or liabilities (or both), and lower interest rates on liquidity support. Forbearance also may be implicit—that is, authorities turn a blind eye to violations of laws, standards, and regulations by either individual banks or the banking system. Cross-country experience shows that forbearance strategies have rarely been successful. As the above empirical evidence shows, forbearance often increases the costs of financial crises, especially in weak microenvironments when authorities are unable or unwilling to stop the transfer of resources out of financial institutions that long ago turned insolvent.

Because of dangers of misuse, some experts propose that forbearance be forsworn completely. One could argue that forbearance has a useful role in special circumstances—in cases of a sharp external shock faced by otherwise sound financial institutions and a good institutional framework (including proper regulation and supervision and monitoring by the market). If used, forbearance should be transparent and accompanied by stringent standards, realistic targets and implementation periods, and strict enforcement with prompt and transparent action in case of violation. It should not be adopted in situations with existing micro weaknesses or where owners are wholly or partly responsible for the bank's predicament.

The Medium-term Rehabilitation and Restructuring Phase

Allocating Losses and Use of Public Resources. When a financial institution is insolvent, the claims of shareholders and subordinated debtholders should be written down entirely before public money is forthcoming. Restructuring can strengthen financial discipline by allocating losses not only to existing shareholders, but also (at least some losses) to creditors and depositors who should have monitored the bank. Allocating losses to creditors or depositors will not necessarily lead to a run on the bank or end in contraction of aggregate money and credit, and output. In some past crises, governments imposed losses on depositors, and there were little (or no) adverse macroeconomic consequences or flight to currency (Baer and Klingebiel 1995). Economic recovery was rapid, and financial intermediation, including household deposits, was restored within a short time (Figure 14.3). Financial discipline was further strengthened when management, deemed to be part of the problem, was changed as well, and banks were operationally restructured.

This does not mean that government support should always be withheld. Rather, it can imply the opposite, that countries need (or must be perceived) to have large enough public war chests to deal with the large costs. Often a government's instinctive reaction to a crisis is to allocate too few public resources. Unsure of the amount of help available, financial institutions tend to hide the true extent of their problems, and existing and potential shareholders will not put up new capital. More generally, insufficient government support undermines the confidence of depositors and investors. Yet public sector capital injections should not be a bailout of existing shareholders. Rather, the aim is to allocate losses transparently and minimize costs to the taxpayers, while preserving incentives for the infusion of new private capital.

If public money is provided, assisted banks should be required to draw up an acceptable business plan, verified by third parties, that covers capital restructuring and operational restructuring to reduce costs and improve profit prospects without taking on additional risks. Adequate safeguards are needed to ensure that banks do not subsequently become undercapitalized, and they should include strict and regular monitoring and supervision, on-site and off-site. In the past, many countries failed to follow these principles. They resolved their financial crises in part through partial or full public bailouts, which reinforced the perception of an implicit government guarantee on deposits and other bank liabilities to the detriment of market discipline. In some cases, bank management, at least partly responsible for the problems, was not even changed for the course of the restructuring, which further undermined incentives for prudent behavior. The lingering effects of such policies contributed to the 1997 banking crisis in East Asia (Alba, Hernandez, and Klingebiel 1999).

Corporate Restructuring. A large portion of nonperforming loans is often just a reflection of overleveraged borrowers and corporate distress. Lowering corporate sector debt is frequently essential to corporate revival and reducing vulnerability to future shocks. This situation portends debt restructuring along with operational restructuring. Countries have used different approaches for corporate restructuring: a *centralized, government-led approach* that concentrates asset recovery in one public agency or asset management company (AMC), or *a*

Figure 14.3. When Depositors Absorb Losses: Estonia (1992), Argentina (1980–82), Japan (1946), and United States (1933)

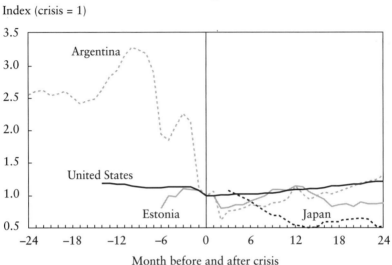

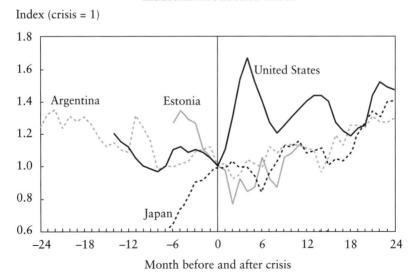

Source: Baer and Klingebiel (1995).

decentralized approach led by banks and other creditors. Both approaches have advantages and disadvantages.

Centralization of assets may permit a consolidation of skills and resources and easier monitoring and supervision of workout practices. As claims are consolidated, more leverage may be obtained over debtors and perverse links between banks and corporations may be broken, allowing better collection on (connected) loans. Yet an AMC holding a large portion of corporate claims is difficult to insulate from political pressures. Moreover, a transfer of loans breaks the links between banks and corporations, links that may have positive value given banks' privileged access to corporate information. And if AMC assets are not actively managed, credit discipline in the whole financial system can be undermined, increasing the overall costs of the crisis. Public AMCs have had a mixed record (Klingebiel 2000) and often have led to higher fiscal costs because assets were inadequately managed and consequently lost value (see Box 14.1).

The decentralized, creditor-led workout approach relies on banks and other creditors to resolve nonperforming loans. Because banks have the institutional knowledge of the borrower and because their own survival depends on asset recovery, they may be better willing and able to maximize recovery value and avoid future losses. Furthermore, banks can provide new loans in debt restructuring. Successful decentralized debt workouts require, however, limited or no ownership links between banks and corporations (otherwise, the same party would be both debtor and creditor), adequately capitalized banks, and proper incentives for banks and borrowers. The very slow speed of restructuring in Japan, for example, has stemmed in part from extensive ownership links among banks, other financial intermediaries, and corporations. As a result, there was a deadlock on claims in Japan, which was not broken for a long time. Similarly, banks need to be adequately capitalized to have the loss absorption capacity to engage in corporate restructuring. If governments allow banks to recapitalize via increased earnings over a longer time horizon—either through implicit or explicit forbearance—banks' abilities to engage in rapid corporate restructuring are limited.

The Incentive Framework. Regardless of whether banks have the resources, the degree and sustainability of corporate restructuring, and therefore the final fiscal costs, will depend on the incentives for proper restructuring. With weak incentives, creditors may be inclined to roll over nonperforming loans rather than to restructure them, hoping for eventual recovery, with the downside risks covered by an implicit government guarantee. The incentives for proper restructuring include adequate accounting and troubled debt restructuring standards that ensure that standards are applied uniformly across all classes of creditors and

---

Box 14.1 The Use of Asset Management Companies in the Resolution of Banking Crises—Cross-Country Experience

In the past, asset management companies (AMCs) have been employed to address the overhang of bad debt in the financial system. Two main types of AMCs can be distinguished: those set up to help and expedite corporate restructuring and those established as rapid asset disposition vehicles. A review of seven AMCs in Finland, Ghana, Mexico, the Philippines, Spain, Sweden, and the United States reveals that they have a mixed record. In two out of three cases, corporate-restructuring AMCs did not achieve their narrow goals of expediting bank or corporate restructuring. These experiences suggest that AMCs are rarely good tools for expediting corporate restructuring. Only the Swedish AMC successfully managed its portfolio, acting in some instances as lead agent in the restructuring process. It was helped by some special circumstances, however: the assets acquired were mostly real estate-related, not manufacturing-related (which are harder to restructure), and were a small fraction of the banking system (which made it easier for the AMC to maintain its independence from political pressures and to sell assets back to the private sector). Rapid asset disposition vehicles fared somewhat better, with two out of four countries—namely, Spain and the United States—achieving their objectives.

The successful experiences suggest that AMCs can be used effectively, but only for the narrowly defined purposes of resolving insolvent and nonviable financial institutions and selling their assets. But even achieving these objectives required many ingredients: a type of asset that can be easily liquefied (real estate), mostly professional management, political independence, a skilled resource base, appropriate funding, adequate bankruptcy and foreclosure laws, good information and management systems, and transparency in operations and processes. In the Philippines and Mexico, the success of the AMCs was doomed from the start, because governments transferred politically motivated loans or fraudulent assets to the AMCs. A government agency susceptible to political pressure and lacking independence finds these assets difficult to resolve or to sell off. Neither of these agencies succeeded in achieving its narrow objectives. (Source: Klingebiel 2000.)

---

that classification is based on the borrower's demonstrated ability to repay. To that effect, bank regulators may need to evaluate all rules, regulations, and policy statements to ensure that they facilitate, not hinder, restructuring by allowing partial debt forgiveness; permitting immediate debt write-off for tax purposes; providing flexibility in valuing payments in-kind and tax relief on such payments; eliminating artificial ceilings on assets acquired by financial institutions through restructuring; eliminating unnecessary taxes, duties, and levies on shares issued as a result of debt-to-equity conversions; and eliminating all taxes on the issues or exchange of debt instruments used in debt restructuring.

Other measures that influence bank and corporate incentives for proper restructuring are liberal foreign investment and foreign entry rules and liberal merger and acquisition policies. During times of crisis, foreign investment can provide much-needed capital and expertise. Adequate bankruptcy procedures are necessary to ensure that debtors can be forced to negotiate in good faith and minimize the transactions costs of resolving financial distress.

Tools for Reducing the Probability of Banking Crises

The probability of banking crises can be reduced by undertaking financial restructuring in tandem with other fundamental reforms—strengthening prudential regulation; adopting internationally accepted accounting, auditing, and financial reporting standards and practices; and toughening compliance and regulation to align the incentives of market participants with prudent banking. The extent to which excessive risk-taking is curbed by regulation and penalized by the supervisory authority as well as by the market greatly influences the behavior of financial institutions. The overall incentive framework in which financial institutions operate significantly affects the risks of a future financial crisis.

Three groups could potentially monitor financial institution managers: owners, the market, and supervisors. The government should strive to ensure that each exerts pressure on managers to engage in prudent risk-taking. In industrial economies, authorities erect entry barriers; they enforce modest capital requirements, usually above the BIS (Bank for International Settlements) minimum of 8 percent (capital to risk-weighted assets); and intermediaries face market discipline in money and capital markets, which usually are weakened by explicit government guarantees and are supervised by one or more government agencies. Industrial country authorities have tended to permit bank exit, though some individual banks still engage in excessive expansions that cause systemic difficulties. In developing and transitional economies, where risks are greater because of the small and often more concentrated economies, where shocks often are larger and volatility greater, and where the market's ability to monitor banks is hampered by poor information, governments need to enhance the ability and incentives of these three groups.

Incentive Structure of Owners, Creditors, and Other Claim Holders

Those who own equity in a bank in principle have both the ability and the incentive to monitor the actions of their bank. They tend to provide effective self-regulation when they have much at risk, in the form of either capital or expected future profits. Moreover, well-capitalized banks are usually better monitored by their shareholders. Small shareholders, however, will tend to free ride, so it is important that government makes sure that there are some large stakeholders, or strategic investors, who will take and bear the responsibility for running the bank. Inside and outside investors need to face the loss of their investment, and they and their managers need to see the possibility of bank failure or exit from the industry to encourage prudent behavior.

Some emerging economies have raised minimum capital ratios above that for most industrial economies to take into account the riskier environment in which banks operate and the difficulty in measuring the economic net worth of a bank using backward-looking accounting measures.[3] Even then, capital adequacy is inherently a backward-looking accounting indicator of the true solvency of the financial institution. Some banks with high measured capital have become insolvent in short periods of time,[4] even in economies with good accounting standards and practices.

The increased incentives to engage in excessive risk-taking when the capital adequacy position is weakened make it all the more important not to rely just on accounting capital adequacy alone. Countries have applied one or more of the following measures: limiting entry or otherwise raising franchise value (future profitability), which can be collected only by banks that remain open; enhancing the liability of directors and shareholders, which New Zealand authorities have undertaken; and requiring the issuance of subordinated debt. Some countries also have enhanced liability beyond current capital levels by applying stiff penalties when bankers violate regulations or agreements with supervisors about how they will take and monitor risks.[5] Developing country authorities need to choose (at least) one of these additional methods for improving the incentives of bank owners to behave prudently. Although some of these methods may be relatively blunt, the costs of not using them can be quite high.

Incentive Structure of Market Participants

Market participants, principally those who enter into a creditor relationship with a bank, monitor and discipline the relationship if they have the ability and the incentives. The ability to monitor banks depends on the reliability and range of information available. The starting point therefore is adequate accounting standards and practices. Authorities in some countries recently put into place extensive disclosure requirements backed up by enhanced liability (New Zealand), mandatory ratings by at least two private rating agencies (Chile), and an online credit reporting system (Argentina). Beyond information, creditors need incentives to monitor in the form of the assurance that they will be allowed to suffer losses. Although small depositors are unlikely to be good monitors of banks, large debt holders have a much greater potential to fulfill this role. At the very least, large debt holders need to be reminded that they are not covered by any explicit or implicit deposit insurance scheme. Mandating that banks periodically issue large blocks of uninsured, subordinated debt, as recently instituted in Argentina, could in some circumstances further enhance market monitoring and also could create a class of future bank owners; if the current owners fail to ensure a safe and sound bank, the subordinated debt holders could take over the bank. The incentives of subordinated debt holders may thus be appropriately balanced.

Incentive Structure for Supervisors

Although owners and markets can be motivated to provide oversight, banks, given their special nature, also are subject to government supervision. Historically, bank supervision in developing and transitional economies was oriented toward ensuring compliance with government directives on credit allocation. Though lagging relative to other parts of financial reform programs, authorities in most developing countries have moved to engage in prudential supervision. Less attention has been devoted to providing supervisors with the incentives both to monitor better and to take actions based on this effort. If there are no incentives to monitor, and thus no consequences for banks for violating a regulatory framework, the trend toward greater supervision will be completely ineffective. It follows, then, that one way to promote better supervision is to give authorities better incentives. In many countries, supervisors are paid poorly relative to their counterparts in banks. At the very least, low pay makes it difficult to attract qualified personnel, and may negate the effects of even the best training programs as skilled supervisors move to the banking sector. Moreover, the lure of eventual high-paying jobs leaves open a form of corruption: less rigorous supervision now in exchange for a lucrative salary later. This disincentive for effective supervision can be reduced only by raising supervisory pay reasonably close to private sector levels.

Furthermore, it may be useful to tie the hands of supervisors and lay down the course of action to be followed. In the context of dealing with weak banks, it has become increasingly common to recommend that countries adopt the "prompt, corrective action and structured, early intervention" approach analogous to that embodied in U.S. legislation. Structured, early intervention calls for (a) higher capital; (b) structured, prespecified, publicly announced responses by regulators, triggered by decreases in a bank's performance (such as capital ratios) below established levels; (c) mandatory resolution of a capital-depleted bank at a prespecified point when capital is still positive; and (d) market value accounting and reporting of capital. Although this approach appears to have yielded promising results in the United States, it is by no means certain that this model works at all times or can be exported to other countries.

Conclusion

Recent experience suggests that the fiscal costs of a banking crisis can be substantial and can, in extreme cases, threaten fiscal stability. On average, a banking crisis in an emerging market has added 14 percentage points to government spending relative to GDP, and in some countries as much as 50 percentage points of GDP. Governments have taken on liabilities in banking sector restructuring because of explicit guarantees—either extensive public deposit insurance or direct government guarantees on bank liabilities—or implicit government guarantees. While many of the causes of banking crises have been identified, it has proven difficult to predict the incidence and exact timing of a financial crisis. It also has been hard to predict with any precision the magnitude of contingent liabilities arising from banking system distress. Existing approaches to measuring contingent liabilities in the banking sector, while they represent a good start, often fall short. Most are based on static models, which focus on the typical causes of a banking crisis, rather than on policy responses. Most important, these models do not analyze what governments can do to control fiscal liabilities arising from the banking sector, because they fail to recognize the dynamic dimensions of managing contingent liabilities.

Recent research has identified more precisely the main policy measures contributing to banking crisis costs. Investigators found that liquidity support, unlimited guarantees, and forbearance contribute the most to costs. These findings suggest some crisis management strategies that can limit the fiscal costs. In addition, cross-country evidence indicates that the comprehensiveness of restructuring efforts can determine the robustness of the banking system in the medium term. The probability of banking crises can be reduced through a variety of instruments that improve the incentive framework.

Notes

1. Honohan and Klingebiel (2000) do not include these medium-term strategies in their empirical analysis because this level of detail would be difficult to cover in a regression framework, but many case studies highlight the value of these principles (see Sheng 1996).

2. It also should be noted that guarantees might not be credible if the scale of the losses is estimated to be so large that the government is perceived to lack the resources and capacity to fulfill the guarantee. This happened in some countries, where a depositor run turned into a currency panic.

3. In Argentina, for example, the minimum capital adequacy requirement is 11.5 percent, with higher requirements for banks engaging in riskier activities and having a weaker risk management capacity. The average actual capital adequacy ratio in Argentina, for example, was close to 16 percent in 1997. Furthermore, before the financial 2001 crisis, banks in Argentina were subject to high liquidity requirements. Singapore also has higher capital adequacy requirements (12 percent). Moreover, most banks in countries with 8 percent capital adequacy requirements have capital adequacy ratios that greatly exceed those: the average capital adequacy ratio in the United States, for example, is about 12 percent.

4. In a world of derivatives, balance sheets can be altered in minutes.

5. In evaluating market risk, supervisors around the world have recently moved toward assessing the quality of the risk management tools banks use rather than the actual positions. Banks are then fined if they violate risk management arrangements ex post.

References

The word *processed* describes informally reproduced works that may not be commonly available through libraries.

Alba, Pedro, Leonarda Hernandez, and Daniela Klingebiel. 1999. "Financial Liberalization and the Capital Account: Thailand, 1988–97." Policy Research Working Paper 2188. World Bank, Washington, D.C.

Baer, Herbert, and Daniela Klingebiel. 1995. "Systematic Risk When Depositors Bear Losses: Five Case Studies." In George G. Kaufman, ed., *Research in Financial Services: Private and Public Policy.* Vol. 7. Greenwich, Conn.: JAI Press.

Barth, James R., Gerard Caprio, Jr., and Ross Levine. 2000. "Banking Systems around the Globe: Do Regulation and Ownership Affect Performance and Stability?" Policy Research Working Paper 2325. World Bank, Washington, D.C..(Forthcoming in Frederick Mishkin, ed. *Prudential Regulation and Supervision: What Works and What Doesn't.* Chicago: National Bureau of Economic Research/Chicago University Press.)

————. 2001. "Bank Regulation and Supervision: What Works Best." World Bank, Washington, D.C. Processed.

Blejer, Mario, and Liliana Schumacher. 1998. "Central Bank Vulnerability and the Credibility of Commitments: A Value-at-Risk Approach to Currency Crises." IMF Working Paper WP/98/65. International Monetary Fund, Washington, D.C.

Bongini, Paolo, Stijn Claessens, and Giovanni Ferri. 2001. "The Political Economy of Distress in East Asian Financial Institutions." *Journal of Financial Services Research* 19 (1): 1–25.

Caprio, Gerard, Jr., and Asli Demirgüç-Kunt. 1997. "The Role of Long Term Finance: Theory and Evidence." Policy Research Working Paper 1746. World Bank, Washington, D.C.

Caprio, Gerard, Jr., and Daniela Klingebiel. 1997. "Bank Insolvency: Bad Luck, Bad Policy, or Bad Banking?" In Michael Bruno and Boris Pleskovic, eds., *Annual World Bank Conference on Development Economics.* Washington, D.C.: World Bank.

————. 1999. "Scope and Fiscal Cost of Banking Crisis: Compilation of Information on Systemic and Non-systemic Crises from 1970s Onward." Financial Policy website <*http://www-int.worldbank.org/jsp/sectors_view. jsp?tab=2&gwitem=473944*>. World Bank, Washington, D.C.

Claessens, Stijn. 1999. "Experiences of Resolution of Banking Crises." In *Strengthening the Banking System in China: A Joint BIS/PBC Conference Held in Beijing, China, 1–2 March, 1999.* BIS Policy Paper 7. October (Bank for International Settlements).

Demirgüç-Kunt, Asli, and Enrica Detragiache. 1998. "Financial Liberalization and Financial Fragility." In Joseph Stiglitz and Boris Pleskovic, eds. *Annual World Bank Conference on Development Economics.* Washington, D.C.: World Bank.

————. 2000. "Monitoring Banking Sector Fragility: A Multivariate Logit Approach." *World Bank Economic Review* 14 (2): 287–307.

Goldstein, Morris, Graciela Kaminsky, and Carmen Reinhart. 2000. *Assessing Financial Vulnerability: An Early Warning System for Emerging Markets.* Washington, D.C.: Institute of International Economics.

Gonzales-Hermosillo, B. 1999. "Determinants of Ex-ante Banking System Distress: A Macro-Micro Empirical Exploration." IMF Working Paper WP/99/33. International Monetary Fund, Washington, D.C.

Hardy, Daniel, and Ceyla Pazarbasioglu. 1998. "Leading Indicators of Banking Crises: Was Asia Different?" IMF Working Paper WP/98/91. International Monetary Fund, Washington, D.C., June.

Honohan, Patrick. 1999. "Fiscal Contingency Planning for Banking Crises." Policy Research Working Paper 2228. World Bank, Washington, D.C.

Honohan, Patrick, and Daniela Klingebiel. 2000. "Controlling Fiscal Costs of Banking Crises." Policy Research Working Paper 2421. World Bank, Washington, D.C.

Kaminsky, Graciela, and Carmen Reinhart. 1999. "The Twin Crises: The Causes of Banking and Balance-of-Payments Problems." *American Economic Review* 89 (3): 473–500.

Keefer, Philip. 1999. "Political Institutions and Crisis: The Effects of Political Checks and Balances on the Dynamics of Financial Sector Distress." World Bank, Washington, D.C., June. Processed.

Kharas, Homi, and Deepak Mishra. 2001. "Fiscal Policy, Hidden Deficits, and Currency Crises." In S. Devarajan, F. H. Rogers, and L. Squire, eds., *World Bank Economists' Forum*. Washington, D.C.: World Bank.

Klingebiel, Daniela. 2000. "The Use of Asset Management Companies in the Resolution of Banking Crises." Policy Research Working Paper 2284. Washington, D.C.: World Bank.

Laeven, Luc. 1999. "Risk and Efficiency in East Asian Banks." Policy Research Working Paper 2255. World Bank, Washington, D.C.

La Porta, Rafael, Florencio Lopez de Silanes, and Andrei Shleifer. 2000. "Government Ownership of Banks." Harvard University, Cambridge, Mass., August. Processed.

Sheng, Andrew, ed. 1996. "Bank Restructuring: Lessons from the 1980s." World Bank, Washington, D.C. Processed.

Standard and Poor's Sovereign Ratings Service. 1999. "Global Financial System Stress: 24 Show Adverse Trends in Credit Quality." New York, May.

World Bank. 1993. *East Asia Miracle*. Policy Research Report. New York: Oxford University Press.

———. 2001a. *Finance for Growth: Policy Choices in a Volatile World*. Policy Research Report. New York: Oxford University Press.

———. 2001b. *World Development Report: Institutions for Markets*. New York: Oxford University Press.

CHAPTER 15

Government Insurance Programs: Risks and Risk Management

Ron Feldman
Federal Reserve Bank of Minneapolis

INSURANCE CAN IMPROVE THE allocation of resources in at least two ways. First, risk-pooling can reduce the likelihood that the insured will suffer a catastrophic loss. Second, the central administration of risk-pooling allows for cost minimization by reducing administrative expenses and transactions costs and exploiting economies of scale. As a result, insurance provides an efficient method for firms and households to manage some of the risks they face.

These benefits explain the long history of insurance provision, the large size of private insurance markets in many countries, and the increasing array of risks for which insurance has become available. But offering insurance is a risky business, and this truism is particularly applicable when the government decides to provide insurance. In particular, governments tend to offer insurance—with a face value in the trillions of dollars in developed countries—for risks that are difficult to insure because of problems of correlated losses, moral hazard, adverse selection, poor data, and limited demand. And partly as a result, governments have suffered very high losses across a range of programs from flood to pension insurance. Indeed, a poorly designed insurance program—deposit insurance, for example—can actually retard a country's growth.[1]

Policymakers thus face difficult tradeoffs. Government insurance offers the potential to improve welfare by providing unique risk management for catastrophes such as natural disasters and banking panics. At the same time, government must avoid the high costs that can arise when it absorbs risks without the policies and institutional capabilities to manage them. To that end, tools are available to government to help manage the exposure created by insurance programs. Many of these tools are commonplace in the private sector's provision of insurance, including risk-based pricing, the use of loss-sharing techniques such as coinsurance, deductibles and caps on losses, discretion in the coverage of risks, and effective verification and adjustment of loss. Government also has unique powers that can assist it in the management of insurance exposure. For example, the government can increase opportunities for risk-pooling by compelling firms and households to participate in insurance programs. The government also can use regulatory powers to try to manage the risk-taking of the insured. At times, however, these techniques have proven ineffective or at odds with the political objectives of policymakers.

The rest of this chapter provides analysis and background specifically on government insurance programs in the hopes of assisting policymakers who face tradeoffs in managing them. The next section discusses the inherent and political challenges that governments face in offering insurance. It is followed by a section that examines some of the methods available to the government insurer to mitigate the risks it assumes. The concluding section emphasizes the need to reassess continually the direct government provision of insurance given advances in private risk-bearing.

Challenges to Policymakers Offering Government Insurance

The challenges to governments providing insurance are twofold. First, insurance programs are more likely to remain solvent if certain conditions hold, but governments typically provide insurance programs when these favorable conditions do not exist. Second, the use of techniques to manage the risks that government insurers assume can reduce the political benefits that insurance programs provide policymakers. As a result, policymakers may not implement these tools (discussed in detail in the next section), thereby increasing the chance the government insurer will become insolvent or distort resource allocation or both.

Inherent Challenges

Several conditions facilitate effective and sustainable provision of insurance. First, the probability that one person or firm in the risk pool will suffer losses should be independent of or uncorrelated with the probability that others in the pool will suffer losses. However, virtually all of the insurance programs offered by governments lack independence of loss. Banks whose deposits are insured, for example, tend to fail in bunches. A similar situation may exist for firms that sponsor pensions insured by the government (for example, many large steel firms with underfunded pensions can face difficulty at the same time). Likewise, large areas of agricultural production can face drought or excessive rain. Conversely, hail is a localized phenomenon, and private insurers offer policies against hail damage. A lack of independence of loss means that government could suffer substantial losses over a short period.

Second, losses suffered by the insured should result from chance and not from the actions of the insured. However, acquiring insurance introduces the moral hazard problem that the insured will more likely engage in behavior that raises their chances of making a claim. Consider the case of government pension insurance. Workers may have previously reviewed the funding of their pension or had an agent, such as a union, do it for them. If future pension benefits were uncertain, workers would typically demand more cash income and fewer pension benefits. The same workers, however, have an incentive to reduce reviews after their benefits become insured. The workers may now agree to lower current compensation in return for guaranteed future benefits. Firm cash flows that used to support current compensation may increasingly benefit equity holders via dividends or increased investment in high-return/high-risk projects. Moral hazard becomes particularly problematic when insurance covers 100 percent of losses, the insured entity is insolvent, and the premiums charged do not vary with the risk-taking of the insured (some government programs have all three characteristics).

Third, the insurer must be able to estimate accurately the expected claims of the insured. An insurer cannot make adequate forecasts if it does not have sufficient data. There may be pressure for the government to step in if private insurance providers do not offer insurance in markets with limited data. The U.S. government took such a role with mortgage insurance (Weicher 1994).

Fourth, and closely related to point three, the insurer must have the ability to distinguish among the insured based on the risk of loss they pose. If not, the insurer will price risk inaccurately and, because of adverse selection, will face higher-than-expected losses.

Finally, limited demand from consumers prevents successful provision of insurance, particularly insurance against natural disasters. A lack of demand has several sources, including the high cost of insurance due to a lack of independence of loss and adverse selection and the low incomes of potential beneficiaries.[2] A second cause of low demand is ex post assistance from government and charities to those who have suffered catastrophic losses from natural disaster. In a recent example, the U.S. government provided ex post assistance to agricultural producers in the summer of 1999 who had explicitly waived the right to such payments when they refused to purchase crop insurance.[3]

The Political Challenge

Policymakers tend to provide insurance to achieve social and distributional objectives. Deposit insurance, for example, supports smaller financial institutions that might otherwise have to pay more for deposits than larger banks with more diversified asset portfolios. Similarly, pension insurance encourages establishment of pensions that provide a fixed or defined benefit to workers.

More generally, governments can use insurance to subsidize certain constituents by charging them premiums below the fair amount needed to cover expected losses. In some cases, the very act of providing insurance generates the subsidy, as no other insurer would offer the constituent an insurance policy at any price. For example, government insurers have been known to offer insurance against a natural disaster when the probability of imminent loss is near 100 percent. Insurance is an especially attractive method for providing subsidies because of its low visibility. Taxpayers have limited information on insurance programs and muted incentives to carry out the challenging analysis needed to determine the long-term costs of such programs.

The bottom line is that methods of creating the subsidy require that the government insurer avoid practices that give it greater control in managing its exposure, such as charging risk-based premiums. The difficulty in monitoring the fiscal position of the insurance program removes a potential check on policymakers' discretion to increase expected losses. As a result, governments may not enact the policies discussed in the next section that guard against fiscal loss and resource misallocation.

Methods for Addressing the Risks Posed by Government Insurance Programs

Government insurers have two sets of tools available to them to manage the risks they assume. One group of methodologies reflects the standard insurance management techniques used by private firms, including risk-based pricing, loss-sharing, and coverage rules. The second set of tools is uniquely available to the public insurance entity and includes compulsion, regulation, and budgeting. Policymakers have pointed to the availability of these instruments of government policy to justify the provision of government insurance. However, these unique attributes of government are not excuses for ignoring generic risk management techniques.

Generic Risk Management Tools for Insurers

Private insurers have had to develop a variety of methods to address effectively the inherent challenges of providing insurance. Insurers must address moral hazard, in particular. Observers have attributed some of the significant losses that government insurers have suffered to a refusal to apply these techniques.

Pricing. An insurance program will ultimately have a cash flow deficit if the assessment charged to a household or firm in conjunction with other sources of income is less than the expected costs of insuring them. But perhaps the more profound importance of the actuarially fair or risk-based premium is its influence on the behavior of the insured. The insured will continue to take actions that increase her expected losses as long as the premium and other marginal costs that she faces are less than the marginal benefit the actions produce. As a result, a fair premium encourages the insured to avoid actions that could increase the chance of claim and loss (Blair and Fissel 1991).

Despite the importance of addressing moral hazard, government insurance programs have at times deliberately charged less than the fair premium. Some programs have charged no premium at all and instead have relied on ex post levies. Governments justify this practice as preventing misuse of funds held in reserve. An alternative common practice has the insurer charging the same premium to all.

Although the setting of risk-based premiums has not been the norm for many government insurance programs, the ability to set them is not beyond the ken of government.[4] Standard actuarial approaches to premium-setting could be appropriate for programs such as crop insurance where data on crop yields and insurance performance go back many years. The crop insurer should establish rates for broad categories of agricultural producers (for example, all wheat growers in a given location). The insurer then adjusts the rates to account for individual differences that influence losses such as the use of irrigation and the variant of crop grown. The insurer can calculate initial rate classification and adjustments based on descriptive statistics—the average loss for wheat farmers in a given location using irrigation, for example—or through statistical techniques that isolate the effect of a given attribute on the probability of loss. Putting the insured into groups based on their general characteristics and charging an appropriate premium to each group are an effective response to the potential for adverse selection.

Premium-setting for insurance against the insolvency of firms (for example, pension and deposit insurance) could benefit from advances in both computing and practices in statistics and finance. Monte Carlo simulations and the use of option-pricing theory provide new avenues for estimating expected claims and fair premium-setting. (For details on modeling the exposure of pension guarantee programs, see Chapter 13 by Pennacchi in this volume.) The utility of these models goes beyond premium-setting in one time period. Analysts could use these models to judge exposure and simulate how changes in insurance policies might alter expected losses. In addition, some government insurers can look to private markets for information that would help in setting premiums. For example, risk assessments of banks captured in fixed-income instrument or equity prices could serve as input into the calculation of insurance assessments. More directly, a government insurer can contract with market participants to bear some of the risk of an insured event occurring. The pricing of such contracts can provide information for the government insurer in setting premiums for other insured entities.

Loss-sharing. Seminal economic analysis of insurance by Arrow and others recognized that insurers address moral hazard by having the insured bear some risk of loss (Arrow 1977). Insurers share losses with the insured in several ways. Capping the losses the insurer will bear fosters risk-sharing. The International Monetary Fund (IMF) identified the provision of a "low" amount of coverage as a best practice in government deposit insurance (Garcia 1999: 9, 12). The insurer can also require the insured to pay a set amount, the deductible, before the insured receives loss protection. Finally, the insurer can split losses through a coinsurance arrangement. For example, the insurer may decide to cover 75 percent of losses. In implementing loss-sharing, governments should consider, among other factors, the ability of private markets to provide supplementary coverage, the benefits of targeting insurance coverage to those least able to bear the risk themselves, the effect of loss-sharing on the risk-taking of the insured, and the amount of exposure the government can manage. Government insurers use loss-sharing to varying degrees, although it appears less often in public programs than in private policies. This reluctance likely reflects social objectives and the potential for loss-sharing to produce an outcome, such as increased instability in the banking system, that is at odds with the goals underlying the establishment of the insurance program.

Loss-sharing policies also require policymakers to create time-consistent commitments for imposing losses, especially if the insurer shifts from a regime where it absorbed all losses, even when not legally required. Potential methods for establishing a credible loss-sharing regime include passing laws that mandate loss-sharing, implementing schemes that punish regulators for not imposing losses, and enacting reforms that limit the damage loss-sharing could cause. Another method for establishing credibility requires policymakers to appoint insurance program managers who are more likely to impose losses than the general populace. Other creative proposals address the time-consistency problem. For example, the government can agree to provide full protection for the first uninsured entity, such as a bank, that suffers loss but not for other uninsured entities. This proposal could assuage policymakers' fears of spillover failures. At the same time, the plan increases creditors' incentives to price risk correctly so that they are compensated in the event that their bank is the first to fail (Stern 2000).

Coverage Limits and Decisions. The expected claims for the government insurer depend significantly on the type of coverage it provides. Each coverage decision depends, in turn, on the particular circumstances of the insurance program. In an obvious example, the insurer would have a better chance at solvency if it insures risks for which it has good data. Without sufficient data, the insurer should take on only a limited amount of exposure and establish tight controls on growth. The government insurer also reduces its chances for solvency if it provides insurance against very high-probability losses or routinely agrees to insure those whose record and behavior indicate a very high probability of making a claim. In fact, the government would discourage future risky behavior by those who are currently insured if it excluded those posing a very high risk of claim from the pool.

Government disaster insurance programs provide numerous examples of the types of coverage decisions the insurer must make. Consider insurance against flood damage. The government must determine at what point prior to the flood it will offer insurance. If the government provides coverage when flooding is imminent, it will be nearly impossible to balance premiums with losses. The government flood insurer in the United States had to increase the time between the receipt of an application and the provision of insurance from 5 to 30 days to limit the number of applicants with very high probabilities of making a claim. The flood insurer also had to restrict coverage on structures that suffered repeated damage over a short period of time. Whatever and whomever it decides to cover, the government insurer must produce a written contract or policy that clearly enumerates its decisions. Exposure can become virtually unlimited without such documentation.

Verification and Adjustment of Loss. The insurer must have a process in place to verify that the loss claimed by the insured actually occurred and to determine the amount rightfully paid under the contract. The absence of a proficient claims adjustment process invites fraud and unnecessary expenses. The adjustment process for government insurance programs involving property damage could be similar to practices by private insurers. In fact, the government insurer could contract with private insurers to benefit from their potentially lower costs and greater expertise. (Such contracting, of course, has monitoring costs and requires incentives for the private provider to meet the government's objectives.)

Adjustment in firm insolvency insurance programs may require different skills. For example, the government insurer needs to acquire expertise in the disposition of assets held by the firm at insolvency. The amount the government may owe the insured can depend on the money the government raises through the sale of assets from the failed firm. The ability of the government to sell assets for higher returns after failure means lower losses to the insurer. Disposition of assets has proven to be particularly challenging in a number of countries, particularly in the aftermath of mass bank failures. Creating the infrastructure to sell the assets is costly and difficult, particularly when the assets to sell are illiquid. Nonetheless, experience suggests that use of private sector firms, financial market innovations such as securitization, and disposition strategies that allow for the quick sale of assets can support cost-effective collection efforts (FDIC 1998). The insurer can also lower losses by recovering funds through lawsuits against the insured firm that has unlawfully dissipated the value of its assets.

Unique Risk Management Tools for Government Insurers

In theory, governments might have a greater ability than private firms to address problems of moral hazard, lack of independence of loss, and adverse selection. These powers arise from the sovereign status of the government and include means to compel participation in insurance pools, regulate the behavior of insured entities, and raise funds through taxes. In theory, these powers would allow the government to provide risk-pooling where private firms could not, although their effectiveness has been less impressive in practice.

Compulsion. Governments can attempt to compel firms and households to participate in risk pools. Governments often try to accomplish this objective by tightly linking receipt of a benefit that the government provides to insured status. In many countries, only the government has the right to grant a banking charter. The bank must then accept deposit insurance in order to obtain the charter. This form of compulsion could help address adverse selection, because the risk pool will contain a larger representation of eligible candidates, not just those posing a higher risk of loss. Uniform coverage could also potentially provide more independence of loss. For example, government could require all those who live near rivers to participate in the government flood insurance program. Losses could be less correlated across a risk pool of all those living near all rivers in a country compared with a risk pool of those living near one river.

This form of compulsion has its limits, especially if the insurer tries to force lower-loss entities to subsidize the higher-loss entities. The lower-loss entities in such a scenario will take steps to reduce their exposure to insurance assessments. Overcharged banks will shift away from the assets or deposits on which premiums are levied toward untaxed items. In the extreme, overcharged insureds will give up the government benefit tied to insurance and shift to untaxed options. This substitution can leave the government in the position it sought to avoid—namely, an insurance pool with an overrepresentation of high-loss entities. Governments can try to limit shifts out of the risk pool by inefficiently banning substitutes or taxing exits, although the latter step will limit pool participation in the first place. More commonly, governments will accompany attempts at compulsion with government regulation of risk-taking.

Regulation. Governments can regulate the behavior of insured entities to address the potential for moral hazard and adverse selection and, more generally, to try to reduce the probability that an insured entity will make a claim. Before granting insurance, the government can set regulatory standards that attempt to limit the expected loss of the insured. Entities that want to receive government protection from natural disaster may have to first mitigate against loss by, for example, ensuring that buildings meet quality codes. Similarly insured financial institutions must meet certain levels of financial strength, often measured by equity-to-asset ratios, before government protection becomes available. The government can also try to manage the amount of risk-taking of the insured through laws and regulations that govern their ongoing operations. The insurer may require that communities prevent new building in disaster-prone areas in order to continue to receive disaster insurance. Likewise, the insurer could limit the asset holdings of insured financial institutions.

In addition to promulgating regulations, the government insurer and its agents could engage in ongoing supervision and monitoring. In one form, the regulator audits the insured to ensure compliance with regulations. But even this basic level of monitoring can be tricky given the inevitable subjectiveness of compliance. A bank's compliance with capital rules, for example, depends on the assessment of hard-to-value assets. Regulators also go beyond checking for compliance and often use quantitative and qualitative inputs to produce assessments of the insured's level of risk. The government insurer may need supervisors to generate such private information on the insured, because, as noted,

344   RON FELDMAN

it may not be able to rely on observable and easy-to-verify characteristics to determine expected losses.

Academics and some policymakers have expressed significant skepticism about the ability of regulation to limit effectively and efficiently the risk-taking of the insured.[5] Moral hazard results when economic agents do not bear the marginal costs of their actions. Regulatory regimes can alter marginal costs, but they accomplish this task through very crude and often exploitable tactics. In particular, reliance on lagging regulatory measures, restrictive regulatory and legal norms, and the ability of insureds to quickly alter their risk profile have often resulted in large claims despite regulation. Moreover, while regulators have access to inside information, there still appear to be areas of profound informational asymmetry between regulators and insured entities.

A second concern focuses on forbearance—that is, the regulator and the insurer may not take action against the insured in the hope that the riskiness of the insured declines in the future. Forbearance can result from political pressure or attempts by the regulator and insurer to avoid damage to their reputations.

Finally, even if regulators had the ability to assess risk-taking accurately, they do not have a sound basis for determining how much risk is too much or too little. Supervision and regulation of insured entities, in other words, should not be expected to result in the economically efficient amount of risk-taking.

Some have used such criticism to call for less, or even an abolishment of, regulation. But, for the most part, analysts have called on the insurer and regulator to augment regulatory assessments of the insured's risk-taking with market assessments. To accomplish this goal, as noted, the government insurer can shift some of the risk of loss to private agents. The price charged for such reinsurance would provide the primary government insurer and regulator with an assessment of risk. A second source for market risk assessments are market participants also at risk of loss from the insured's actions. The prices that these market agents set on debt issued by the insured firm, for example, could provide useful information. A variant of this form would rely on the credit ratings of the insured. The insurer could use these market signals to set premiums or determine eligibility for insurance. The signals could also trigger regulatory restrictions on the insured's actions. The market risk assessments also have the advantage of being visible to the public. They could therefore make it difficult for the government to ignore or cover up potential exposure to the insurance program.[6]

Loss Absorption and Smoothing. Some governments can withstand larger losses than private firms. In private markets, the more uncertain the costs of providing the insurance and the larger the expected claims, the more capital the insurer will have to hold to ensure it can survive large claims. But most government programs do not raise funds from private investors to withstand losses. Most government insurers raise cash to pay for future losses through the government's taxing authority and benefit from de facto taxpayer support. As a result, the government insurer may not have to hold any funds to ensure that it can pay off losses. Instead, the government could borrow funds and repay these funds with future premiums and taxes if current premium income falls below current claims. This means that governments could provide insurance even if there were not independence of loss in the risk pool. U.S. Treasury Secretary Lawrence Summers summed up this position, noting that "the Federal government is uniquely capable of spreading risk over time. A private insurer . . . can only lose so much money in any given period without being declared bankrupt. By contrast, the capacity of the Federal government to borrow for the purpose of meeting short-term contingencies dwarfs that of any private sector entity."[7]

Two very important caveats accompany this observation. In particular, the government must have a near uninterrupted ability to access funds, through taxes or borrowing, at a "manageable" cost. If this is not the case, the government insurer may be no better off than a private firm in absorbing large losses. Moreover, even if the insurer does not hold capital, it must still incorporate the lack of independence of loss in its pricing if it wants to manage future losses and have premium income pay for claims.

Public Budgeting and Management Strategies. A well-designed public budgeting regime can give policymakers incentives to manage the exposure of the government to expected insurance losses. Budgetary rules and accounting that require policymakers to face the opportunity costs today of potential costs in the future could achieve that objective.

Accounting for the finances of government insurance programs on an accrual rather than a cash basis could make opportunity costs more explicit.[8] As noted, many public budgeting systems do not provide useful data on future exposures. In Chapter 3 of this volume, Allen Schick describes how short-term, cash-driven recognition of government budgets can make insurance programs appear to be cash generators until the moment they suffer massive financial losses. Conventional budgeting systems do not give policymakers reason to act to limit fiscal, and related deadweight, losses.

In a similar vein, policymakers can structure the incentives of those running the government insurance program to facilitate management of claims exposure. Managerial strategies must address the fact that insurance programs require frequent modifications to keep losses within desired ranges. Elected bodies with rules designed to foster debate and inclusion are often incapable of making the timely decisions required to keep insurance programs in fiscal shape. Environments in which managers have the contractual incentives and the power to make necessary adjustments could prove more effective. Establishing clear objectives, agreeing how to measure achievement of the objectives, and linking rewards and performance are important steps in shifting insurance management responsibilities from policymakers to managers. These steps could also help address the principal-agent concerns that such a delegation will produce.

Public Information Campaign. Public information campaigns describing the risk of loss from rare events could increase the demand for government insurance programs, particularly in cases where underestimation of such losses helps explain limited demand. Some government disaster insurance programs attribute an increase in participation rates to more extensive and more effective advertising. In particular, government insurers have shifted from more traditional and staid warnings about risk to advertising campaigns that are closer in spirit to those used by firms with well-known consumer brands. And there are several reasons why the government may need to provide such information. Information on the probability of a natural disaster could serve as a public good. The public cannot easily verify the quality of forecasts and could discount those provided by private insurers as biased toward insurance purchase. The government forecasts usually come from an agency with no clear ties to or financial gain from insurance purchase. Finally, marketing efforts could convey the steps the government is taking to reduce the chance residents will receive ex post assistance.

Importance of Regularly Reassessing Direct Insurance Provision

The previous discussion focused on designing and managing government insurance programs to increase their probability of remaining solvent. That discussion implicitly presumed underlying social or economic justifications for government provision of insurance. However, these justifications may never have been strong and may have become weaker with advancements in private insurance markets. Policymakers thus have a strong reason to review insurance programs regularly and to determine whether alternative, more attractive methods to achieve their goals exist. In terms of social objectives, a direct subsidy program may prove more effective and efficient than government insurance. Additionally, improvements in insurance and risk-shifting technology may allow private firms to offer insurance where government had previously. In another option, the government could regulate private insurance markets in order to increase coverage. However, such regulation could have significant drawbacks.

Alternative Methods of Subsidization

Several attributes of insurance that have been discussed suggest it is not a good distribution method for subsidies. Policymakers cannot target the subsidy very well through insurance. The benefits of government insurance often go to unintended parties (for example, the managers of insured firms) and those who could otherwise protect themselves from loss. In addition, the policies that create the subsidy, such as mispricing, lead to poor resource allocation and increased chances of program insolvency. Finally, the overhead to deliver a subsidy through an insurance program makes it an expensive option relative to direct payments, vouchers, or tax credits. For the recipient, cash payments have a higher value than in-kind transfers.

This discussion juxtaposes direct subsidies with direct provision of insurance. But, for example, how does insurance as a subsidization tool compare with ex post disaster assistance? This comparison depends on the actual management and structure of the insurance program. Poorly designed government insurance programs can produce the same moral hazard problems associated with disaster assistance. Moreover, the provision of insurance may not make delivery of ex post disaster assistance less likely. As such, it is not clear that replacing ex post assistance with government insurance will reduce the government's fiscal exposure.[9]

Technological Advancements in Private Risk-Shifting Markets

The private markets that can absorb risk of loss from uncertain outcomes have become much larger and more robust over the last decade. It is now more feasible for these private markets to bear risks that government may have assumed previously. Some of the private market expansion has occurred in traditional risk-bearing organizations. In particular, consolidation in the insurance industry has led to larger firms, some of which have increased cross-national exposure.[10] The resulting firms should have more capital and diversified portfolios. The growing liquidity of capital markets and increased ability to evaluate risk have also led to increased capital for the primary and reinsurance markets. This increased capacity has been accompanied by lower prices, making reinsurance more widely available for primary insurers (Standard and Poor's 1999b). In total, U.S. property and casualty insurers, for example, significantly increased their capacity to finance major catastrophic property loss during the 1990s (Cummins, Doherty, and Lo 1999).

There has also been significant growth in traditional financial instruments that allow firms and households to better manage their exposure to loss. For example, the volume of agricultural options traded on the Chicago Board of Trade has more than doubled over the last decade, and the volume of agricultural futures has gone up by about 30 percent.[11] Despite this growth, there remains ample opportunity for expansion as only a small minority of agricultural producers, in the United States at least, make use of financial contracts to manage their risk. And financial contracts are not the only traditional yet underused method that producers can utilize to manage exposure to loss. For example, farmers can hedge risk of loss through planting diversification, vertical integration, and marketing contracts.[12] In addition, advances in financial modeling have made it more feasible for producers, in fields such as agriculture, to simulate future revenue and optimize risk management strategies (Falloon 1999).

In addition to growth in traditional markets, advancements in the technology of insurance provision have increased the private market's capacity to absorb loss, especially with regard to natural disasters.[13] Huge strides in computing and analytical techniques have made it more feasible to model and forecast the likelihood and cost of natural disasters (although limited historical data remain a concern). Advances in financial technologies in areas such as securitization and derivatives have led to the development of financial instruments that shift the loss caused by catastrophic events to capital market investors. Property catastrophe put and call options are exchange-traded derivatives that would allow an insurer to transfer risks above some limit, based on the total claim payments made by the insurance industry for property damage due to catastrophe, for example, to investors. Another choice with increasing appeal is a catastrophe or act-of-God bond. Issuers structure the bonds so that the bonds reduce principal and interest payments when a catastrophe occurs. Thus the holder of the bond takes on some of the risk of loss. In addition, there are markets for catastrophe swaps where those bearing risk can exchange exposures to loss.

All of these financial instruments, and there are other examples not mentioned here, tap into a much deeper pool of capital with a greater ability to diversify than is available to a single firm. Moreover, capital market investors can diversify their portfolios more completely than an insurer. In combination, these developments increase the ability of the private insurance markets to bear risk and reduce the likelihood that capacity and pricing will fluctuate as much as they have in the past.

Many of the new financial instruments discussed are geared to insurers themselves, but innovation has also allowed producers to transfer risk directly to capital markets. For example, producers have a greater ability to hedge against weather-related loss directly in financial markets through so-called weather options. In the past, these producers may have been able only to hedge or insure against more general changes in the price of their output.[14] The combination of these developments could dramatically change how governments provide insurance. Rather than bearing all the risk from weather loss through crop and flood insurance programs, the government could make use of the increased capacity of the insurance industry and the new technology of risk-shifting to purchase reinsurance from a private firm or share the risk of loss through a financial instrument. The government could eventually encourage or require the insured themselves to go directly to private markets.

It is not only recent developments in insurance markets that make private insurance substitution for government programs possible. Some scholars believe that market-based solutions to the problem of banking panics have developed in the past and could develop again in the future if government stopped providing deposit insurance (see Bentson and Kaufman 1995; Calomiris and Mason 1997). Provision of pension insurance by private firms could also be more feasible as a result of developments in insurance markets and the experience gained through the government insurance program (Weaver 1997: 157).

While private markets will not offer every insurance product a policymaker may want for society, the trend is clearly toward a more complete array of private risk-bearing options. Policymakers should therefore regularly assess the viability of private market alternatives to government insurance. Indeed, the greatest impediment to private risk-bearing solutions may come from government. In particular, the public may not believe that the government would actually allow firms or households to bear large losses. As noted, previous government support and the likelihood that governments will provide support in the future could discourage firms and households from purchasing private insurance, encourage riskier behavior, and even lead insurers and their creditors to believe that the government will bail them out if they do suffer large losses. The steps for establishing credibility discussed in the previous section would be particularly important for a transition to more private risk-bearing.

Regulation in Place of Direct Provision

Governments can also expand insurance coverage for its residents by regulating the private market. Regulation can take the form of price-setting/rate suppression or requirements that insurers provide certain types of coverage or that private firms accept all applicants for coverage. These steps have significant drawbacks as replacements for a direct insurance provision that has run its course. For one, regulation may simply shift the government's exposure to loss rather than reduce it. Some governments provide guarantees to the policyholders of private insurance firms and may offer implicit coverage for creditors of large insurance firms. The chance of a claim to the government may increase if rate suppression or mandatory coverage rules make private insurance providers more likely to fail. In addition, there are virtually no sound justifications for price regulation, and the actual manner in which governments force mandatory coverage reduces the benefits that such programs might theoretically produce.[15] For some of these very reasons, there has been a growing call for movement away from inefficient economic regulation of insurance firms.[16] Finally, government could more effectively and transparently achieve social goals through direct payments or vouchers than through regulation.

These points argue against rate regulation and forced coverage, but do not preclude other government actions that could indirectly reduce the need for government insurance provision. On the most general level, governments can create and enforce legal and financial infrastructures that have been shown to lead to a growing financial sector.[17] These steps seem to have significant rewards, especially for developing countries. Part of this basic legal structure could include measures that address fraud in the provision of financial services, such as insurance, and perhaps provide for some limited regulation of insurers' safety and soundness.[18] Governments could also ensure that other policy tools, such as taxation, do not unnecessarily thwart the development of private sector firms. At a later point, the government could determine whether additional legal rules governing insurance products and firms such as supplementary disclosure would prove beneficial. In total, the steps the government can take to increase the depth and scope of private insurance markets should prove most beneficial in the shift away from government provision of insurance.

Notes

1. The World Bank notes, "There is a strong positive correlation between economic development and the growth of [private] insurance utilization" (World Bank 2001).

2. For evidence of the effect of financial resources on the demand for disaster insurance, see Browne and Hoyt (1998).

3. Schnepf and Heifner (1999) discuss the limited demand for crop insurance in the United States despite subsidized premiums.

4. Details on estimation methods for federal insurance programs are found in U.S. GAO (1997: 152–217).

5. For important discussions of regulation, moral hazard, and insurance, see Ippolito (1989) and Kane (1989).

6. The use of market signals with regard to deposit insurance reform is discussed in Stern (1999)

7. Lawrence H. Summers, testimony before the Committee on Banking and Financial Services, U.S. House of Representatives, April 23, 1998.

8. See Redburn (1993) for a discussion of budgeting and accrual accounting.

9. For a similar view, see Harrington (2000b). For more discussion on disaster risk, see Chapter 20 by Alcira Kreimer in this volume.

10. Standard and Poor's (1999a) characterized recent mergers and acquisitions in the property and casualty insurance market as significant and driven by factors including the desire for increased scale and globalization.

11. Data from Chicago Board of Trade <*www.cbot.com/market_info/*>.

12. A discussion of the many methods producers can use to manage uncertainty can be found in Harwood and others (1999).

13. This discussion is largely based on Froot (1999) and Borden and Sarkar (1996).

14. A discussion of financial instruments to protect against weather-related loss is found in WeatherRisk (1999).

15. A detailed analysis of regulation to increase coverage can be found in Harrington (2000a).

16. For a discussion of the current state and trends in regulation of insurance firms, see OECD (1998).

17. Levine (2000) discusses the importance of legal structures for economic and financial growth.

18. See Savage (1999) for a discussion of implementing insurance regulation. Savage argues that financial regulation could help establish public confidence in insurance systems in developing countries.

References

Arrow, Kenneth. 1977. "Insurance, Risk and Resource Allocation." In Kenneth Arrow, *Essays in the Theory of Risk-Bearing.* New York: Elsevier.

Bentson, George, and George Kaufman. 1995. "Is the Banking and Payments System Fragile?" *Journal of Financial Services Research* 9 (December): 209–40.

Blair, Christine E., and Gary Fissel. 1991. "A Framework for Analyzing Deposit Insurance Pricing." *FDIC Banking Review* (fall): 26.

Borden, Sara, and Asani Sarkar. 1996. "Securitizing Property Catastrophe Risk." *Current Issues in Economics and Finance* (August), Federal Reserve Bank of New York.

Browne, Mark, and Robert Hoyt. 1998. "The Demand for Flood Insurance: Empirical Evidence." Paper presented at the 25th Seminar of the Geneva Association, Geneva, September.

Calomiris, Charles, and Joseph Mason. 1997. "Contagion and Bank Failures during the Great Depression: The Chicago Banking Panic." *American Economic Review* 87: 863–83.

Cummins, J. David, Neil A. Doherty, and Anita Lo. 1999. "Can Insurers Pay for the 'Big One'? Measuring the Capacity of an Insurance Market to Respond to Catastrophic Losses." Wharton Financial Institutions Center Working Paper 98-11-B. Philadelphia.

Falloon, William. 1999. "AgRisk: Farm Quants Plant a New Model." *Risk* (July): 31–33.

FDIC (Federal Deposit Insurance Corporation). 1998. *Managing the Crisis: The FDIC and RTC Experience.* Washington D.C.

Froot, Kenneth. 1999. "The Evolving Market for Catastrophic Event Risk." NBER Working Paper 7287. National Bureau of Economic Research, Cambridge, Mass.

Garcia, Gillian. 1999. "Deposit Insurance: A Survey of Actual and Best Practices." IMF Working Paper 99-54. International Monetary Fund, Washington, D.C.

Harrington, Scott E. 2000a. "Insurance Deregulation and the Public Interest." AEI-Brookings Joint Center for Regulatory Studies, Washington, D.C.

———. 2000b. "Rethinking Disaster Policy." *Regulation* 23: 40–46.

Harwood, Joy, Richard Heifner, Keith Coble, Janet Perry, and Agapi Samwaru. 1999. "Managing Risk in Farming: Concepts, Research, and Analysis." USDA Agricultural Economic Report 774. Economic Research Service, U.S. Department of Agriculture, Washington, D.C.

Ippolito, Richard. 1989. *The Economics of Pension Insurance.* Homewood, Ill.: Irwin.

Kane, Edward. 1989. *The S&L Insurance Mess: How Did it Happen?* Washington D.C.: Urban Institute.

Levine, Ross. 2000. "Bank-Based or Market-Based Financial Systems: Which is Better?" Paper presented at the World Bank Conference on Financial Structure and Economic Development, Washington, D.C., February 10–11.

OECD (Organisation for Economic Co-operation and Development). 1998. "Competition and Related Regulation Issues in the Insurance Industry." *Roundtables on Competition Policy* 19.

Redburn, F. Stevens. 1993. "Measuring Revenue Capacity, Effort and Spending: How Should the Government Measure Spending? The Uses of Accrual Accounting. "*Public Administration Review* 53 (May/June): 228–36.

Savage, Lawrie. 1999. "Re-engineering Insurance Supervision." Policy Research Working Paper 2024. World Bank, Washington, D.C.

Schnepf, Randy, and Richard Heifner. 1999. "Crop and Revenue Insurance: Bargain Rates but Still a Hard Sell." *Agricultural Outlook* (August): 15–19.

Standard and Poor's. 1999a. "Standard and Poor's Maintains a Negative Outlook for the U.S. Property/Casualty Insurance Industry through 2000." Standard and Poor's Insurance Rating Service Commentary. April.

———. 1999b. "U.S. Reinsurance Pricing Is Expected to Firm in 2000." Standard and Poor's Insurance Rating Service Commentary.

Stern, Gary. 1999. "Managing Moral Hazard with Market Signals: How Regulation Should Change with Banking." *Proceedings of the 35th Annual Con-*

ference on Bank Structure and Competition. Chicago: Federal Reserve Bank of Chicago.

———. 2000. "Designing Credible Policies to Address TBTF and Moral Hazard after Financial Modernization." Speech presented at the George J. Stigler Center for the Study of the Economy and the State Conference on the Future of Finance: Globalization, the Internet, and Regulatory Reform, April 2000.

U.S. GAO (General Accounting Office). 1997. *Budgeting for Federal Insurance Programs.* Washington D.C.

WeatherRisk. 1999. *A Risk Special Report.*

Weaver, Carolyn. 1997. "Government Guarantees of Private Pension Benefits: Current Problems and Market-Based Solutions." In Sylvester Schieber and John Shoven, eds., *Public Policy Toward Pensions.* Cambridge, Mass.: MIT Press.

Weicher, John. 1994. "The New Structure of the Housing Finance System." *Economic Review* (July/August): 47–65.

World Bank. 2001. "Financial Sector: Insurance and Contractual Savings" *<wbln0018.worldbank.org/html/FinancialSectorWeb.nsf/generaldescription/1insurance+and+Contractual+Savings?opendocument>*.

CHAPTER 16

Contingent Liabilities of the Central Bank: Analyzing a Possible Fiscal Risk for Government

Mario I. Blejer
Central Bank of Argentina

Liliana Schumacher
International Monetary Fund

CENTRAL BANKS, NO MATTER HOW independent from the fiscal authorities, may become a source of fiscal risk for the government. Should the central bank's net worth drop below zero, fiscal authorities will be called on to act. As it turns out, the major risk to the central bank's financial position arises from its contingent commitments. Although central banks have frequently undertaken contingent commitments as part of their regular operation in the economy, it is only recently, through central bank involvement in the derivatives markets, that these transactions have drawn the attention of policymakers, market participants, and international agencies. This renewed interest and the fact that these contingent operations came to light in the aftermath of the 1997 East Asian financial crisis increased the interest in the analytics and the measurement of these commitments.

The goal of this chapter is twofold. First, it seeks to explore the rationale for central banks to undertake this type of commitment—in particular, to intervene in derivatives markets—and to assess the arguments that are commonly made for and against this sort of involvement. Second, it seeks to suggest a methodology for analyzing the whole spectrum of central bank contingent liabilities. Specifically, we aggregate all on- and off-balance sheet transactions in a single framework in order to draw meaningful conclusions about the consequences of these central bank operations for important policy issues such as the volume of the central bank's available reserves, the potential burden arising from instability in the banking sector, and the overall solvency of the central bank.

The chapter is organized as follows. The next section briefly classifies the different types of contingent liabilities that central banks typically undertake. It is followed by a discussion of the rationale for central bank operations involving contingent liabilities and of some of the advantages and disadvantages of these operations. The next two sections apply general finance principles to the problems of valuation, aggregation, and measurement of the risk arising from contingent liabilities. The chapter concludes with a description of some policy implications.

Central Bank Contingent Liabilities: A Classification

The general definition of central bank contingent liabilities coincides with the standard concept used to classify government contingent liabilities in the context of the fiscal accounts. However, some distinctive central bank commitments require a specific conceptual treatment. Moreover, the *concrete quantitative valuation* of certain types of central bank obligations requires a special analytical approach.

One point is important to stress at the outset. An analytical distinction exists between the lack of proper economic accounting of some assets and liabilities that would result in off-balance sheet items (such as implicit credit subsidies) and the conceptual and practical consequences of contingent assets and liabilities—that is, the management of items that have an uncertain value because their financial implications hinge on the realization of conditions that depend on future uncertain events (such as the provision of credit guarantees).

Like government contingent liabilities, central bank contingent liabilities can be divided into *implicit* and *explicit* ones, depending on whether they arise from a legal or contractual source. *Explicit* central bank contingent liabilities originate in formal statements in regulations or in contracts entered into by the central bank with specific counterparties. These liabilities can be divided into three types.

The first type is liabilities that arise from formal central bank commitments to supporting the soundness of the banking sector. These commitments include providing liquidity to individual institutions (the central bank's role as lender of last resort), as well as providing specific deposit and other guarantees.

The second type is liabilities created by central bank operations in non-spot foreign exchange and other financial markets. Specifically, when the central bank intervenes in derivatives markets, these operations give rise to potential gains and losses that are contingent both on the state of the world and on other central bank actions. These types of operations could be a very important source of contingent liabilities because they include not only straight intervention in the markets for forwards, futures, options, and currency and interest rate swaps, but also monetary operations involving foreign exchange swaps and repurchase agreements (repos). The focus of contingent liability analysis, however, is on the use of derivatives as *policy tools*—that is, operations designed to influence variables such as the exchange rate or the interest rate. In particular, currency forwards and options and foreign exchange swaps can be used as instruments in the foreign exchange market to affect the exchange rate, and repurchase agreements can be used in the money market to influence the interest rate. It is important to distinguish these operations from the use of derivatives undertaken as part of the central bank's routine management of its own foreign exchange reserves.

The third type of contingent liabilities is other potential guarantees to private sector activities, such as guaranteed repayment of directed credit to selected sectors and export and investment guarantees.

Among the *implicit* central bank contingent liabilities, the most salient is the commitment of central banks to ensuring the *systemic* solvency of the banking (and financial) sector, over and above the explicit commitment to providing liquidity to individual institutions and to guaranteeing certain types of deposits or other private sector bank assets. These commitments would include providing financial coverage over and above the legal guarantee scheme and the bailout and recapitalization of banks and nonbank financial institutions.

It could be argued that certain macroeconomic central bank commitments such as the preservation of a stable exchange rate regime or, more generally, the attainment and maintenance of price stability also should be considered, in themselves, implicit contingent liabilities and, consequently, also should be subject to quantification. While in principle this argument would seem consistent with the general framework suggested here, we submit that they should not be part of the same analytical framework. Our reason: the financial consequences of the event (that is, deviations from implicit central bank policy targets) are hard, if impossible, to quantify because they can give rise to numerous types of responses. We postulate, therefore, that only *when specific policy actions can be taken to protect the implicit commitment* and they are embedded in legal norms (such as a stock of repo transactions or forward exchange market operations), the implicit commitment should be considered part of the framework suggested here.

The Rationale for Central Bank Operations Involving Contingent Liabilities

The rationale for the involvement of the central bank in activities that result in contingent liabilities varies according to the type of operation.

Much has been written about what motivates central banks to assume specific commitments to strengthening the soundness of the financial markets—for example, about the role of the central bank as lender of last resort or the rationale for deposit insurance. The main arguments in favor of these institutional devices include the illiquid nature of banks, together with the potential for systemic risk (Diamond and Dybvig 1983) and the existence of asymmetries of information and the protection of the small depositor (Tirole and Dewatripont 1994). Similarly, the issuance of guarantees for private sector activities has been the subject of abundant inquiries. In general, the view is that such activity is in fact clearly quasi-fiscal in nature, and therefore its rationale also is fiscal in nature. In particular, central banks may be induced to undertake these types of operations to hide undesirable budget outcomes from public scrutiny.

What has been much less well researched is the rationale for central bank intervention in derivatives markets. Therefore, in what follows we develop in more detail the main arguments that could be used to justify the implementation of these operations. In general terms, it is possible to assert that central banks tend to engage in derivatives operations for the following reasons: (a) to provide additionality to incomplete or illiquid markets; (b) to defend a fixed exchange rate regime or an exchange rate band; (c) to alleviate the conflict between the defense of an exchange rate regime and the stability of the financial system; (d) to act as an automatic stabilizer of the foreign exchange market; and (e) to act as an alternative instrument for monetary management under some specific circumstances.

Providing Additionality to Incomplete or Illiquid Markets

In many countries, the derivatives market is not deep enough and therefore does not provide the range of instruments needed for appropriate hedging and risk management. In these circumstances, the rate of growth of the underlying market would tend to be lower than desired, and the central bank's provision of additional innovative instruments and liquidity could be seen as a means of developing both the spot and the derivatives markets and of eliminating, or at least smoothing, volatility in the spot market.

Defending a Fixed Exchange Rate Regime
or an Exchange Rate Band

A central bank's engagement in derivatives operations, including forward and swap operations, has also been used repeatedly to reduce exchange rate fluctuations and, more specifically, to protect a fixed exchange rate regime or an exchange rate band. Central banks have two important reasons to prefer this form of intervention over intervention in the spot market. First, derivatives allow defense of the exchange rate without an immediate use of foreign exchange reserves and without an impact on the money supply. Such a defense is therefore similar to sterilized intervention, but it has ex ante an opposite—that is, a positive—fiscal outcome.

Second, intervention in the derivatives market is an efficient way of releasing some of the pressure that dealers and banks may exercise on the foreign exchange spot market at times of particularly heavy speculative stress. During normal times, banks and dealers can easily find counterparts for hedging their foreign exchange operations. But at times of uniform expectations, when there is a widespread market belief that the exchange rate would likely change in one particular direction, they may find it difficult to hedge in the derivatives market. Clearly, when the generalized expectation is that the domestic currency is bound to depreciate (or will be devalued), market participants will seek to shorten the domestic currency, buying put options or taking short forward positions. However, banks and other foreign exchange dealers will take the long side of the market only if they can hedge their exposure. But hedging in these circumstances could mean facing some impediments. In the absence of agents that need to hold a natural long position in the domestic currency, banks and dealers may be able to hedge only synthetically. In a synthetic hedge, dealers aim to replicate, with an opposite sign, the cash flows that emerge from the derivatives transactions to which they have committed. There are two cash flows to hedge: (a) a long position in the weak currency equal to the total amount of their forward commitments plus their put options commitments times the probability that the put options will be exercised (the hedge ratio); and (b) a short position in the strong currency for an amount equal to the long position times the forward rate. As can be seen easily, these two cash flows, with an opposite sign, can be easily replicated in the spot market by, for example, taking a loan in the weak currency and opening a deposit in the strong currency.

While hedging synthetically could be, from the point of view of risk management, satisfactory for the dealers, it may create a problematic situation from the central bank's perspective that provides the motivations for stepping into the derivatives markets. Several of the major concerns that central banks have with synthetic hedging are of particular interest. The first one relates to the impact of synthetic hedging on the foreign exchange spot market. As for the second, synthetic hedging can distort the response of agents to increases in the domestic interest rates.

Impact of Synthetic Hedging on the Spot Market. Clearly, during times of turbulence in the foreign exchange market, it is reasonable to expect that a central bank committed to defending a peg would try to avoid additional selling pressures on the domestic currency. However, a dealer hedging synthetically will tend to do precisely that by short-selling the domestic currency and using the proceeds to buy foreign currency. This would indeed put additional pressure on the spot market that can only be released by increasing the liquidity of the derivatives market. The central bank's willingness to sell forward contracts or to write put options is therefore intended to provide dealers with appropriate hedges, removing in this manner the additional pressure that synthetic hedging exerts on the spot market. In other words, central banks may intervene in the derivatives markets to prevent speculation from spilling over immediately into the cash/spot markets.[1]

Synthetic Hedging and Interest Rates. Central banks also are interested in containing synthetic hedging, because it is well recognized that these types of operations tend to disrupt the typical central bank defense of a pegged foreign exchange system. Garber and Spencer (1995) show that an increase in the domestic interest rate results in an increase in the hedge ratio (that is, in the inverse of the ratio between the number of puts and the units of foreign currency necessary to hedge those puts).[2] This situation means that an increase in interest rates *raises* the demand for foreign exchange in the spot market on the part of the synthetically hedged agents. Therefore, whether a higher domestic interest rate will succeed in reducing speculation, by inducing market participants to continue to hold the domestic currency, depends on the relative importance of market agents that are synthetically hedging versus the rest of the market participants that are caught in the interest rate squeeze.

Alleviating the Conflict between the Defense of an Exchange Rate Regime and the Stability of the Financial System

The conflict may arise when expectations of devaluation accelerate, provoking a surge in capital outflows. Given the importance of banks in the intermediation of capital flows, the intensifying pressures in the foreign exchange market could result in serious liquidity problems for the banking system. These problems might be further complicated by the fact that the increase in the expected rate of devaluation will lead to higher domestic interest rates. The central bank, in its role as lender of last resort, would tend to provide liquidity loans to banks that have experienced losses because of the higher interest rates[3] in the interbank market or because of the fire sale of bank assets when the interbank market dries up. However, because the lender of last resort cannot discriminate among banks with a legitimate liquidity problem of this sort and other banks that may attempt to borrow from the central bank in order to hedge or to speculate in the foreign exchange market, the provision of liquidity by the central bank may end up feeding the short-selling of domestic currency, increasing in this way the pressure on the foreign exchange market. In other words, central banks may prefer to step into illiquid derivatives markets in order to provide banks and dealers with an alternative way to speculate, through forwards or options, without exerting further pressures on the foreign exchange spot market.

Acting as an Automatic Stabilizer of the Foreign Exchange Market

The money (American or European) put option written by the central bank on the reserve currency serves as an automatic stabilizer of the foreign exchange market.[4] When there is an inflow of foreign currency and the exchange rate appreciates, the put buyers exercise the option and deliver the reserve foreign currency to the central bank. In addition, to stabilize the market, this mechanism allows the central bank to accumulate reserves precisely when the foreign currency weakens and avoids the negative signaling effect of open central bank intervention in the spot market. The foreign currency reserves accumulated during such episodes of appreciation can be used to reduce outstanding foreign currency liabilities or, when there are pressures on the exchange rate to depreciate, to provide the additional supply required by the market.

Acting as an Alternative Instrument for Monetary Management under Some Specific Circumstances

Some arguments have also been voiced justifying the use of foreign exchange swaps as an instrument for domestic liquidity management. In particular, in countries running fiscal surpluses or where the outstanding stock of public—including central bank—debt is low, central banks may find it expensive (or disruptive) to inject domestic liquidity using repos based on domestic bonds. For that reason, some countries have resorted to the use of foreign exchange swaps, which are basically repos in foreign exchange currency, as a temporary mechanism for managing domestic liquidity.[5] These operations do not change the level of net international reserves, but they do temporarily increase domestic liquidity.

Conclusion

There is therefore a positive policy rationale for central banks to accumulate contingent liabilities through intervention in the derivatives market. However, these operations carry significant risks. A proliferation of contingent liabilities distorts the financial statements of central banks. The solvency of the central bank also can be compromised by potential losses. Moreover, intervention in the derivatives market may have serious drawbacks. They could be difficult to support when these markets are very thin, and they are bound to result in a loss of the informational content provided by these markets. In addition, the ability to intervene in the derivatives markets at a low cost, and the lack of a material constraint to the intervention levels, could lead to a potential postponement of important policy decisions.

Valuation and Aggregation

One of the main problems posed by contingent liabilities is the issue of how to record them and, in particular, how to aggregate these contingent liabilities (which are by definition off-balance sheet) with the on-balance sheet central bank transactions for valuation purposes.

Valuation

We propose here using a portfolio approach to all central bank transactions, as the only way in which both on- and off-balance sheet transactions can be aggregated and as a way of providing some meaningful information on variables such as the central bank's available reserves, the potential burden caused by preserving banking sector stability, and the overall solvency of the central bank. In a portfolio approach, transactions are aggregated according to their sign (short or long) and their value. The theory of financial instruments provides the tools needed for pricing these transactions, and therefore the procedures are not reviewed here in detail.[6] However, for illustration, and because some operations are particularly relevant for central banks, we discuss here two specific cases: the value of a currency forward contract and the value of a deposit insurance commitment. Then, we discuss some examples of proper aggregation in the central bank portfolio.

   The Value of a Currency Forward Contract. The economic value of a currency forward contract can be derived from covered interest rate parity

(16.1) $$e^{-r_{f,0}}F_{0,T} = S_0 e^{-r_{d,0}}$$

where $F_{0,T}$ is the forward rate for the foreign currency, for maturity T, as of the day the contract is signed; S_0 is the spot rate for the foreign currency as of the day of the contract; $r_{d,0}$ is the domestic interest rate as of the day of the contract; and $r_{f,o}$ is the foreign interest rate as of the day of the contract.

The meaning of (16.1) is that according to the covered interest rate parity, a forward contract can be viewed as two zero coupon bonds. The left-hand sign of the equality represents a zero coupon bond denominated in domestic currency, with a face value equal to the forward rate of the foreign currency for maturity T, as of the day of the contract, and with maturity T. The value of this zero is found by discounting the forward rate by the domestic interest rate. The right-hand side of the equality represents a zero coupon bond denominated in foreign currency, with a face value equal to one unit of the foreign currency (converted into domestic currency using the spot price of the day of the contract). The value of this zero is found by discounting the unit of the foreign currency by the foreign interest rate.

We can now rearrange (16.1) to find the value of the forward contract, any day after the contract was signed, as the difference between the value of the two zeros—that is,

$$(16.2) \qquad e^{-r_{d,t}}F_{0,T} - e^{-r_{f,t}}S_t \neq 0.$$

Equation 16.1 revealed that the value of a forward, as of the day of the contract, is zero. But for any other day after the original date, the value of the forward contract in the book of the central bank can be different from zero and can be determined by calculating equation 16.2 with information that is generally readily available.

Deposit Insurance. Following Merton (1977), deposit insurance can be seen as the equivalent of a put option held by the banks and written by the central bank on each unit of bank assets, with a strike price equal to the value of bank-insured debts. The equivalence goes as follows: if banks become insolvent, the value of bank assets by definition is lower than the value of bank debts. Given limited liability for the shareholders, bank debts will suffer the full loss. But in the presence of deposit insurance, banks have the ability to "exercise the put option"— that is, they "sell" their assets (the underlying asset of the put) to the central bank and they get in exchange an amount equal to the face value of the insured liabilities (the strike price), which is used to pay for bank-insured debts.

Following this equivalence, the value of deposit insurance is

$$(16.3) \qquad G(T) = TBe^{-rt}\phi(X_2) - V\phi(x_1)$$

where $X_1 = \{\log(B/V) - [r + (\delta^2/2)^T]\}/\delta\sqrt{T}$; $X_1 = X_2 + \delta\sqrt{T}$; $B =$ face value of bank liabilities (exercise price); $V =$ value of the banks' assets; $\delta =$ volatility of the banks' assets; $T =$ maturity of bank liabilities; and

ϕ ($\cdot$) = cumulative probability distribution function for a standardized normal variable—that is, the probability that such a variable will be less than ($\cdot$).

As Merton (1977) indicates, (16.3) also can be applied to valuing a government guarantee of loans made to private (financial or nonfinancial) corporations.

Aggregation

Based on an economic valuation of the off-balance sheet contingent positions of the central bank, as described above, all central bank transactions can be aggregated. We now illustrate this procedure using eight hypothetical central bank portfolios, which are described in Tables 16.1 and 16.2. Table 16.1 contains the basic information used to construct the on-balance and the off-balance sheet accounts of the assumed central bank, together with the prices and interest rates used to value the positions. We chose the British pound (GBP) as the domestic currency and the German mark (DEM) as the foreign currency. Table 16.2 is an estimate of the portfolio values of the central bank positions, and

Table 16.1 Hypothetical Central Bank Portfolio: Data

On-balance sheet items:
Reserves are invested in a one-year zero coupon bond denominated in DEM.
Face value of reserves: DEM118
Domestic debt: GBP30
The central bank holds a loan against the Treasury for GBP30.
Monetary base: GBP10

Off-balance sheet items:
The central bank is short DEM30 in the forward market. The maturity of the forward is one year.
For the calculation of the deposit insurance guarantee, the following data were used:
- Bank leverage (ratio of bank liabilities to bank assets) = 0.8.
- Volatility of bank assets (measured by the standard deviation of annual changes of the value of bank assets) = 0.5.
- X1 = 0.5964.
- Value of one put = 0.0515.

Prices
Spot exchange rate 1 DEM = GBP0.338.
Interest rate (GBP) = 0.1000.
Interest rate (DEM) = 0.0839.
Forward rate 1 DEM = GBP0.333.

Source: Compiled by the authors.

Table 16.2 Hypothetical Central Bank Portfolio: Values

Positions in the central bank portfolio	Value
1. Base case	
Foreign exchange reserves	GBP36.9
Domestic debt	GBP27.27
Long leg of forward	
Loan to Treasury	0
Monetary base	GBP100
Short leg of forward	
Financial sector guarantee	
Value of portfolio	−35.84
2. Base case + forward	
Foreign exchange reserves	GBP36.9
Domestic debt	GBP27.27
Long leg of forward	GBP9.09
Loan to Treasury	0
Monetary base	GBP100
Short leg of forward	GBP9.36
Financial sector guarantee	
Value of portfolio	−36.21
3. Base case + guarantee	
Foreign exchange reserves	GBP36.9
Domestic debt	GBP27.27
Long leg of forward	
Loan to Treasury	0
Monetary base	GBP100
Short leg of forward	
Financial sector guarantee (bank assets: GBP400)	−20.62
Value of portfolio	−56.39
4. Base case + 2* guarantee	
Foreign exchange reserves	GBP36.9
Domestic debt	GBP27.27
Long leg of forward	
Loan to Treasury	0
Monetary base	GBP100
Short leg of forward	
Financial sector guarantee (bank assets: GBP800)	−41.23
Value of portfolio	−76.95
5. Base case + 3* guarantee	
Foreign exchange reserves	GBP36.9
Domestic debt	GBP27.27
Long leg of forward	
Loan to Treasury	0
Monetary base	GBP100
Short leg of forward	
Financial sector guarantee (bank assets: GBP1,200)	−61.85
Value of portfolio	−97.5

(Table continues on the following page.)

Table 16.2 (continued)

Positions in the central bank portfolio	Value
6. Base case + guarantee + forward	
Foreign exchange reserves	GBP36.9
Domestic debt	GBP27.27
Long leg of forward	9.09
Loan to Treasury	0
Monetary base	GBP100
Short leg of forward	9.36
Financial sector guarantee (bank assets: GBP400)	20.62
Value of portfolio	−56.76

Source: Compiled by the authors.

from these economic—rather than accounting—values the true valuation of the central bank equity is calculated. The economic values of the balance sheet items were calculated by converting all notional amounts into British pounds and discounting these amounts by the relevant interest rate. For the forward positions and the deposit insurance, we used the formulas just described.

The base case or Case 1 is the simplest one, where the central bank issues monetary base in exchange for foreign reserves or domestic debt. In addition, there is a loan to the Treasury whose economic value is assumed to be zero.[7] In Case 2, the central bank, in addition to its activities in Case 1, is active in the forward market for foreign currency. The central bank intervenes in the forward market in only one direction: it buys domestic currency forward. In Case 3, the central bank also provides deposit insurance to the banking system. Cases 4 and 5 are identical to Case 3, except for the size of the banking system: in Case 4, the assets of the banking sector are twice as large as in Case 3, and in Case 5, the bank assets are three times those in Case 3. Finally, Case 6 combines intervention in the forward market for foreign currency with deposit insurance.

The value of the portfolios, when properly accounted for the economic value of assets and liabilities, is negative in all cases and becomes more negative as contingent liabilities are added to the portfolio. The fact that the central bank's equity is negative is not an anomaly. In fact, it is interesting to note that a central bank with negative economic equity is a likely outcome, because the usual *accounting* approach to the value of central bank activities does not consider the economic value of explicit or implicit commitments such as a deposit insurance guarantee and a forward contract. In addition, most central bank assets are registered at nominal values and are not economically valued (for example, the probability of repayment of certain loans, the time value of domestic and foreign assets, and the credit risk of reserves invested abroad are not considered). The standard approach therefore usually results in an overestimation of central bank equity.

Using a methodology based on economic valuation rather than on nominal accounts, we also can estimate the value of specific components of the portfolio. For example, for Case 2, we could compute the value of reserves net of forward contracts (in domestic currency) as 36.90 + 9.09 − 9.36 = 36.36. It is easy to see in this example that as the domestic currency (the pound) depreciates in the spot market, the economic value of the reserves net of forward contracts decreases. The same happens if the interest rate in pounds goes up. This is so because the value of the long leg of the forward that is worth 9.09 in this example decreases as the pound depreciates and the interest rate in pounds increases.

In another example, the unit value (per unit of bank assets) of the deposit insurance is GBP0.0515 (see Table 16.1). Note, however, that the value of the insurance depends on the size of bank assets. When bank assets are GBP400 (Case 3 in Table 16.2), the insurance is worth GBP20.62; when bank assets are GBP800, the insurance is worth GBP41.23; and when bank assets are GBP1,200, the insurance is worth GBP61.85.

The risk of the bank system also has an influence on the value of the contingent liability. Consider the case of a rapid deterioration in the quality of bank loans. The value of bank assets, adjusted by risk, goes down and the leverage ratio goes up, making the value of the central bank contingent liability higher.

Concluding Remarks

Central banks perform a large variety of operations that give rise to contingent liabilities, defined as financial commitments that are triggered by the occurrence of an event whose realization is uncertain. Because these operations cover a wide array of areas, the motivation for central banks to engage in this type of activity stems from a myriad of reasons. In this chapter, we provide a taxonomy for classifying these operations and elaborate on their analytical aspects, as well as on the operational motivations that induce central banks to utilize these instruments.

We conclude that although some of a central bank's contingent liabilities arise from anomalous circumstances,[8] some positive reasons explain their apparent popularity. Some of these positive implications are well recognized—particularly those that arise from the central bank's role in guaranteeing the stability of the banking sector—but the constructive aspects of central banks' involvement in derivatives markets are less understood. We attempt here to provide a broader and more positive perspective, but, at the same time, we must stress that, because most of the operations that give rise to contingent liabilities also tend to be off-balance sheet, they reduce the transparency of central bank accounts. This, in turn, may result in serious problems regarding the proper assessment of the financial position of the monetary authority and, by implication, of the overall macroeconomic conditions of the country. We suggest, therefore, that a comprehensive portfolio approach that values, in an economic rather than purely accounting sense, all off- and on-balance sheet assets and liabilities of the central bank be adopted. We provide some examples of how this could be done, particularly for some contingent liabilities that are characteristic of central banks.

Note, however, that even though proper valuation and aggregation of central bank financial positions would solve some of the transparency problems posed by contingent liabilities, their presence in the central bank portfolio also would tend to increase financial risks. In addition to reducing, ceteris paribus, the net equity of the central bank, as shown in our illustrative simulations, formal risk indicators would tend to rise in tandem with the volume of this type of liabilities. It would indeed be a useful research endeavor to attempt a full quantification of these effects, using available central bank information.[9]

Notes

1. Examples of such interventions are the Bank of Spain intervention in the options (put) market during the 1992–93 European exchange rate mechanism crisis and the Bank of Thailand's sale of forward contracts in 1997.

2. This also can be interpreted as the probability that the put will be exercised.

3. When banks have positive duration gaps, an increase in interest rates will lead to bank losses.

4. This was the case in the stabilization scheme adopted by Mexico in July 1996.

5. The Reserve Bank of Australia has resorted to this mechanism with relative frequency. For example, the need to increase liquidity arising from the Y2K problem led to the doubling of the stock of outstanding forward obligations, matched by a similar increase in the total holding of official reserve assets.

6. One of the many textbooks that have addressed this topic is Hull (1999).

7. Under the assumption that the Treasury will not repay the loan, the discount factor is infinite.

8. Such as those that simply reflect quasi-fiscal operations transferred from the government budget to the central bank for purely political or "cosmetic" reasons.

9. One possibility is to utilize risk measurement methodologies such as value at risk. For a framework of this type of application in the context of central bank portfolios, see Blejer and Schumacher (1999).

References

Blejer, Mario I., and Liliana Schumacher. 1999. "Central Bank Vulnerability and the Value of Its Commitments: A VaR Approach." *Journal of Risk* (fall).

Diamond, Douglas W., and Philip H. Dybvig. 1983. "Bank Runs, Deposit Insurance and Liquidity." *Journal of Political Economy* 91: 401–19.

Garber, Peter M., and Michael G. Spencer. 1995. "Foreign Exchange Hedging and the Interest Rate Defense." *IMF Staff Papers* 42: 490–516.

Hull, John. 1999. *Options, Futures and Other Derivative Securities.* Englewood Cliffs, N.J.: Prentice Hall.

Merton, Robert. 1977. "An Analytic Derivation of the Cost of Deposit Insurance and Loan Guarantees. An Application of Modern Option Pricing Theory." *Journal of Banking and Finance* 1: 3–11.

Tirole, Jean, and Mathias Dewatripont. 1994. *The Prudential Regulation of Banks.* Cambridge, Mass.: MIT Press.

Practice

CHAPTER 17

Contingent Liabilities in Infrastructure: Lessons from the East Asian Financial Crisis

Ashoka Mody*

International Monetary Fund

FOR EAST ASIAN GOVERNMENTS in the midst of financial crisis in 1997 and 1998, the transformation of their contingent liabilities into immediate obligations proved to be an additional blow in an already challenging situation.[1] In all crisis countries (Indonesia, Republic of Korea, Malaysia, and Thailand), the banking sector was the major source of such liabilities. However, except in Korea, infrastructure projects also added to the fiscal stress. Specifically, in so-called public-private partnerships, governments had contingent contractual obligations—and these became due as the crisis worsened. With ongoing economic recovery, the fiscal pressure from these obligations will likely decline. The pressures will remain, however, where the problems stemmed from inadequate project design and ineffective sector strategy and regulation.

This chapter draws on the experience in Indonesia and Malaysia, both of which adopted a distinctively Asian style of infrastructure privatization.[2] Indeed, throughout East Asia, governments sought private capital and private management skills, yet they also provided contractual commitments to enhance the financial attractiveness of the projects. Some of the government commitments were in the form

---

*The author was with the World Bank when he wrote this article; he is currently with the IMF.

of cash subsidies, but most were contingent in nature, promising, for example, to top up revenues if they fell below a threshold or promising to honor a pricing formula.

The principal guarantees provided by the Philippines government, summarized in Table 17.1, represent the types of commitments made by governments throughout the region. The commitments were based on two premises. First, the transition from government infrastructure monopoly to multiple private infrastructure providers requires significant investment in regulatory capacity. Second, because such capacity cannot be built overnight, contractually specified public-private partnerships are necessary intermediate steps in a rapid infrastructure development strategy. The World Bank's 1994 *World Development Report* endorsed the Asian approach as an appropriate transitional strategy (World Bank 1994). Transport and power projects were identified as especially suitable for applying the approach.

Based on the Indonesian and Malaysian experiences, this chapter argues that contingent liabilities are not intrinsically associated with privatized infrastructure. Their manifestation in East Asia reflects a specific privatization strategy undertaken in a period of rapid growth

Table 17.1 Main Sources of Infrastructure Contingent Liabilities, the Philippines

Item guaranteed	Cost	Sector
Buyout clause or termination	Buyout or termination price	Power and transport
Force majeure	Buyout or termination price	Power, transport, and water
Minimum revenue ("Take-or-pay" contract for the power sector)	Payment obligation to meet the minimum revenue threshold	Power and transport
Toll changes; automatic toll adjustment formula	Costs of inability to implement toll adjustments	Transport
Assumption of "old" (preprivatization) loans being paid by concessionaire	Cost of principal and interest	Water
Loser of appeal to pay total cost of appeals process for both parties	Cost of appeals process	Water

Source: Reside (2000).

with the objective of rapid new investment in infrastructure. However, even where justified, transitional structures created with government's direct support and contingent commitments should give way to competitive infrastructure provision with greater risk shifted to the private sector (World Bank 1994). This has not yet happened in East Asia. Latin American economies—especially Argentina and Chile—demonstrate the practical implementation of privatization without the government acquiring contingent liabilities.

The rest of this chapter is organized as follows. The sources of contingent liabilities are discussed first for the transportation sector, then for the power sector, and briefly for the water and sanitation sector. Each section critiques the sector strategy pursued and outlines alternatives based on international experience. The chapter concludes by emphasizing that it would be a mistake to view the postcrisis realization of contingent liabilities as mainly due to the crisis and urges a systemic reform that can both improve efficiency and lower government risks.

Transportation

In the mid-1990s, transportation projects dominated private infrastructure projects in East Asia, both in numbers and especially in dollar outlays (World Bank 1994). These projects were typically built and operated by the private sector, with the assets to be transferred to the government after a contractually agreed on period. Several legal variations of the build-operate-transfer model exist, but these are not economically significant. Private debt and equity, supported by specific government financial support, financed the projects. For transportation projects, governments provided some direct subsidies, often in the form of rights to land. More controversial was support that guaranteed minimum revenues to the project sponsors.

The East Asian crisis notwithstanding, few countries worldwide have succeeded in using a stand-alone build-operate-transfer model to deliver a significant transportation network. Especially in the early stages of implementation, demand projections have proven to be overly optimistic and cost overruns have proven to be endemic. A major toll road program in Mexico suffered from both problems. In Bangkok, Thailand, private expressway and urban rail financing has been scaled back, because the government and private concessionaires failed to agree on and adhere to contractual terms. Even on heavily traveled roads, such as the one from Guangzhou to Shenzhen in southern China, cost overruns have led to unanticipated financing requirements. Overall, the number of private transportation projects has fallen sharply. In 1998, in the aftermath of the East Asian crisis, only one new toll road—in Croatia—was brought to successful financial closure in non-OECD (Organisation for Economic Co-operation and Development) countries.

Malaysia

In Malaysia, contingent liabilities have arisen principally from two Kuala Lumpur light rail projects and an extensive toll road program. The light rail projects have suffered much lower-than-expected demand. By October 1998, concessions were signed for 26 expressway and toll bridge projects. Of these, 12 projects were open to traffic, 6 were under construction, and the remaining 8 were under negotiation. The full program was expected to create about 1,700 kilometers of toll roads. Although the roads under the toll road program represent only about 2 percent of the total length of the country's road network, they are important economic arteries. Some roads constructed earlier, including the major North-South Expressway, enjoyed initial financial success. Problems have arisen in part because of the crisis-related economic downturn that reduced demand, especially for new highways, and also affected users' willingness to pay tolls. However, the long-term economics of the new generation of toll roads is suspect.

Because a comprehensive account of the government's contingent liabilities is not possible, estimates were obtained for three transportation projects essentially underwritten by the government. Failure by the project to make its commercial debt payment required a declaration of a default and the takeover by the government of the commercial debt and therefore of the project. The government consequently had significant financial exposure to these projects (Figure 17.1).

A Monte Carlo simulation approach was used to estimate the government's exposure. Under this approach, the stochastic (uncertain) cash flows are projected into the future, and 2,500 scenarios are run. Under some scenarios, the project is economically viable and no default occurs. Under other scenarios, the project defaults on its commercial debt and is taken over by the government. The estimated *expected* cost to the government is the average cost over all the scenarios—or the cost the government can expect to pay out on average. However, if some unfavorable factors coincide, such as low ridership and higher-than-anticipated costs, the payout can be larger. The *unexpected cost* is defined as the amount paid out in the 95th percentile case (that is, there is only a 5 percent chance that such an eventuality would occur). In addition to these costs arising out of project default, the government is committed to subsidies, such as low interest rate loans, that would have to be paid.

As Figure 17.1 shows, the government's financial obligations in transportation projects are highly sensitive to the assumption on ridership/ traffic flows. For the light rail projects, traffic projections had been steadily revised downward after initiation of the projects. Each revision raised the costs to the government substantially. Since the 1997 crisis in East Asia, ridership has been even lower than the latest precrisis

Figure 17.1. Monte Carlo Estimates of Contingent Exposure to Transport Projects in Malaysia

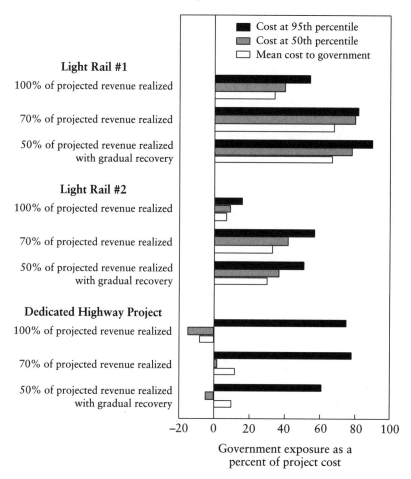

projections. If ridership is about half of the most recent projections, then the expected costs to the government for one of the projects could be as high as about two-thirds of project costs. The dedicated highway project is performing better than the light rail projects. Assuming 50 percent less traffic than projected by the project and a gradual recovery after the crisis, the average cost to the government will be around 10 percent of the total project.[3]

The estimates suggest that about half of the expected postcrisis costs arise from the optimistic projections made when the projects were initiated and the other half are the result of the downturn. These estimates do not take into account obligations from the freezing of tolls on certain highways, which have created significant payments by the government to the project sponsors (Box 17.1).

Indonesia

In Indonesia, the government's obligations for toll road projects are more modest than those in Malaysia and also are more modest than those in Indonesia's own power sector. This is the case for two reasons. First, many of the roads carry intraurban traffic, which is relatively well established and steady. These roads, therefore, have not been seriously affected by the economic crisis. Second, the government has few explicit guarantees, unlike in Malaysia where typically the government must pay the outstanding debt when a project defaults on its loan and take over the project. However, the full extent of the obligations may be larger than is apparent. Much of the financing of the toll roads came from domestic banks. The nonperformance of the toll roads would show in the nonperforming portfolio of the banks, which in turn are backed by the government. Thus there may actually be more exposure to the government from the toll road projects than is evident.[4]

Lessons for Private Transport Concessions

Because individual toll road and rail projects rarely generate positive cash flows in their early years, a possible approach lies in creating

---

Box 17.1 From Contingent to Real Liabilities: Malaysia's North-South Highway (PLUS)

Under the 1986 concession agreement for the North-South Highway, automatic toll increases equal the greater of 6 percent or the annual increase in the consumer price index. If the eligible toll increase is denied, the concessionaire must be compensated an equivalent amount. Thus permitting a formula-driven toll rate increase creates a contingent liability for the government that grows with each additional year the eligible increase is denied. Since 1996, the government has denied the full increase permitted under the concession agreement. The government budgets for this expense, which for the PLUS concession was a total of MYR161 million for 1996 and 1997 and which increased sharply to MYR145 million for 1998 (because of the cumulative denial of rate increases for successive years).

regional transport utilities that are able to cross-subsidize the different transportation segments within their jurisdiction. Such cross-subsidization could be justified on the basis of network externalities. In China, this model has been piloted by the provincial communications ministries in toll highway development. In several provinces, provincial toll road companies securitize existing toll road assets on the domestic and Hong Kong stock exchanges, using the proceeds to finance new toll highway development.

Lessons from France and Spain, which have among the more extensive toll road programs, also may be relevant. In particular, they have experimented with private toll road companies that operate multiple roads (Gomez-Ibanez and Meyer 1992). In France, three of the four toll road companies went bankrupt in the 1970s, after the energy crisis, and were taken over by the government. The one remaining private company, which was the largest, has maintained efficient operations. Since then, France has used a system of cross-subsidization across companies to assist the investment programs in the underdeveloped regions. Spain has dispersed its toll road holdings among about a dozen or so companies. The impact of the 1970s energy crisis also was felt in Spain but with a less devastating effect. The government took over some of the smaller companies; however, the bulk of the toll road network continues to be in private hands. Spain has avoided cross-subsidization of companies on the grounds that it reduces the incentives for improved efficiency. In both France and Spain, initial tolls were set at different levels, but the subsequent increases were based on a common formula. For example, in France the tariff increase allowed is 95 percent of the increase in the consumer price index.

Lessons from the Metropolitan Transportation Authority (MTA) in New York, an example of a relatively successful transport utility, may be relevant for urban public transport. The MTA operates the subway, bus, and commuter railroad systems, which run chronic operating deficits, and also owns the Triborough Bridge and Tunnel Authority (TBTA). TBTA generates operating profits well in excess of half a billion U.S. dollars a year, which subsidize transit operations or enable infrastructure investments. The experience highlights the importance of coordinating the different transport modes.

Lessons from the international experience therefore caution that the objective of speeding up the development of urban and intercity city transportation networks through private capital may be untenable except in select circumstances. As such, while the economic crisis, and the consequent fall in ridership and traffic, undoubtedly created additional fiscal stress in Malaysia (and in Thailand), the very basis of a strategy of accelerated development that does not take into account the integrated nature of transport networks must be reexamined.

Power Sector

Government contingent obligations in the power sector arise mainly through long-term "take-or-pay" contracts with independent power producers (IPPs). Under these contracts, the government-owned power utility makes a commitment to buy ("take") a minimum amount of power at a prespecified price or pay for that contracted power in any case. Typically, the power utility is financially strained, and so the utility's obligation is backed by the sovereign government, creating a government contingent liability. In developing countries, the IPP strategy was pioneered in the early 1990s by the Philippines (World Bank 1994). The Philippine government also waived sovereign immunity against claims made by international creditors.

The IPP strategy is attractive because it facilitates the rapid installation of power generation capacity at no immediate cost to the government. The government takes on a contingent obligation, which may never be called, especially if the high economic growth projections materialize. The cost of not adding to capacity can be large, because the lack of power can constrain growth. Following the Philippine example, other countries contracted with IPPs, especially Indonesia, Pakistan, and Thailand. But, except in the Philippines, disagreements and contract renegotiations have been a serious problem.

Malaysia

In Malaysia, the obligations for IPPs are not borne directly by the government but by Tenaga Nasional Berhad (TNB), the partially privatized power utility.[5] These obligations arise in the context of long-term take-or-pay contracts with IPPs. If the exchange rate is allowed to float, the depreciation also can increase the costs of imported inputs and debt denominated in foreign currencies. These costs (unlike those for hikes in interest rates) are contractually passed on to Tenaga. How well Tenaga is able to bear these costs depends on its financial condition.

In the run-up to the banking crisis, Tenaga's financial situation was conditioned by its large U.S. dollar-denominated borrowings, which resulted in significant foreign exchange losses as the Malaysian ringgit weakened (Box 17.2). As a consequence, while demand growth remained surprisingly strong after the crisis, Tenaga's internal funding resources shrank, requiring fresh additional foreign borrowings. Although Tenaga sought to renegotiate its commitments to five IPPs, they did not accept the proposal. In a small gesture, however, they agreed to receive payments monthly instead of weekly.

Box 17.2 Tenaga's Approach to the Financial Crisis

The government of Malaysia continues to be the principal shareholder of the electricity utility Tenaga Nasional Bhd, which suffered cash losses for 1998 that were significantly higher than in the previous year (see table). The big loss stemmed from the currency depreciation. Demand growth slowed, but it continued to be surprisingly strong. Electricity demand is expected to grow between 6 and 8 percent annually.

	For financial year ending August 31(billions of ringgit)	
	1997	*1998*
Turnover	10.0	11.4
Operating profit	1.4	0.6
Foreign exchange loss	(1.3)	(3.5)
Loss after tax	(0.1)	(3.1)

As a utility, Tenaga normally has access to significant internal funding sources. Recently, however, these sources have been limited, requiring fresh foreign borrowings. To reduce its debt service burden, Tenaga swapped part of its dollar-denominated debt for yen-denominated debt, thereby reducing its dollar exposure from 40 to 30 percent. The yen debt carries a significantly lower interest rate. However, Tenaga now takes on the risk of possible yen appreciation. (Source: *Star* [Kuala Lumpur], November 11, 1998.)

Indonesia

In Indonesia, concerns existed prior to the crisis about the country's capacity for excess power generation and the unsolicited, long-term take-or-pay contracts that the government-owned utility, Perusahaan Listrik Negara or the PLN, signed with some of the 26 independent power producers. The cost of this power is high by international standards and, more to the point, in relation to the tariffs that can realistically be charged the final consumers. The banking crisis aggravated the PLN's debt burden in two ways. First, the rupiah value of its U.S. dollar-denominated obligations (including debt service to the government of Indonesia on on-lent loans, gas purchases for its own plants, and contracted purchases of power from IPPs) skyrocketed as the rupiah depreciated. Second, demand growth fell. For example, energy sales in Java-Bali (80 percent of the PLN's market) are now projected to remain flat. The PLN's current weak financial situation implies that it will be unable to meet all its contractual obligations.

The PLN's obligations may ultimately be the government of Indonesia's obligations. It remains true that the government's "letter of comfort" to the sponsors of private projects does not oblige the government to pay creditors and IPPs on behalf of the PLN under the take-or-pay contracts. However, as more IPPs come onstream, the PLN's fiscal situation is likely to come under increasing pressure. As a state-owned entity, the PLN would have recourse to the government on at least some of its other obligations.

The implications of the crisis are serious. The IPP capacity contracted for by the PLN is just coming onstream. During fiscal 1999/2000, additional monthly payments of about US$50-60 million (about 0.4 percent of GDP) came due. These payments will continue to increase for the next four to five years as successive IPPs get ready to deliver power. Because virtually none of the new capacity that comes onstream will be used in the next four to five years, given the high level of contracted capacity and the sharp decline in demand, these new obligations will present a huge drain on the financial resources of the PLN.

The PLN and the Indonesian government also are exposed to risks associated with legal action. In view of the PLN's growing obligations, the government has put on hold some negotiations for additional capacity (*Keppres 39/97*, September 1997). In principle, that is the right decision. However, some of the negotiations were at a relatively advanced stage. One promoter of such a project has taken the view that a commitment already existed on the part of the government and has sought claims under the United Nations Commission on International Trade Law.

Beyond IPPs: A More Competitive Model

As with the transport infrastructure, some of the problems faced by Indonesia (and also other countries such as Pakistan and Thailand) stem from the underlying strategy. While negotiations of project terms to lower the prices paid to the IPPs can help, ultimately far-reaching sectoral reform will be required. Such a strategy will entail more active steps toward containing the generating capacity and creating a sector structure that permits the transfer of more risks to the private providers.

The recent international experience offers several pointers. First, to create more competition in power generation, countries that have contracted with IPPs will have to deal with the stranded assets from past contracts—assets whose economic value will potentially decline after deregulation, either because the market test shows IPPs are no longer needed or because they face greater market risks. Considerable controversy surrounds how much compensation is due to the owners of the stranded assets and how the compensation will be funded—the two choices are the taxpayers or the consumers. In general, the consumer pays through a levy on the electricity bill. This need not raise the cost of electricity if competition lowers the basic charges, but it will delay the benefits of lower overall bills.

Second, creating and operating an independent system operator (ISO) are crucial. The ISO ensures equal access to transmission lines and the economic utilization of generation assets through overseeing the functioning of a spot market for electricity. Although the details of the spot market vary somewhat across countries, the principle is the same everywhere. Generators bid for defined time slots by declaring their marginal cost of supply. The ISO dispatches requirements for that slot, choosing the generators with the lowest marginal costs; all generators receive a price equal to the marginal cost of the lowest-cost supplier, thus creating an incentive for efficiency. The price paid by the electricity distributor for electricity received from the ISO is regulated and equals some variable cost elements (including the spot price of the electricity in the relevant time periods) and transmission charges, which are limited through a price cap formula.

Third, competition also occurs through direct contracting between generators and the larger users of electricity as well as with distributors who then sell power retail to the final consumers. Typically, these contracts are not regulated, and thus the price charged and the length of the contracts are determined through direct negotiation between the buyer and the seller. The spot market for electricity and the direct contracts provide benchmarks for each other, and, where competition is effective, the average prices in the two markets should converge. A key regulatory issue, however, does arise. The generator will not typically transmit electricity to the customer buying the power. Rather, the customer "will take physical service from the local utility which will deliver power commingled from an undifferentiated array of generators who are making common, simultaneous use of the transmission grid and distribution facilities" (California Public Utilities Commission 1996). Thus the generator requires the agreement of the local utility to conclude its obligation to its customer, and the pricing of such access requires regulatory oversight.

Finally, distribution rates are typically regulated through a price cap formula. Once again, certain variable costs of the energy are passed through, while the fixed charges for distribution (for connection and making capacity available) are capped. Competition among distributors is increasingly permitted, especially for larger consumers, although, as the Argentine example shows, small consumers are increasingly benefiting from a choice of energy sources (see Box 17.3).

Box 17.3 Competitive Power in Argentina

Just prior to its recent crisis, Argentina may well have had the most competitive power industry in the world. At the end of 1997, generation capacity of 19,000 megawatts was shared by over 40 generation plants. Another 14 plants with total capacity of over 5,000 megawatts planned to be operational by the end of 2001. Most of the new plants were expected to employ the combined cycle technology, which allows greater operational efficiency and is economical at smaller scales than traditional thermal and hydro-powered generation.

Distribution concessions were awarded to 17 principal distributors plus several smaller ones. Distributors are organized largely in line with state boundaries. Large consumers are able to bypass the distributors. In fact, because Argentina has one of the most liberal definitions of large users, many relatively small users are able to contract directly with generators. Two categories of large users are recognized. In the first are those with a requirement of more than 1.0 megawatt and a minimum annual consumption of 4,380 megawatt-hours; they must contract directly for at least 50 percent of their needs. In the second are those with peak requirements of between 0.1 and 2.0 megawatts; they must contract directly with generators for all of their energy needs. Most contracts, in practice, are of relatively short duration because prices have been falling.

The competitive system is held together by a transmission and dispatch system and an overall regulatory framework for ensuring coordination and efficient pricing. The National Interconnected System covers about 90 percent of the Argentine population, and the rest is served by a smaller grid. The system is managed by Compania Administradora del Mercado Mayorista Electrico S.A. (CAMMESA), which is owned half by the government and half by various suppliers and users. Although CAMMESA has been successful in operating the spot market for electricity, through which the various generators supply power to the transmission grid, expansion of the network has been more difficult to coordinate, because it needs joint approval by several parties.

The regulatory task includes setting price caps for the transmission and distribution segments of the network. The regulator also is supposed to supervise the periodic reauctioning of the distribution networks. To augment the independence of the regulator, the government has set high standards for qualifying as a regulator, the regulators have fixed terms and cannot be easily removed, the terms are staggered in the style of U.S. public utility commissions to provide continuity to the regulator's activities, and an independent source of funding has been created through a levy on the various industry participants. (Sources: Duff and Phelps 1998 and Estache and Rodriguez-Pardina 1998.)

Malaysia's National Sanitation Project

Malaysia has made important strides in using the private sector for delivery of water and sanitation services (Haarmeyer and Mody 1998). Several water supply and treatment projects have been constructed on a build-operate-transfer basis. In addition, the Indah Water Konsortium (IWK) national sewerage project demonstrates both the benefits and limits of the Malaysian approach. Prior to the IWK concession, local governments bore responsibility for providing sewerage services. However, they often lacked the necessary financial or technical resources, and, as a result, the existing physical plant was very neglected and needed investments were not undertaken. The unsolicited project proposal offered an innovative approach to dealing with an increasingly urgent sewerage problem. IWK's proposal was processed and approved very rapidly by the government, and the award in 1994 yielded a dramatic improvement in the level of investment and in the quality of service.

However, IWK quickly began to encounter problems that became more serious over time and threatened the financial viability of the concession. Consumers protested against the rates charged soon after the concession was awarded, well before the economic crisis. As a result, IWK's contractually agreed to tariff structure was disallowed without clear compensatory arrangements and was not reestablished until 1997 at much lower levels. Indeed, it appears that several important details relating to the tariff and compensation structure, interim performance targets, and contract management were not addressed with sufficient detail in the concession agreement, perhaps in part because of the speed with which it was processed.

Notwithstanding the tariff structure change, poor collection rates are a critical ongoing problem, complicated by the economic slowdown and the lack of an effective enforcement mechanism. The economic crisis also prompted a 30 percent reduction in charges to commercial sector customers in July 1998. Compounding the revenue woes, the full magnitude of the physical rehabilitation needed was not anticipated, and IWK's management was further disrupted by three ownership changes during its first four years. As a consequence, the government has had to make more than MYR450 million in long-term soft loans to IWK, in addition to other support.

Though many of IWK's difficulties are not uncommon, the approach taken has aggravated them. At least in four respects, the Malaysian approach runs counter to international trends:

- By eschewing a competitive bidding process in favor of a speedier negotiated transaction, the government compromised the legitimacy of the prices charged. Consumers are more likely to agree to pay for services where the prices charged are perceived as fair.

• By awarding a nationwide contract, the government further limited its capacity to regulate the private supplier. In the United Kingdom and in some developing country cities such as Manila and Mexico City, benchmarked competition has been employed. By splitting the concession area into distinct jurisdictions, the regulatory authority is able to compare and assess the performances of the different operators, even though the operators do not directly compete with each other.

• By guaranteeing a minimum rate of return, the government went against the trend of using "incentive" regulation. As is well known, under a guaranteed return the operator has no incentive to control costs. In contrast, under incentive regulation such as a price cap, there is a stronger incentive to limit costs.

• A final unusual feature of the contract was the separation of sewerage from water. In major concession contracts (such as those in Buenos Aires and Manila), water and sewerage have been jointly awarded to the private concessionaire. This allows charging for sewerage services as an add-on to the water service. In Malaysia, water services are under the provincial authorities and sewerage is under the national authority. The inability to reconcile these two authorities led to the separate award of sewerage services to private operators. This represents a missed opportunity from a financial standpoint, insofar as water utilities generally have much better success collecting revenues, thereby possibly resolving a very serious problem for IWK.

From the Crisis to the Long View

The financial crisis in East Asia presents governments with a challenge—and an opportunity—to rethink their strategies in key infrastructure sectors. It is possible, as in Malaysia, to view the postcrisis problems as temporary and seek financial engineering solutions to tide over. This approach requires the assumption that the projects and the sector structures are basically sound and that with the recovery of growth the projects will be financially viable. Under this interpretation, a thorough overhaul of sector strategies is not required as a response to the crisis; a more modest effort will provide short-term relief. Alternatively, the governments could undertake a more fundamental review of project and sector economics to create a sounder basis for future operation and investment decisions. Even after recovering from the crisis, East Asian growth rates are unlikely to achieve the high levels they reached just before the crisis. As such, the policy emphasis needs to shift from the creation of new assets to the more efficient use of current assets. As Argentina demonstrated in the early 1990s, a crisis allows a fundamental questioning of old infrastructure strategies and presents an opportunity to mobilize the political will to take difficult decisions.

A longer view also is desirable from a risk management perspective. Risk management entails three complementary tasks: mitigating the risk at source, transferring the risk to parties better able to bear the risk, and monitoring and managing any residual risk that cannot be mitigated or transferred.

Ultimately, risk mitigation is the most desirable long-run strategy, because it reduces the vulnerability of the economy to shocks and thus reduces the government's direct and indirect contingent liabilities. Mitigation is also beneficial because it can be typically associated with strategies that enhance efficiency of resource use, thereby enabling faster growth and lower risk. For example, a power sector that is organized to permit competitive generation and distribution will foster efficient use of resources while lowering the risks arising from excessive installation of capacity. Risk also would be more effectively transferred to private providers than under the current system.

Here a comparison of sector strategies in Malaysia and Chile might be useful. Malaysia is unusual in targeting its privatization initiatives to the "hard" sectors: transportation and water/sanitation. Although the shares of privatized infrastructure investment in Malaysia and Chile are at comparable levels, significant sectoral differences exist between the two countries (Figure 17.2). In interpreting Figure 17.2, however, note that the true extent of private participation in Malaysia is exaggerated, because the figure more closely reflects the share of project value under private operation than the financial risk borne by private operators (see Box 17.4).

Malaysia and Chile differ in their philosophical motivations for privatization. Whereas Chilean privatization is integrally linked to a competition policy, competition within the infrastructure sector is virtually absent in Malaysia. Instead, privatization in Malaysia has been, and continues to be, driven by the aim to fill a perceived financing gap, although other considerations including socioeconomic factors are at play as well. In Chile, the power sector is almost entirely private but transportation and water/sanitation investments continue to be largely in public hands; by contrast, Malaysia has pursued nearly the opposite strategy. Chilean privatization of transport and water has been limited, because competition in these sectors is difficult to achieve. Also contrast the differences in the privatization approaches of the electric power sector. In Chile, power generators compete to supply to power grid. In Malaysia, the five private power producers have long-term take-or-pay contracts with Tenaga, giving them a virtually assured market for the power they produce irrespective of efficiency. So while Chilean authorities have been concerned with maintaining adequate separation between the generation, transmission, and distribution of electricity, until recently unbundling power sector services has not been a high priority policy matter in Malaysia.

Figure 17.2. Public and Private Investment in Infrastructure Across the World, 1995

(percent of total investment)

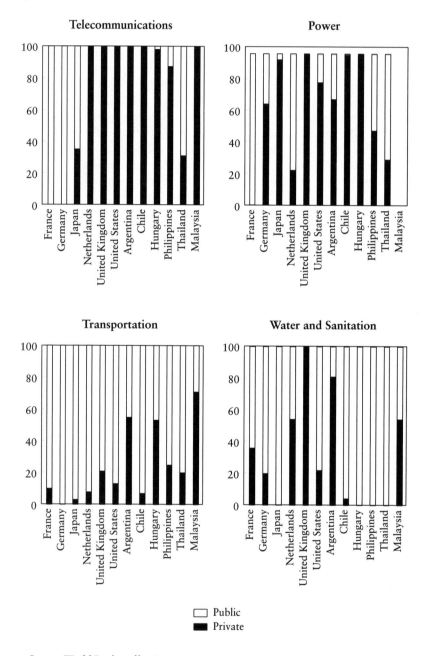

Source: World Bank staff estimates.

Box 17.4 How Much Risk do Malaysian Project
Sponsors Really Take?

As in many countries, the true extent of private participation in Malaysia is less than the value of the "private" projects. The private capital at risk is substantially lower than the project cost, because the government has provided support through several mechanisms: "soft" loans, equity investments, directed lending through banks and provident funds, and various explicit and implicit guarantees.

  • *Government soft loans* carry low interest rates (between 0 and 8 percent a year, long grace periods of 10–15 years, and maturities as long as 25 years). These loans often finance the acquisition of land and are justified on the grounds that the projects would not otherwise be economically viable and, by contract, are transferred to the government at the end of the concession period.
  • *Equity participation* is carried out through government-owned holding companies and corporations, such as Khazanah, Employees Provident Fund (EPF), Petronas, and Tenaga.
  • *Government guarantees* take different forms. In some transportation projects, the minimum revenue or traffic volume is guaranteed, while minimum revenue levels are assured to IPP project sponsors in the take-or-pay capacity payment arrangements. The government also stands ready to compensate lenders and project equity providers in the event of project termination. In the Indah Water Konsortium (IWK) concession, the government's guarantee is technically broader and assures a minimum rate of return to the equity holders.
  • *Lending* by domestic financial institutions (including EPF and other government-directed entities) has been a strength of Malaysian infrastructure development, because it has reduced reliance on foreign currency borrowings, a significant source of financial dislocation in other developing Asian nations. However, although such borrowing was intended to take place on "commercial terms," lending institutions lacked incentives and, in some cases, perhaps the sophistication to exert extensive due diligence given the government's support and sponsorship of projects.

Conclusion

Much of the discussion of guarantees for infrastructure in East Asia was initially conducted in terms of "optimizing" the guarantees (Johnston, Mody, and Shanks 1996). The assumption was that guarantees, in one form or another, were likely to be a permanent (or, at least, a long-term) element of infrastructure financing. As such, the focus was on paring down the guarantees from the relatively extensive obligations taken on by governments in the early stages to more limited obligations that constituted a "core" minimum. The core obligations, in turn, were defined as those that reinforced government regulatory commitments for rights of operation and pricing formulas. Financial guarantees were a device to hold governments to their word. Proposals in vogue included one that recommended a timetable for reducing the lists of risks for which governments provided guarantees and also the benchmarks (such as credit rating upgrades) that would trigger the reductions.

The East Asian financial crisis can be treated as an unusually extreme event unlikely to repeat itself and thus having no bearing on the basic approach to infrastructure privatization and so no additional bearing on the forms of government commitment. However, in this chapter I argue that that would be a mistake. It is likely that the contingent liabilities that governments will eventually have to pay for will be less than thought at the height of the crisis. But that should not lull governments into assuming that the infrastructure strategy being pursued is without significant risks. Throughout the region, as in other parts of the developing world, projects based on government contingent support (either implicit or explicit) have encountered problems even outside of crisis conditions, with significant fiscal costs to governments. Long-term sustainability, for both risk management and efficiency reasons, requires a shift to a new model rather than tinkering with the old one.

Notes

1. This chapter builds on inputs provided to World Bank (1999) and World Bank (2000). For comments and suggestions, I am grateful to Hana Polackova Brixi, Sudarshan Gooptu, and Mona Haddad. The chapter also reflects ideas developed in long-running collaboration with Christopher Lewis and Robert Shanks.

2. Other Asian countries that adopted similar strategies include China, India, and Thailand. Thai contingent liabilities are discussed in Arthur Andersen (1999). In contrast, Korea undertook limited infrastructure privatization. In Latin America, Colombia adopted the "Asian" strategy with several stand-alone public-private infrastructure projects (Lewis and Mody 1997), as did Mexico for a major toll road program and a more modest independent power program.

3. For an earlier application of a similar Monte Carlo simulation to estimate contingent liabilities in Colombia, see Lewis and Mody (1997).

4. To the extent that this is already part of the overall bad debt portfolio of the troubled banks in Indonesia, it is not an *additional* liability for the government.

5. Electricity is supplied in Malaysia by three entities, each operating in its own area. In Peninsular Malaysia, the partially privatized Tenaga Nasional Berhad (TNB), formerly the National Electricity Board, is responsible. The Sabah Electricity Sdn. Bhd, under the majority ownership of TNB with the state government retaining a minority share, supplies power in Sabah. Finally, the Sarawak Electricity Supply Company, wholly owned by the state government, supplies power to Sarawak.

References

Arthur Andersen. 1999. *The Fiscal Costs of State Enterprises and Private Participation in Infrastructure.* Draft Report. Bangkok.

California Public Utilities Commission. 1996. "Executive Summary and Introduction" *<www.cpuc.ca.gov/restur.dec/chap1.html>*.

Duff and Phelps Credit Rating Co. 1998. *Latin Power.* New York.

Estache, Antonio, and Martin Rodriguez-Pardina. 1998. "Light and Lightning at the End of the Public Tunnel: Reform of the Electricity Sector in the Southern Cone." EDI Regulatory Reform Discussion Paper. World Bank, Washington, D.C. *<www.worldbank.org/wbi/reform/ref_pdfs/light.pdf>*.

Gomez-Ibanez, José A., and John R. Meyer. 1992. "Toll Roads and Private Concessions in France and Spain." John F. Kennedy School of Government, Harvard University, Cambridge, Mass.

Haarmeyer, David, and Ashoka Mody. 1998. "Tapping the Private Sector: Approaches to Managing Risks in Water and Sanitation." *Journal of Project Finance* 4 (2): 1–28.

Johnston, Felton Mac, Ashoka Mody, and Robert Shanks. 1996. "A House of Cards: Government Guarantees." *Project and Trade Finance* 154 (February).

Lewis, Christopher, and Ashoka Mody. 1997. "The Management of Contingent Liabilities: A Risk Management Framework for National Governments." In Timothy Irwin, Michael Klein, Guillermo Perry, and Mateen Thobani, eds., *Dealing with Public Risk in Private Infrastructure.* World Bank Latin American and Caribbean Studies. Washington, D.C.: World Bank.

Reside, Renato E., Jr. 2000. "Estimating the Philippine Government's Exposure to and Risk from Contingent Liabilities in Infrastructure Projects." School of Economics, University of the Philippines, Manila.

World Bank. 1994. *World Development Report: Infrastructure for Development.* Washington, D.C.

———. 1999. *Malaysia: Public Expenditure Review.* Washington, D.C.

———. 2000. *Indonesia: Public Spending in a Time of Change.* Washington, D.C.

CHAPTER 18

Monitoring Fiscal Risks of Subnational Governments: Selected Country Experiences

Jun Ma*

Deutsche Bank in Hong Kong

IN MANY COUNTRIES, SUBNATIONAL (hereafter local) governments are charged with responsibility for delivering most public services.[1] The fiscal health of local governments is thus essential to the stability and efficiency of the country's entire public finance system. The central governments, however, often have limited information on local public finance for the purpose of assessing local fiscal risks and planning for fiscal emergencies. In a typical developing country, the ministry of finance receives monthly reports on budgetary revenues and expenditures from local governments on a cash basis, but does not have sufficient information on many extrabudgetary activities, especially local government guarantees, extrabudgetary and off-budget capital expenditures and associated borrowings, operations of local financial institutions, pension funds, unemployment insurance funds, and other transactions that could generate government liabilities.

Some countries have recognized the need to establish a monitoring system to record and assess local government obligations (both direct and contingent liabilities) and local fiscal risks in general. This system can potentially be used to generate a ranking of local governments by fiscal health and serve as a basis for central government intervention and emergency financial assistance. Over the longer term, this monitoring system—the database and analytical indicators—can provide

*The author was with the World Bank when he wrote this article; he is currently with the Deutsche Bank in Hong Kong.

a useful information base for a local government credit rating system, a prerequisite for opening up subnational borrowing and developing a municipal bond market.

This chapter provides some relevant international experiences and suggests an illustrative set of risk indicators for a hypothetical developing country. It also includes a brief discussion of what is needed institutionally for a system of monitoring local fiscal risk to work effectively. Specifically, it points out the need to widen the coverage of fiscal reporting, strengthen auditing, and, over the medium term, establish a legal framework for dealing with fiscal emergencies and a clearer division of expenditure responsibilities between levels of government.

Rationales for Monitoring Local Fiscal Risks

Unlike private companies, subnational governments provide basic public services—such as education, health, police, infrastructure—that are essential to the general welfare of the population in their jurisdictions and to the functioning of the regional economy. In most cases of local government default or bankruptcy, the resolution is not to cease the operation of the government and sell its assets, but to restructure its debt and other obligations. In many unitary states, if private creditors are not willing to restructure or reschedule subnational debt, the central government is pressured to provide a financial rescue package. In some countries, local governments are not permitted to borrow from banks or issue debt, but when local financial institutions fail, local governments and major local government corporations default on guarantees as well as on wage, pension, and unemployment benefit payments, or local governments become unable to provide basic services at minimum standards, the resulting social pressures may force the central government to step in. *This mechanism serves as an implicit guarantee by the central government for local government liabilities.* This type of guarantee leads to a serious moral hazard problem—that is, local governments (or corporations owned by local governments) have strong incentives to borrow, issue guarantees, and even incur arrears, because the costs may be borne by the central government. The central government therefore needs to be aware of the size of the subnational obligations, its capacity to meet payments obligations, and its future expenditure profile in order to prevent local government defaults and protect its own fiscal position. Otherwise, the central government's own fiscal stability could be jeopardized.

In many developing countries where the municipal bond market and private credit rating systems are not developed, local governments are not subject to market discipline. In addition, the lack of transparency of local fiscal operations in many countries exacerbates the tendency for local governments to engage in imprudent fiscal activities.

These problems further strengthen the need for the central government to monitor and exert control over local liabilities.

Local fiscal emergencies do not arise without causes. Therefore, it is possible to design an early warning system that monitors the fiscal health of local governments and predicts potential fiscal crises. Through experience, many countries' central or provincial governments recognize that local fiscal crises are often caused by, among other things, a rapid increase in expenditure relative to revenue, persistent deficits, high government debt, and liquidity problems (short-term liabilities exceed liquid assets). By closely watching indicators of this sort, the higher-level government may detect which local government is on the brink of financial trouble and take measures (such as providing financial planning advice, tightening expenditure control, improving revenue collection, and limiting future borrowing) to prevent it from slipping deeper into fiscal trouble.

Local Fiscal Monitoring Programs: The United States, Brazil, and Colombia

This section briefly describes the local fiscal monitoring systems in the United States, Brazil, and Colombia. Among these, the U.S. model (more specifically, the Ohio model) appears to be the most sophisticated one; it was explicitly designed to provide an early warning system. The Brazilian and Colombian systems aim to provide a basis for central government control over local indebtedness. Similar systems exist in many other countries where subnational borrowing is permitted up to certain limits and requires central government approval (see Table 18.1).

These monitoring systems do have important limitations, however. The risk indicators used in the fiscal monitoring systems described in this section are basically static and backward looking. They do not reflect the dynamics of government revenue, expenditure, and debt and, as a result, do not provide a direct assessment of fiscal sustainability. These problems can be addressed by requiring local governments to produce medium-term fiscal projections. A more fundamental flaw of this type of monitoring system is that most indicators are based on traditional fiscal accounting—government cash flows and direct debt obligations. They do not, or only to a very limited extent, reflect government contingent liabilities. In this chapter, the examples of New Zealand and Australia (and the example of the Czech Republic discussed in Chapter 9 by Brixi, Schick, and Zlaoui in this volume) illustrate how fiscal analysis can incorporate contingent liabilities.

The United States: Ohio's Fiscal Watch Program and Fiscal Emergency Law

The United States experienced some significant local government defaults in the 1970s and 1980s, including the 1975 New York City note

Table 18.1 Limits on Local Borrowing, Selected Countries

Country	Debt service ratio	Debt-to-"revenue" ratio	Some kinds of restrictions
Japan	Three-year average ≤ 20 percent of general revenue; more restrictions if exceeding 20 percent	None	Mainly for local infrastructure projects; no foreign borrowing
India[a]	None	None	No foreign borrowing; long-term credits for investment only; case-by-case approval by state government
Italy	≤ 25 percent of own revenue net of certain earmarked funds		Only for capital expenditure; no foreign borrowing
Russia	≤ 15 percent of general revenue	≤ 30 percent for provinces ≤ 15 percent for municipalities	
Lithuania (proposed)	≤ 15 percent of general revenue	≤ 30 percent of total revenue	No state guarantee; ministry of finance able to approve lower ceiling for municipalities; long-term credits for investment only
Spain	≤ 25 percent of total revenue		Long-term credit for investment only; approval required for foreign borrowing

a. There is a proposal to impose quantitative limits on subnational borrowing.
Sources: Council of Europe (1993); Ma (1994); Peterson (1997); Ter-Minassian (1997); Budget Code of the Russian Federation, Federal Law No. 145-FZ, July 31, 1998.

default, the 1978 Cleveland default, and the Washington power supply system default in 1983. As a response, the U.S. Advisory Commission on Intergovernmental Relations (ACIR) conducted a series of studies on local fiscal emergencies and recommended to the states that they improve the monitoring of local government fiscal health and prevent or correct local fiscal emergencies (see ACIR 1985 and Box 18.1). Ohio is one of the states that has adopted much of the commission's advice and developed a local government monitoring system, the Fiscal Watch Program. Ohio's Code on Local Fiscal Emergencies, originally passed in 1979 and amended in 1985, stipulated the

---

Box 18.1 ACIR Indicators of Local Fiscal Health

Between 1945 and 1969, 431 state and local debt defaults occurred in the United States. In the early 1970s, the financial stability of America's cities became a matter of public concern. In response, in 1973 the U.S. Advisory Commission on Intergovernmental Relations (ACIR) conducted a study of city financial emergencies and proposed some measures as warning signals. These measures were modified and applied in its 1985 follow-up report "Bankruptcies, Defaults, and Other Local Government Financial Emergencies"(ACIR 1985). The eight measures developed in the 1985 report are:

- *deficits:* general fund expenditures exceeded revenues by more than 5 percent;
- *persistence of deficits:* general fund expenditures exceeded revenues for two consecutive years with the second year larger;
- *trend of deficit growth:* expenditure growth rates exceed revenue growth rates;
- *balance sheet gap:* general fund-accumulated deficits (net liabilities) as a percentage of general fund revenues;
- *liquidity:* net liquid assets (cash and liquid assets minus short-term debt outstanding) as a percentage of general fund expenditures;
- *debt maturity:* existence of short-term debt as of the end of the fiscal year;
- *tax compliance:* property tax collection rate; and
- *unfunded pension liabilities:* (a) net amount of payments for benefits and withdrawals, shown as a percentage of receipts; (b) benefit and withdrawal payments from the local fund as a percentage of the total assets of the fund.

---

procedure for implementing this monitoring system.[2] Similar to a "Watch" issued by the National Weather Service, the Ohio Fiscal Watch Program acts as an early warning system to prevent local governments—including counties, municipalities, school districts, state universities and colleges—from slipping further into fiscal distress.

The Fiscal Watch Program, implemented by the Office of Auditor of State, conducts fiscal watch reviews to determine whether a local government is approaching a state of fiscal emergency. Any of the following conditions constitutes grounds for a fiscal watch:

- The existence of either of the following situations: (a) all accounts that were due and payable from the general fund and had been due and payable for at least 30 days at the end of the fiscal year, less that year-end balance in the general fund, exceeded one-twelfth of the general fund budget for that year; (b) all accounts that were due and payable for at least 30 days from the general and special accounts at the end of the fiscal year, less that year-end balance in the general fund and the respective special funds, exceeded one-twelfth of the available revenues—excluding nonrecurring receipts—during the preceding fiscal year.

• The aggregate of deficit amounts of all deficit funds at the end of the preceding fiscal year, less the total of any year-end balance in the general fund and in any special fund that may be transferred to meet such a deficit, exceeded one-twelfth of the total of the general fund budget for that year and the receipts to those deficit funds during that year other than from transfers from the general fund.

• At the end of the preceding fiscal year, moneys and marketable investments in or held for the unsegregated Treasury of the local government, minus outstanding checks and warrants, were less in amount than the aggregate of the positive balances of the general fund and those special funds, and such deficiency exceeded one-twelfth of the total amount received into the unsegregated Treasury during the preceding fiscal year.

Upon determining that one or more of the conditions just described are present, the auditor of state issues a written declaration of the existence of a fiscal watch to the local government. The fiscal watch remains in effect until the auditor determines that the conditions are no longer present and cancels the watch, or until the auditor determines that a state of fiscal emergency exists.

This Fiscal Watch Program—as an early warning system—provides a major impetus for local governments to improve their fiscal management. It also triggers the state government's advisory service. In many cases, after receiving a warning signal, local authorities and institutions immediately began to increase their cash reserves instead of spending down their funds at the fiscal year-end. At the same time, the Office of Auditor of State provides immediate advisory help at no cost to local governments under watch. For example, in 1997 it provided guidance on improving the city of Silverton's accounting system, and within three months the office issued a performance audit with several options for budget reduction and operational improvement. These advisory services were greatly welcomed by local governments in fiscal distress, because they could not afford to obtain consulting and other support services from the private sector (Petro 1997).

The Ohio Code on Local Fiscal Emergencies sets out in detail the conditions constituting a fiscal emergency. Some of these conditions were tailored to fit the unique budgeting and accounting characteristics of Ohio local governments. They can be summarized as follows:

• *test 1 (default on debt)*: the existence of a default on a debt obligation for more than 30 days;

• *test 2 (wage arrears)*: failure to pay employees within 30 days of when such payment is due unless two-thirds of the employees have agreed to a delay of up to 90 days;

• *test 3 (request for transfers)*: the need to reallocate tax levies, within the constitutional tax limitation, from other local governments to the municipality;

• *test 4 (payments arrears to vendors)*: accounts payable that are delinquent by more than 30 days in either the general fund or all funds that, after deducting cash available to pay them, exceed one-sixth of the prior year's general fund or all funds revenues;

• *test 5 (deficits)*: total deficit for a combination of funds, less balances in any other funds that can be transferred to reduce such deficits, exceeds one-sixth of the prior year's revenues of those funds that are in deficit; and

• *test 6 (cash shortage)*: uncommitted cash and investments in the general cash accounts of the government are less than the book balances of the funds by an amount greater than one-sixth of the total cash received in those funds in the prior year.

The results of applying the fiscal emergency tests to the ten local governments declared to have financial emergencies during 1979–85 (Table 18.2) reveal that test 5, the measure of fund deficits relative to receipts, was failed by eight of the ten governments. By contrast, no

Table 18.2 Local Fiscal Emergency Tests Failed, Ohio, 1979–85

Local government	Test 1	Test 2	Test 3	Test 4	Test 5	Test 6
Niles				X	X	X
Cleveland	X			X	X	X
Norwood					X	X
Plymouth	X				X	X
Ashtabula					X	
Freeport				X		
Ironton	X	X			X	X
Lincoln Heights				X	X	
East Liverpool				X		X
Manchester				X	X	
Total number of failed tests	3	1	0	6	8	6

Source: ACIR (1985).

governments failed test 3. Only one government failed to meet its pay-roll for 30 days (test 2) and that failure occurred after the government had already been declared to be in a state of fiscal emergency.

According to the Fiscal Emergency Law, as soon as a local government is declared to be in a state of emergency, the state of Ohio shall establish a "financial planning and supervisory commission" to assume the supervisory power of the locality's fiscal management. Within 120 days of the commission's first meeting, the chief executive of the local government (also a member of the commission) shall submit a financial plan that contains actions to:

- eliminate all fiscal emergency conditions;
- eliminate the deficits in all deficit funds;
- restore to construction funds and other special funds moneys that were used for purposes not within the purposes of such funds;
- balance the budgets;
- avoid any fiscal emergencies in the future; and
- restore the ability of the local government to market long-term general obligation bonds.

The main powers and functions of the commission include:

- reviewing all tax, expenditure, and borrowing policies to require that they are consistent with the financial plan;
- bringing civil actions to enforce the fiscal emergency law;
- ensuring that books of account, accounting systems, and financial procedures and reports are in compliance with the auditor of state; and
- assisting the municipal executives in the structuring of the terms of, and the placement or sale of, debt obligations.

Brazil: Limits on Subnational Borrowing

Over the past decades, Brazil has experienced three subnational debt crises, resulting in considerable cost to the national government (this section is based on Dillinger 1999). In most of these cases, the national government had to take over a large portion of subnational debt. In a response to the most recent debt crisis, in 1998 the Senate issued Resolution 78, which significantly tightened the central government's monitoring and control over subnational borrowing. This resolution consists of a set of extremely restrictive controls on both the demand for and supply of subnational debt. The main provisions of this resolution include the following:

- Subnational governments are not permitted to borrow from their own enterprises or suppliers.
- Borrowing must be equal to or less than the capital budget.

- New borrowing cannot exceed 18 percent of net current revenue; debt service cannot exceed 13 percent of net current revenue; and the debt stock must be less than 200 percent of net current revenue.
- Any borrowing government must have a primary surplus; defaulters are not permitted to borrow.
- The total outstanding guarantees issued by the government must be less than 25 percent of net current revenue.
- Short-term revenue anticipation borrowing may not exceed 8 percent of net current revenue.
- New bond issues other than rollover are prohibited.
- At least 5 percent of any bond issue must be retired at maturity, and any borrowing government whose debt service obligations are less than 13 percent of net current revenue must retire up to 10 percent of bonds at maturity or spend 13 percent of net current revenue, whichever is less.

Passage of Resolution 78 was followed in September 1999 by Resolution 2653 of the national monetary council, which imposed a complementary set of restrictions on the supply of credit to subnational governments. This resolution has two major components. First, it authorizes the central bank, in its capacity as supervisor of the domestic banking system, to control the supply of credit to subnational governments by the domestic banks.[3] Second, it authorizes the central bank to enforce Senate Resolution 78's controls on subnational borrowing. Specifically, all borrowing petitions for Senate approval must be submitted first to the central bank, which has 30 days to analyze the petitions and forward its recommendations to the Senate. If the central bank's analysis shows that the borrowing government is violating the criteria listed in Resolution 78, it has the right to refuse to forward its loan request to the Senate.

The new system appears to have significantly reduced new borrowing, because only subnational governments that have little existing debt and little capital investment are qualified to borrow. There are, however, two concerns. First, the current system relies heavily on restrictive government regulations rather than on market dicipline. This may reinforce the perception that the federal government stands behind all subnational credit operations. Second, even under the new system, the Senate is still free to ignore its own resolutions, making the control mechanism highly vulnerable to political pressures from the states.

Colombia: The "Traffic Light System"

The government of Colombia is divided into 32 provinces (departments) and 1,064 municipalities. It is one of the most decentralized governments in Latin America, with about 40 percent of total government spending at the subnational level (this section is based on Rentaria, Steiner, and Echavarria 1999).

Until 1993 Colombia's subnational government borrowing was under no control by the Ministry of Finance, other than a registration requirement. In 1993 Law 80 forced financial intermediaries to monitor the destination of loans and the indebtedness capacity of subnational governments. Banks became responsible for grading loans to government and for monitoring the nature and quantity of acceptable guarantees. In 1997 Law 358 limited subnational debt to payment capacity, by means of associating payment capacity with the generation of operational savings. One ratio (interest payment/operational savings) proxies the liquidity of the subnational government. The other ratio (debt/current revenue) evaluates debt sustainability in the medium and long run. For each new loan, the above indicators act as traffic lights and must be calculated (Table 18.3).[4] When the test result is yellow or red, the loan requires permission from the Ministry of Finance, and the borrowing government must sign a performance agreement with the financial institutions (lenders).

Table 18.4 presents an estimation of the legal capacity of indebtedness of the provinces and municipalities of Colombia for 1998. Of the 27 provinces for which there are estimates, 17 are in red, 1 in yellow, and 9 in green. Most of the liquidity problems can be tracked down to negative savings. Of 26 provincial capitals, 13 have a red light, 4 have yellow, and 9 have green.

A typical performance agreement consists of a series of targets with which the local government must comply, within a predetermined time frame. These include increases in own resources, expenditure cuts, generation of current surpluses, and an improved debt profile. When the local government does not comply, its access to future credit will be limited. For example, the performance agreement signed by Valle, the most indebted province, with 23 financial institutions includes the following conditions:

- The province must contract an irrevocable trust deposit with a fiduciary society, which will administer all the provincial government's funds.
- The province must contract an irrevocable trust deposit with a fiduciary society, which will administer and sell shares of the two main corporations owned by the provincial government.
- The province must have authorization from the central government to roll over or refinance its short-term loans, to increase its level of indebtedness.
- The province must, in 1999 and 2000, reduce personnel and other current expenditures by at least 5 percent a year. Any increase in current revenue must first be used to service debt. Only if the current revenue increase in real terms exceeds 2.5 percent a year can the province allocate 50 percent of the additional revenue.

Table 18.3 Indebtedness Alert Signals (Traffic Light System), Colombia

Indicator	Autonomous indebtedness (green light)	Intermediate indebtedness (yellow light)	Critical indebtedness (red light)
Debt interest/ operational savings (liquidity indicator)[a]	< 40 percent	Between 40 percent and 60 percent	> 60 percent
Debt stock/ current revenue (solvency indicator)	< 80 percent	< 80 percent	> 80 percent
Effect	Local government is allowed to contract new credit autonomously.	(a) If the new loan does not increase debt stock by more than the inflation target set by the central bank, local government can contract new credit autonomously. (b) Otherwise, the indebtedness authorization of the Ministry of Finance is required, with the following condition: the signing of a performance plan with the lending financial institutions.	Authorization is required to start credit operations, and a performance agreement with the lending financial institutions must be signed.

a. Operational savings is defined as current income minus operational expenses and transfers paid by the local government. Current income mainly includes tax revenues, nontax revenues, royalties and fees, transfers from the central government, national revenue sharing, and interest income. Operational expenses include wages and salaries, honoraria, social welfare benefits, and social security expenditures.

Source: Law 359, 1997.

Accounting for Government Contingent Liabilities: Australia and New Zealand

In the cases just discussed, governments build their local monitoring systems only on information about government cash flows (such as revenues and expenditures) and explicit and direct liabilities.[5] Contingent

Table 18.4 Legal Capacity of Indebtedness of Subnational
Governments, Colombia, 1998
(millions of Brazilian reals)

Province	Liquidity	Solvency	Liquidity	Solvency	Situation
Valle	−23.7	22.3	Red	Red	Red
Antioquia	−163.4	46.9	Red	Green	Red
Atlántico	339.0	65.2	Red	Green	Red
Tolima	−13.1	86.6	Red	Red	Red
Nariño	−64.7	186.5	Red	Red	Red
Magdalena	−18.2	57.0	Red	Green	Red
Huila	−30.5	11.5	Red	Green	Red
Cesar	70.6	38.0	Red	Green	Red
Santander	106.9	11.1	Red	Green	Red
Caldas	−7.6	16.0	Red	Green	Red
Bolívar	273.5	5.2	Red	Green	Red
Sucre	233.8	22.7	Red	Green	Red
Quindío	−4.8	12.2	Red	Green	Red
Amazonas	−1.2	101.3	Red	Red	Red
Vaupés	−0.5	81.2	Red	Red	Red
Vichada	−4.2	28.0	Red	Green	Red
Córdoba	−326.3	—	Red	Green	Red
N. de Santander	47.4	10.9	Yellow	Green	Yellow
Cundinamarca	9.6	30.8	Green	Green	Green
Risaralda	19.8	39.6	Green	Green	Green
Guajira	12.7	76.9	Green	Green	Green
Arauca	16.8	14.8	Green	Green	Green
Cauca	30.1	18.3	Green	Green	Green
Boyacá	17.4	11.6	Green	Green	Green
Caquetá	7.2	9.2	Green	Green	Green
Putumayo	27.5	13.6	Green	Green	Green
Meta	30.7	—	Green	Green	Green
Municipality					
Medellín	−87.5	26.4	Red	Green	Red
Barranquilla	94.2	29.2	Red	Green	Red
Santafe De					
Bogota DC	105.9	7.0	Red	Green	Red
Cartagena	−72.6	44.7	Red	Green	Red
Tunja	78.3	27.5	Red	Green	Red
Florencia	209.5	36.5	Red	Green	Red
Popayán	67.4	42.7	Red	Green	Red
Montería	103.9	333.9	Red	Red	Red
Neiva	−12.3	32.6	Red	Green	Red
Santa Marta	102.5	44.6	Red	Green	Red
Bucaramanga	128.7	94.3	Red	Red	Red
Pasto	−18.5	48.5	Red	Green	Red
Inirida	−7.3	99.5	Red	Red	Red

Province	Liquidity	Solvency	Liquidity	Solvency	Situation
Pereira	52.9	26.1	Yellow	Green	Green
Manizales	45.9	74.0	Yellow	Green	Yellow
Sincelejo	44.0	35.6	Yellow	Green	Yellow
Ibagué	43.1	5.1	Yellow	Green	Yellow
Cali	49.7	53.6	Yellow	Green	Yellow
Villavicencio	22.7	19.5	Green	Green	Green
Armenia	16.8	19.2	Green	Green	Green
Arauca	27.1	63.7	Green	Green	Green
Yopal	30.0	67.2	Green	Green	Green
Mocoa	16.4	31.6	Green	Green	Green
Leticia	21.4	15.6	Green	Green	Green
Mitú	—	26.8	Green	Green	Green
Puerto Carreño	5.2	6.4	Green	Green	Green

— Not available.
Source: Renteria, Steiner, and Echnavarria (1999).

liabilities are not taken into account in assessing local fiscal risks because, in most cases, data are difficult to collect or even do not exist. Australia and New Zealand are two of the very few countries that have developed a system for accounting and reporting government contingent liabilities. This section briefly describes the systems used in the state of Victoria in Australia and by the New Zealand central government. I have not found good cases in developing and transition countries, but a series of recent World Bank studies on Eastern European countries provides some relevant experience for other transition countries about the types of government actions that have led to contingent liabilities. The Czech Republic case presented in Chapter 9 in this volume is a good example. Although the New Zealand and Czech cases are at the central government level, the concept and methodology of these exercises also could provide useful references for local governments.

Victoria, Australia: A Statement of Fiscal Risks

The state of Victoria requires that the state treasurer include a statement of risks in his or her annual and semiannual budget reviews presented to Parliament and the public. This statement describes the factors that could have a significant effect on the fiscal outcome of the state, including:

• changes in economic parameters such as the generalized system of preferences (GSP), employment, wages, prices, and interest rates;

• fiscal risks associated with the occurrence of identifiable events that affect specific revenues or expenditures but that are of uncertain likelihood or timing; and

• the realization of contingent liabilities arising from nonquantifiable commitments made by the government.

The risk statement of the 1999–2000 midyear budget review discusses some quantifiable and nonquantifiable events that form contingent liabilities of the government. These events involve, among others, lawsuits against the government, government guarantees, environmental damage, and possible changes in demand for public services. What follows are a few examples:

• The State Revenue Office has a contingent liability of about AUD93 million related to the possible outcome of the appeal against the Supreme Court's decision of 1998 in the case of *Drake Personnel v. Commissioner of State Revenue* (subject: payroll tax).

• In May 1994 the Public Transport Corporation (PTC) entered into contracts with the OneLink Consortium, which will provide automated ticketing and fare collection services to the PTC over a period of 10 years. The treasurer has guaranteed the payment obligations of the PTC under the service contract. The service provider has a contractual right to claim compensation for any losses stemming from public transport reform and privatization of the PTC.

• Some properties have been identified as potentially contaminated sites. Although the state does not formally admit any liability with respect to these sites, remedial expenditures may be incurred to restore the sites to an acceptable environmental standard if they are developed in the future.

• Key services provided by the Department of Human Services such as acute care in public hospitals are experiencing strong demand growth. There is a risk that this growth will require unplanned additional funding of these services by the department.

New Zealand: A Statement of Contingent Liabilities

New Zealand's Fiscal Responsibility Act of 1994 requires the central government to include, on an annual and semiannual basis, a statement of contingent liabilities in its financial statements. Reporting government contingent liabilities is thought to be essential to ensuring the robustness of the reported fiscal position and outlook. All financial statements, including those on contingent liabilities, are submitted to Parliament and also published on the government's website.

A summary form of New Zealand's contingent liability table is presented in Table 18.5. The coverage of the contingent liabilities includes those of the Reserve Bank of New Zealand (the central bank), state-owned enterprises, and Crown entities (central government budgetary institutions). The important examples of contingent liabilities included in these statements are as follows:

- *Guarantees and indemnities:* government guarantees for local government or enterprise borrowing from foreign or domestic sources; claims for indemnification from private corporations/individuals for property damage or loss of value; and a government guarantee for deposits.
- *Uncalled capital:* the government's uncalled capital subscriptions to international financial institutions such as the Asian Development Bank (ADB), European Bank for Reconstruction and Development (EBRD), and International Bank for Reconstruction and Development (IBRD).
- *Legal proceedings and disputes:* interest and principal costs that may be claimed if legal cases were decided against government agencies (for example, ministries, police, defense force, tax authorities, social welfare agency) and state-owned enterprises.
- *Other quantifiable contingent liabilities:* contingent liabilities relating to fulfillment of conditions for payment by government agencies of grants and compensation; claims against the government for people's personal injuries; promissory notes issued by the government to international financial institutions; other claims against state-owned enterprises.

In addition to the above, the Crown government also is obliged to provide details of those contingent liabilities that cannot be quantified.

Table 18.5 Statement of Government Contingent Liabilities, New Zealand, 1997–99
(millions of New Zealand dollars)

	June 30, 1997	June 3, 1998	June 30, 1999
Guarantees and indemnities	496	373	541
Uncalled capital	2,922	2,250	2,820
Legal proceedings and disputes	362	669	464
Other contingent liabilities	1,286	1,203	1,373
Total quantifiable contingent liabilities	5,066	4,495	4,902

Source: Financial statements of the government of New Zealand, 1997, 1998, 1999, New Zealand Treasury.

Lessons from Experience

This section draws several general lessons from the above case studies.

Definition of Fiscal Emergencies/Crises

Two types of definitions are used in the countries studied here. A broad definition is used in ACIR (1985), which suggests that fiscal emergencies generally fall into one of the following categories:

- *Bankruptcy:* applies only to instances in which there has been a formal filing of a bankruptcy petition under Chapter 9 of the federal 1978 Uniform Bankruptcy Reform Act. To file for bankruptcy, the government must declare itself insolvent.
- *Default on government bonds/notes/bills:* failure to pay interest or principal when due.
- *Failure to meet other obligations* (such as payrolls, payments to vendors, pension obligations).

A narrower definition of fiscal crisis refers to the second bullet only—that is, the local government defaults on explicit and direct debt. This is a typical interpretation in countries where the bankruptcy law does not apply to governments and fiscal accounting does not provide adequate information on payments arrears.

For countries where local governments have not been permitted to borrow (except for central government on-lending), there have been no defaults on local government debt. A local fiscal emergency would therefore be better described as a local government running large payments arrears (including wage, pension, and unemployment benefits arrears) and failing to deliver basic public services at minimum standards. These events often generate sufficient social pressures on the central government that it will provide a rescue package.

Selection of Early Warning Indicators

Debt service burden, deficits, debt levels, and liquidity positions (for example, cash balances as a percentage of expenditure), and their medium-term projections, are indicators commonly used for measuring solvency and liquidity risks. However, these indicators suffer from two major problems. First, for the selection of specific indicators, most countries seem to base their design on the principles of data availability, relevance (based on experience), and simplicity. Most of these systems lack a solid theoretical foundation and often are not supported by rigorous statistical tests.

Second, this system works relatively well in countries where the budgets of the local governments cover most of their fiscal activities and where contingent liabilities are relatively unimportant in relation to the size of the budgetary operations. This is the case in the United States. In developing countries, where off-budget and contingent liabilities are presumably significant, the traditional indicators do not necessarily reflect the possibility of a sudden increase in debt service obligations due to contingent liabilities. Therefore, identifying and accounting for the major contingent liabilities would be essential if the monitoring system is to become a meaningful early warning system. In most Western countries, government guarantees, unfunded public pension and insurance liabilities, and legal claims against the government are the most important items. For developing and transition countries, insolvent financial institutions and state enterprise debt are likely to be significant government liabilities as well.

Accounting, Auditing, and Reporting of Local Fiscal Activities

Unsound fiscal management is one of the most significant causes of the fiscal crises of local governments. In many countries, inadequate accounting and reporting have caused some local governments to drift into fiscal crisis without realizing how serious their problems had become. By the time they became aware a crisis was imminent, the size of the problem had already made fiscal adjustment (that is, a sharp increase in taxes and a reduction in services) politically impossible.

Without a sound fiscal reporting system at the local level, an early warning system, no matter how well designed, does not work effectively. Any useful risk measurement must be supported by reliable financial data and have sufficiently broad coverage. Significant efforts by the central government, along with its political will, are required to provide technical assistance to local governments, to widen the coverage of fiscal reporting, and to strengthen the auditing of local government reports (including independent auditing). Budget reforms, including establishment of a single Treasury account, introduction of departmental budgeting, and reform of budget classifications, should all help improve the quality and coverage of local fiscal reporting. In addition, certain requirements for publicity, such as publication and local congressional review of detailed local budgets, execution reports, and off–balance sheet government transactions (such as guarantees) will further improve local accountability.

Central Government Intervention in Local Fiscal Emergencies

Establishing a local monitoring system is not a self-serving task. It should act as a trigger for central government intervention and should provide incentives for local governments classified as "highly risky" to take quick and decisive actions to adjust their fiscal positions and reverse the tendency toward default.

In terms of administrative intervention by a higher-level government in local default or near default, country experiences differ widely. Most countries do not have a formal legal framework that governs the procedure for dealing with local defaults, and, as a result, each situation is handled on a case-by-case basis. This legal ambiguity often goes hand in hand with uncertainties in the areas of revenue and expenditure assignments as well as negotiation-based intergovernmental transfers. As a result, crisis resolutions often call for the central government to extend additional transfers and loans, reschedule or write off local government debt, or assume local government debt and other payment obligations, and for state banks to provide credits to local governments. Such a system is often understood as providing implicit guarantees by the central government on local government obligations, and it generates incentives for local governments to pursue excessive spending through borrowing or provision of guarantees.

Good examples exist of legally formulated procedures for higher-level government intervention in local fiscal emergencies. In the United States, although the federal government does not have the legal responsibility to intervene in municipal defaults (with a few exceptions such as Washington, D.C.), some states have developed formal legal frameworks for state government intervention. Most noteworthy is the two-phase approach of Ohio, based on the state's Code of Local Fiscal Emergencies. In Ohio, if a local government's fiscal position is close to but does not yet qualify as an "emergency," the state auditor would announce that the local government is included in the Fiscal Watch Program, and the auditor's office would provide it with advisory services on improving local fiscal accounting, auditing, and expenditure control. In many cases, after receiving such a warning signal, local authorities immediately begin to increase their cash reserves instead of spending down their funds at fiscal year-end. If a local government's fiscal health further deteriorates (that is, it suffers significant defaults and arrears), it would be declared an "emergency." In this case, the state would establish a fiscal planning and supervisory commission, which would temporarily take over the fiscal authority of the distressed government. This commission would be charged with responsibility for restoring the distressed government's debt service capacity by cutting expenditures (including freezing salary and staff levels), raising additional revenues, and building up reserves. In recent years, legal procedures involving a "control board" or "performance agreement" have been put in place in some developing and transition countries, including Argentina, Colombia, Hungary, and South Africa.

An important advantage of having a transparent procedure for identifying and handling local fiscal emergencies is that local governments
know in advance the conditions that will trigger an emergency declaration and the higher-level government actions that will ensue. Otherwise,
they cannot be sure whether, when, and how the higher-level government will act. International experiences tend to indicate that the existence of a set of criteria for determining fiscal emergencies helps to reduce
the severity of the problems, because it permits the resolution of these
problems at a stage at which they are still manageable.

Toward a More Comprehensive Reform of Intergovernmental Relations

In many countries, a fundamental difficulty in implementing a credible local fiscal warning system and the ensuing central government
intervention—both aimed at reducing the local government's incentive to engage in short-sighted and imprudent fiscal activities—is the
lack of a clear division of labor between levels of government in revenue sources and expenditure responsibilities. Without a clear and transparent legal framework for these relationships, the central government
has to fill the gap, which encourages local spending increases, reduces
local revenue efforts, and results in excessive bargaining.

Another important aspect of transparency in intergovernmental
relations is that the central government ensure that the rules for determining grants and loans to local governments are known and understood by all local governments. This can serve as a useful device by the
central government for fending off local government requests for supplementary grants and loans that are not justified by the announced criteria (for example, central government policy changes, natural disasters).
The rationale for the effectiveness of this device is simple: should the
center grant additional resources to a local government with poor fiscal management, it needs to defend this decision in front of all other
localities.

Establishing an Implementable Monitoring System

This section illustrates how a developing country can draw from relevant international experiences and design a monitoring system that
meets the following criteria:

- the indicators reflect the fiscal risks associated with major quantifiable contingent liabilities;
- the measurement of fiscal risks reflects the potential pressures on
the central government for rescue packages; and
- the system's predictive power is testable with empirical data.

Measuring Contingent Liabilities

Most countries' ministries of finance receive information on local budgetary revenues and expenditures, extrabudgetary revenues and expenditures, nonlending from the central government (including from the proceeds of central government bonds and foreign loans), and debt service payments. These data provide a basis for calculating local governments' current fiscal positions, but do not necessarily reflect future expenditure obligations and borrowing requirements. To build a useful early warning system, the central government also must compile information on contingent liabilities of local governments.

Because different countries may have very different sets of local government responsibilities—explicit and implicit—it is impossible to design a system that can be applied universally. This section considers a sample developing country with significant state involvement in the banking and productive sectors, a vague definition of legal responsibilities for the central and local governments, substantial de facto fiscal autonomy at the local level but no legal right to borrow, and accounting and reporting mechanisms. Under this system, at least four major sources of contingent liabilities should and can be captured by some simple measures:[6]

- *Solvency gaps of local government-owned financial institutions.* These financial institutions mainly include local government-owned commercial banks, credit cooperatives, and nonfinancial institutions such as investment and trust corporations. While there are several different resolution strategies for problem local financial institutions,[7] the worst scenario, from a fiscal cost perspective, is that the solvency gaps (between the current levels of net worth and zero solvency) are filled with government funds (or debt).[8] In the case of a large state bank absorbing failed local financial institutions, the central government in fact directly assumes the fiscal cost of recapitalizing (or purchasing nonperforming loans from) the state bank. The central bank that regularly receives financial statements from all local financial institutions (albeit of dubious quality) should be able to provide the solvency information to the ministry of finance.

- *Guarantees provided by local governments.* Many local governments view issuing guarantees as a zero- or low-cost approach to mobilizing resources for their jurisdictions. In countries in which local government borrowing is prohibited or restricted, the incentive to issue guarantees tends to be stronger. These guarantees have increasingly become a main source of local government contingent liabilities. While difficult, it is possible for the central government to require that all guarantees be registered with local fiscal bureaus and their aggregates be reported to the ministry of finance. The ministry of finance can then calculate the total amount of outstanding local government guarantees that are to mature within a certain period weighted by some measures of default risk (see the case of the Czech Republic in Chapter 9 in this volume).[9]

• *Unfunded pension liabilities.* In many countries, local governments own and operate public pension funds. When these funds begin to run deficits (under cash-basis accounting) and arrears, they are often met by local or central government budgetary transfers. These deficits or arrears are likely to widen further as a result of population aging and persistent unemployment problems. However, because of the complexity of actuarial projections for many pension funds with a large number of varying assumptions, it is not feasible to estimate accurately the unfunded pension liabilities for all pension funds. Therefore, the ministry of finance can consider a simplifying assumption that the current levels of pension fund deficits plus will persist over the next three years and that they need to be financed/cleared with budgetary resources.[10]

• *Unfunded unemployment benefits.* In some countries, local governments are responsible for providing unemployment insurance. When the benefits levels mandated by government regulations cannot be fully met with contributions, the financing gap becomes a local government liability. Again, any accurate measure of the financing gap/deficit requires detailed forecasts of the unemployment rates, contribution bases, collection compliance, and benefit rates in all cities, and will be difficult to implement. For a rough estimate, one can assume that the financing gaps of the unemployment insurance will continue for the next three years at the current levels.

Other sources of contingent liabilities also are worth considering. For example, environmental degradation in many regions poses a major risk to local government budgets. It is clear that, to reach the national environmental standard, a region with poorer environmental indicators will need to spend more on cleaning up than other regions. In theory, some formulas for calculating the cleanup cost can be developed. This factor is not listed as a quantifiable government liability for the current exercise, however, because its estimation is complicated by the fact that different regions have different compositions of financing sources for environmental projects. This can be a task for future research.[11]

Selection of Risk Indicators

This section first discusses the basic data requirements and then describes a set of indicators to measure local fiscal risks. The basic data set will look like that in Table 18.6.

Table 18.6 Summary Data Sheet: [Name of Local Government]

	1998	1999	2000	*Data source*
1. Revenue and transfer (R)				
Total revenue				MOF
Current revenue				MOF
Higher-level government transfers				MOF
2. Expenditure (E)				
Total expenditure				MOF
Current expenditure				MOF
Wage and pension payments				MOF
Interest payments (I)				MOF
Expenditure on contingencies (EC)[a]				Local FB
3. Deficit				
Overall deficit (OD)				MOF
Current deficit (CD)				MOF
Primary deficit (PD)				MOF
4. Financing				
Central government on-lending				MOF
Other (specify)				MOF
5. Cash balance in reserve funds				Local FB
6. Outstanding debt, end of period (D)				
6.1 Loans on-lent by the CB				MOF
o/w: Local currency-denominated				MOF
Foreign currency-denominated				MOF
o/w: Short-term				MOF
Long-term				MOF
6.2 Loans contracted by the LG				Local FB
6.3 Bonds issued by LG corporations[b]				SSC
6.4 Payments arrears				Local FB
7. Outstanding contingent liabilities, end of period (CL)				
7.1 Solvency gap of local financial institutions[c]				CB
7.2 Risk-weighted guarantees provided by LG, maturing by 2003[d]				Local FB / Local FB
7.3 Three times 2000 pension fund deficits[e]				MOL, local BOL
7.4 Three times 2000 unfunded unemployment benefits[f]				MOL, local BOL

Note: MOF = ministry of finance; FB = fiscal bureau; CB = central bank: LG = local government; SSC = state securities commission; MOL = ministry of labor/social security; BOL = bureau of labor/social security; o/w = out of which.

a. Spending on financial sector restructuring, payments to creditors on behalf of defaulted borrowers, and transfers to cover pension and unemployment benefits.

b. For public infrastructure projects.

c. This number should be backed up by a separate table showing the solvency gaps of all locally owned financial institutions and the percentage of shares owned by the local government.

d. To be supported by a separate table showing all outstanding guarantees and their maturities. The MOF should define the criteria for LG corporations in this category.

e. To be supported by a separate table showing deficits of all public pension funds.

f. To be supported by a separate table showing deficits of all reemployment centers and unemployment insurance funds.

Source: Compiled by the author.

Most of the data in Table 18.6 are available in the local financial reports submitted to the ministry of finance, or they can be obtained from the local fiscal bureaus. The difficult part of data collection is that of contingent liabilities, listed in section 7 of Table 18.6. These data are to be collected from the central bank, the ministry of labor or social security, local fiscal bureaus, and local departments of labor or social security. Detailed data sheets will have to be designed to permit the calculation of the summary numbers in Table 18.6.

Using the above data, one can calculate indicators to assess government fiscal risks (see Table 18.7). Some of these are familiar ratios, such as the debt-to-revenue ratio, debt service-to-revenue ratio, and current surplus-to-revenue ratio, which are used by many countries' central governments and by credit rating agencies. However, none of these ratios will fully reflect the future obligations of the government (especially those arising from contingent liabilities) and provide a projection of the pressure on the central government's budget created by a local government (see the Appendix for a fuller discussion on the advantages and disadvantages of these ratios).

To address this problem, I propose two new measures as the main criteria for ranking local governments in terms of fiscal risk: (a) expected minimum borrowing requirement ($MINBR_{t+1}$) as a percentage of current period revenue; and (2) expected maximum borrowing requirement ($MAXBR_{t+1}$) as a percentage of current period revenue. The Appendix presents a detailed derivation of these two measurements. In this exercise, I assume that the central government considers two planning periods—the current period (t) and the next period ($t + 1$)—and wishes to use information available at the end of period t to assess the fiscal risks facing a local government during period $t + 1$. As an example, period t can be interpreted as 1998–2000 and period $t + 1$ as 2001–2003.

Intuitively, $MINBR_{t+1}$ estimates the expected level of pressures from a local government on the central government for a rescue package (loans or grants) under an optimistic scenario—that is, the local government can roll over all realized contingent obligations with payments only covering the interest in period $t + 1$. $MAXBR_{t+1}$, on the other hand, estimates the expected level of pressures for such a rescue package under a pessimistic scenario—that is, all realized contingent liabilities need to be paid off with cash within period $t + 1$.

Local governments with higher revenue capacities tend to face less difficulty in achieving the fiscal adjustment needed to eliminate BR. This suggests that MINBR and MAXBR as a percentage of local government revenue (denoted by minbr and maxbr) are better indicators for local fiscal risk and its resulting pressure on the central government budget.

The ministry of finance can determine the cutoff thresholds for minbr and maxbr based on experience (for example, the observed relationship

Table 18.7 Selected Indicators for Local Fiscal Risks

Indicator	Definition	Remarks
Debt-to-revenue ratio (t)	Stock of direct debt at year-end 2000 divided by total revenue in 2000.	Total revenue can be replaced with current revenue (which applies to all items below). The ratio of net debt defined as debt minus liquid assets)-to-revenue ratio also can be calculated.
Debt service-to-revenue ratio (t)	Three-year average (1998–2000) of ratios of debt service (interest and principal payments) to total revenue.	
Overall deficit-to-revenue ratio (t)	Three-year average (1998–2000) of overall deficits-to-revenue ratios.	Includes arrears in overall deficits. Also applies to the following two items.
Current deficit-to-revenue ratio (t)	Three-year average (1998–2000) of current deficit (current expenditure minus current expenditure)-to-revenue ratios.	
Primary deficit-to-revenue ratio (t)	Three-year average (1998–2000) of primary deficit (noninterest expenditure minus total revenue)-to-revenue ratios.	
Payments arrears-to-revenue ratio (t)	Outstanding payments arrears at year-end 2000 divided by total revenue in 2000.	
Balance in reserve funds-to-revenue ratio (t)	Three-year average (1998–2000) of ratios of balance of budgetary reserves to revenue.	Can also calculate the ratio of reserves to expenditure.

Risk-adjusted contingent liabilities ($t + 1$)	Risk (r)-weighted contingent liabilities that are to mature within the next three years (2001–03). For solvency gap of locally owned financial institution, r can be interpreted as the percentage of the financial institution's shares owned by the local government; for a guarantee, r represents the default probability of the guaranteed borrower; for pension deficits and unfunded unemployment benefits, r should be set at 1.	
Expected minimum borrowing requirement ($t + 1$)	The expected level of local government borrowing from the central government under an optimistic scenario—that is, the local government can roll over all the contingent obligations with payments only covering the interest. See Appendix for formula.	Note that the minimum borrowing requirement can only be measured in a probability sense—that is, using the value-at-risk approach. This indicator—expected maximum borrowing requirement—produces a value based on the assumption of a fixed set of risk weights (r_i).
Expected maximum borrowing requirement ($t + 1$)	The expected level of local government borrowing from the central government under a pessimistic scenario—that is, all realized contingent liabilities need to be paid off with cash within period $t + 1$. See Annex 18.1 for formula.	Note that the maximum borrowing requirement can only be measured in a probability sense—that is, using the value-at-risk approach. This indicator—expected minimum borrowing requirement—produces a value based on the assumption of a fixed set of risk weights (r_i).

Source: Compiled by the author.

between these two indicators and the frequency of local requests for additional central government lending and transfers beyond the original budget). If a local government exceeds either of these two thresholds, it should be declared on the watch list and qualify for certain intervention (such as fiscal policy advisory service by the central government and tightening of central government monitoring over debt-financed capital expenditure; see the earlier discussion of these interventions in this chapter).

Empirical Tests and Future Work

In the future, as data on local defaults/arrears become more available, the ministry of finance can construct a model to predict local government defaults, with minbr, maxbr, and other financial ratios as independent variables. This model will then permit the ministry to determine, more scientifically, the predictive power of the proposed indicators and their cutoff thresholds for risk classification purposes. For example, these cutoff thresholds can be derived by minimizing the combination of type I and type II errors of a logistic default predictive model. Many readily available techniques, such as those used in credit risk models in commercial banks and early warning models for predicting currency and banking crisis, can be easily adapted to model local defaults.

Consideration also should be given to the following extensions of the above-described monitoring system: (a) in compiling data on liquid government assets (such as marketable securities, deposits, and cash) and using this information to calculate net government debt (gross debt minus liquid assets); (b) in developing a set of indicators to assess the interest rate, currency, and rollover risks of government debt; (c) in estimating future borrowing requirements, taking into account extraordinary expenditure needs; and (d) when data on local government defaults/arrears become available, in estimating the probability distribution of defaults on contingent liabilities, and applying the value-at-risk (VAR) approach to generate a more precise description of fiscal risks associated with contingent liabilities.

Annex 18.1: Derivation of Expected Minimum and Maximum Borrowing Requirements in the Presence of Contingent Liabilities

This derivation considers two periods of a local government's operation: the current period (t), and the next period ($t + 1$). The objective of designing the indicators is to predict the borrowing requirement—that is, the demand of the local government for central government lending[12] in period $t + 1$, using information available at the end of period t. Under the current Chinese system, local governments are not permitted to borrow from banks or issue public debt. Therefore, any local government borrowing requirement can be met only by central government lending or transfers if the central government does not want to see a local government default. Compared with any other indicators discussed in Table 18.8, the local borrowing requirement best reflects the magnitude of pressures placed on the central government by local fiscal operations.

In this exercise, let us assume that each period lasts for three years; period t being 1998–2000 and period $t + 1$ being 2001–03. The borrowing requirement in period $t + 1$ can be written as

$$(18.1) \qquad BR_{t+1} = (PD_{t+1} - EC_{t+1}) + I_{t+1} + EC_{t+1}$$

where PD_{t+1} is the primary deficit in period $t + 1$, I_{t+1} is the interest payment on formal debt (excluding promissory notes, see below) in period $t + 1$, and EC_{t+1} is the expected expenditure on contingencies in period $t + 1$. Let us assume that $PD_{t+1} - EC_{t+1}$, or the noncontingency primary deficit (deficit excluding expenditure on contingencies) in period $t + 1$, grows at the same rate as revenue growth a—that is, $PD_{t+1} - EC_{t+1} = (1 + \alpha) (PD_t - EC_t)$. This is a simplifying but plausible assumption for the purpose of cross-locality comparison given that no information on future revenue and noncontingency expenditure is available. This assumption gives rise to

$$(18.2) \qquad BR_{t+1} = (1 + \alpha) (PD_t - EC_t) + I_{t+1} + EC_{t+1} .$$

To calculate EC_{t+1}, one first needs to know the magnitude of the contingent liabilities that are likely to become direct government obligations during period $t + 1$. Denote this amount by $RACL_{t+1}$ (risk-adjusted contingent liabilities). It can be written as

$$(18.3) \qquad RACL_{t+1} = \Sigma_i r_{i^*} CL_{i, t+1}$$

where r_i is the estimated risk weight attached to the ith contingent liability $CL_{i, t+1}$. For the solvency gap of a locally owned financial institution, r can be interpreted as the percentage of the financial institution's shares owned by the local government; for a guarantee, r represents the default probability of the guaranteed borrower; for pension deficits and unfunded unemployment benefits, r should be set at 1, because experience shows that budgetary transfers are the only major source of financing.

EC_{t+1} can range between two extremes. The expected lower limit can be derived by assuming that all realized contingent liabilities are

Table 18.8 Comparison of Various Indicators
for Fiscal Health

Indicator	Advantages	Disadvantages
Debt-to-revenue ratio	Indirectly reflects future debt service burden.	A high but stable debt level may still be sustainable. This measure does not fully reflect the impact of overall/primary fiscal balance on sustainability.
Debt service-to-revenue ratio	Reflects part of government obligations.	Current debt service may not reflect future obligations. This measure does not fully reflect the impact of fiscal balance on sustainability.
Deficit-to-revenue ratio	Reflects current borrowing requirement.	Does not fully reflect future borrowing requirements.
Total contingent liabilities	Partially indicates future obligations.	Fails to discount for default risk and adjust for revenue capacity.
Liquid assets/expenditure needs	Captures liquidity risk.	Does not reflect revenue capacity, overall balance, and debt sustainability.
MINBR and MAXBR as percentage of revenue	Directly measures the fiscal pressure on the central government budget. Reflects risks arising from the debt stock, future service burden, and the current fiscal balance. Unlike the above indicators, br is sensitive to all relevant fiscal health measures: debt stock, contingent liabilities, default risks, interest rate, current fiscal balance, and revenue capacity.	The selection of coefficients (the revenue growth rate and interest rate) is somewhat arbitrary.

Source: Compiled by the author.

met by government promissory notes to the creditors (including bank depositors, pensioners, and the unemployed) with a maturity longer than the length of period $t + 1$. The only government payment obligation stemming from the realization of contingent liabilities during period $t + 1$ is the interest payment on the promissory notes. The lower limit of EC_{t+1} can thus be written as $EC_{t+1} = i^*RACL_{t+1}/2$, where i is the average interest rate for period $t + 1$.[13] With the above assumptions, the expected minimum borrowing requirement (to be met by the central government) that corresponds to the expected lower limit of EC_{t+1} can be derived from

$$(18.4) \quad \text{MINBR}_{t+1} = (1 + \alpha)\,(PD_t - EC_t) + i^*[D_t + (D_t + \text{MINBR}_{t+1})]/2 + i^*RACL_{t+1}/2.$$

Note that the interest payment on formal debt (excluding promissory notes) is derived by multiplying i by the average debt stock during period $t + 1$. Solving equation 18.4 yields

$$(18.5) \quad \text{MINBR}_{t+1} = [(1 + \alpha)\,(PD_t - EC_t) + i^*D_t + i^*RACL_{t+1}/2]/(1 - i/2).$$

The expected upper limit of EC_{t+1} is derived on the assumption that all realized contingent liabilities during period $t + 1$ need to be financed with cash outlays from the local government's budget, because creditors do not accept any promissory notes offered by the local government—that is, $EC_{t+1} = RACL_{t+1}$. This assumption gives rise to the equation for the expected maximum borrowing requirement (to be met by the central government):

$$(18.6) \quad \text{MAXBR}_{t+1} = (1 + \alpha)\,(PD_t - EC_t) + i^*[D_t + (D_t + \text{MAXBR}_{t+1})]/2 + RACL_{t+1}.$$

Solving equation 18.6 yields

$$(18.7) \quad \text{MAXBR}_{t+1} = [(1 + \alpha)\,(PD_t - EC_t) + i^*D_t + RACL_{t+1}]/(1 - i/2).$$

Intuitively, MINBR_{t+1} estimates the expected minimum level of pressure exerted on the central government by the local government for a rescue package under an optimistic scenario—that is, the local government can roll over all the contingent obligations with payments only covering the interest. MAXBR_{t+1}, on the other hand, estimates the expected maximum level of pressure for such a rescue package under a pessimistic scenario—that is, all realized contingent liabilities need to be paid off with cash immediately.

Note that local governments with higher revenue capacities tend to face less difficulty achieving the fiscal adjustment needed to eliminate

BR. This suggests that MINBR and MAXBR as a percentage of local government revenue (denoted by minbr and maxbr) are better indicators of local fiscal risk and its resulting pressure on the central government budget.

In measuring local fiscal risks, BR as a percentage of revenue (br) has the following desirable features:

- a higher debt stock implies a higher br;
- a higher current fiscal deficit implies a higher br;
- a higher interest rate implies a higher br;
- higher contingent liabilities imply a higher br;
- higher default risks associated with the contingent liabilities imply a higher br; and
- a higher revenue capacity implies a lower br.

Table 18.8 compares br with other indicators in other countries' local monitoring systems. It concludes that all existing indicators only partially reflect local government fiscal sustainability or default risk, while br captures the impact of most measures of fiscal symptoms on local government risk.

Notes

1. The author would like to thank Phillips Dearborn, Dana Weist, David Shand, Robert Ebel, Bill Dillinger, Eleoterio Codato, Fernando Rojas, Sergei Shatalov, Ed Gomez, Nobuki Mochida, Tom Richardson, David Shand, Hana P. Brixi, E.C. Hwa, Homi Kharas, Christine Wong, Zhang Chunling, Wang Weixing, Zhang Tong, Guo Chuiping, and Xiang Zongzuo for helpful discussions and comments. The views expressed in this paper are those of the author, and do not necessarily represent those of the World Bank.

2. The code may be found online <204.89.181.223/cgi-bin/>.

3. For example, it stipulates that a domestic bank's outstanding loans to the public sector may not exceed 45 percent of its equity. It also sets a ceiling of BRL600 million on the total exposure of the banking system to the public sector, with any amount below this ceiling allocated among banks on a first-come, first-served basis.

4. Note that the presentation of the Colombian example does not imply that the author recommends these specific thresholds to other countries. See other country cases for a comparison (Table 18.1).

5. According to Polackova (1998), government liabilities can be classified into four categories: explicit and direct (such as formal government debt, budgeted expenditure), explicit and contingent (such as government guarantees and deposit insurance schemes), implicit and current (such as social insurance expenditures), and implicit and contingent (such as defaults by state-owned enterprises, banks, social insurance funds).

6. One may argue that some of the following items—for example, the solvency gaps of local government-owned financial institutions, would be better labeled implicit liabilities than contingent liabilities. In reality, the dividing line between implicit and contingent liabilities often is not clear. In the case of solvency gaps, they are government implicit liabilities in the sense that the insolvency has already occurred, but they also can be contingent because the actual amount of government support needed at a particular future date depends on the macroeconomic conditions, the loss-absorptive capacity of the private sector, and the bank restructuring strategy adopted, none of which are deterministic.

7. Some typical forms of local government support to problem local financial institutions are: (a) for liquidated institutions, the local budget pays off individual deposits; (b) the local government requests other locally owned state enterprises to inject capital into problem local financial institutions, imposing an indirect cost to the local budget through a reduction in tax revenues from these enterprises; (c) the local government offers tax concessions to the problem local financial institutions; (d) the local government accepts deposit certificates in failed local financial institutions as payment to the government; (e) because of the liquidation of local financial institutions, local budgetary institutions lose their deposits, resulting in a demand for additional budgetary allocation or arrears; or (f) the local government pays off foreign debt owed by local financial institutions (for example, some trust and investment companies).

8. If data are available, off–balance sheet guarantees provided by financial institutions also should be taken into account in the projection of solvency gaps.

9. To the extent possible, the ministry of finance also should consider the inclusion of other implicit forms of guarantees extended by local governments. Examples include: (a) local government agreement with foreign investors that guarantees the purchase of services over an extended period; and (b) local government agreement with foreign direct investors that guarantees a minimum rate of return and the repayment of the initial investment within a certain period of time.

10. A slightly more complicated but accuracy-enhancing assumption is that the deficit level in each of the next three years is the 1999 deficit multiplied by a coefficient (uniform across regions), determined by projected changes in the demographic structure, wage level, unemployment rate, benefit rates, and so forth. This alternative also applies to the estimation of unfunded unemployment benefits (see the next bulleted section).

11. Here the Bulgarian experience provides some useful lessons. Bulgaria's Ministry of Environment and Water estimates that the 1999–2015 cost of containing past environmental damage and financing the required treatment of water supplies, management and disposal of solid and hazardous wastes, and air cleanup will come up to US$8.5 billion. Assuming equal annual amounts, the government will need nearly $570 million (about BGN1 billion)

annually. The 2000–06 Public Investment Program envisages annual amounts of $400 million (for discussion, see Chapter 9 by Brixi, Schick, and Zlaoui in this volume).

12. This also can be interpreted as a demand for a budgetary transfer from the central government. In terms of the impact on the central government's overall fiscal balance, lending and offering grants to local governments do not make a difference. Therefore, I concentrate on the case of local borrowing from the central government to cover its deficit.

13. Let us assume the interest rate applies to the average stock of realized contingent liabilities during period $t + 1$.

References

The word *processed* describes informally reproduced works that may not be commonly available through libraries.

ACIR (U.S. Advisory Commission on Intergovernmental Relations). 1985. "Bankruptcies, Defaults, and Other Local Government Financial Emergencies." Washington, D.C.

Council of Europe. 1993. *Borrowing by Local and Regional Authorities.* Strasbourg: Council of Europe Press.

Dillinger, Bill. 1999. "Brazil: Regulations on Subnational Borrowing." World Bank, Washington, D.C. Processed.

Ma, Jun. 1994. "Intergovernmental Fiscal Relations: The Cases of Japan and Korea." Working Paper 41-1994. Economic Development Institute, World Bank, Washington, D.C.

Peterson, George. 1997. "Measuring Local Government Credit Risk and Improving Creditworthiness." World Bank, Washington, D.C. Processed.

Petro, Jim, Auditor of State (Ohio). 1997. "The Ohio Fiscal Watch Program." Columbus. Processed.

Polackova, Hana. 1998. "Contingent Government Liabilities: A Hidden Risk for Fiscal Stability." Policy Research Working Paper 1989. World Bank, Washington, D.C.

Renteria, Carolina, Roberto Steiner, and Juan José Echavarria. 1999. "Bailout of Territorial Entities by the Central Government in Colombia." World Bank, Washington, D.C. Processed.

Ter-Minassian, Teresa, ed. 1997. *Fiscal Federalism in Theory and Practice.* Washington, D.C.: International Monetary Fund.

CHAPTER 19

Guarantees as Options: An Evaluation of Foreign Debt Restructuring Agreements

Sweder van Wijnbergen
University of Amsterdam and
Centre for Economic Policy Research

Nina Budina
World Bank

GUARANTEES ARE CONTINGENT LIABILITIES that come into play once a specific guarantee clause is triggered.[1] As such, the associated payment streams can often be duplicated using a properly structured series of option contracts. In that way, option-pricing techniques can be used to price guarantees.

In fact, public debt itself has option characteristics, because of the option the government has not to service the debt in the years that the debt servicing requirements exceed the country's ability to pay. Thus option pricing also can be used to model the secondary market discount of sovereign debt. This chapter adopts and applies an approach to debt pricing, based on option-pricing theory, to estimate the market values of different menu options available under Bulgaria's debt and debt service reduction (DDSR) agreement concluded in 1994 with the London Club.

In Bulgaria, a part of the principal and interest payments of the discount bonds and the front-loaded interest arrears bonds are secured by 30-year, zero coupon U.S. Treasury bonds. Claessens and van Wijnbergen (1993) show a way to account for the principal and interest collateralization. The principal collateralization is equivalent to an unconditional guarantee of the full repayment at maturity and can be presented as a put option written by the guarantor to the creditor on the repayment capacity in every period, with a strike price equal to the contractual obligation. Thus full collateralization of the principal will fully offset the put option representing the sovereign risk on this payment.

Pricing the interest guarantees is more complicated, because the guarantees are not fully backed to their maximal exposure; rather, they are backed by a fund with much less coverage. Thus the interest guarantee is conditional on the existence of at least one payment in the fund. Pricing therefore requires a derivation of that probability. This can be done using the same model used to price the nonguaranteed debt.

This chapter is organized as follows. The next section discusses the issues surrounding foreign debt management and the terms of the 1994 Bulgarian DDSR agreement with the London Club. It is followed by sections that present the results of our model and our conclusions.

An Option-Pricing Approach
to Sovereign Debt Valuation

How are the benefits of the injection of official funds as part of debt restructuring exercises divided between the debtor country and its creditors? The answer to this question depends on estimates of the market value of commercial claims both before and after the agreement; the difference in market value then represents the value accruing to the banks. It is tempting to use the secondary market prices quoted by traders and brokers before and after the agreement as a starting point for such an analysis (see Bulow and Rogoff 1989 for such an attempt). One would then equate the gains of the banks associated with the injection of official funds to the difference in the market value of the commercial claims between, say, the announcement of debt restructuring and the actual time that the agreement was concluded and the claims were reduced.

The result of such an exercise, however, could be far off, because for this kind of analysis secondary market prices suffer from several shortcomings. First, until recently, volumes of trade in the secondary market were often low, and the market has been illiquid for claims on smaller countries and is easily influenced by a single, relatively small trade. Second, the regulations under which commercial banks operate heavily influence prices and often change over the period considered. Third, the prices over the period of time in which an agreement is negotiated are often influenced by exogenous factors such as the price of oil. This influence clearly contaminates the comparison between ex ante and ex post prices as a measure of gains accruing to banks. Fourth, ex ante prices incorporate the market's anticipation of the upcoming debt reduction agreement, further contaminating them. Moreover, secondary market prices for sovereign debt are often very volatile in the period leading up to debt negotiations as rumors about defaults do the rounds. Finally, agreements often involve the creation of claims with different seniority status (the new money claims are junior to the debt relief bonds). This factor too makes an evaluation using secondary market prices alone difficult, because not all claims are quoted.

The use of secondary market prices is further complicated by the fact that ex post no prices of pure commercial claims are quoted. The only market prices available are those of the debt relief bonds, which have third party guarantees in the form of principal collateralization and rolling interest guarantees. Consequently, the prices of these bonds will reflect the expected repayment by the debtor as well as expectations about the repayment from the collaterals. Simply comparing the ex ante market value of the commercial claims with their ex post market value would involve comparing claims that differ greatly in the nature of the risk.

These considerations point to the need for an analytical pricing model of sovereign claims with and without third party enhancements. Such a model would allow setting benchmarks by pricing the claims before the deal and the new instruments afterward using the same model. The choice of a particular pricing model should be led by the nature of the repayment behavior on a sovereign claim, the different seniority structures of the old and new claims, the particular enhancement schemes used, and the contingent nature of some of the repayment obligations (the recapture clauses).

Option pricing is a logical choice. Methodologies developed in finance for pricing contingent claims can be adapted to the problem of pricing sovereign debt (see Claessens and van Wijnbergen 1989, 1991, 1993).

The main issue with option pricing is to specify the underlying stochastic process driving the debtor country's repayments to the commercial banks. In general, repayments will be difficult to predict; they will be the result of a complex bargaining process between the country and its banks. Repayments will be influenced by factors such as export earnings, terms of trade shocks, the benefit of future access to international capital markets, the position of other lenders, and domestic political and economic factors (Cohen 1989).

Claessens and van Wijnbergen (1991, 1993) used the following procedure to derive the stochastic process for the net amount of financing available each period to service foreign commercial bank debt. First, they model nonoil exports, import requirements, and net scheduled capital in- or outflows consistent with the constraints imposed by domestic economic and political factors to obtain the expected nonoil, noninterest current account (see Claessens and van Wijnbergen 1989).

Second, they adjust the nonoil, noninterest current account for debt service to more senior claim holders, for foreign direct investment flows, and for capital account transactions such as reserve accumulation (see van Wijnbergen and Pena 1989). Third, oil earnings are added to the flows. In accordance with the large share of oil in total exports and the very high variance in oil prices, the behavior of oil exports introduces the stochastic element in the net amount of financing available to service the commercial bank debt.

The net amount of financing available for debt service may itself depend on the debt reduction agreement and the provision of third party guarantees. However, theory gives no clear indication which way this effect goes. On the one hand, because of moral hazard strategic interactions could reduce the financing available from the country once a guarantee is provided. On the other hand, such interactions may increase available financing because of the stronger bargaining power of the third party providing the guarantee (see Bulow and Rogoff 1989 for a multilateral bargaining framework). Or financing might increase because of the country's incentive to avoid a possible adverse signal associated with defaulting. In the absence of strong analytical support either way, we assume that the derived process is not altered by the conversion of commercial bank debt into claims with guarantees.

Pricing Sovereign Debt

Within the above framework, we now introduce the option-pricing model. Each period, the debtor country will pay to its creditors as much as available financing allows, but never more than its contractual obligations in the period—that is,

$$(19.1) \qquad R^*(t) = \min[R_t, FX_t]$$

where $R^*(t)$ is the actual repayment, R_t the contractual obligation, and FX_t the resources available to service commercial debt, all in period t. Equation 19.1 can be rearranged to yield

$$(19.2) \qquad R^*(t) = R_t - \max[0, R_t - FX_t].$$

But $\max[0, R_t - FX_t]$ equals the value of a put option written on FX_t with a strike price of R_t. Thus the uncertain repayment can be represented by a certain repayment, R_t, minus a put. Having thus replicated the payoff stream at maturity, we can obtain its current value, V, as the current value of the certain repayment R_t minus the current value of the put—that is,

$$(19.3) \qquad V(R_t) = \exp(-rt)^* R_t - P(FX_t, R_t, r, t, \sigma)$$

where r is the (continuously compounding) interest rate and $P(FX_t, R_t, r, t, \sigma)$ is the current value of a put written on FX_t with exercise price

R_t, interest rate r, maturity t, and standard deviation σ.[2] The current value of a loan with a series R_t falling due over time (where R_t can be different for each period, depending on the terms of the loan) is then simply the sum of the current values of a series of these claims over the maturity of the contract.

Pricing Guarantees and Recapture Clauses

The option-pricing framework also allows for straightforward pricing of the various guarantees and recapture clauses if the latter exist. Consider the principal and interest guarantees first.

The principal collateralization is equivalent to an *unconditional guarantee* of the full payment, R_T, at maturity. The implicit guarantee is equivalent to a put option with an exercise price R_T, maturity date T, and written on FX, provided by the guarantor to the creditor. This put exactly offsets the put option representing sovereign risk on this payment (see the discussion in the previous section).

Pricing the interest guarantee is more complicated. Recall that this is done through an escrow account with a fixed number of interest payments, say N, in it and no retention of interest earned in the account. This is clearly a *conditional guarantee*, of value only if there is in fact money left in the escrow account at the time it is called. This would not be the case if in the intervening years there were at least N calls on the fund. If there is at least one payment left in the account, the pricing *conditional on there being at least one payment in the fund* is the same as the unconditional guarantee pricing.

Thus if FX_t is serially independent over time, as assumed here, the pricing of the conditional put, PC, for the rolling guarantee in year t is

(19.4) $PC(FX_t, R_t, r, t, \sigma) = O_N(t, R_{\{t'\}}, FX_{\{t'\}}, \sigma)^* P(FX_t, R_t, r, t, \sigma)$

where $\{t'\}$ is the set of t' preceding t. $O_N(t, \ldots, \sigma)$ denotes the probability that the guarantee has been called at most $N - 1$ times during $\{t'\}$, leaving at least one payment in the account. The value of $O_N(t, R_{\{t'\}}, FX_{\{t'\}}, \sigma)$ can be derived using a simple recursive formula on the level of the funds in the escrow account in conjunction with some obvious initial conditions.[3] The total value of the rolling interest guarantee provided through the escrow account is then equal to the summation of equation 19.4 over all years that interest payments are scheduled.

Pricing the Various Options

To obtain the values of the various options, we adopt the Black option-pricing formula, which uses as its inputs forward prices for the underlying state variables (Black 1976). This is in contrast to the Black-Scholes model, which uses the spot price as input. We therefore need the forward prices for the foreign exchange available, the volatility of the forward prices, and the interest structure. As noted, the variability of *FX* stems predominantly from the uncertainty of the price of oil. We therefore model the maturity structure of forward prices to be consistent with market expectations for forward oil prices at the time of agreement.

For the forward prices, lognormality could not be rejected at reasonable confidence levels, so the options can be priced using the Black option-pricing formula (see Black 1976). We obtain an estimate of the standard deviation of the forward prices by calculating the volatility of futures prices for contracts of all maturities that were consistently quoted on the New York Mercantile Exchange between July 1986 and July 1990. This excludes the effects of the Persian Gulf crisis. We use daily (settle) prices. The resulting term structure of volatilities for different maturities (number of months to expiration) indicates that the volatility of the longer maturity contracts is much below that of the nearby contracts and that volatility converges to a level of about 22 percent. In accordance with this decline in volatility, commercial institutions priced long-dated options using volatilities of about 20 percent at the time the agreement was concluded. A standard deviation of about 20 percent is also confirmed by the standard deviations implied by actual market prices of oil options at the time the agreement was reached. We therefore use a volatility of 20 percent as input in our option-pricing model.

The Brady Debt Restructuring Package

The Brady plan for heavily indebted developing countries, announced for the first time in 1989 and named after Secretary of the Treasury, Nicholas Brady (1988–1993), sought to remove inefficiencies caused by a debt crisis. The plan was based on a combination of commercial bank debt reduction and adjustment lending programs designed by the international financial institutions (IFIs). Commercial bank debt reduction was to be achieved through market-based debt instruments (see Krugman 1989) using the menu approach to debt rescheduling and combining the concerted and voluntary characteristics of commercial lending, thus keeping the advantages of pure market and pure concerted mechanisms. The main role of the IFIs in these debt and debt service reduction programs is to provide adjustment lending, conditional on specific adjustments and policy reforms in country debtors, which would allow them to utilize fully the benefits of such a debt reduction (see Diwan and Rodrick 1992).

At the outset of its transition to a market economy, Bulgaria faced difficult conditions produced mostly by the inherited heavy debt burden, the collapse in exports stemming from the breakup of the former Council for Mutual Economic Assistance (CMEA), and the overvalued domestic currency. These difficult initial conditions resulted in a deep economic recession and the virtual collapse of the country's repayment capacity, which prompted Bulgaria to announce a debt moratorium in 1990. During 1990–1996, economic reforms were implemented in a stop-and-go fashion, and inconsistent macroeconomic policies triggered domestic currency and banking crises (see Dobrinsky 1996, 1997b; Budina 1997). These factors contributed to lengthy negotiations on Bulgaria's foreign debt reduction, which began in 1992, when Bulgaria partially resumed servicing its commercial debt, and were concluded only in March 1994. Since then, both the principal and the interest on the foreign debt have been reduced through exchanging the liabilities for new instruments using U.S. Treasury bonds as collateral. The subject of the agreement was all the Bulgarian Foreign Trade Bank (BFTB) debts in foreign currency and the debts to foreign creditors guaranteed by BFTB as of March 1990 when the moratorium on Bulgarian foreign debt was announced (Alexandrov 1995).

Table 19.1 shows the structure of the foreign obligations and the amount of different options chosen. The 1994 DDSR agreement converted US$8.3 billion, which included the original debt and the past due interest (all dollar amounts are in current U.S. dollars). The market-

Table 19.1 Structure of Bulgaria's Foreign Debt Subject to the DDSR Agreement

	Face value (millions of U.S. dollars)	Percent of debt eligible for DDSR
Debt eligible for DDSR agreement	8,088.0	100.00
Original debt[a]	6,186.2	76.49
Buybacks	798.2	9.87
Discount bonds (DISCs)	3,730.4	46.12
Front-loaded interest reduction bonds (FLIRBs)	1,657.5	20.49
Past due interest (PDI)	1,901.8	23.51
Interest down payment	63.8	0.79
Buybacks	223.3	2.76
PDI bonds	1,614.7	19.96
Up-front debt reduction[b]	179.3	
Debt prior to DDSR[c]	8,267.2	

a. Original debt represents the face value debt to the London Club before the debt moratorium period.

b. Up-front debt reduction is a World Bank estimate of the face value of the interest reduction from the favorable treatment of interest since September 1992, the debt moratorium period (see World Bank 1994: 11–12).

c. Debt prior to DDSR refers to what would have been the face value debt to the London Club if interest arrears had been accumulated based on market interest rates, or it would be just the debt eligible for the DDSR plus the face value of up-front debt reduction.

Sources: Ministry of Finance and the World Bank.

based debt and debt service reduction was estimated at about 42 percent in present value terms or at about 38 percent when excluding the up-front costs of the deal.

Here "original debt" refers to the face value of the debt to the London Club before the announcement of the debt moratorium, or about $6.2 billion. Past due interest includes all unpaid interest on this original debt since declaration of the debt moratorium in 1990. Since September 1992, Bulgaria has resumed partial interest payments. Up-front debt reduction is a World Bank estimate of the face value of the interest reduction from favorable treatment of interest since September 1992, the debt moratorium period.[4] Debt prior to the DDSR ($8.3 billion) refers to what would have been the face value debt to the London Club if interest arrears were accumulated based on market interest rates, or it would be just the debt eligible for the DDSR agreement ($8.1 billion) plus the face value of up-front debt reduction ($0.179 billion). Thus the DDSR agreement contained some reduction of accrued interest for the period in which partial interest payments were made.

The debt allocated to each of the available debt reduction options as a share of debt eligible for the DDSR agreement ($8.1 billion) was: debt buybacks, 9.87 percent buyback of the original debt and about 3 percent mandatory buyback of the adjusted interest arrears; discount bonds (DISCs), 46.12 percent; front-loaded interest reduction bonds (FLIRBs), 20.49 percent; and past due interest, out of which past due interest bonds (PDIs) were 19.96 percent and about 1 percent of past due interest was down paid (see World Bank 1994: 12, table 3).

A graph of the pre-debt deal secondary market price appears in Houben (1995). This price, which was extremely low in the beginning of the 1990s, was estimated by the World Bank to be about 20 cents per U.S. dollar. After Bulgaria's agreement in principle with the deal, the secondary market price went up to about 30 cents per dollar.

Menu of Options

The menu of options available was standard for such an agreement: cash buybacks (total of about $1 billion); FLIRBs (approximately $1.7 billion) with lower interest payments in the first seven years; DISCs ($3.7 billion) with a 50 percent discount, but carrying market interest rates; and PDIs covering interest arrears ($1.6 billion). Table 19.2 provides a detailed description of the menu of options under the DDSR agreement (see Alexandrov 1995 and Houben 1995).

Under the *cash buyback* option, agreement was reached for the repurchase of $1.02 billion, or 12.63 percent of the qualified foreign debt, at a buyback price of 25.8 cents per dollar face value debt. The *collateralized discount bonds* (DISCs) were issued at $250,000 par value with a 50 percent discount from the face value of the principal.

Table 19.2 Bulgaria's Brady Debt Agreement with the London Club: Menu of Options

Instrument	Maturity	Interest rate (percent)	Collateral	Comments
Cash buy-backs				25.8 cents per U.S. dollar of original debt plus related unpaid adjusted interest
FLIRBs (par exchange)	18 years (8 grace)	Year 1: 2.00 Year 2: 2.00 Year 3: 2.25 Year 4: 2.25 Year 5: 2.50 Year 6: 2.75 Year 7: 3.00 Year 8: LIBOR + 13/16	One-year interest initially at 2.6 percent rising to 3.8 percent. Interest collateral is required only for the first seven years. No principal collateral.	Bearer bonds Limited to no more than 30 percent of original debt 30 percent of bonds issued for short-term debt will carry a 0.5 percent higher interest rate.
DISCs (50 percent discount on face value)	30 years bullet	LIBOR + 13/16	Principal secured by zero coupon U.S. Treasury bonds. Twelve months interest guarantee calculated at 7 percent interest rate.	Registered bonds. 30 percent of bonds issued for short-term debt will carry a 0.5 percent higher interest rate.
Past due interest				
Cash payment (3 percent)	n.a.	n.a.	n.a.	3 percent of interest arrears, paid on the closing date
PDI bonds (par exchange)	17 years (7 grace)	LIBOR + 13/16	None	Bearer bonds Amortization is payable semi-annually as the following scheduled installments: 1–6, 1 percent 7–11, 3 percent 12–16, 6 percent 17–31, 9.8 percent

n.a. Not applicable.
Note: FLIRBs = front-loaded interest reduction bonds; DISCs = discount bonds; LIBOR = London interbank offered rate; PDI = past due interest.
Source: World Bank (1994).

They have a maturity of 30 years and a bullet amortization. The principal and one year of the interest payment of the DISCs are collateralized with U.S. Treasury zero coupon bonds. The DISCs also are subject to the value recovery clause. Finally, the DISCs yield a six-month LIBOR (London interbank offered rate) plus 13/16 percent and their interest payments are made semiannually. Under the third option, the *FLIRBs*, the overall principal bid was exchangeable one to one with the overall loan principal. The FLIRBs were issued in two tranches at $250,000 par value with maturity of 18 years and were subject to a mandatory buyback in 21 semiannual installments. The first buyback is due in July 2002 and the last one in July 2012. Interest payments are due each January and July. Seventy percent of the bonds issued under the first tranche were in exchange for short-term debts with maturity of up to one year. The FLIRBs yield lower interest payments in the first seven years: years 1–2, 2 percent; years 3–4, 2.25 percent; year 5, 2.5 percent; year 6, 2.75 percent; year 7, 3 percent. After that, they yield the market interest rate of LIBOR plus 13/16 percent a year. One year of their interest payments is collateralized.

Bulgaria accumulated a large amount of *interest arrears* between the announcement of the debt moratorium in mid-1990 and the initiation of debt negotiations with the London Club. Several schemes were used to deal with the unpaid interest. First, part of the interest arrears were written off (the interest payments due were calculated by using a lower fixed dollar interest rate of 3.5 percent). The estimated face value of the written-off interest was $0.1793 billion. Second, $0.223 billion of the interest due was subject to the buyback. In addition, Bulgaria had to make a down payment of $0.0638 billion of the interest due. The rest of the interest arrears, $1.615 billion, was converted to PDIs. PDI*s*, the last option, were issued on the closing day of the agreement at $250,000 par value and were used to purchase all adjusted interest arrears on the qualified debts or related to them, which were exchanged for FLIRBs or DISCs. The PDIs mature in 17 years and are subject to buyback requirements. They yield LIBOR plus 13/16 percent a year. Their principal and interest are not secured. Although it was proposed that the FLIRBs and DISCs be accepted in debt-equity swaps (one to one for DISCs and for FLIRBs at a 50 percent discount), this proposal was not embodied in the regulations on privatization through foreign debt conversion.

Up-front Costs of the DDSR Agreement

At the time of the debt deal negotiations, the Bulgarian government was faced with conflicting objectives: achieving greater debt reduction—but at the lowest cost. Table 19.3 lists the up-front costs of the Bulgarian debt and debt service reduction agreement.

Table 19.3 Up-front Costs of DDSR Agreement
(millions of U.S. dollars)

	Buybacks	PDIs	DISCs	FLIRBs	Closing date
Down payment	257	64	n.a.	n.a.	321
Principal collateral	n.a.	n.a.	220	n.a.	220
Interest collateral	n.a.	n.a.	131	43	174
Total	257	64	351	43	715
Foreign exchange reserves, excluding gold	n.a.	n.a.	n.a.	n.a.	1,300

n.a. Not applicable.
Note: PDIs = past due interest bonds; DISCs = discount bonds; FLIRBs = front-loaded interest reduction bonds.
Source: World Bank (1994).

The most important question is whether Bulgaria succeeded in achieving an efficient agreement. Houben (1995) expresses the view that the Bulgarian foreign debt reduction was comparable to the average reduction with the other debt deals. Because this reduction has been achieved at a remarkably low cost, it has, on average, received a positive evaluation. Yet Houben points out some important lessons for the other countries that plan to initiate the Brady-type debt restructuring agreements. First, the debtor country must orient its macroeconomic and financial policies toward preserving financial stability throughout the debt restructuring process. In addition, to conclude a debt deal that ensures the desired outcome, the debtor country must look for the necessary external financing before reaching the final debt restructuring agreement. Last but not least, the debtor country must specify explicitly in the debt agreement the amount of debt reduction it would like to obtain.

Estimation Procedure

Now it is necessary to estimate the underlying stochastic process driving Bulgaria's repayments to the commercial banks. Figure 19.1 presents the daily data on the secondary market prices of various Brady bonds from their issue on October 14, 1994, to July 10, 1997. Secondary market prices of various Brady bonds are expressed as ratio to 1 U.S. dollar face value debt. For example, low secondary market prices would represent deep discounts of face value debt and often reflect low demand to hold debt instruments of the particular country debtor. Frequently, they reflect the low credibility of domestic macroeconomic

Figure 19.1. Secondary Market Prices of Bulgarian Brady Bonds

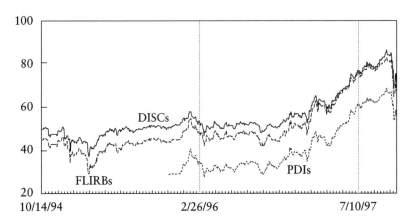

Note: DISCs = discount bonds; FLIRBs = front-loaded interest reduction bonds; PDIs = past due interest bonds. Secondary market prices of various Brady bonds are expressed as ratio to 1 U.S. dollar face value debt.

Source: Authors' calculations.

policies, but at times they also may be subject to external shocks, such as contagion effects from financial crises in other countries.[5]

Secondary market prices also reflect the presence of third party guarantees. Brady bonds often have (partial) guarantees on the principal or interest. Because various claims differ, we cannot compare directly the debt of different countries because they have different contractual terms. And these contractual terms can differ over time—for example, bonds that yield variable versus fixed interest rates. For these reasons, raw data on the secondary market prices cannot be used as an approximation of the underlying stochastic process that drives the debtor country's repayment capacity.

Our approach to this problem follows that of Claessens and van Wijnbergen (1993). They used the prices of forward oil contracts as underlying the stochastic process of Mexico's noninterest current account, because Mexico is an oil exporter. First, we estimate the volatility of prices of the dominant import commodity, oil; Bulgaria is an oil importer. Then we estimate the initial value and growth rate of the underlying process, *FX*.

Determination of the Repayment Capacity, *FX₀* and Its Growth Rate

The next parameter needed to apply the option-pricing model is the starting value of the noninterest current account balance. We use the actual and estimated data on external capital and debt and the DDSR agreement from the World Bank (see World Bank 1994: 55, annex 3). Working with the actual and projected current account in millions of U.S. dollars for the period 1991–2002, we net it out with the interest payments to obtain the noninterest current account for the same period. In addition, we subtract the net transfers to the official creditors.[6] Then we average the noninterest current account over the period 1994–2002 to obtain the initial value for Bulgaria's repayment capacity, $0.26 billion. However, when we include the debt moratorium period, 1991-1993, in our average value for the repayment capacity, we obtain $0.142 billion. We use this amount to value the pre–debt deal original debt, including the period of the debt moratorium. When we take the average of the noninterest current account without the official creditors' disbursements for the period 1994–2002, we obtain $0.26 billion, which we use as an estimate of Bulgaria's repayment capacity to value the debt restructured through DDSR. We also use the two different estimates for Bulgaria's repayment capacity to assess the changes in the secondary market price of the pre–debt deal debt stemming from resolution of the interest arrears problem.

The next problem is the growth rate of the noninterest current account. For our analysis so far, we have assumed that the drift in the repayment capacity is equal to the risk-free interest rate, which is the assumption of the Black-Scholes formula.

Risk-free Interest Rates

We approximate the risk-free interest rates by using the U.S. Treasury bond yields and calculate the term structure of future interest rates on the U.S. Treasury bonds. Data on the interest rates on U.S. Treasury bonds with maturities of 1, 3, 5, 10, and 30 years were used to derive the term structure of future interest rates.

If we assume that the interest rate on a one-year bond is the same for years $t + 2$ and $t + 3$, and because we know the one-year bond rate in the current year and the three-year bond rate in the current year, we can express the future interest rate on the two-year bond. In this way, we are able to provide the annualized interest rates on bonds with maturities of from zero to 30 years.

According to the term structure hypothesis of the interest rates, the interest rate on the three-year U.S. Treasury bond is represented as

(19.5) $$(1 + i_3^t)^3 = (1 + i_1^t)(1 + i_2^{t+1})^2$$

where i_3^t is the yield on a three-year U.S. Treasury bond that is known at time t; i_1^t is the yield of a one-year U.S. Treasury bond at time t; and i_2^{t+1} is the future yield of a two-year U.S. Treasury bond. Therefore, we can determine the future interest rate of two- and three-year bonds from (19.1).[7] The future yield of a four-year U.S. Treasury bond is determined by

$$(19.6) \qquad (1 + i_5^t)^5 = (1 + i_1^t)(1 + i_2^{t+1})^2(1 + i_4^{t+1})^2$$

where we assume that the interest rates of a four- and a five-year U.S. Treasury bond are the same.

Next, we can represent the current yield on a 10-year U.S. Treasury bond as

$$(19.7) \qquad (1 + i_{10}^t)^{10} = (1 + i_1^t)(1 + i_2^{t+1})^2(1 + i_4^{t+1})^2(1 + i_6^{t+1})^5$$

where we assume that the future yields of 6- to 10-year U.S. Treasury bonds are the same.

Finally, we represent the current yield on a 30-year U.S. Treasury bond as

$$(19.8) \qquad (1 + i_{30}^t)^{30} = (1 + i_1^t)(1 + i_2^{t+1})^2(1 + i_4^{t+1})^2(1 + i_6^{t+1})^5(1 + i_{11}^{t+1})^{20}$$

where we once again assume that the future yields of 11- to 30-year U.S. Treasury bonds are the same. In this way, we are able to determine all future yields on U.S. Treasury bonds with different maturities (see Figure 19.2).

Figure 19.2. Future Annual Interest Rates on U.S. Treasury Bonds with Different Maturities

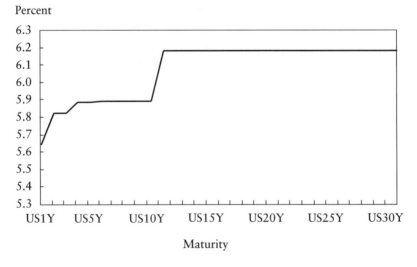

Source: Authors' calculations.

Market Valuation of Bulgaria's Foreign Debt
before and after the DDSR Agreement

We begin with the market valuation of the external debt before the debt deal. Based on our model, we are able to present the effect of the changes in the starting value of the repayment capacity and changes in its volatility on the secondary market price of the debt. Next, we analyze the relationship between the face value and the market value of the debt. In doing so, we present the impact of different face value discounts on the secondary market price and the market value of the debt. We then price separately a 50 percent discount bond with a face value equal to the original debt. We also evaluate the total Brady package and compare it with its pre–debt deal value and price. The debt deal will be beneficial for Bulgaria if the market value of the claims without enhancements falls because of the agreement, which also means a reduced foreign debt burden. If the enhancements are included, the market value may still go up, but by less than the full value of the enhancements. The debt deal will not be beneficial for Bulgaria if the market value goes up with the full value of the enhancements. This implies that there was no debt relief and that all the benefits accrue to the private creditors at the expense of the third party's enhancement effort. We also calculate the gross and the net debt relief and its equivalent buyback price.

Valuation of Bulgaria's External Debt
before the DDSR Agreement

Here we apply the option-pricing approach outlined earlier in this chapter to the value of the original amount of Bulgaria's external debt before the DDSR agreement. However, one should be careful in determining the original value of the debt; there are two different measures for it. This difference can be explained with the interest arrears that accumulated between the announcement of the debt moratorium and the beginning of the negotiations between the Bulgarian government and the London Club. According to the DDSR agreement, the country was obliged to recognize partially the interest arrears incurred since the announcement of the debt moratorium. These interest arrears were treated favorably, because the interest rate applied in this period was fixed at 3.5 percent in dollar terms. This would therefore imply an up-front debt reduction of about $0.179 billion. We use these two different values for the pre–debt agreement debt, as well as our calculations of Bulgaria's repayment capacity as explained in the previous section, in order to find out the pre–debt deal secondary market price. To value the pre–debt deal original debt, including the period of the debt moratorium, we estimate Bulgaria's repayment capacity as the average of

the noninterest current account without the net disbursements to the
official creditors, using both actual values and projections for the period 1991–2002, or $0.142 billion. To value the DDSR restructured
debt, we estimate the repayment capacity as the average of the
noninterest current account without the official creditors' disbursements for the period 1994–2002, $0.26 billion.[8] We start by using the
option price model discussed earlier in this chapter to value the debt
prior to DDSR agreement ($8.27 billion). In doing so, we use the higher
estimate of the present value of the repayment capacity ($0.26 bil-
lion), which is obtained after excluding the debt moratorium period.
This simulation yields a market value of $2.4 billion, which corre-
sponds to an implied secondary market price of 29 cents per dollar of
face value debt (after settlement of the interest arrears).

We then use the same model to calculate the market value and the
implied secondary market price of the debt prior to the DDSR agreement ($8.27 billion) before the official settlement of the accumulated
interest arrears. In this case, we also use the lower value for Bulgaria's
repayment capacity, estimated at $0.142 billion. Thus we obtain 20
cents per dollar face value debt as an estimate for the secondary market price of the original debt, $8.27 billion, during the period of the
debt moratorium. This means that the market value of the original
debt before the official settlement of the interest arrears was equal to
$1.65 billion.[9] Houben (1995) presents a graph with the secondary
market prices of Bulgaria's external debt. The secondary market price
of the foreign debt during the period 1990–1992 was about 20 cents
per dollar of face value. However, once the agreement was reached in
principle in 1993, but before the agreement was signed, the secondary
market price went up to the high twenties.

Table 19.4 presents the secondary market price and market values
of the pre–debt deal debt during the debt moratorium period and after
resolution of the interest arrears problem. Thus, to analyze the benefits of the DDSR agreement, we compare the results for the new secondary market price and market value with the two different market
prices of the old debt—first, before the settlement of the interest arrears and, second, after the agreement on the interest arrears was
reached.

Market Value of the Foreign Debt after the DDSR Agreement

In this section we analyze the total impact of Bulgaria's DDSR agreement with the London Club. We obtain the market value of the post–
DDSR agreement debt by summing up the market values of the
individual instruments. When we price each instrument, we take into
account its share of the total original debt, any principal or interest
guarantees, and the present value of Bulgaria's repayment capacity[10]

Table 19.4 Secondary Market Price and Market Value
of Original Debt before and after Debt Management

	Including the debt moratorium	*Without the debt moratorium*
Face value	$8.27 billion	$8.27 billion
Secondary market price	$0.20	$0.29
Market value	$1.65 billion	$2.40 billion
Repayment capacity	$0.142 billion	$0.26 billion

Source: World Bank and authors' calculations.

and its volatility. We also take into account the interest arrears down payment and the amount of buyback and its price.

Figure 19.3 presents the market value of the debt derived from our valuation model. The first column represents the market value of the pre-DDRS agreement debt ($8.27 billion), prior to settlement of the interest arrears problem, which is estimated at $1.65 billion. The implied secondary market price, therefore, is 20 cents per dollar face value debt. The second column represents the market value of the pre–DDSR agreement debt after the resolution of the interest arrears problem, estimated at $2.40 billion. This yields an implied secondary market price of 29 cents per dollar face value debt. This estimate is consistent with the actual secondary market price of the Bulgarian foreign debt

Figure 19.3. Pre– and Post–Debt Deal Market Value
of the DDSR Debt

Market value (billions of U.S. dollars)

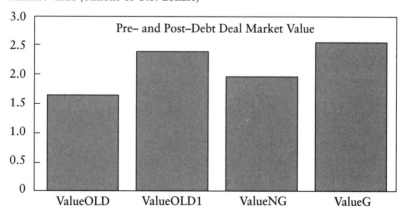

Source: Authors' calculations.

when the DDSR agreement was concluded in principle. The third column represents the market value of the reduced debt after the DDSR agreement, but without the value of the principal and interest guarantees. The face value of the new debt is now equal to $5.13 billion. The secondary market price of the reduced debt after the DDSR agreement, but not taking into account the collateral, amounts to 38 cents per U.S. dollar face value debt, which means that the market value of the debt after the DDSR agreement without enhancements is now $1.97 billion. However, the price of the debt after the DDSR agreement with guarantees increases up to 50 cents per U.S. dollar, and the market value of the reduced debt with enhancements rises to $2.56 billion. Thus, although the face value of the debt has been reduced with the DDSR agreement, its market value with enhancements has increased from $2.40 billion to $2.56 billion. Without guarantees, the market value of the debt is lower ($1.97 billion) as compared with $2.40 billion before the DDSR.

Amount of Debt Relief Implied. Table 19.5 lists the absolute amount of the debt reduction provided under the different options, the debt reduction for the various instruments expressed as a percentage of the new face value ($5.13 billion), and the percentage of debt relief relative to the old face value ($8.27 billion). Note that in the debt reduction provided by the DDSR agreement we include the up-front debt relief and a favorable treatment of the interest arrears accumulated

Table 19.5 Debt Relief Implied by All Options

Debt instrument	Debt relief (billions of U.S. dollars)	Debt relief as percent of new face value ($5.13 billion)	Debt relief as percent of old face value ($8.27 billion)
DISCs	1.86	36.2	22.5
FLIRBs	0.32	6.2	3.9
Buybacks	1.02	19.9	12.3
PDIs	0.00	0.0	0.0
DIAP	0.06	1.2	0.8
Subtotal	3.27	63.6	39.5
Up-front debt reduction	0.18	3.5	2.2
Total	3.44	67.1	41.7

Note: DISCs = discount bonds, FLIRBs = front-loaded interest reduction bonds; PDIs = past due interest bonds; DIAP = interest arrears down payment.

a. The up-front debt reduction is made by capitalizing the nonpaid interest using a lower dollar interest rate of 3.5 percent. This estimate is provided by the World Bank.

Source: Authors' calculations.

between the moratorium announcement in 1990 and settlement of the arrears before the debt deal was concluded with the commercial creditors. This relief amounts to $0.179 billion. Therefore, we calculate the percentage of debt relief, taking into account what the original debt would have been without such a favorable treatment, $8.27 billion. Thus the total value of the gross debt relief amounts to $3.4 billion, or about 42 percent of the pre–DDSR agreement face value debt. This suggests that Bulgaria's debt deal was on average successful.

The largest percentage of debt relief was provided by the discount bonds, 22 percent of the original face value; the next type of instrument, buybacks, accounted for about 12 percent of the original face value. The FLIRBs accounted for about 6 percent of debt relief as a percentage of the new face value, or as 3.9 percent of the old face value. Finally, the favorable treatment of the interest arrears provided in debt relief 3.5 percent of the new face value and about 2 percent of the old face value.

Secondary Market Valuation of the New Instruments. This section describes the results of applying the option valuation model for the market values and the secondary market prices of various instruments available under the DDSR agreement. The face value of DISCs that yield 50 percent debt reduction accounts for the largest share of the face value of the pre-DDSR debt. Both the FLIRBs (interest reduction bonds) and the PDIs (new money claims) account for about 20 percent in the face value pre-DDSR debt.

Table 19.6 presents the percentage share of market value (with and without guarantees) of different instruments in the total pre– and post–

Table 19.6 Projected Secondary Market Valuation of New Instruments
(share of the new instruments)

	Without guarantees		With guarantees	
	Percent of old face value[a]	*Percent of new face value*[b]	*Percent of new face value*[a]	*Percent of old face value*[b]
DISCs	13.19	21.24	30.59	18.99
FLIRBs	7.74	12.47	14.61	9.07
PDIs	2.90	4.68	4.68	2.90
Total	23.83	38.72	49.88	30.97

Note: DISCs = discount bonds; FLIRBs = front-loaded interest reduction bonds; PDIs = past due interest bonds.
a. The pre-DDSR face value of $8.27 billion.
b. The new face value of restructured debt, $5.13 billion.
Source: Authors' calculations.

debt deal debt. A comparison of the second and the third columns reveals the impact of the guarantees on the market value of the debt. The difference between the two columns stems from the principal and interest collateral of the discount bonds—their market value increases from 21.2 to 30.6 percent of the new face value debt. The difference of about 10 percent in the two market values is due to the effect of the principal and interest guarantees. The market value of the FLIRBs increases from 12.5 to 14.6 percent of the new face value debt. The increase in the market value in this case is smaller because only one year of payments is guaranteed.

Assessment of Bulgaria's DDSR Agreement with the London Club

The debt deal will be beneficial for Bulgaria if the market value of the claims without enhancements goes down because of the agreement, which also means a reduction in the burden of the foreign debt. If the enhancements are included, it may still go up but by less than the full value of the enhancements. The debt deal will not be beneficial for Bulgaria if the market value goes up with the full value of the enhancements. This means that there was no debt relief and that all the benefits accrue to the commercial banks at the expense of the third party's enhancement effort.

Figure 19.4 presents the pre– and post–debt deal market value of the Bulgarian foreign debt subject to the DDSR agreement. The first two columns of the graph represent the market value of the debt deal before the DDSR agreement. The first column is calculated under the assumption that during the debt moratorium in the early 1990s, the secondary market price of the debt was 20 cents per dollar. Given the original face value, this yields a market value of $1.65 billion during the time of the debt moratorium. However, during the DDSR negotiations the secondary market price of the old debt went up—our model estimates it at 29 cents per dollar face value debt. This was the situation in 1993, when Bulgaria had recognized the interest arrears incurred in 1991 and 1992 and there was an agreement in principle on the debt reduction. Given the original face value of the debt, this price implies a market value of the debt of $2.40 billion. We have used the second value, $2.40 billion, as a basis for our comparison, because the debt moratorium is not sustainable in the long run.

The third and the fourth columns of Figure 19.4 represent the market value of the debt after the DDSR agreement, without and with the enhancements. The difference between the market value of the post-deal debt with and without enhancements represents the market value of the enhancements, $0.59 billion—that is, $2.56 billion minus $1.97 billion. Assuming that Bulgaria has borrowed all the funds to provide

Figure 19.4. Evaluation of the Benefits of the DDSR
Agreement, Including Guarantee Costs

Market value (billions of U.S. dollars)

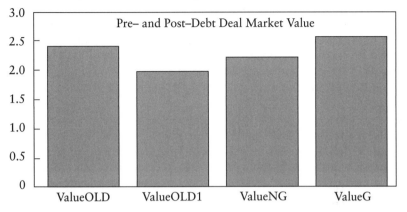

Source: Authors' calculations.

the guarantees, we now look more closely at how the benefits from
these third party enhancements are distributed between Bulgaria and
its commercial creditors.

First, we compare the market value of the debt before the deal,
$2.40 billion, with the market value of the debt after the debt deal but
without enhancements, $1.97 billion. The difference of $0.43 billion
represents the benefits accrued to Bulgaria. Second, we compare again
the pre-debt deal market value of the debt, $2.40 billion, with the
market value of the debt after the deal, but including the enhancements, $2.56 billion. The difference of $0.16 billion represents the
benefits accrued to the commercial banks. In terms relative to the total
market value of the guarantee funds, Bulgaria has gained approximately 73 percent of the total benefits, and the commercial creditors
have gained about 27 percent. This result suggests that the DDSR agreement was beneficial for Bulgaria, and it is comparable with the Mexican debt deal (see Claessens and van Wijnbergen 1989, 1993).
According to Claessens and van Wijnbergen (1993), Mexico struck a
very good bargain because its benefits from the agreement varied between 76 and 97 percent of the provision of official funds.

The situation looks very much different once we realize that not all
of the guarantee funds were provided by the official creditors. If we
assume in the extreme case that Bulgaria provided all the guarantee
funds from its own resources, then the result is that all the benefits
from the increase in the market value due to the guarantees went to

the commercial banks, not Bulgaria. However, this is not a plausible conclusion, because, for one thing, Bulgaria was partially reimbursed for its up-front costs. According to the World Bank figures (1994), the total up-front costs of the DDSR agreement amounted to $0.715 billion. Of that amount, $0.22 billion was used as principal collateral on the discount bonds; $0.174 billion was used as interest collateral on both the discount and FLIRB bonds; and the rest, $0.321 billion, was used for buybacks and the interest arrears down payment. Therefore, the total up-front cash used for guarantees is $0.394 billion, whereas we estimate their market value at $0.59 billion.[11] The total official support for the DDSR agreement was $0.241 billion,[12] or approximately 61 percent of the total up-front costs of the guarantees. If we assume that the market value of the official support is again 61 percent of the market value of the total guarantee costs, $0.59 billion, this implies that the market value of the third party guarantees fund is equal to $0.35 billion. This means that Bulgaria has to add the part of the market value of the guarantees that was not covered by the international institutions to the market value of the nonguaranteed debt, implying that the debt reduction in this case is much lower. This is also shown in Figure 19.4.

In this case, the difference is that the direct benefit to Bulgaria is now much lower: Bulgaria now gains only $0.19 billion, as compared with $0.43 billion, which represents the potential gains for Bulgaria if the country had been reimbursed in full for these up-front costs. The gain accrued to the commercial banks is the same as before, $0.16 billion. The total amount of the benefits is $0.35 billion. Thus the distribution of the benefits is as follows: 54.3 percent of the benefits accrue to Bulgaria and 45.7 percent to the commercial banks. This result shows that if we account for the fact that part of the guarantee funds were paid by Bulgaria, the debtor country succeeded in capturing a much lower share of the total benefits from the DDSR agreement.

However, such a debt reduction agreement also has indirect benefits, including future access to the official credits after the debt deal. Currently, Bulgaria has gained access to World Bank and IMF loans intended to provide the foreign exchange needed to introduce the currency board system and to speed up the structural reforms.

Conclusion

We have applied the option valuation approach outlined to assess the benefits of Bulgaria's DDSR agreement with its commercial creditors. Under the assumption that Bulgaria has borrowed all the up-front cash needed for the guarantee funds, our analysis shows that Bulgaria succeeded in retaining most of the benefits (about 73 percent of the market value of the guarantee funds). Commercial banks also gained from the DDSR agreement (approximately 27 percent of the funds). In this respect, the Bulgarian DDSR agreement is comparable with the Mexican agreement, which was rated favorably among other debt restructuring agreements. However, if we take into account that Bulgaria provided about 40 percent of the total costs of the guarantee funds from its own sources, lower debt relief is revealed, as well as a different distribution of the benefits between commercial banks and the debtor country: Bulgaria now captures slightly above half of these benefits, as compared with 73 percent in the previous case.

Bulgaria's DDSR agreement provided a gross debt reduction of 42 percent of pre–debt deal face value debt, and about 38 percent net debt reduction, accounting for up-front costs of the deal.

The agreement can lead to less uncertainty about future fiscal and foreign exchange developments associated with the debt overhang. It can therefore increase the probability of success of the reform program and can lead to restoration of future growth through regaining access to the international capital markets. Bulgaria benefited in three ways: the debt overhang was reduced significantly; the maturity structure of its debt obligations was improved; and the future uncertainties associated with the debt overhang were reduced, making it possible to regain access to the international capital markets and renew growth recovery prospects.

However, slow structural refoms and frequent political and financial instability prior to 1997 resulted in negligible external commercial inflows and a relatively low level of foreign direct investment compared with that in relatively more advanced transition economies. Furthermore, although the debt overhang was decreased significantly, the debt burden remains high, which means that during the next decade Bulgaria must undertake significant fiscal tightening to be able to service its debt without difficulties.

The introduction of the currency board system in 1997 (see Dobrinsky 1997a), together with the strong political commitment toward radical restructuring, will give Bulgaria an opportunity to grow out of its debt.

Notes

1. The authors thank the European Commission for the financial support provided through the ACE Phare Research Project 1996 Programme (ACE-PHARE Research Project P96? 6028-R).

2. We use a constant interest rate r for notational convenience only. In the application, we allow for the maturity structure of interest rates. Even though the state variable FX is a nontraded asset, and as such is not priced directly in

the market, it is likely spanned by instruments that are traded and whose current values are known. For example, forward and futures contracts on oil can span Mexico's oil earnings. As a result, the option-pricing model can be used identically as in the case of traded assets. In particular, we use the Black (1976) formula for commodity-based options, which uses forward prices for FX rather than the spot price as in the more standard Black-Scholes pricing formula.

3. Note that $O_N(t, R_{(t')}, FX_{(t')}, \sigma) = 1$ for $t < N$. Also note that it is logically impossible to get more than $N - 1$ calls in less than N payment periods.

4. For more details, see the description of past due interest bonds at the end of this section and World Bank (1994: 1112).

5. For a more detailed discussion and empirical analysis of the determinants of the secondary Brady bond prices of Bulgaria's debt, see Budina and Mantchev (2000).

6. We calculate the net transfers to official creditors as repayments due to official creditors minus the disbursements from the official creditors plus the interest owed the official creditors.

7. We assume that the future yields of the two- and three-year U.S. Treasury bonds are the same.

8. The use of the two different estimates for Bulgaria's repayment capacity to assess the changes in the secondary market price of the pre–DDSR agreement debt is needed to account for the impact of resolution of the interest arrears problem on the secondary market price of the debt.

9. Our results are consistent with the World Bank estimates and with data shown in Houben (1995).

10. The present value of the repayment capacity is calculated as the average noninterest current account, without the net disbursements to the official creditors for the period 1994–2002.

11. The difference accounts for the fact that the up-front cash payment for interest collateral is smaller. According to the World Bank (1994), at the beginning the interest payments are collateralized at a level of 2.6 percent, and the earnings on the interest collateral are to be retained until the interest collateral reaches 3 percent of the outstanding amount of FLIRBs. The earnings on the interest collateral in excess of 3 percent are to accrue to the Bulgarian government.

12. The main official creditors were the IMF, the World Bank, and the government of the Netherlands.

References

The word *processed* describes informally reproduced works that may not be commonly available through libraries.

Alexandrov, S. 1995. "Bulgarian Brady Bonds." *Bank Review, Quarterly Journal of National Bank of Bulgaria* (1).

Black, Fischer. 1976. "The Pricing of Commodity Contracts." *Journal of Financial Economics.* January–March.

Budina, Nina. 1997. "Essays on Consistency of Fiscal and Monetary Policy in Eastern Europe." Ph.D. diss. Tinbergen Institute Research Series No.145.

Budina, Nina, and T. Mantchev. 2000. "Determinants of Bulgarian Brady Bond Prices: An Empirical Assessment," World Bank Working Paper 2277. Washington, D.C.

Bulow, J., and K. Rogoff. 1989. "Sovereign Debt Repurchases: No Cure for Overhang." NBER Working Paper No. 2850. National Bureau of Economic Research, Cambridge, Mass.

Claessens, Stijn, and Sweder van Wijnbergen. 1989. "An Option-Pricing Approach to Secondary Market Debt (Applied to Mexico)." International Economics Department and Latin America and the Caribbean Country Department II, Working Paper WPS 333. World Bank, Washington, D.C.

———. 1991. "The 1990 Mexico and Venezuela Recapture Clauses: An Application of Average Price Options." *Journal of Banking and Finance* 17: 733–45.

———. 1993. "Secondary Market Prices and Mexico's Brady Deal." *Quarterly Journal of Economics* 108 (November): 965–82.

Cohen, D. 1989. "A Valuation Formula for LDC Debt with Some Applications to Debt Relief." World Bank, Washington, D.C. Processed.

Diwan, I., and D. Rodrik. 1992. "Debt Reduction, Adjustment Lending, and Burden Sharing." NBER Working Paper No. 4007. National Bureau of Economic Research, Cambridge, Mass.

Dobrinsky, R. 1996. "Monetary Policy, Macroeconomic Adjustment and Currency Speculation under Floating Exchange Rates: The Case of Bulgaria." *Economics of Transition* 4 (1): 185–210.

———. 1997a. "The Currency Board in Bulgaria: First Experience." Sofia. Processed.

———. 1997b. "Transition Failures: Anatomy of the Bulgarian Crisis." Paper prepared for the ACE Workshop on Exchange Rate and Capital Flows in Transition Economies. Sofia.

Houben, A. 1995. "Commercial Bank Debt Restructuring: The Experience of Bulgaria." IMF Paper on Policy Analysis and Assessment PPAA/95/6. International Monetary Fund, Washington, D.C.

Krugman, P. 1989. "Market-Based Debt-Reduction Schemes." In J. A. Frenkel, M. P. Dooley, and P. Wickham, eds. *Analytical Issues in Debt.* International Monetary Fund, Washington, D.C.

van Winjbergen, Sweder, and S. Pena. 1989. "Mexico's External Debt: Structure and Refinancing Options." World Bank, Washington, D.C. Processed.

World Bank. 1994. "Proposed Debt and Debt Service Reduction Loan to the Republic of Bulgaria to Support DDSR Program of Bulgaria." Report No. P-6403-BUL, September 7. Washington, D.C.

CHAPTER 20

The Fiscal Risk of Floods: Lessons of Argentina

Alcira Kreimer
World Bank

TYPICALLY, AFTER A DISASTER OCCURS in a developing country its government is forced to reallocate funding from development activities to relief and reconstruction efforts. In many countries, devastating natural disasters are a frequent occurrence. A natural disaster occurs when an extreme event such as a flood affects vulnerable investments or structures and the consequences surpass the society's ability to respond. In Argentina, like in other countries, accelerated changes in demographic and economic trends have disturbed the balance existing in ecosystems, increasing the risk of human, social, economic, and financial losses. Rapid population growth in vulnerable areas increases pressures on natural resources and the environment and raises the consequent risks associated with human activities. Major disasters not only damage capital assets but have long-term effects on the economy as well. Disasters can seriously dislocate a country's economy and trigger shortfalls in tax revenues, create fiscal deficits, increase levels of public debt, and affect the overall economic performance measured by negative changes in the gross domestic product (GDP), balance of payments, and gross capital investments

Despite the repeated experience of disasters, government officials often react with surprise at the results of an "act of God." Awareness of risk to extreme natural events is not well established in the process of public and private investment decisionmaking. According to Munich Re (1999), in the decade of 1988–97 floods accounted for over half of the 390,000 recorded fatalities and a third of the damage from all natural catastrophes worldwide. Kunreuther and Linnerooth-Bayer

(1999) found that, despite the far greater capital stock in the developed world, most of the US$233 billion in global flood losses over the past decade occurred in developing countries (all dollar amounts in chapter are current U.S. dollars).

While the precise scale, time, or location of disaster events cannot be predicted, areas of hazard and vulnerability can be identified. Aggregate losses can be anticipated at the national level, and contingent provisions can be made for extreme events. Governments can then incorporate disaster losses into the economic and fiscal planning process, as indicated in the sections that follow.

Assessing the Risk: Exposure of the Argentine Government to Flood Risk

Flooding is the major natural hazard in Argentina, where the phenomenon poses a major challenge to development. Floods have destroyed human, social, and physical capital, and they have derailed economic and fiscal planning, because funds are reallocated from ongoing programs to finance relief and reconstruction assistance.

The most distinctive geographic feature of Argentina is the delta formed by the conjunction of three great rivers: the Paraguay, Paraná, and Uruguay. The waters of the combined Paraná and Uruguay Rivers, which drain one-fourth of the waters of South America for a watershed that covers more than 4.1 million square kilometers, flow into the Río de la Plata and then out to sea. Heavy precipitation throughout the year and the country's flat topography often combine to inundate the floodplains of all four rivers. The coastal areas of the northeastern and central parts of the country also are at risk, and storm surges pose a threat to regions along the coast.

Dangerous conditions occur alarmingly often. For example, hydrological data for the city of Corrientes reveal that flooding takes place in two of every three years. Since 1957, Argentina has had 11 major floods. The floodplains in the country cover more than a third of Argentina. Within that area are the nation's most developed agricultural and industrial zones, an extensive transportation network, and two major hydroelectric dams (Kreimer, Kullock, and Valdés 2001). Of the 11 major floods in Argentina, three of them have caused direct damage in excess of $1 billion: the 1983 flood with damages of $1.5 billion; the 1985 flood with damages of $2 billion; and the 1998 flood with damages of $2.5 billion. According to statistics developed by Swiss Re (1998), Argentina is among the top 18 countries worldwide with potential flood losses in excess of $3 billion. As for measuring flood losses as a percentage of GDP, Argentina is one of 14 countries whose potential losses to floods are greater than 1 percent of GDP (Freeman 2001). In

Latin America, only Ecuador has a higher GDP exposure from flood risk. In pure economic loss terms, Argentina has the highest risk in Latin America; however, not all members of society perceive the risk as high and respect safety in planning and development.

Incorporating Catastrophic Exposure into Government Fiscal Planning

A model incorporating the impact of floods into Argentina's national economic and fiscal planning estimates that the country faces an annual contingent exposure of $650–950 million in lost capital stock due to flooding (Freeman and others forthcoming). The model traces the potential sources of replacement capital finance and shows how incorporating contingent catastrophe losses can lead to better estimation of macroeconomic performance.

Using estimates of $2 billion in losses from one-year flooding events, $9 billion in losses from 100-year events, and $12 billion in losses from 1,000-year events, Freeman and others (forthcoming) trace the macroeconomic costs of those losses assuming that Argentina rebuilds immediately after a catastrophe. Incorporating catastrophes into macroeconomic planning indicates that accounting for flood exposure contributes to the following effects:

- Increases estimates of required public investment by an average of $801 million a year.
- Reduces projected levels of government consumption by $200 million a year.
- Decreases private consumption projections by as much as $1,647 million a year, or increases private consumption projections by as much as $1,671 million a year. In the year of a catastrophe, private consumption drops dramatically. If, however, the catastrophe is followed by inflation and an appreciation of the real exchange rate, then in the years following the catastrophe imports will increase, exports will decrease, and private consumption will increase, to the detriment of an already deteriorating resource balance and growing foreign debt.
- Increases import projections by, on average, $429 million a year and decreases export projections by, on average, $211 million a year.
- Increases foreign debt projections by $2,689 million a year.

Risk Reduction

Because government exposure to flood risk has such an important impact on fiscal planning, it is important to understand what can be done to reduce such exposure. Efforts to prevent flood losses consist of (a) protecting existing development through flood control works (for example, reservoirs, channel improvements, diversions, flood warning and evacuation, and flood proofing); (b) removing existing development through public acquisition, urban redevelopment, public nuisance abatement, nonconforming uses, conversion of use of occupancy, and reconstruction; (c) discouraging development through public information, warning signs publicizing hazards, tax assessment practices, public facility expansion, and flood insurance; and (d) regulating floodplain uses through zoning ordinance districts, special floodplain regulations, subdivision ordinances, and building codes (United Nations 1976). Early on, the predominant efforts in Argentina focused on structural measures, such as the construction of dams, embankments, or levees.

But structural mechanisms to control floods are not enough; they must be coupled with nonstructural measures. Furthermore, some flood control projects may be counterproductive, because they may foster unrealistic expectations that all flooding can be prevented and stimulate people to move onto floodplains, thereby increasing total catastrophic exposure. For example, investigators found that in the part of Argentina affected by the floods of 1991, works implemented in the past, such as makeshift protective earthworks, had been built without a well-thought-out plan or a basic understanding of the local topography. Thus settlements commonly protected themselves by building a levee along the river, but then they did nothing to protect themselves from the nearby creek that fed into it. Rising water in the river raised the level of the creek, and floodwaters came into the settled area from an unanticipated direction.

Recent efforts such as the Argentina Flood Rehabilitation Project, prepared by the government with financing from the World Bank in 1992, have moved from purely structural measures to support for the development of a national strategy to help the country cope more effectively with the recurrent floods. Thus, in addition to financing flood recovery needs, the project financed the development of an institutional framework for the coordination and implementation of government rehabilitation efforts (World Bank 2000).

Risk Management: Legal and Institutional Framework

River basin and floodplain management in Argentina is a fragmented, disorganized sector that lacks adequate infrastructure, appropriate environmental standards and regulations, and institutional capacity. The two most generic and notable features of the sector can be summarized as follows. First, the provinces have primary jurisdiction over water resources (except for navigation) even though many river basins are interprovincial, and the national legal and institutional framework does not adequately address this imbalance. Second, the characteristics of water resources vary greatly among the country's regions and provinces, and there is no consolidated policy and institutional framework, which has resulted in significantly uneven and poorly coordinated infrastructure development.

Although Argentina has significant national water legislation, it lacks the basic framework that would allow provinces to establish consistent regulations for users' rights and obligations, the economic value of water, the river basin as the primary management unit, and multisectoral user's organizations, among other things. At the provincial level, legal frameworks are unevenly developed and inconsistent. Some provinces have well-developed regulations, while others have no specific laws on some of the issues that affect them. In other cases, existing legislation is very old and does not incorporate new concepts such as multisectoral management, economic criteria, institutional development, and so forth.

Gaps in the management of the flood problem are twofold. On the one hand, there is a lack of norms for environmental management for flood risk. For example, the resources devoted to meteorological and warning systems are not well used, and the programs of public investment in water resource management are not part of an overall integrated planning system. The fiscal policy system exerts only a minimal degree of efficiency in the ex post assistance efforts to support recovery after floods. Finally, the handling of flood management issues by government agencies is characterized by weak coordination, poor financial control, and poor programming of public investments and fiscal policy. On the other hand, there are important gaps in the coordination among the different jurisdictions that administer the flood problem. In the metropolitan area of Buenos Aires, which is at high risk from floods, 14 municipalities, in addition to the provincial government and the federal government, have jurisdiction over the flood problem. There is a duplication of functions in some of these institutions, and resources are devoted to similar functions, but they are applied in the context of government policies that are often opposed and that are defined independently of each other. There is no articulation of policies and programs, and resources and knowledge are not shared across institutions. Furthermore, a unified and integrated fiscal policy on government exposure to flood risk is lacking.

Risk Transfer

Kunreuther and Linnerooth-Bayer (1999) identify two mechanisms available to governments to fund the costs of recovery: hedging instruments and financing instruments. Hedging instruments are predisaster arrangements in which the government incurs a relatively small cost in return for the right to receive a much larger amount of money after a disaster occurs. Insurance and capital market-based securities are examples of hedging instruments. Financing instruments are arrangements whereby the government either sets aside funds prior to a disaster or taps its own funding sources after the event occurs. An example of a predisaster measure is a public catastrophe fund in which the government implicitly self-insures by setting aside money to finance some of the recovery needs after a disaster. An example of this type of mechanism in an emerging economy is a calamity fund, such as FONDEN in Mexico (Kreimer and others 1999). Funds earmarked for relief and reconstruction by the federal government are maintained in FONDEN, which provides funds for the repair of uninsured infrastructure, immediate assistance to restore the productivity of subsistence farmers, and relief to the low-income victims of disasters. There is no such fund in Argentina.

Flood insurance has been introduced successfully in many parts of the world, and it is particularly effective in areas where floods are frequent. However, in most developing countries the full cost of insurance in high-risk areas is beyond the means of many property owners. Insurance premiums must be based on a full assessment of risks by using flood hazard maps for the flood-prone areas. In some developed countries such as the United States and Australia, the national governments have introduced subsidized flood insurance programs to provide some relief for disaster-prone areas. In the United States, flood insurance is tied to measures to reduce losses. Flood-prone communities may buy subsidized flood insurance only if both the homeowners and the community make efforts to reduce the risk of the insured structures to floods.

Historically, and like other emerging markets, the government of Argentina has absorbed the losses from floods. In principle, flood coverage is available as a supplement to fire insurance, because noncommercial and commercial risks are covered under fire policies. However, even though private insurance that can absorb a portion of the costs of flooding is available in the country, the penetration of the private market is minimal. Farmers absorb most losses from floods. However, as Freeman (2001) notes, multiperil crop insurance has been available in the country since 1990. This coverage, which includes losses from floods occurring from excess of rain, builds on the 100-year history of hail insurance in Argentina. As with fire insurance, the penetration of the market has been very small. The total premium for multiperil crop insurance is less than $1.5 million a year. Stand-alone flood coverage is no more than $180,000 a year.

Currently in Argentina, the costs of catastrophes are absorbed by the victims of the disaster and by the federal, provincial, or municipal governments. In turn, the federal government, which is the primary source of recovery funding, has relied on borrowing from international lending institutions (mainly the World Bank and the Inter-American Development Bank) to fund flood losses. Under the procedures now in place, the federal government pays 60 percent of the costs of the reconstruction of flood-damaged infrastructure, and the provincial governments pay the remaining 40 percent. Essentially, those funds cover the immediate needs of the population and infrastructure projects, and no funds are allocated to reimburse agricultural losses. Thus the flood recovery plans proposed by the provinces have an emphasis on infrastructure: roads, bridges, sanitation, schools, hospitals, and low-income housing projects for people living on floodplains.

Additional funding for disaster relief is provided in a fragmented fashion. However, a procedure is in place to declare an emergency area and to make budget allocations to fund disaster relief. Often, these allocations are accompanied by additional taxes to fund the relief process. Yet this procedure certainly causes budget and fiscal problems, is subject to political manipulation, and brings about reallocations from developmental initiatives to relief.

Alternatives to Flood Insurance

Alternatives for risk transfer exist. One alternative is the creation of an insurance system for the government along the lines of the one proposed for FONDEN in Mexico. Another alternative is to explore the feasibility of using risk transfer based on weather indices.

A program similar to the one proposed to modify FONDEN in Mexico would be based on providing transfer and financing options for the government for losses from catastrophic flooding. Instead of the government being the primary insurer for flood risk, which it is now, there would be ex ante financial planning for flood losses. The program would entail a budget allocation for flood losses, as opposed to the post-event financing options currently employed. This early allocation would provide more stability for the budgeting process, enabling funds for other programs to be more effectively managed. Moreover, it would provide a consistent set of resources for dealing with major catastrophic flood losses. And it would demand a systematic risk assessment by the government of the essential infrastructure subject to flood losses. The program would include cooperation between the federal government and reinsurance companies to absorb a portion of the federal government's flood risk. The program also would define the financing required for the portion of the risk not subject to transfer. In this alternative, the government would retain a portion of the risk (about 50 percent). The reinsurers would provide a credit facility to offer liquidity in the event of a flood with damages in excess of the amount covered by the government. For this layer of risk, the government would pay an annual premium to the reinsurers. The program would cover losses from property damage for which the Argentine government is now responsible—that is, the government is responsible for reconstruction, mainly of infrastructure: roads, bridges, schools, hospitals, dams, and dikes. The program also would require that the Argentine government undertake steps to reduce its exposure to flood losses. A financial guaranty by a third party or international organization or a similar instrument may be required to initiate the program.

As noted by Freeman (2001), this type of program could have significant benefits for both the Argentine government and the international lending community. The process of lending for natural disasters after a disaster occurs is both inefficient and disruptive for the federal government. The process eliminates the benefits of risk-spreading as an effective policy tool. As mentioned earlier, in the developed world risk transfer is regarded increasingly as a relatively effective and efficient tool for dealing with the costs of catastrophes. In the developing world, the ready availability of post-event lending may be a disincentive for exploring the benefits of pre-event risk transfer. Furthermore, the repetitive financing of infrastructure projects destroyed by flood reduces lenders' abilities to fund new projects with their poverty-reducing benefits. In Argentina, the issuance of loans to restore the same infrastructure from flood loss twice within a decade is an inefficient use of scarce lending resources. This is particularly the case when a private market option exists to deal with the problem. The program would create an incentive for the government to encourage the use of private insurance by other governmental agencies, industrial firms, and commercial enterprises. By quantifying the cost of flood risk, and paying current budget funds to absorb the risk, the government would have a powerful incentive to force those who incur the risk to bear their fair share of the cost of the risk.

Another potential strategy for transferring disaster risk that could be explored in the future would build on pilot work currently being conducted in Morocco, Tunisia, Ethiopia, and Nicaragua, and a proposed project in Nicaragua. These initiatives are targeted to crop protection and develop the idea of insurance based on a weather event rather than on actual losses such as crop failure. The underlying assumption is that certain weather events (such as rainfall above or below a specified amount) are highly correlated with crop failures and therefore the income risks of rural people. Drought insurance is one example. Insurance contracts are written against severe rainfall shortfalls (say 30 percent or more below the norm) that can be measured by a regional weather station. The key advantages of this kind of insurance are that the trigger event (in this case rainfall shortages) can be independently verified, and therefore are not subject to the possibilities of manipulation that are present when insurance payouts are linked to actual farm losses.

Conclusion

Argentina is among the top seven countries in losses from floods as a percentage of the gross domestic product. Managing the risk requires an integrated approach that entails risk identification, risk reduction, and risk transfer. A major aspect of risk management is a coordinated and well-established institutional and legal system and a program of risk reduction that incoporates structural and nonstructural mechanisms. In addition, in Argentina feasible private sector options for transferring risk are available. All of this, however, requires moving from a fatalistic approach to dealing with floods to a culture of prevention; from a system of bearing the losses to a more efficient system of managing the risk.

References

Freeman, Paul K. 2001. "Recomendaciones para la transferencia de los riesgos de inundactions." In Alcira Kreimer, David Kullock, and Juan B. Valdés, "Inundaciones en el Area Metropolitana de Buenos Aires." Disaster Risk Management Working Paper Series No. 3. World Bank, Washington D.C.

Freeman, Paul K., Leslie A. Martin, Reinhard Mechler, Koko Werner, with Peter Hausman. Forthcoming. *Catastrophes and Development*. Disaster Risk Management Series No. 3. Washington, D.C.: World Bank.

Kreimer, Alcira, Margaret Arnold, Christopher Barnham, Paul Freeman, Roy Gilbert, Frederick Krimgold, Rodney Lester, John D. Pollner, and Tom Vogt. 1999. *Managing Disaster Risk in Mexico*. Disaster Risk Management Series No. 1. Washington, D.C.: World Bank.

Kreimer, Alcira, David Kullock, and Juan B. Valdés. 2001. "Inundaciones en el Area Metropolitana de Buenos Aires." Disaster Risk Management Working Paper Series No. 3. World Bank, Washington, D.C.

Kunreuther, Howard, and Joanne Linnerooth-Bayer. 1999. "The Financial Management of Catastrophic Flood Risks in Emerging Economy Countries." Paper presented at the Conference on Global Change and Catastrophic Risk Management. International Institute for Applied Systems Analysis, Laxenburg, Austria.

Munich Re. 1999. "Natural Disasters. Annual Review of Natural Catastrophes, 1998." Munich Reinsurance Company, Munich.

Swiss Re. 1998. "Floods—An Insurable Risk?" Swiss Reinsurance Company, Zurich.

United Nations. 1976. "Guidelines for Flood Loss Prevention and Management in Developing Countries." Department of Economic and Social Affairs, United Nations, New York.
World Bank, Operations Evaluation Department. 2000. "Performance Audit
Report: Argentina Flood Rehabilitation Project." Washington, D.C.

Toward a Code of Good Practice on Managing Fiscal Risk

Allen Schick
University of Maryland

THE STUDIES PRESENTED IN THIS book indicate that countries differ greatly in their treatment of contingent liabilities and other fiscal risks. There are no generally accepted risk management principles, no model practices to guide governments that want to go beyond conventional budget and debt data to analyze their fiscal performance and regulate their financial exposure to contingencies. Many, perhaps most, countries have taken no significant steps toward analyzing and managing such risks, and those that have had to invent their own means of dealing with the problem. There is as yet no agreement on what should be reported on, or annexed to, financial statements, nor on the extent to which contingent liabilities should be recorded in budget documents prior to the point where payment occurs. The difficulty of codifying practices is greatest when the liability is implicit, but problems also emerge when a government's obligation is explicit.

The conceptual studies in this book mirror the divergence in practice. Although the conceptual boundaries have been stretched and some of the ideas proposed by various contributors may find future application, at present there is no agreement on what is good or feasible practice. In contrast to risk management in the market sector, which is highly developed, the stockpile of ideas for government is disparate. Much work lies ahead before the concepts will solidify into practical guideposts.

Given the disarray in theory and practice, one might conclude that it is premature to propose normative rules for managing contingent liabilities. This concluding chapter, however, takes the opposite position. Precisely because practices are so disparate and the risks of doing nothing so high, we believe it prudent to move forward with advice on regulating government's exposure. As the title of this book indicates, contemporary governments are at risk. The absence of concrete standards means that many governments may not take even the most elementary steps toward cushioning their fiscal position against the types of shocks and disturbances that have destabilized the finances of emerging market, developing, and transitional countries.

Fiscal risks do not evaporate just because government fails to recognize them. In good times, the risks hibernate "below the line," off the books and out of sight; when they come due in bad times it is too late to do anything about them. It is likely that fiscal risks will escalate in the years ahead, especially in developing and transitional countries where national governments will become more active in stabilizing economic conditions and household income. Moreover, as Maastricht-type fiscal norms spread, governments may be impelled to substitute contingent liabilities for cash payments—for example, by providing guarantees rather than payouts. If this occurs, the short-term budget situation may become more favorable, but the longer-term outlook will deteriorate. The temptation to behave in this manner is great, because contingent liabilities rarely come due in the same fiscal period in which they are entered.

Taking the initial steps to codify good practice would spur many governments to improve their management of fiscal risks. It also would provide usable benchmarks for assessing existing benchmarks and for identifying matters in need of correction. Furthermore, over time it may lead to greater convergence in country practices and to more refined standards. The guidelines set out in this chapter are provisional; with additional experience, it should be possible in due course to specify widely accepted principles for managing fiscal risk.

Two issues have to be faced in this first effort to devise standards. One is whether the recommended norms should be limited to explicit liabilities or also should cover implicit ones. The other is whether the norms should reflect the most commonly used practices or should go beyond these to novel approaches that may offer the most promise in controlling fiscal risk. With regard to the first issue, it bears noting that standards are better suited for commitments formalized in law or in contracts than for those arising out of expectations or informal understandings. For one thing, it may be hard to identify implicit liabilities or to assess the extent to which they may be called; for another, recognizing implicit liabilities may spur the affected parties to behave in morally hazardous ways and thereby increase the government's exposure. Yet commitments embedded in expectations should not be ignored. After all, doing so will not diminish expectations or eliminate the prospect of future payment. The position taken here is that explicit and implicit liabilities should be identified separately, and that implicit liabilities should be recognized only to the extent that it is strongly probable that government will be called on to make payments. In no case should they be recognized when doing so would materially increase moral hazard or the risk to government. On this basis, some implicit liabilities would be covered; others would not. For all implicit contingent liabilities, however, government should examine its exposure, take steps to reduce the associated risks (such as improving banking regulation and supervision systems), and prepare confidential contingency plans that would offer guidance to policymakers in case of failure.

Proposed Standards

The standards proposed here build on the discussion of actions that a government may take to control its risks, which was presented in Chapter 1 as well as in the chapters that describe specific country experiences. The standards are based on existing methods; they do not require technical breakthroughs. It does little good to set the standards so high that few countries will strive to reach them. The aim should be to promote practices that can be adopted without undue difficulty by most countries. For this reason, the standards do not include some promising ideas, such as the credit budgeting system introduced in the United States (and explained by Schick in Chapter 3), or the reserve fund conceived by Daniel Cohen (see Chapter 6).

Standard 1. Before it accepts a new contingent liability, a government should assess the risk to its fiscal condition, including the probability of future payouts. The assessment should be conducted by an independent entity.

The best, and often the only, time to regulate fiscal risk effectively is before it is taken. Some countries—including Canada, Colombia (see Chapter 12 by Echeverry and others), the Netherlands, South Africa, Sweden, the United States (see Chapter 3)—have implemented this requirement. This is not easy to do, because the parties to the risky transaction have an incentive to underestimate risk, sometimes insisting that guarantees are costless because no money is leaving government hands, or that the cost will be amply covered by the future dividends of a burgeoning economy. In good times, it is easy to forget that contingent liabilities and other risks typically come due when conditions turn adverse; in bad times, it is tempting to argue that things will get better if the government provides guarantees or other assistance that enables enterprises and households to stay afloat. In other words, the whole process is skewed in favor of underestimating the government's exposure. This is especially so when the same government agency is responsible for tendering the guarantees and assessing the risk.

To counter these tendencies, it is essential that governments separate risk-taking and risk assessment by placing them in different organizations. The entity that processes guarantees or other contingent risks should have no role in assessing the probability of default or of other adverse events. This task should be entrusted to an independent unit that has no decisionmaking authority. Separation of the two functions is standard procedure in prudently managed financial institutions, but it is still rare in government. In fact, few governments have formal risk assessment rules or procedures; many treat this as a policy decision that is taken regardless of the risks involved. Moreover, many governments see themselves as a guarantor of last resort, assuming risks that would otherwise be held by weak enterprises or poor households. Because they knowingly take on bad risks, governments are indifferent to the losses they face, especially when these do not appear in current budgets or financial statements.

The standard proposed here is based on the principle that government should assess risk even when it has already decided to provide guarantees, and even when it does so because the beneficiary is a bad risk. It should do so in order to have an accurate picture of its financial condition and of potential downstream losses and payments. Ideally, it should use this information to estimate the money needed to cover losses in the current budget or future ones.

These assessments should be conducted independently; if they are not, they will be tainted by conflicts of interest, misassessments of risk, and increases in avoidable losses. Several alternative organizational arrangements may be appropriate for assuring independence. One would be to assign responsibility to a specialized, independent unit whose only task would be to carry out objective risk assessments. Alternatively, responsibility might be assigned to an existing entity that enjoys independence from political considerations. For example, in countries that have an autonomous debt management office, such as Sweden and Ireland, this office would be a good candidate. In other countries, it may be the supreme audit office, as it is in the United States.

A third option would be to assign overall risk assessment to a central unit and responsibility for particular actions to the agency running the program. For example, a central agency might analyze programs to promote home construction or ownership, while the housing agency assesses applications for guarantees from builders or home purchasers.

Standard 2. The government should periodically compile an inventory of outstanding contingent liabilities and report on the volume of these liabilities, their legal basis, and the probability of losses.

This standard recognizes that even if government is prudent is taking new risks, it already has a portfolio of contingent liabilities and other risks that may come due in the future. In this regard, practice in Australia and New Zealand (described by Petrie in Chapter 2) and in the Czech Republic (see Chapter 9 by Brixi, Schick, and Zlaoui) is exemplary. In managing its finances, a government must be cognizant of these commitments and take them into account in budget plans and other policy statements. It would be sensible for government to report annually on outstanding liabilities and the risks associated with them. The report may be appended to financial statements (in those countries that regularly publish such statements) or be published as a free-standing document. It would be preferable for the report to be reviewed by auditors who would comment on the adequacy of the methods for documenting contingent liabilities and estimating their costs.

Many governments may have difficulty at the outset compiling such a report, but the requirement to do so should spur them to improve their database. A government should describe risks even when it lacks sufficient data to measure their volume or probable cost reliably. Moreover, the report should distinguish between quantifiable and nonquantifiable risks. Quantifiable risks would be those whose volume or probability of loss can be estimated with reasonable confidence; nonquantifiable risks would be those that lack a basis for measuring these amounts. But even risks that cannot be measured should be described in the report.

In many cases, it would be prudent for the report to specify a range within which the risk is expected to occur rather than to provide point estimates. Point estimates often turn out to be wrong, and they can mislead government so that it takes inappropriate action. It is preferable to estimate a range of possible outcomes and to discuss the factors that may determine the actual liability or cost. Finally, the report should project the fiscal period(s) during which the government may be called on to indemnify losses.

Standard 3. Government fiscal analysis published in the annual budget or other documents should discuss the major risk factors affecting revenues and expenditures for the next fiscal year or beyond.

Every budget is subject to an array of risks that may result in actual revenues and expenditures that deviate significantly from the planned levels. This fact has been elaborated in the fiscal vulnerability framework proposed by Richard Hemming and Murray Petrie in Chapter 7. The risks generally do much more damage to fiscal stability in developing and transitional countries than in developed ones. In developed countries, unbudgeted losses may compel the government to make relatively minor adjustments in revenue or spending plans; in developing and transitional countries, variances may be so large that they force the government to discard the approved budget and prepare an entirely new one. In some poor countries, the government does not bother to prepare a new budget, but pretends to be implementing the approved one, while it covertly spends different amounts.

Many of the risks to the estimates are known when the budget is tabled, but the near-universal practice is to ignore them, either in the hope that things will turn out better or in the expectation that the budget will have to be remade during the year. Commenting on major risks would prepare the government for events—such as a shortfall in revenue, deterioration in exchange rates, or natural disaster—that will upset its budget plans, and also spur it to prepare more realistic revenue and spending estimates. Doing so should not be difficult, because governments typically are required to discuss risk factors in offering statements or similar documents when they seek private financing. These documents have narrow circulation and receive none of the attention that is given the annual budget.

Fiscal analysis is incomplete if it omits government contingent liabilities and other fiscal risks. Speaking to this point, Chapters 1, 6, 7, 8, 9, 10, and 11 illustrate the weaknesses of conventional fiscal analysis, outline possible frameworks for a more comprehensive analysis, and apply such frameworks to the analysis of the fiscal position of several countries. Although it may be difficult for governments to analyze the risks associated with their whole portfolio of assets and their contingent as well as direct liabilities (as advocated by Brixi and Mody in Chapter 1 and by Easterly and Yuravlivker in Chapter 8), or to assess all sources of their fiscal vulnerability (as encouraged by Hemming and Petrie in Chapter 7), it may be relatively simple to calculate the government's hidden deficit and hidden debt (as was done for the Czech Republic in Chapter 9). Consistent with government accounting practice, expenditures and revenues that occur outside the budget can be taken into account. In addition, for noncash programs such as guarantees, the present value of the expected fiscal cost, and the likely cash consequences for the budget in the years ahead, can be estimated in a simple manner. This is illustrated for the Czech Republic, Bulgaria, and Hungary in Chapter 9 and for Thailand in Chapter 11 (and, later, with the help of options-pricing methodology, for pension guarantees in Chapter 13 by Pennacchi, for central banks in Chapter 16 by Blejer and Schumacher, and for credit guarantees in Chapter 19 by van Wijnbergen and Budina). Other fiscal risks, such as those arising from the country's banking sector (discussed by Claessens and Klingebiel in Chapter 14), from government insurance schemes (surveyed by Feldman in Chapter 15), and from private participation in infrastructure (outlined by Mody in Chapter 17), also may be analyzed in simple terms, reflecting their face value and possible scenarios (as was done for Indonesia in Chapter 11). As data and analysis improve, it will be feasible to give fiscal analysis a longer-term perspective and to expand the coverage fiscal sustainability analysis (as presented by Cohen in Chapter 6 and applied to China by Krumm and Wong in Chapter 10).

The budget discussion should cover at least the next fiscal year and should reflect not only the risks arising from the levels and structure of government budget and debt, but also those outside the budget and debt portfolio. Governments that have a medium-term framework or multiyear projections should extend the coverage to the next several years and present different scenarios showing the possible impacts of the various risks on the budget according to the macroeconomic, policy, and other underlying variables. The discussion need not be comprehensive; it should concentrate on those risks that have the greatest capacity to force the budget to veer off course.

Standard 4. The government should establish a risk management strategy to guide public organizations when they take actions that expose them to financial liability.

In contrast to most direct spending decisions that are made through regular budget procedures, governments often take on contingent liabilities in an ad hoc manner, without regard for the impact on their financial condition. Each guarantee program, and sometimes each guarantee, is treated as a special case, with its own rules and procedures. The result is a hodgepodge of contingent liabilities that lack uniformity but add up to a significant risk to government. Some governments impose initiation (or origination) fees, but most do not. Some have rules and procedures for recovering assets in case of default, but most do not. Some assess the government's exposure before a commitment is made, but most do not. The standard recommended here (and elaborated by Brixi and Mody in Chapter 1) would have the government develop a policy that would have to be followed before new liabilities are undertaken. In some countries, it may be appropriate to codify the policy in legislation, but in most an administrative decree could suffice. Ideally, the policy should be comprehensive, covering all contingent liabilities, but, as a practical matter, there are likely to be exceptional cases that are guided by expediency rather than by rules.

The recommended standard is neutral on the question of whether government, or an entity related to government such as a municipality, state-owned enterprise, or agency benefiting from any kind of government guarantee (such as export guarantee funds, agriculture guarantee funds, state insurance entities), should take on risk. It focuses instead on the procedures to be followed and the data to be compiled and reviewed before government, or such entities, accept these liabilities. As envisioned here, the guidelines should cover issues that arise when contingent liabilities are proposed, including:

- procedures to assess the risk of loss;
- initiation or origination fees;
- form of guarantee contracts and the role of the finance ministry or others in reviewing contracts before they are executed;
- risk- or cost-sharing arrangements;
- procedures for monitoring performance under guarantees or other contingent liabilities; and
- what protection the government or entity should have in case of default or other events that cause losses.

These and other issues should be addressed in an authoritative manual that covers all the main steps in the contingent liability process and pertains both to programs that expose the government to risk and to specific transactions. Few countries currently have comprehensive guidelines. Canada and the Netherlands (see Chapter 3) appear to be among the most advanced in this area. In these countries, central agencies operate a process for reviewing and implementing guarantees that parallels the direct expenditure process. Their guidelines cover most of the steps, from proposal through financing, and emphasize the importance of mitigating the government's risk. Although the guidelines are designed to discourage the issuance of guarantees, they can be easily modified to suit countries that prefer to use this policy instrument in a prudent manner. It is perhaps more difficult, however, to regulate and ensure proper risk-taking incentives in entities outside the framework of the central government. Krishna Ramaswamy in Chapter 5 and Jun Ma in Chapter 18 point to some possible approaches for state-owned enterprises and subnational governments.

Because policy without enforcement would be a hollow gesture, it is essential that implementation of the guidelines be entrusted to a central agency, such as the finance ministry, which, in most countries, already has responsibility for direct expenditures. Another possibility would be to assign responsibility to the debt management (or similar) office (as in Colombia, Sweden, and Thailand), which is experienced in assessing the risk associated with government borrowing. In rare cases, the government may wish to establish a special agency for handling contingent liabilities. The important thing is not that an agency be established but that it have sufficient authority and resources to safeguard the government's interests.

Standard 5. The government should promote cost- and risk-sharing to discourage moral hazard, ensure the economic viability of guarantees, and reduce the probability and amount of loss.

Even if it takes the position that contingent liabilities are appropriate policy instruments, a government should be cognizant both of the impacts of its actions on the behavior of others and of the risk it is assuming. All guarantees change behavior, and all impose costs. If they did not, the market for guarantees would dry up quickly. Even though a government cannot fully escape moral hazard and the prospect of loss when it assumes contingent liabilities, it can take steps to greatly diminish its exposure. The steps are technically easy (and have been discussed in several chapters, including Chapter 4 by Sundaresan), though they may be politically difficult. They involve shifting some portion of the cost and risk to those who benefit from guarantees and other contingent liabilities.

As a general rule, government should charge risk-based premiums or establish deductibles for compensating losses. These premiums recognize that not all contingent liabilities are equally risky. In some cases, a guarantee may merely lower the cost to the beneficiary without adding much to the government's risk. For example, a borrower who can obtain funds privately may nevertheless seek a government guarantee in order to obtain lower interest charges or other more favorable terms. More commonly, credit-unworthy borrowers seek government guarantees because they cannot obtain private loans. In these cases, it would be appropriate for the government to charge premiums that reflect its true cost (that is, the present value of the expected fiscal cost). If the government decides to charge premiums lower than the true cost, it should openly acknowledge the size of the subsidy. There may be instances in which government subsidies, such as a reduced premium or government support through guarantees, are appropriate. Yet such subsidies and support should be subject to the same scrutiny as any spending items in the budget.

Government also can reduce its exposure by paying for the last, rather than the first, loss—that is, by setting high deductibles that must be satisfied before it makes payment. The problem, however, is that because risky borrowers cannot otherwise obtain capital, they have a strong incentive to lobby government for special treatment. Government also can seek to mitigate moral hazard and loss by regulating the actions of those benefiting from guarantees and other forms of contingent assistance. It is common business practice for lenders to impose covenants that restrict risky behavior by firms. A government should act in the same way to protect its interest, by restricting those who might otherwise behave in a morally hazardous manner. Finally, a government can safeguard its interests by monitoring the actions of borrowers and other insured parties and by giving its claims seniority over those of other parties. These practices are common in business, but still rare in the public sector.

Standard 6. The budget should limit the amount of guarantees and other contingent liabilities to be tendered during the year, as well as the total amount that each institution authorized to issue guarantees may have outstanding.

As explained by several contributors to this book, the budget is inherently a weak tool for regulating contingent liabilities. In cash-basis budgeting, losses are recognized when the payment is made, not when the liability is incurred. Accrual-basis budgeting provides for recognition when the liability is incurred, but rules and practices for treating contingent liabilities have not yet been standardized. Few countries have accrual-basis budgets, and fewer systematically provision for losses. For this reason, efforts to strengthen budgetary control of contingent liabilities will likely develop through cash-basis budgeting.

The cash basis enables government to control the volume of guarantees issued during the year or the total outstanding. These amounts may be specified for the budget as a whole as well as for each institution authorized to issue guarantees or to enter into other contingent commitments. These controls are easy to apply because they do not depend on estimates of losses or payments; rather, the control is exercised over volume, without regard for the riskiness of the transaction. This method has been applied in Hungary (see Chapter 9) and in some other countries where the annual budget specifies the maximum amount of guarantees that may be tendered during the year. These aggregates are then parceled out among institutions authorized to make guarantees, much in the same manner that direct spending is allocated among government departments and ministries.

Standard 7. The budget should set aside funds, within an overall fiscal constraint, for expected losses during the year.

Although limits on the volume of guarantees can be separate from the expenditure budget, the government should provide in the budget for payments expected to be made during the year. These reserves should be included in calculations of total expenditure and of the surplus or deficit. Of course, the provisions are not effective constraints, for the government would have to pay for losses that exceed the budgeted levels. Nevertheless, setting aside funds in the budget would serve two laudable purposes: it would sensitize the government to the fact that contingent liabilities entail costs, and it would induce the government to devise more reliable procedures for estimating risk.

Conclusion

Implementing these standards may appear to be a daunting task, yet they are within reach of most governments. The critical step involves collecting the information on outstanding contingent liabilities, estimating the government's exposure, and incorporating the information into fiscal analysis and government budgets and financial statements.

The task is ongoing, for it is a rare government that knows all that it should about guarantees and other contingent schemes. In the same way that governments monitor and regulate direct expenditures, updating their information on a regular basis, they should invest in the capacity to identify, measure, and update information on contingent liabilities. If they do so, the quality and relevance of their information will improve rapidly.

Where some standards are beyond immediate attainment, government should seek corrective action—first, by imposing the standards on new contingent commitments, and, second, by making strong efforts to identify the most critical risks, those that pose the greatest threat to fiscal stability. Ideally, governments should strive for a comprehensive accounting of risks. But they should move ahead even when there are gaps in their database.

The standards themselves should be moving targets. Efforts should be made both through government action and through policy research to elaborate fuller standards and practices. In terms of action, governments at the cutting edge of practice, with strong fiscal institutions, should devise fuller means of dealing with risks. Some may wish to apply the business-type or experimental practices discussed in this book. It is especially important that accounting standards be devised to deal with fiscal risks. With the rapid spread of financial reporting, one can expect that financial statements will be a powerful conduit for disseminating standards in the future.

Finally, there is much need for research both on existing and on experimental practices. For example, it would be fruitful to study systematically how New Zealand uses statements of contingent liabilities to manage risk, the manner in which Hungary budgets for expected losses, and the credit budget model introduced in the United States. The study of fiscal risk is still in its infancy; much research remains to be done.